I Spe<br>in the Mines

# I Spent My Life in the Mines

## The Story of Juan Rojas, Bolivian Tin Miner

June Nash

Columbia University Press
New York

COLUMBIA UNIVERSITY PRESS
NEW YORK   OXFORD

Copyright © 1992 Columbia University Press
All rights reserved

Library of Congress Cataloging-in-Publication Data

Rojas, Juan.
    [He agotado mi vida en la mina. English]
    I spent my life in the mines : the story of Juan
Rojas, Bolivian tin miner / June Nash [editor].
       p.   cm.
    Includes bibliographical references and index.
    ISBN 0-231-07936-2.
    ISBN 0-231-07937-0 (pbk.)
    1. Rojas, Juan.   2. Tin miners — Bolivia —
Biography.   I. Nash, June C., 1927–   .   II. Title.
    HD8039.M72B66513   1992
    331.7'6223453'092 — dc20
    [B]                                                   92-26276
                                                              CIP

Book design by Teresa Bonner
Printed in the United States of America

    c   10   9   8   7   6   5   4   3   2   1
    p   10   9   8   7   6   5   4   3   2   1

# CONTENTS

20   Juan                                      334
21   Juan Manuel                               356
22   Elena                                     364
23   Epilogue                                  373

REFERENCES CITED                               377
GLOSSARY                                       379

I Spent My Life
in the Mines

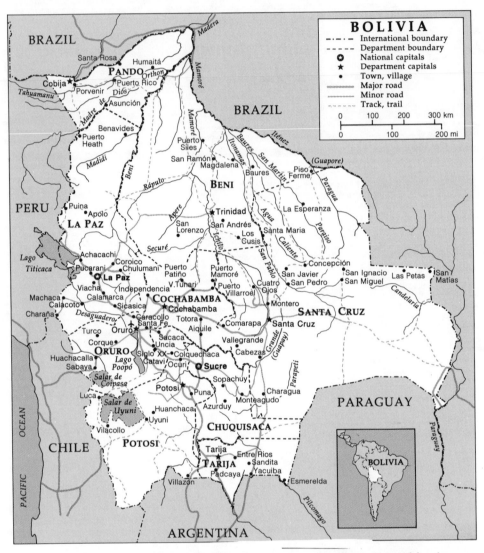

From *Bolivia: New Mining Investment Opportunities*, a brochure prepared by the United Nations Department of Technical Cooperation for Development under a mineral investment promotion project (BOL/87/012) funded by UNDP, February 1991.

# PART ONE
# 1926–70

# 1

# Introduction: Revolutionary Parallels in a Life History

Social movements of the twentieth century have drawn more people into the mainstreams of history than at any other time. The actions of peasants and workers up to the present century were sporadically mentioned in history, usually as participants in episodes of violent outbursts, and more often than not they figured as the victims, not the architects of events. In the past half century, peasants and workers have been involved almost continuously in sustained political action and have acquired the responsibilities of power. Their resistance to colonial and postindependence national movements to destroy their economy and draw them into wage work often resulted in armed conflict. Wolf captures this paradox in his study of peasant wars of the twentieth century when he states that "it is the very attempt of the middle and free peasant to remain traditional which makes him revolutionary." (1969:292)

Those peasants who failed to hold on to the land and became wage workers in the mines, plantations, and factories of the developing countries retained many of the rituals and beliefs that sustained them in their rural village life. These customs and concepts were as important in formulating their struggles as the new revolutionary ideologies to which they were exposed in the industrial setting. Moral imperatives rather than socialist rationality dominated their consciousness as they sought for collective solutions to their problems of survival.[1]

Bolivia's uncompleted revolution of 1952 (Malloy 1970) brought to

[1] I have tried to substantiate this statement in the monograph I wrote on the Bolivian mining communities (Nash 1979; republished 1992) and summarized in an article on ritual and revolutionary movements for Susan Eckstein's *Power and Popular Protest* (1989).

the front stage of its national history miners and peasants who, before that, had made newspaper headlines only when they were massacred in large enough numbers to draw attention, or when major shifts in employment opportunities brought about large-scale migrations or massive hunger. After their backing of the National Revolutionary Movement (MNR) brought Victor Paz Estenssero to power in 1952, the Bolivian Workers' Center (COB) provided two vice presidents, twenty state representatives, one hundred senators, and ten presidents and directors of independent enterprises in the first decade of power (Canelas 1966:77). In the period of President Siles Zuazo's term of office from 1956 to 1962, labor leaders held a majority in the Chamber of Deputies. They led the move to counter the stabilization program calling for wage limits and austerity for workers that was promoted by the United States and international banks as the price for continued credit. Following the military coup led by Colonel Hugo Banzer in 1971, peasants joined the miners in resistance to military oppression. In 1974 peasants set up blockades on the major highway connecting La Paz and the oil rich province of Santa Cruz in order to express their objection to the low prices for the subsistence crops they raised in a time of rampant inflation (Nash 1980). Their resistance movement and that of the miners went underground when they were met by military force that killed more than a hundred protestors. A hunger strike begun by women from the mining community in November 1978 brought their struggles to international attention and finally toppled the military dictatorship.

Siles Zuazo's attempt to reestablish democracy during his presidency from 1983 to 1985 was subverted by a shaky economic base and contradictory policies arising from the diverse forces loosely joined in the Popular Democratic Unity, or UDP (Eckstein 1988). It succumbed to a series of military coups in the interim until Siles Zuazo was again installed as president in 1983. With the fall in price of both tin and oil — from which the major revenues of the government were derived — and with the mounting interest owed on a five-billion-dollar debt incurred under the military rule, the country reached what one analyst called "terminal breakdown" (Goslin 1985; see also Strengers 1985; Dunkerly & Morales 1986). Unable to control the inflationary wave resulting from loss of revenues from nationalized industries, devaluations of the currency, and runaway costs for servicing the debt run up by the military, President Siles Zuazo relinquished control to Victor

Paz Estenssoro, who had previously served two terms as president, and who was elected to yet a third term in 1985 (Laserna 1985; Ramos Sanchez 1986).

In one of the many paradoxical turns of Bolivian history, President Paz Estenssoro, who had decreed the nationalization of the mines in his first term of office in 1953, ushered in the new era of privatization of national enterprises and austerity. In response to the International Monetary Fund's conditions for repayment of the national debt he set forth his "New Economic Policy" shortly after he came into office. Among the provisions was Decree Number 21060, calling for the closing of mines operating at a loss, the sale of profitable mines to private companies, and the transfer of others to cooperatives. These policies led to the laying off of thousands of miners. By 1986, 460,000 people, or 60 percent of the work force, were unemployed: twenty thousand miners were laid off from national mines, six thousand from private mines, ten thousand from public administration, and two thousand from banks; and 118 factories were closed. From over twenty-five thousand workers in COMIBOL (the Bolivian Mining Company) in 1986, the ranks were reduced to four thousand. The gross national product was 40 percent of the 1940 level, and debt payments took 51 percent of exports (CEDOIN 1987). The price of monetary stabilization was hunger and misery for the workers.

To their desperation many miners who had been promised land in the new colonizing areas at low altitudes found themselves deceived once again by the government of Paz Estenssoro. Some went to Chapare to work in coca production, which had become the major source of revenue in the country. Even after they had lost their base in the mines, laid-off miners organized the Association of Relocalized Miners led by Filemón Escobar. In 1987 the association had more members than the Federation of Bolivian Mine Workers Unions (CEDOIN 1988a). On March 3, 1988, eight hundred miners relocated to tropical zones initiated a march in search of subsistence labor on the coca plantations. They demanded that the fight against drugs be directed toward cocaine processors and traffickers rather than the coca producers (CEDOIN 1988b, 1988c). The women of the mining communities who belonged to the Association of Housewives joined with wives of factory workers as they tried to organize street sellers and others in the informal labor force. (CEDOIN 1987).

The accounts of social movements occurring throughout the world, no matter how finely tuned to informants' recordings of their under-standings, cannot capture the historical moment in which conscious-ness is formed. This requires the full replay of the life stories of people who became part of those social movements. The life stories we have, such as Sidney Mintz's *Taso: trabajador de la cana* (1988), Judith-Maria Buechler and Hans Buechler's *Carmine* (1981), Domitila Barrios de Chungara's *Let Me Speak* (1977), Rigoberta Menchu's *I, Rigoberta* (1984), and Filemon Escobar's *Testimonio de un militante obrero* (1981), reveal the process of the formation of consciousness regarding the changing world into which those people were thrust. Decisions regard-ing marriage, whether to bear a child already conceived, choices of ca-reer, and participation in social movements reveal the multitude of cir-cumstances that enter into comprehension of life conditions. One approach to analyzing the development of these attitudes is that of the "family autobiography" as developed by Oscar Lewis in his collabora-tive works with Mexican subjects, *Pedro Martinez* (1964). Through the eyes of family members differing in age and sex, we can see the differ-ential impact of events on the individuals and how the events influenced his or her actions. Yet Lewis failed to inform his readers of the cues he used to stimulate the narrators, or of the liberties he took as editor. This is particularly true of the life story *Children of Sanchez* (1961) where we are left wondering where Sanchez's narrative leaves off and Lewis's be-gins. Vincent Crapanzano's *Tuhami: Portrait of a Moroccan* (1985) cul-tivates the reflexive view of the elicitor/editor that is an essential ingre-dient in personal testimonies.

The generative base for major social movements emerges as people respond to and engage in action to influence change. The distinct in-terpretations of events that each member of the family experienced give an insight into the interplay of consciousness formation and social change. Their collective responses as a family to turbulent social change show the continuing significance of this institution in human survival. Readers will discover for themselves the many contrasts and contradictions in the accounts of each member of the family as the var-iables of age, gender, and position in the occupational hierarchy define the parameters of their consciousness.

During my fieldwork in the tin mining center of Oruro, Bolivia, I collected a number of autobiographies as a means of analyzing the de-velopment of consciousness among workers. This work proved to be more rewarding than I had expected. In recounting and interpreting past events, the subjects revealed the unconscious values that motivated their actions. Their usual tendency to self-censor and conform to what they assume the anthropologist wants to hear was suspended as they became caught up in the narrative aspects of their life history. These narrative accounts of workers and peasants are of special importance because their actions are usually not recorded by historians.

In publishing personal testimonies — a term I take from Vincent Crapanzano, Yasmine Ergas, and Judith Modell (1986) — the editors/ elicitors take some liberties in making the account accessible to a general public. First they (and I) feel obliged to eliminate repetition and confusion, on the part of both the elicitor and the narrator. The decisions here were made in relation to the cultural parameters in which the elicitor operates. This means that the published narrative has been sifted through cultural sieves that make it accessible to the readership of at least one and possibly two cultures. I tried to minimize intervention both in the initial Spanish transcription and in the English translation, with which I was ably assisted by Elizabeth Hansen and Cassandra Torrico. We tried to reflect the style as well as the meaning of the accounts of the various members of the family. The startling metaphors and vivid recall of actions present in many of Juan's chapters are his own, not an editor's embellishment. Carmen de Dandler, who assisted me in preparing the first edition of Juan's testimony in Spanish (Nash & Rojas 1976), was equally sensitive to the language in which Juan and Petrona — in her two chapters — express themselves. I have retained my interjections during the narration so that the reader will be aware of the prompts that influenced the discourse. I neglected to record the extended discussions we had before and after each session. At the time I thought of these as pump-priming and paid attention only to the flow that resulted.

In many ways I feel that I was selected by Juan to be the medium through which he could narrate his life story. He was one of the dozen individuals selected by the personnel manager of the San José, Oruro COMIBOL mines to talk with me when I first started my study in the mines. Juan's conformity to protocol, his courteous, though never obsequious, behavior toward superiors — which he himself recounts in his chapters and which I observed — made them confident that he would not reveal any subversive material. Yet in our first interview, sitting in the antechamber of the superintendent of mines, he spoke eloquently of the disasters in the mines and even invited me to his home.

In the course of many visits to his household I learned to appreciate the open hospitality and lively intelligence of all the members of his family. Juan lived in the new Barrio Minero Sante Fe, built by the National Housing Company (CONAVI). There I met his wife, Petrona, and their six children, who ranged in age from twenty years to infancy. It was the first of many visits I made to the little house that was then on the outskirts of the advancing barrios of working and retired miners. In 1969, the year that I met Juan and Petrona, the oldest child, Filemón, had just graduated from secondary school at the age of twenty and was enrolled in the Cochabamba School of Agronomy. I became María's godmother at a Mass for her health on her fifteenth birthday. Aníbal was ten, Elena eight, Anita four, and Juan Manuel had not yet celebrated his first birthday. Juan's greatest ambition was to see all of his children graduate from secondary school.

When Petrona subsequently asked me to be godparent at a Mass for the health of their year-old, Juan Manuel, it confirmed the enduring relationship that involves mutual support and advice. Often when the family encountered difficulties, they called upon me to give advice or even mediate disputes. Three of the children arrived one evening to ask me to come and help quiet Juan who was enraged at the transgressions of a co-worker. The co-worker had charged Juan with negligence while on guard duty that resulted in the loss of dynamite. The children were afraid that he would get a stroke from the extent of his raving.

Once when I was upset by the claim of one of the company spies that I was a CIA agent, he and Petrona tried to placate me so that I would not "burst a spleen" and then counseled me to go to another godparent to determine a strategy to avoid any negative reaction in the mining community (Nash 1974). Even when I left Bolivia for an extended period, I received letters from them announcing the arrival of their last child and requests for help when the economic crisis was most severe.

Yet I did not consider collaborating in a life history with Juan until he was laid-off from work after the doctor declared that he had "100 percent silicosis." I was working with a much more flamboyant miner who was reputed to have been the chief political force in Oruro during the MNR period. But since Juan had no income until his pension was to begin, I suggested that he come each day to work for me, recounting his memories of work in the mines. He arrived conscientiously every day at nine in the morning and we would begin taping a dialogue that increasingly became a monologue. At lunch we would discuss some of the incidents and then return to clarify or expand points that had been raised.

I was continually surprised that it took so little to evoke an extended narrative. This was particularly true of Juan in comparison with Petrona, and I think it reflects cultural prompts that both encourage men to be more vocal than women and also provide them with experiences that are considered to be of greater social import. On my return trip fifteen years after I had elicited the Spanish version of the family biography in 1970, I found that Petrona, the mother/wife, was far more engaged in the discourse than she had been earlier. This was, in part, related to her emergence as a greater force in maintaining the collective unity of the family once the children were married and involved in their own homes, and, in part, to her greater involvement selling that brought income to the family after Juan had retired.

The memories of the three generations in the family span the time from the Chaco War in 1934 when Juan began to work at the age of eight, to the 1985 elections when the family voted for Paz Estenssoro for the third time. Their strength in enduring the violent changes of government that characterized Bolivian politics and the disastrous economic cycles that occurred in the declining mining centers is the core of the story they tell.

Both Juan and Petrona came from mining families who had been recruited from the *campesinos* of Cochabamba by Simon I. Patiño, the great tin magnate, to work in the mine known as Siglo XX. Petrona's father had worked in the mines until he injured his arm setting off dynamite for a celebration. He then opened a barber shop where, many years later, Petrona met Juan, who was a customer. All her brothers worked in the Santa Fe mines until their retirement in the 1980s.

Juan's father tried to escape the mines by going to the colonization area in Santa Cruz that the government had opened up in the 1930s, in the interest of maintaining the frontiers during the Chaco War. But he was already affected by the silicosis that shortens the life of most workers, and his lungs were unable to bear the greater atmospheric pressure at the lower altitude.

After Juan's father's death his mother married a miner who took the family to Taniani, a small mine where Juan, at the age of eight, worked as a "parrot" warning miners in the open pits of landslides. When Juan's stepfather died, the family moved to the Siglo XX mines where his older brother worked. Juan clerked in a store until he enlisted in the army. He was stationed at the Chilean border at the time that President Villarroel was assassinated and his body hung in public. When his year's service was over, he returned to Santa Fe mines where his other brothers worked.

There he met Petrona, the daughter of one of his mother's friends. Like most Bolivian couples, they lived together for several years before marrying. In 1952 they took advantage of a layoff to get married in Cochabamba. The National Revolutionary Movement (MNR) had just succeeded in seating Victor Paz Estenssoro as president. Juan was called back to the mines and given a power drill to work as an explorer-driller.

Juan was not a leader in the revolution or in the organization of the Federation of Mine Workers Unions, yet his support of those leaders when they were in hiding, and the help he and Petrona gave to the families of the leaders when they were forced into exile, sustained and gave credibility to those movements. Ultimately it is the consciousness of people like Juan and Petrona in the rank and file that determine the success of fledgling unions and of revolutions.

I found many instances in which the versions of an event contrasted sharply in Juan's and Petrona's account. For example, Juan says in his chapter on his marriage that he decided in 1952 to marry Petrona. She states that her uncle initiated the marriage ceremony. I suspect she was correct, since they were living in her uncle's house at the time and the uncle paid for feast. Juan's daughter Elena also departs from her father's account regarding her decision not to marry the father of her child. Juan's account emphasizes his own acceptance of the pregnancy and his disassociating it from the need for a marriage contract; she tells of how hard it was to convince her father that she should not marry at that time in her life.

Juan measured national leaders in relation to the broader spectrum of political and social changes they initiated, while Petrona tended to evaluate them in terms of what they delivered. Thus, he was more skeptical of the succession of presidents that played a role in the MNR period, while his wife accepted Paz Estenssoro because she credited his National Construction of Housing program with the house they lived in. There are internal contradictions in Juan's statement of his beliefs and practices; while he can in one chapter excoriate the military massacres in the mining communities, in another we learn of his forcing his son to return to the army post from which he fled in fear of his life.

I left Bolivia in 1971, just a few days before the Banzer coup that ushered in a dozen years of military rule. I returned briefly in 1973 while Banzer was still in office, arriving at Juan and Petrona's house late in the evening. I was afraid that my presence might be noticed by the spies in the mining communities, since I had heard that my name was on a list of persona non grata because of articles I had written. I did not wish to involve the family in any political problems. I showed Juan the manuscript of his autobiography and he agreed that "everything was the truth," and that he would use the pseudonym "Juan Rojas." Petrona also agreed to that designation and to the names we gave to the children to avoid discovery in case of recriminations.

Despite my fears for their safety after Juan's retirement, they seemed to be prospering. Petrona had even acquired a red three-piece sofa and a coffee table. Filemón had taken his father's place in the mines and contributed to the family his wages and supplies he could obtain from the mine store. He and his wife slept in the room that used to be Juan and Petrona's bedroom. "He is the father of us all," Petrona asserted. The other children were still enrolled in school. The mines were under military control, but they were producing at a high level and the price of tin was good.

In the intervening years we kept up a sporadic correspondence. I learned that another child, Victor Hugo, had been born and sent some money to ease the desperation I sensed. I returned briefly in 1983 when Ernesto Siles Zuazo, the same man who had served in the period from 1956 to 1960, had just been installed again as president. I hardly recognized the house when I arrived at ten o'clock in the morning. It was now in the center of an expansion of housing that had spread even to the denuded hills that people had avoided in the past because of the sharp cold winds in August. A two-story extension was attached to the original house, which was surrounded by the trees Juan had planted in 1970, now taller than the adobe wall enclosing the entire compound.

Filemón had moved to an apartment in his wife's family's courtyard and Aníbal had taken over his brother's role of bringing in supplies from the commissary, once he went to work in the mines. María lived nearby with her husband, Guido, who worked in the petroleum refinery in Oruro. Guido's parents lived and worked in the Santa Fe mines where Juan and Petrona had spent so many years of their lives. Elena had a two-year-old son, Israel, but was continuing her studies in nursing. Juan Manuel, still a playful, gawky thirteen-year-old, towered over his parents. Victor Hugo, now eight, was almost forgotten as his nephew, Israel, attracted the attention of all.

Within minutes after my arrival, the whole family congregated. Petrona had installed a telephone: this acquisition overwhelmed me more than any other. We spent the day catching up on the decade that had elapsed. The remarkable unity and integration of the family and its ability to survive in the face of economic disasters and political upheavals impressed me, and I was determined to return to update their book.

When I returned in the summer of 1985, elections were underway and the country was experiencing its most violent economic changes of the century. Activity in the mining centers had almost come to a standstill, since there had been little exploration for new veins during the period of military control. With price ceilings imposed on most agricultural products, the only profitable trade was in cocaine, which did not bring the government any revenue.

In the declining economy the government was unable to repay even the interest on the huge debts run up by the military regimes during the 1970s. This further devalued the Bolivian currency in relation to the dollar and drove prices up in the national and international markets. When I arrived in June the official rate of exchange was $b67,000 to the dollar, with a "parallel," or black market, price of 350,000 to the dollar. Within a month the parallel exchange rate rose to 1,000,000!

In this precipitous economy a July election was called. Banzer had returned to run against Paz Estenssoro in one of those electoral contests that could only happen in Bolivia. Jaime Paz Zamorra, who was one of the triumvirate of young Revolutionary Left Movement leaders who had discredited themselves in the early months of Siles Zuazo's term in office, was a third runner-up. There were a dozen other candidates of the left.

Juan had just recuperated from his second paralytic stroke; this one occurred during the celebration of the marriage of Aníbal to the daughter of one of the labor leaders who had been exiled to Sweden and had returned with the advent of democracy. Juan's relapse occurred during the ceremony, at which he drank and danced. The celebration ended when he was taken to the hospital and put on oxygen.

Petrona was in jail at that time; her partner in real estate sales had issued more contracts than there were lots and had run off, leaving her to face the authorities. In jail she busied herself, knitting woolen bonnets for her grandchildren and even selling a few knitted caps to the other inmates. Since she was the only woman interned in quarters that did not have separate cells for women, the jailor would let her leave at night and return early in the morning, before the superintendent showed up.

I lived with the family for a month, catching up with their lives. Petrona had become the financial mainstay of the family after Juan's retirement, although in his narration he does not once refer to her earnings from the sale of lots in the mining barrios, or her sale of the jewelry that she brought to Santa Fe. When I got her out on bail, we went to La Paz to find her partner, and she succeeded in serving him with the summons. The trial resulted in her having to repay one-third of the down payments that he had embezzled.

Juan Manuel, now sixteen, had just run away from the army. His father had sent him there after he failed his school examinations. Juan Manuel had seen a young recruit killed by a sergeant while he stood at attention with other soldiers in a training field. Subsequently, the brutal sergeant who had killed the youth whipped and kicked Juan Manuel repeatedly when the latter failed to return on time from a leave, because the buses had not run on schedule. Yet Juan left his sickbed to take his son back to his post — only to have Juan Manuel escape again, fearful that the vengeful sergeant would kill him too.

Aníbal had just left home to live with his new wife, María, in her father's house. She had gone to Sweden with her parents and, throughout their exile, had corresponded with Aníbal. She felt lonely and estranged in Sweden despite the formal hospitality extended to political exiles. She was often taken to be a gypsy and treated as a potential thief in stores. The only friendships she had were with "guest workers," Turks who, she said, kept their women in seclusion and treated them very badly. She wanted to marry a Bolivian, and within two weeks of her return to Bolivia she became engaged to Aníbal. She hoped to return with Aníbal to Sweden where she could work in a nursery and where he could pursue his studies in electronic repair.

Elena had switched her course of studies from nursing, in which she had failed to pass her exams, to music. Juan felt that she could succeed in this field if only she could purchase an accordion.

Anita had returned to complete her bachelor's degree after dropping out for a year. María lived nearby and visited regularly with her two little girls and baby boy. The baby, born prematurely, was saved by the constant attention of the family members who had camped out in the pediatrics ward of the local hospital. Filemón, who was working in the mine commissary, reported that fewer supplies were coming in each day. He now had five children and still lived with his in-laws.

Each evening we gathered in the bedroom where Juan and Petrona slept with Victor Hugo in their big bed, next to Elena and her son in a single bed and Juan Manuel on a cot. I was given the seat of honor squarely in front of the television set, tucked in with shawls and lap blankets. Petrona arrived home each evening shortly after dark – her jailor did not want his supervisor to see that he had released her for the night – and would get into bed with Juan, who lay propped on pillows still wearing his suit, sweater, and felt hat. Between them was Victor Hugo, now nine. He was a serious child who hardly ever spoke, not even trying to compete with Israel for the admiring attention of the family. There we would eat the supper that Anita prepared after she came home from secondary school: vegetable soup, heaps of rice, and occasionally a little meat.

Usually Petrona's comadres would arrive about eight o'clock to watch television and sew on her machine. Throughout the month of July a television version of the Mexican novella *Viviana* was featured. When I entered the household, Viviana was in jail, having been unjustly accused of killing the madam of a bordello who was the sister of the woman who employed her, Viviana, as a housemaid. In the course of the novella, Viviana's husband deceives her into signing divorce papers and then marries another woman for her wealth. When Viviana discovers she is pregnant, three men – her ex-husband, the father of her husband's new wife, and the grandson of her employer – try to save her honor by marrying her.

Television ads for the candidates interrupted the episodes of *Viviana*. Banzer had the most paid ads, and he promised a return to the prosperity of the 1970s when Bolivia, like most Latin American countries, was able to get unlimited credit because of the petrodollar glut in international banks. Paz Estenssoro returned from obscurity to promise "more of what he had brought to the Bolivian nation." No one was quite sure what that was. There were also sixteen parties of the Left, fragments of the old National Revolutionary Movement (MNR), the Revolutionary Left Movement (MIR), the Communist Party, the Socialist Party, the United Left Front, the Tupak Katari Liberation Party of Miners and Peasants, and a host of contenders for each of these fragments. The Socialist Party was, in effect, running a dead man, Marcelo

Quiroga Santa Cruz, who had been cruelly murdered during Banzer's coup. He had been gunned down after his assassins had torn out his tongue to make sure that he would never speak. In the Socialist Party's ads the current candidate was shown speaking to crowds in front of a huge blowup of Marcelo's face.

Big problems confronted us as we sat in front of the television set. Would Viviana get out of jail? (she did) have her child? (yes, a boy) and remarry her husband? (I left before this last question was satisfactorily answered.)

We also were questioning whether Petrona would get a prison sentence along with a fine for the sale of the lots. Would Juan Manuel get his discharge papers despite his desertion from the army? Would Aníbal go to Sweden with his wife and abandon the family? Would Banzer seize the presidency in a coup to forestall a victory by *"El Mono"* (Paz Estenssoro) in the elections? Would María's husband, Guido, a labor leader in the National Petroleum Works, be jailed and tortured if Banzer carried out the coup? Would Juan suffer another stroke if he drank at the saints' day celebration that María and Guido were planning? Would Elena get an accordion and become a music teacher?

While we ruminated about these problems, María and her husband were making preparations for the saints' day celebration which was to take place in Juan's house.

One afternoon I came back from a critical meeting of the Housewives' Association to find the wall between the dining room and kitchen totally torn down. Fearing the worse, I ran upstairs and found out what had happened. Elena announced that they had torn down the wall so that the orchestra for the great fiesta could be housed inside, while the dancing would take place in the dining room and on the patio.

Suddenly all my years of practiced cultural relativity fell away, and I felt completely at a loss as to how to deal with their behavior. How could they think about having a fiesta with all these impending disasters? I left for La Paz and then returned to my own home a week short of my planned stay. I realized at an ethnographic level that having the celebration was precisely the thing that made it possible for them to survive the crises they faced every day. Celebrations give meaning and purpose to lives that are subject to threatening circumstances. I knew this, but still I felt the limitations that my own cultural outlook, which strives for order and security, had imbued in me.

The following year I returned briefly in August, when the March for Life (see Nash 1992) was organized. This demonstration was an attempt on the part of miners and civic committees in the mining communities to reverse decree 21060 that closed the mines. I went to the Rojas' house in Barrio Minero Santa Fe and found Anita alone. The house was rented except for one room where all of Petrona's possessions were piled up—the refrigerator, the red three-piece suite, the beds, and the television set. Anita was tidying up to receive the Mormon missionaries who arrived a few minutes after I did. Before they came, Anita told me where each member of the scattered family was living. Then I left the compound for the last time.

Most discussions about class are metatheories that put the conditions observed in a set of propositions the theoreticians would derive if they were experiencing those conditions. Or they derive notions about what workers should think from a theoretical construct that proposes what their historical role should be. The family autobiographies give a sense of the actual ideas people hold about class. They reveal the contradictions workers experience in their daily lives as they try to respond to the demands that class allegiance pose at the same time that they balance the claims put upon them by their family responsibilities. This juggling act reduces the heroic dimensions of everyday behavior, resulting in the compromises that plague the lives of workers who take their family responsibilities seriously.

Juan's life is fraught with these dilemmas. He sent his son Juan Manuel into the army, even knowing that the army is used mainly to fight workers' movements, and when Juan Manuel fled from the savage attacks of the sergeant, it was Juan that took him back so that he could receive his workbook.

Petrona accepts the compromises of working-class status with less concern for abstract principles. She voted for Paz Estenssoro because it was he who brought about the housing program from which they benefit. Her selling activities sustained the family during their most difficult years after Juan's retirement. However Juan does not once mention these activities when he speaks of all the other survival mechanisms undertaken by himself and his sons.

The children live out some of these same contradictions, caught in the web of the illusion that they could escape a life of toil through education, a goal that Juan set forth, yet one that became ever more elusive as the declining economy promised ever less even for professionals. Like Mother Courage, Juan reinforced the social system in which they were trapped with his often futile attempts to inspire his children to pursue an education. Elena is the one most caught up in this fantasy; she gave up marriage to the father of her child so that both of them could pursue their studies. My mere presence created another fantasy that cropped up when Anita announced that she wanted to be an anthropologist.

Juan recognizes the contradictions in the advice he gives his children, but he cannot avoid these since he wants them to live. And so he sent Juan Manuel into the army so that he could get his discharge papers and be rewarded with a job in the national mining company. When I asked him what kind of advice he gave to his children about the nature of military regimes, he responded

> I explained to them all that had happened in the past. For example, in this recent period, when Juan Manuel was in the army, he said that the military leaders of his regiment gave instructions saying that they were going to shut up the miners. Juan Manuel told me, "The military are going to seize the miners and machine-gun them down. They are going to go to work with the bullet at their throats." And I said to Juan Manuel, "This father of yours is a miner, a worker. Are you going to raise your hand against your father and your brothers? That is what your officers are saying, but you ought never to take it seriously. That is a bad thing for you." That's what I said. And I went on, "If anything serious happens, like a revolutionary battle, and if the workers take their stand, then you have to liquidate all the officers that command you to fire. So it ought to be."

Yet when Juan Manuel went AWOL after he was severely beaten by a noncommissioned officer who threatened to kill him, his father personally escorted him back to the barracks.

Juan, like most workers in Third World countries, has a greater sense of what is the historically appropriate moment for "taking a stand" and turning against their oppressors. But it is a problematic situation that the younger generation may find harder to deal with than their seniors have.

In speeches and publications leaders, like Domitila Barrios de Chungara (Barrios de Chungara, with Viezzer 1977) defy the everyday compromises of living in repressive countries, yet their survival depends upon people like Juan and Petrona to feed them when they are in hiding and to follow them when they call on workers to take a stand. It is as important to understand *their* lives as to understand those of the leaders; *they* are the ballast that provides the stability in historical progress.

Chapters 1 through 10 were translated by Elizabeth Hansen, 11 through 16 by Cassandra Torrico, and chapters 17 through 21 by me. I reviewed and revised all translations, with the help of comments from Adriana Garcia and from anonymous readers as well. The translations attempt to be true to the speech patterns of Juan and Petrona. I am indebted to the Professional Staff Congress Research Program of the City University of New York for a grant that enabled me to prepare the English translation of the book published in Spanish by Nueva Visión under the title *He agotado mi vida en la mina*, and also for the funds that made possible the return field trip I made in 1985 to update the narrative.

# 2

# From the Countryside to the Mine

Like many mining families, the parents of Juan and
Petrona were recruited into the mines from the Cochabamba valley area. Population growth and the selling off of land left many peasants without a livelihood;
some were disinherited by their own families, as Juan
recounts, while others were left penniless by national
policies that favored large landowners over small plot
cultivators. Even after these peasants left their villages
to work in the mines, they maintained continuing relations with family and community. These links were
kept alive by the women who traveled continually to
the agricultural valleys to purchase supplies for their
families' use and to resell in the mining community.
Juan's mother epitomizes the resilience of women in
the face of widowhood and frequent relocations from
one mining center to another or even back to their rural origins. It is through their efforts to maintain kin
and fictive kin relations that workers brought conti-
nuity to a transient society.

In this chapter, Juan recalls his earliest memories of
his life in Cochabamba and how his father entered the
mines.

My mother came from a very rich family. They had estates in the plains
of Cochabamba, where they planted potatoes, corn, wheat, *papalisa* [a
kind of potato], *oca*, and everything. My grandmother, my mother's
mother, had lost her husband by the time she was called for the distri-

bution of her family's lands. When she got to her brother's house, he asked her, "Which of the haciendas do you want? Do you want the hacienda at Ichuichu or the one at Arrumuri?"

My grandmother answered, "What do I want with a hacienda? It would be better to give me money. With money I will be able to live until the hour of my death. My oldest son is no longer at my side, so there is no one to work the hacienda. Haciendas are for men."

My grandmother's older brother told her, "Justina, I will give you money and horses and bulls if you like. Whatever you ask for, I will give you, and I will take over the running of the hacienda at Arrumuri."

My grandmother was satisfied and accepted the offer. After some time she received twelve horses, twenty bulls, and a sum of money. In this way she gave up her claim on the hacienda at Arrumuri. To this day, my grandmother's brother is working that hacienda. Well, with the agrarian reform, they took away most of it, but he continues working what is left.

*How many acres was it?*

I can't tell you precisely, but it was a very big estate. I remember that it included the ranches of Chacapaya, Lampayani, Totrani, Ichuichu, Arrumuri, Ch'ulpu Casa, and Mallku Rancho.

The money that my grandmother got from her brother was used up soon. She didn't die as soon as she thought she would. She started to sell other land, including the lands in Mallku Rancho. Then she died, and my mother became an orphan and was always poor until the hour of her death.

They say my father was a very disobedient son. When he was young he fought with his brothers. Since they could not agree, he left home. From that day on he never returned. His older brothers looked for him when their parents died, but did not make a thorough search since they wanted to divide up the land only among themselves. They kept half the houses on the Plaza Calacota, some of which should have been given to my father.

That's the reason my father lived in the streets. There he met my mother, and they married. My mother's first husband didn't marry her — he only lived with her. When she was still single she had a son, Leonard, who is the oldest of us. He was recognized as a son by my father, but I don't know what name he uses. He is still living in the Republic of Argentina. Later on she lived with another man. She had another son, Felix, but she says that the man was a bit of a sissy, and that her parents wouldn't let her stay with him and separated them. For this reason we are brothers only through my mother. We don't share a father, and we hardly know each other.

I was born in the year 1926 in the mining district of Morococala. My father worked in the mine until I was six months old, and then we went to Cochabamba. I lived there until I was five years old. My memories begin from that date. I understood things.

After that year's harvest, two gentlemen came to my house and hired my father to go work in the Siglo XX mine. In those days when the ex-magnates of the mining oligarchy like Patiño, Aramayo, and Hochschild were around, there was plenty of work in the mines and everywhere, in the countryside and in the cities. People were afraid to work in the mines, so the mining companies had to go to the countryside to hire workers. Consequently, all the mining administrators sent out labor contractors to hire workers. On these recruiting trips they would bring back at least sixty, one hundred, one hundred and twenty or one hundred and fifty workers. I don't know how much they paid, but they earned lots of money. They came from everywhere, offering work. It wasn't like now; now it is we, the workers, who look for work, not the mining companies who look for workers.

My father contracted to work in the Siglo XX mines. He took us with him by train. We got to the Llallagua station and got off the train. He took us to the Siglo XX mess hall, and there we were given enough food to satisfy each of us. That night he took us by truck to Cancañiri. We slept in a room that had beds for each of us. The next day they took my father to the office for his registration and then to the hospital for the examination. Later on, a man took my mother and father to show them a house in the mining camp. They gave him a house with a kitchen. This was in May of 1931.

In the month of August of the same year there was the fiesta of the Virgin of the Assumption, which they celebrated for three days — the fourteenth, fifteenth, and sixteenth. My father took us to the fiesta to see the events. There were bands of dancers representing devils, llama herders, *cullawas*, *tundiques* — now we call them "Negritos." There were lots of people, lots of things for sale, such as food and alcoholic beverages. There was lots of everything.

The next year, in 1932, my mother put me in school. I was six years old. I went to school for the first time at Siglo XX's school in the camp of Cancañiri. I was a little frightened and timid when I went to school.

There was a boy who told me, "Here in school, we don't play much. If you are going to play this way, they will take you to that house and lock you in with the skulls."

According to what my father told me when I was older, I was a very playful boy, always active. Instead of going to school, I would go behind the hill called Convento, and when I thought it was twelve o'clock, I would go home. Finally the teacher sent for me at home, and they found my father, who was still sleeping since he worked the second shift. They told him I hadn't been going to school. Hearing this news, my father went out to look for me and surprised me on the hill where I was playing. He drove me to school with whip lashes. From that time on, I attended school all the rest of 1932.

Once, while passing near the workers' houses that were by the school, I found a pocket watch. I don't know what kind of watch it was. I was excited, and I told the boys, "I found a watch!"

There was a blond man at the door of one of these houses, who ran up the street shouting, "A boy found a watch!"

Immediately a woman came out of one of the houses, but she didn't claim it. In the afternoon the teacher called me in and said, "Let me see, bring out the watch." I showed it to him, clutching it in my hand. No one was going to take it away from me. Then the teacher said, "We are going to punish you if you don't give up that watch."

I preferred the punishment to giving up the watch, which was mine now. I didn't return it, and the teacher didn't punish me either. He called for my father, but when he came my father told him, "If he found it, and it has no owner, what can we do? It belongs to him from now on."

The teacher wanted to keep it until someone claimed it. But I wouldn't let anyone take it away from me under any circumstance. I held it tight in my hand until I let my father have it. And on each payday my father gave me five or ten cents because I had given him the watch. With these few pennies I bought myself candies, bread, and whatever I wanted. I didn't like candies as much as bread, so I almost always bought bread.

There was a fierce teacher — we called him "*Pícaro* de Virvala." I don't remember his real name, but he was very mean and frightening. He would grab us by the ear or the hair, so whenever I saw him, I would hide. I would go into class only with large groups of boys; that gave me protective cover. There was also a woman teacher, dark and quite nice. She lived next to us in the camp.

In those days we all lived together: there was no particular method of assigning houses. Later they organized separate housing for the teachers and other employees, and there were special camps for the miners; in other words, they always tried to isolate us.

*How many other boys were in your school?*

Well, there were many of us in school. There were three pupils to a desk — very uncomfortable. The mining company wasn't as attentive as it is today. There was always a shortage of desks. I sat in the middle, because I was small; two larger boys were on either side of me. The teacher moved me from there, because I was always fighting with the other boys, and she put me in the first row, closer to her. But there were so many mischievous boys that she mixed us together with the girls. She would seat us with a girl on either side of us and that did it.

In October, before the final exams, our teacher pressed us with work. We couldn't have recess because we had to study. Since there were so many students, we were falling behind.

I was more interested in playing than in other things, and she punished me a lot. The teacher told me to bring my father in so that he would discipline me. That made me think, but I never told him. I went home as though nothing had happened and, at school, I lied and said that my father would come. She waited for him, but he never came. Finally, with all the studying she was making us do, she forgot. Also, I stopped being such a troublemaker and concentrated on my studies. In this way I saved myself. I passed the first grade of primary school.

On one occasion, a bunch of boys suggested we go swimming in Catavi. I remembered that we had passed an iron gate, but in my enthusiasm, I didn't remember much.

We had a good swim and left about eleven o'clock, when we met the mother of one of my friends who had come to Catavi to buy her supplies at the store. I was absent-minded and stayed outside. The boy didn't say "we are going in, wait for me" or anything, he just went off with his mother. Then I thought, How will I go home? I don't know the way. It was a long way from the camp at Siglo XX to Cancañiri. I decided to go alone, and after walking a long way I arrived at one encampment. However, we hadn't come that way with my friend, but around the edge of the hill. I went to the center of the camp, but was so nervous, I couldn't understand the people there.

It was late, about two o'clock. I was frightened. How will I get home? I thought. Finally I arrived at the Siglo XX camp. Just then I realized we had come from below, and I was on the wrong side of the hill. I went down again while it was getting later. It was about five in the afternoon. I continued walking, looking for the way, lost. Soon I met a lady who told me, "In a little while I am going to Cacañiri. I have to go to sleep at my father's." But I was so worried now, I continued walking. I was crying.

Suddenly my father appeared, coming down the path, calling, "Juanito, Juanito, Juanito." I heard my father's voice and ran to him. I was above and he was walking up the path from below. My father grabbed me and beat me with a whip. "Who told you to go," he shouted. I continued crying until he took me home. When I got home my mother beat me too. They were so angry they almost skinned me, because they were worried and they cared for me. They punished me because I left home without telling my mother and they didn't know where I was.

Some time after this incident, I left the house because my parents were arguing. Then my father said to my mother, "Juanito is going out on the street. I think he is running away because he is scared." He followed me, but he fell, whether from rushing or from anxiety because he was afraid I was running away. His whole face was scraped; it was very ugly, as though we had cut a piece of meat off it with a knife.

Seeing all the blood, I screamed, "What's going on?" I thought my mother had done something to him when he came out, but it was from scraping his face on the grading ramp on a corner.

My mother and I took him to the hospital right away. My older sister stayed with the babies. In the hospital, they scolded him and accused him of being drunk, but there was a doctor who thought he wasn't drunk and said, "It was a fall. Surely he was in a hurry and slipped on the ramp and fell down."

My father leveled all those gradings when he fell. My brothers and I have also fallen and leveled them since. They were made of dirt and were very steep. During the rains, though, it was martyrdom for us, it was awful, because they turned to mud and were very slippery. When he was well, my father threw out all that dirt and made new steps.

*Can you describe a mining camp in those days?*

My father's house had a room and a separate kitchen, and we all slept in the main room. Everyone's house was the same; even if a family had eight children, it had only a single bedroom. The bedroom served for everything: to eat in, a living room, everything. We had only three beds and there were four of us children. We all lived in no more than a single room because it wasn't the custom to give rooms the way people now have. The rooms had no windows at all. Some had doors with two glass panes, but most had doors made of corrugated zinc. In those days people suffered a lot in the encampments. A few lived with another family in a single room, all together. Many fights broke out. There were not enough houses, and the company didn't think it necessary to have more built so that its workers could live in peace. It wanted to make money, not provide houses for its workers.

We lived far away from the main mine entrance. But we could hear the workers passing because it was a very steep ramp to descend. At that time, the company didn't give people boots for working in the mine. The workers made their own *p'olqos*. These are boots made with cowhide from the head of the animal. The mine was damp and ordinary shoes would not last longer than two or three days, while the *p'olqos* lasted a lot longer. Miners went to work at five o'clock in the morning. Women had to begin cooking at two or even one o'clock in the morning, so that their husbands could go to work well fed. In those days, the miners did not come out to eat a meal, nor did the women send them food; they ate in the mine. From seven in the morning they were down the mine working continuously until three in the afternoon. At three in the afternoon they would come out.

In the early morning I could hear them entering the mine as I lay in my bed, I could hear them hollering *"Uuja"* ("that way"), some were singing, others whistling and yelling like that whenever they went to work. There are always some workers who are noisy and a bit crazy. Those are the talkers, those who drink a lot, the ones who skip work. Always, in all work crews, there is at least one worker who makes the other workers laugh.

In September, my father married off his godson, Filomeno Camacho. He started working a bit before my father, but he worked no more than two years. My father's goddaughter was a bit lazy. She didn't feed this godson of my father well. So very soon he got the mine sickness and died in the hospital in a terrible frenzy. He breathed in his bed as though he had just run up a mountain at full speed. He couldn't rest anytime, day or night. He was always in a frenzy. Even when he was sleeping, this heavy breathing continued.

*Did you see him?*

I saw him. I was almost six years old. I watched him until he died. I was always at his side, with his wife, because I was a boy. My older sister was not sent to accompany him because she was a girl.

So this godson of my father died. Seeing this, my mother said to my father, "Manuel, I don't want you to work here anymore. You have seen our godson. He worked only two years and died of the mine sickness. We had better go dedicate ourselves to agriculture. We have a bit of land, and there you will plant and we will help you somehow."

My father left the mine in December, and we went to Cochabamba. That year we planted no seed because our land was already rented to others. The harvest came and yielded good produce from the land. It was divided and we received half. I was still not strong enough to help my father, but I earned some money by weeding carrots. It was little, but it seemed fair to me, for in those days money was worth a lot. Five cents always helped at my house, and I was paid on the same day. I would take it to my house and give it to my mother, and she would tell my father. He was pleased.

*During the feast of All Saints' Day we talked with Juan about the souls and how they visit houses. He had prepared a feast for the spirit of his mother and was waiting for her visit this first year with her family. He recalled the following event:*

When we were still small — I remember as though I were dreaming — my mother got sick. My little sister Ricarda was still nursing. My mother got sick with yellow fever, which in those days killed many people. My father was not with us; he had gone to earn money in Chimore, working on the highway. They took my mother to the hospital in Cochabamba. When she would get crazy with delirium they would submerge her in cold water. Then, taking off her wet clothes, they gave her dry clothes and put her in bed. My mother said this helped people with yellow fever sleep. When the fever would return another round of delirium would begin.

On one of those days, my mother died, but only for about five hours. Seeing that she was dead, the nurses took her to the death room to prepare her for burial. They covered her with sheets only. In her dreams, my mother said, she began to wander across a flat plain. She was very thirsty and was looking for water to drink, but couldn't find any. That field ended and another field, covered with big and little bushes appeared. How will I get to the end of this field? she asked herself. Then laboriously she continued crossing those stretches. Another prickly field appeared. She said that the thorns ripped her dress on the sides. A bit beyond some blue appeared, like water, but my mother didn't cross this field. A big house appeared, with a very narrow path to pass by. On one side there was nothing to bother her, but on the other side there were burning flames. It was the only way to go. You must go, thought my mother in her nightmare. She went by the left side and the fire almost burned her. She crossed a large, wide stretch. When she got to a door a man was standing there with a staff. He barred the way with his staff and looked at my mother, and my mother also looked at this man. Then he lowered his staff and she passed. At a second door another man was standing, holding a large key. He put his key into the door, but wouldn't let her pass. At that instant, said my mother, she woke up, five hours after having died.

My mother screamed, "*Alalitawan! Alalitawan! Imaraykutaj hinata wuichurpari wanchis sabanas llatawanri chay wañuchisaj, wañaka taykuri-waychis.*" This means "*Alalaway,* I am cold. Why did they put me on the table like this with only a sheet, as though I were dead? Cover me now. Now, I am cold."

She said that the nurses were frightened and no one came near her because they said that she was damned, having come back from death. Then three doctors came in and gave her an injection. They ordered the nurses to take her to bed and give her a hot water bottle. The nurses put her to bed, covered her well, and put a hot water bottle to her feet. My mother reacted and got sick again.

She got up with delirium one day, and they say that she wandered through the streets, wearing no more than a shift. People stared at her, laughing. (Many sick people wandered like that, the men in their underwear and the women in their shifts. They didn't know what they were doing, a reaction to having a fever of forty degrees.) They grabbed my mother in the street and took her in an ambulance to the hospital where they again put her in the pool of cold water. Then she was put to bed where she remained for two more days.

The final time that my mother went out in her shift, without an overskirt, she got on the streetcar and came to Vinto. No one stopped her. Nothing happened. She got off the streetcar where there was a shack, a very dangerous place because thieves often killed people who went there to sell cattle or paired donkeys. Here my mother saw two men who came down from the mountain above. She got frightened, and again the madness overcame her. She began to sing a carnival song.

We were at home at three in the afternoon that day, playing in the yard. My older brother was sick in bed, but the rest of us were well, including the baby.

(We would get milk for the baby by pasturing our neighbor's sheep.

Our neighbor was my mother's god-parent and my sister Francisca's godmother. We knew how to pick good grass to feed to the sheep so it would have lots of milk, and the neighbor milked it and made cheese. Sometimes this woman was mean and we pastured her sheep in vain. Since none of us had any money, when she would not give us milk we had to give the baby sugar water in a bottle and make her suck on that.)

Suddenly we saw my mother at the door of her god-mother Costa and god-father Liborio's house, singing carnival music, clapping and twirling and dancing. I called to my sister, "Francisca, our mother has come home drunk. She is singing as she comes. She is very drunk."

When my sister came out, she saw her and we ran to hold my mother by the arms while we took her home. There was no smell of alcoholic drink, nothing. We realized that she had escaped from the hospital with her illness. My mother got into bed and the fever passed. We kept her here in the *sovacos* with leaves of *andresuella*, soaked in my younger brother's urine. With this, my mother fell asleep.

When she came to her senses, we said to her, "*Mamitaj, junan kay wawaykitay manaña ñunuykita conquinachi. Korillayña ari kay chika unayñaga,*" in Quechua. This means, "Now you must give your breast to this baby. It took so long for you to come back. These two months the baby hasn't sucked, hasn't tasted, *mamita*. Why do you hide it? This way the baby will be all right, but without the breast he will die."

My mother answered in Quechua, "*Manañoqaypatachu ni ima bala umaswawaspis waway kanchu pitaj nokaman wawata kowaska? Maypi ñoga wawayoj karkani.*" "You are nothing to me. I have neither children nor a baby. Who would have given me a baby? Since when would I have a baby with a bullet head?" Saying this, she got angry.

My sister was crying, we were all crying at her side, and this made my mother remember that she had her little baby. She took the baby and made it suck, but she had no milk. Her breasts were dry because two months had passed. The baby became worse and she almost died.

Suddenly my father arrived with lots of money. He went to Cochabamba and found a good doctor to help my mother get well. He brought the doctor on a horse and he came on foot. The doctor told him how to give injections to my mother and stayed until six in the afternoon at our house. And my father made my sister cook a chicken stew for the doctor, who ate and then left. The next day he came back and treated my mother again. He came for three days. I don't remember how much he was paid, but my father gave a sum of money to this doctor.

My mother got well, but she had to learn how to walk with a stick. She would go out in the sunlight, to the street or to the yard, my sister and I holding her by the arms. When she combed her hair, it came out as though it had been cut with scissors. After my mother got well, my father went again to where he was working, to earn a little money so that we could go with him.

So it was that my mother told me of when she died for five hours and walked on the path to heaven. That is surely the way we will all go, for many people have spoken of these same fields she saw. Those of us who aren't such sinners don't know about the fire; nothing burns us. But for those bad people, they say there is fire.

My mother must have been bad; certainly she was always very strict. She controlled us children with nothing more than her eyes. When people were with her, we had to obey her glances. And if no one was around, she would chastise us with whip lashes.

For this reason we have all followed a straight path and we feel proud. We know how to respect people and we also know how to make ourselves respected. If my mother had raised us like other children without fathers, we would have become ill-mannered, lazy, or drunkards. We are proud because my mother was able to educate us, although not in schools, but she showed us the morality of living in the world. This is why my mother was bad and strict, and surely why she saw that hell that burned her when she passed, burning her on one side.

She said that when she returned from that path, she thought to herself in Quechua, *Kunan kay kitiytiyka kay uj ladutañataj kunan kay uj laduytañataj rupayjuwanka ari.* "Now as I return by one path, I won't burn myself again." She didn't go back the same way, but returned directly to the hospital's death room where she had been taken prematurely.

In the month of August, or thereabouts, my father got sick. I was not in school, because there was no money to send me. We went to the city of Cochabamba to the house of an aviator who was a relative of my father. This man had us in his house for three months. My mother would go to the countryside to plant our lands. During those three months, my father was in the general hospital at Cochabamba, recuperating from the mining sickness; his sickness wasn't so advanced, but he knew that he was ill.

That year we raised many rabbits in the field. We never bred a black buck rabbit, but when the females got impregnated and gave birth, the offspring were all black. Some does had two rabbits, both black. Others four, all pure black. Some had just one, each also black. My father said, "*Caramba*, I don't know which one of us will die."

He got well and we went to Mallku Rancho. The maize shoots were coming out of the ground. They were already big, with three leaves. Seeing this, my father set to work taking care of the plants. The harvest was admirable.

In February my father got sick again. Although he was sick he went, together with many men who had encouraged him to join them, to the east, where lands were being divided into plots of the size that people wanted. In Mallku Rancho we had a very small plot of land to plant, and the harvest didn't last us the whole year. My father went to check whether it was true that they would give him more land. There he again got sick. He stayed a week.

While he was there the little rabbits began to whistle. They would stand on two feet, putting their front paws up like this, and they would whistle like people — one by one, not all at once. There were also other animals, ones that we called *chuseka*, or owl, that came to whistle at our door at dawn, unfailingly, every morning. And our roosters began to crow after five o'clock in the afternoon. A cock should never crow at that hour. If they do, it means that something serious is going to happen in our family, or to some of our neighbors that we like, or even to the nation; some bad luck will happen. That's why the cock crows.

People said, "*Uuuy, kay chica puni cowisniyki yana kaska; luta kayka mayquen niyquichischa wañunquichij.*" This means "*Uuuy*, there have been so many black rabbits. It must mean mourning. Who can it be that will die?" Moreover, my mother told us that in her dream her front teeth came out, all of them except those in the corners. She thought, Why did I have them out now? What will I eat meat with? Then she woke up and told us all.

My father stayed for a week in Puerto Todos Santos and returned even sicker. He told my mother, "María, we have to go as soon as possible. We will leave our harvest to our neighbors. They will harvest it and sell it and send us the money, or else you will come back. There, in Puerto Todos Santos, the life of a peasant is marvellous. There we will live in peace and we will become rich again the way we were before."

We prepared ourselves to go. My mother sold all the animals. A fat woman, named Cristina, helped us. She made *phiri*, a dish made of maize flour to eat with our meat, so that we children wouldn't be asking for bread or food from our mother. We had just enough money to go so we left. I took a little chicken. I didn't know whether it was a male or female when I left, but we later learned it was a female.

We got there and stayed for a day and a night in a house where nobody lived. The next day a gentleman named Serapio, came. He was sick in one eye. This man was in charge of a stretch of land seven kilometers from town and he took my father to show him some land. I don't remember precisely how much, but a lot. He showed him a high place and said, "Here you can build a house and you can clear all of this and prepare it for seeding. This place has no owner. You can plant whatever you like anytime. You can plant everything except potatoes. Instead of potatoes, here we plant *balusa*, it is like yucca." In this way, he gave my father instructions.

But my father got much sicker and couldn't work. The flood came. The camp was flooded. The houses had some hooks to hang our charms against witchcraft. All the houses in the camp were the same. Above, almost at the eaves of the roof, there was a place to sleep that one reached by a ladder with hemp rungs. When we slept we would pull up the ladder on one side, and when we woke up in the morning we lowered the ladder and came down.

When the flood came there was no reason to go anywhere. My first cousin, Simón Rodrigues, and I went to get food for my mother to cook. We got green papayas, green plantains, and yucca *balusa* to eat; That season there was no rice on sale, because it had all been taken to the town.

We were there a month and a half at most. The harvest was still in the ground — the maize had not yet been cut. But my father got sicker, and we went to Cochabamba again.

When we got there I also got very sick. For some fifteen days I didn't get out of bed. We stayed at an inn and put my father in the hospital. We had no money to pay for the lodgings, but we could not return to the country while I was still sick. On one of those days, my sister went out in the street and found a bank note. She brought it to my mother and it was enough to get me medicine. I wanted to walk; I had strength for everything. With this money we went to our house in the country, leaving our father in the hospital. There was plenty of food because the plantings we had left had been harvested. Only a small part had been stolen, and with this we were content.

My mother went to Cochabamba to see my father every week, often every three days. After two months of this my mother no longer had enough money to go. She said to me, "Since you pay less, it's better that you go to see your father." I went there to the general hospital and found that my father's bed was empty. One of the gentlemen in that room spoke to me, in Quechua. *"Qan chay caballerojta wawan kanki?"*

I answered, *"Ari, wawan kani. Hamuni desde kampumantapacha watukuy, mamitay mana hamunchu por que ruwan tianku hakaypi."*

He said, *"Tatayquitaka ch'isi parti wañuskata apaykunku misericordiaman. Wañupuñacha kunan kamaka yajkuspa watukukullay chay muyuykunitallapi."* He had said to me, "You are his son, right?"

I answered, "I am his son."

"Your father is not here. This morning they took him very early. Last night your father died. They took him to the morgue in the last agonies of death."

I went back and looked in the morgue and I saw the face of my father, open-mouthed, his eyes open as though he were looking at the door, waiting for us to come. At this moment, I ran from the hospital to the trolley car station on the highway.

I got to Vinto and from Vinto I ran to my house to tell my mother that my father was dead. My mother sent my older brother Felix to go get money from my uncle Aurelio, my father's brother. He gave Felix five pesos and with this he went with my mother to Cochabamba to bury my father.

To this day I have not seen his tomb, but I know that those two alone buried him. They didn't tell my father's relatives because they had put him out on the street. And so my father died, within four months after the rabbits were born black and whistled, and the cock began to crow at sundown.

We continued living in Mallku Rancho. When I was eight years old, in 1933, I was strong enough to work. My mother hired me out to a man named Luis Rojas to plow the land with an oxen team. When he was plowing, I told him he should teach me and he taught me to work the land. Little by little, watching him, I learned and I worked other lands. I did the sowing on our lands because my mother had no money to pay peons. Luis Rojas helped me for nothing because he saw that we were poor, and he, too, was poor. Finally my mother lived with this man, who was single.

Luis Rojas went to the mines at Taniani and was there nine or ten months. He went to earn money to improve our house in the country and to buy a bull to work the land. I took care of everything that had to be done in the house. I have always been a worker, since I was very small. I have worked hard.

We bought a donkey with the money we made selling grapes, peaches, everything. I went with the donkey to the fields at Mormontarnos to get potatoes. That place was very far away. We would leave at five in the morning from Mallku Rancho, get there at eight or nine at night without resting anywhere. Not so many people came to this place so there were lots of potatoes.

We took a half bushel of peaches and in return, we obtained more than a bushel of potatoes—but there was no one to help load the donkey.

My mother and I were crying and cursing the hour of my father's death. My mother and I pushed some large stones next to the donkey so that I could stand on them and lift the load on to the donkey's back. The donkey was quite tame, it didn't run away. My mother subdued it and held the donkey's head. A boy was passing by that place, and I called to him, "Hold the donkey, so I can heave the load up on its back." The two of us and my mother, with a lot of effort and the help of this boy, put the load on its back. We tied it on tightly and went peacefully to Chacapaya.

Before we got to Chacapaya, it rained heavily, a very strong rain, and the San Antonio river rose dangerously. We saw the river and didn't dare cross it. We slept there and didn't arrive in Chacapaya until six or seven the following evening. We had a dog with us, a big dog who was like a person. That dog always made us respected by everyone. While we slept the dog stayed awake taking care of the donkey and the load. He had only to bark and I would run and see, but nothing happened all night.

The water receded the next day. We were looking for the boatman who guided people rowing across the river. We waited until about eleven in the morning. My brother Felix went up the mountain to bring a *Yuracari*. These are ugly men who have spots on their faces, coffee colored, or white or reddish spots. He brought two *Yuracari* and these two men helped us cross the river.

These men of the jungle don't understand money. When you give them money, they take it with pleasure, because they don't understand how much you are giving. They like silver pennies more than larger quantities of money; they don't know if it's five or ten cents. You have to have the money in change because if you give them bills, they'll take it and won't return any change. You would certainly lose it.

We crossed the river and we walked until about one in the afternoon. The heat was strong, we were thirsty, and there was no water to drink. We met a traveler driving a mule train who knew where there was water. He went to get it and gave us some. He was used to drinking *chiri*. When we got home, the donkey gave birth. We had no sooner unloaded it than it gave birth. It was a male.

*Was that the first time you saw a birth?*
Yes, that was the first time.

*Were you afraid?*
Yes, I was very frightened. My mother said, "Our little donkey is going to give birth, and then we will have two. Let us take good care of the donkey. You must go cut grass and bring it to her. We have no alfalfa." As she said this, I saw the donkey born.

Seeing the birth, I reacted by crying, but I was very happy. "Now we have two donkeys," I cried, and right away I went for grass in the maize fields. There I cut green grass for the animal. I got one load and fed the donkey.

We went on several trips for potatoes, leaving the donkey's offspring behind. We would go in the early morning to exchange peaches for potatoes and we would return at dusk. We knew the baby donkey was waiting for us at home. The donkey had a great deal of milk, so I milked her. My mother said, "When men drink donkey milk, they get strong and become very forceful." Hearing this, I milked the donkey and, except for adding some sugar, took it straight. I drank almost a liter of milk from the donkey and then released her to nurse her offspring.

*What friends did you have in Mallku Rancho?*
I had a first cousin, Simón, the son of my Aunt Salomé, my mother's sister. This boy was older than I. We walked arm in arm, as though we were brothers. There were other boys above us, our houses separated by an irrigation ditch. They were our rivals.

The feast of All Saints came. We went to Cahupisu to pray because there were good offerings.[1] In Mallku Rancho people were the owners of their own fields, while in Cahupisu, they were peons on a large hacienda. There they made good *urpus*[2].

[1] On All Saints' Day, everyone lays a table in their main room with food offerings for the dead of their household. Those who come and sing for the souls of the dead are given bread and cake.
[2] *Urpus* are butterfly-shaped loaves of bread.

We met the boys who lived above. What happened was that we saw ourselves as small and the others as big. We felt we couldn't defend ourselves in any way. Simón said to me, "Let's go, Juanito, because I don't know what they will do to us here. They are big and the ditch is right next to us. They don't know if the water is flowing or dammed. This way they won't know if it is us running down or if it is the water. Above, everything is quiet." One of the boys wanted to throw us in the water. "They will drown us in the water. The ditch is deep. Let's go!"

My brother started running, and the others ran after him, and I, also wanting to run, jumped and fell in the middle of the ditch. My brother leaped over and passed easily. I wanted to do the same, but I did no more than fall in without being thrown in by anyone. I could hardly get out. They were throwing things at my brother, but they didn't see me because I was in the water; otherwise they would have thrown things at me, too. Well, the thought came into my mind: *Caray*, my mother is to blame. I had told my mother before we left, "We will go pray on the upper side."

She had said, "Go, it is better on the upper side, they pay more." She didn't know we were enemies with the other boys. I said to myself, one by one these *carajos* will pay.

The next day the boys from the upper side came in a single group to the cemetery of Viloma and Mallku Rancho. We didn't let any of them pray because they were in our territory and we got our own back. A few came close to pray and we stood in front of them. We wouldn't let them get close to the table offerings. We threw them out of our territory. They went to the other side, but finally they all disappeared.

Once I was carving a top out of *jarka*, a fairly hard wood. I had had a little top made out of willow, but when we played with it, it split in two, so I didn't have a top. I am going to make myself a hardwood top, I thought, and so I made it out of *jarka*. While I was doing this, my mother was making *mukj'u*, jerked beef, to ferment to make *chicha*. The chickens came near while I was carving the wood for the top, and my mother was pulling weeds where the carrots were growing. She saw a chicken eating the *mukj'u* and ran over. As soon as I felt her whip, I noticed that chicken. *Caramba!* I grabbed a rag and used it to put a sign over the breast of the chicken: "This chicken is a thief!" The chicken went for a long time with that sign. (After all, the whip lashes on my legs had hurt a lot.) Everyone who read the sign laughed.

Another time my mother was boiling potatoes and again gave me a lash of the whip because the pot turned over and the fire went out. That time I couldn't avenge myself on anything. My mother went to work, leaving the potatoes cooking. This pot is to blame, I thought, and I grabbed the pot and — pam — I threw it to the ground together with the potatoes.

My mother was nearly speechless when she saw. "What am I going to do?" she said. "This boy is very stupid." But, she didn't punish me anymore; I was just irresponsible when I was young.

I now remember many things which happened in the school at Mallku Rancho. When he was still living Uncle Severino wanted to send me to school to help my mother. I didn't like to go to school because I was used to the street. Nevertheless, he put me in school.

During recess we played with *chuwis*.[3] There were children who would come to bother us. Passing our little mounds of beans, they would step on them. Screaming, "Why did you step on it for me, *carajo*," I would grab the boys and punch them.

Another time a girl from Viloma did the same thing. I gave her a punch in the eye and closed it for her, as though I were her husband. The next day her mother noticed that she was getting a black eye and asked her, "Who did it to you?"

"Doña María's son did it to me because, as I was passing, I stepped on his *chuwis*. That's why he hit me," she told her mother.

Her mother went to the police, and they told my mother and the teacher who asked me, "Why did you do this?"

"She stepped on my *chuwis*. That's why I punched her in the eye. I didn't want to hit her in the eye, but she gave it to me," I told them.

The teacher, Jose Luis Zambrán, laughed and asked, "She gave you her eye so that you could punch it?"

"Yes, sir, she has always given me the eye," I said, and it made him laugh.

He said, "You have to go to your house. You are too mischievous. You don't want to learn anything. You don't want to do anything but play."

"Then I won't come anymore," I said, leaving the school. I stayed behind the wall until it was time to go home. The next day I didn't go to school and, to this moment, I have not gone back. I have learned everything just from working.

[3] *Chuwis* are colored beans that children play with.

# 3
# Entry into the Mines

Juan's early acquaintance with death recounted in the first chapter is sharpened as he enters the mines to work at the age of eight. His total recall of accidents and casualties in this and subsequent chapters reveals an acceptance of human fate but not the development of a callousness to it. Mario Erdheim, a Swiss-Colombian ethnopsychiatrist, remarked on the quality of direct confrontation with death, completely unmystified or distanced, when he read Juan's autobiography. All Souls' Day, one of the most important celebrations in mining communities, is a time to relate to the dead through communal sharing of meals. After a death, when people congregate at the wake, they are given a full banquet to partake of with relatives of the deceased, and this is repeated for at least three years in succession after the death on All Souls' Day when the spirits of the dead are believed to return. Following that, they are offered just the cakes and bread formed into butterflies, babies, ladders (to climb to heaven), and other imaginative representations of their changed condition. Juan tells of his work in Cataricagua and how he tried to support his mother in this chapter.

My stepfather, Luis Rojas, came back from Taniani, where he had gone to work in the mine. He brought money, not much, but enough to take us there. I was eight years old in 1933 when I, too, entered the mine.

I worked as a "parrot" — that's what they call the children who watch for danger. They gave us a whistle to blow to warn the workers if a load was falling when they were working below. When we would blow the whistle, the workers would look up, and when they saw the load come down, they would defend themselves with their shovels. If it was a big load, we would whistle a lot, "Corh . . . corh . . . corh . . . ," and they would know they had to find shelter on either side of the shaft. Many times the rock would flow down like a river, and the workers had to barricade themselves from this with their shovels. It was a wolfram [tungsten] mine. Later they worked it from the outside.

I was still eight years old when I first saw an accident. I was sitting above the men who were working with the pickaxes. They would make trenches five or six meters deep and would enlarge them. They were making a mound to set off a big charge of dynamite. I heard the assist-ant driller saying in the morning: *"Caramba! Maskaynaypikaj soldados presos apayjuywanky, nanay."*

And the others answered, *"Pununkichaypeka, carajo!"* The master driller told him to bring some powder for the explosion.

Right away he brought a fifty-pound bag of powder to set off. He was already loading all of it with a scoop, with the detonator in position. While they were putting it in, they must have bumped it hard. The charge exploded.

I looked down there. *Caramba!* The other workers were down below, resting, waiting for the charge to go off. Some escaped under the rocks where they had their hiding places. I saw two bodies falling with the stones. One fell toward the river, and the other halfway down the slag-pile along with rocks to the place where the others were working.

There was nothing I could do. I couldn't get down to warn anyone. When they looked up, I was at my post, because there was no chance to go down by the stairs. I stayed alone. I became dizzy. They couldn't see me because I was protected by the rock. I didn't see them either. They were scared and shouting, and I answered with my whistle, be-cause I was afraid if I shouted I would dislodge the large rocks above me. I thought they were going to fall on top of me, or something. Then I went to my hiding place.

My spirit was heavy because of that explosion. I did nothing but stay where I was. There the hollowed rock gave me some protection. There was just a little room for me, and I didn't go out. It was lucky for me, because I, too, would have died. Stones were falling where I had been sitting and there was no one below on guard. I felt the explosion. I put my head out and saw the rocks were still falling, so I pulled my head in and stayed crouched in the same place.

After the explosion, I looked and there was still dirt coming down for a long while. The place was full of smoke and dust. The supervisor came up, tied to the stairs with the wire the men carry at their belts just in case of such accidents. Tying me with the wire, he lowered me. The men asked me what had happened.

I told them what I had seen. I saw everything, how the charge exploded, everything, because I was no further than thirty meters away. I saw an accident for the first time when I was eight years old in 1933.

They buried the two dead men in the cemetery of Taniani. The feast of All Saints came in November and we went to pray in their houses. I also went to earn *urpus* [bread shaped in the form of butterflies] by praying. With the little money I had earned working, I bought myself a heavy suit. We always wear a new suit for the important fiestas. In Taniani, the feast which people look forward to most is All Saints'. I wore the suit for the first time on the second of November, the day of the souls' farewell. There were many people who prayed in a different way, but we children of the mine met, and we knew all the songs by heart and we sang in harmony. Everyone wanted us to pray. They didn't want the other children because they didn't pray as well as we did, just one tune, without any harmony.

*Were you praying for your father or for other people?*

Oh, I didn't pray for my father. The praying was for all the people who had died, or for their families who prepared their tombs. We had to pray for other people and not for our own relatives.

*Why?*

Because it is said that when a son prays for a dead father, God does not receive the prayer. A person who is not related to the family has to pray for him.

*When your father died, did you prepare a tomb for the feast of All Saints' Day?*

For my father's first All Saints' Day feast we had a party in his memory. People who were not related, as well as family members, came to eat. But the relatives did not pray. We prepared a replica of a tomb, waiting for my father's soul to arrive. We made a large effigy out of dough and put it in the middle of the tomb. Then we put a roasted turkey biting a hot pepper in the middle of the table, and a cooked rabbit set on potatoes, biting a leaf of lettuce. On either end of the table we put *urpus*.

On the first day our guests prayed for him and no one else. The next day, the second of November, we prayed until noon for all our relatives who died. We cooked food, a hot pepper and chicken stew at midday for the day of the souls' farewell. We offered it to everyone who came. Not a single person who came, either a child or an adult, was left without food.

The feast of All Saints passed, and by the end of November I already knew the foreman. He said to me, "You can take metal away from here and sell it to the company."

During rest periods I would look for metal in the slagpile, collect it, and sell it. I went out at five in the afternoon, and immediately set to work searching for metal with a lamp like *jukus*, the ore thieves, use here. We had to sell it to the company. If we sold it to another company, they would fire us.

*Wasn't it against the law as it is here?*

No, it was done openly; we would put it in our pockets while the overseer was watching us. He wouldn't say anything because what we were taking was for the company itself.

*Could the companies earn more if they let you do this now, instead of having a mining police force?*

Yes, they pay more to the mining police than they save from theft. The police watch for a while, then they sleep, and the company gets robbed just the same. Even if they kept watch every night, the jucus would get hold of some minerals.

The whole mountain had wolfram. It was a black mineral like coal. On one occasion I found myself a large hollow that held a lot of it. I had climbed on top of a large rock when suddenly a flood in the river came rushing down like an avalanche. My stepfather and my brother-in-law were still above carrying this mineral. I saw the river and screamed, "The river is coming!"

There were large ravines, fifteen or twenty meters high, pure rock, and foaming water was coming down. I was frightened. I was far above it, and could see it clearly. That metal saved me. If I had not climbed on to that rock, the river would have taken me. I think we sold the metal for five bolivianos [Bolivian national currency], about fifty cents, but it was worth it.

In the middle of December of 1933 there was another accident, that

of Simón — I don't remember his last name. He was passing by where
the dynamite was, smoking a cigarette. Just below there were eight or
nine hundred sticks of dynamite, lots of it. The passageway was so narrow that we could only get by sideways. There was a wide path below,
but it was far away, and to save time, he was going this way. I don't
know if a spark fell from his cigarette as he went by, or what; I was
standing at the edge of the pit, watching something else. Soon, when
we went up to work, there was an explosion and we saw smoke as
though someone were going up and then down in a parachute. What
happened was that the blast threw that man up high, and then he fell
to the ground, his clothing smoking. He was all burned. People went
up to him to pick him up, and his hand fell away from his body. He was
cooked, screaming, "Ay, Ay!" and unable to move.

There was no fast means of transportation to take him to the hospital. We carefully loaded him on a mule, and took him to Huelchi, and
from Huelchi to Oruro by a car — ordered by radio. I came back from
Huelchi riding the mule, and the others went on to Oruro. Before they
got to Oruro, they said, around Paria, the man died. When I got to
Taniani, the relatives of the dead man asked me, "What happened?
How did he get there, alive or dead?"

"On the road he was alive, and he arrived at the highway still alive.
I don't know if he will reach Oruro alive," I told them.

After a while, the foreman came to my house. "You're back," he said.
"Let's go to work," and he took me with him.

During the rest period, I fell asleep. They had started to work below.
I must have slept a bit, and suddenly, as though the man was still
screaming, I awoke and heard stones falling. Frightened, I saw men on
the slagpile, some falling into a large pit. Others seemed to be escaping.
At that moment I whistled loudly. The rocks had almost buried them.
I was very frightened. I was very sick for some three months. I didn't
work. Finally my mother cured me.

*What type of sickness was it?*

I don't know what sickness it could have been. My mother cured me
of the *jap'eqa.*

*Did you have a temperature?*

A very high temperature, and I couldn't walk.

*Were you paralyzed?*

It was like paralysis. I couldn't move my feet.

*How were you cured?*
I don't know with what things. My mother tied my head here, my chest like this.

*Did she use the millu?*[1]
Yes, my mother cleaned me with the *millu* and she burned it in the fire to diagnose the illness. She cured me that way. She went to a *yatiri* [native curer] and he called back my soul from where it had wandered.

After I got well, we went back to Cochabamba in 1934. I had more sensation in my legs and I was a bit stronger. I used to climb the eucalyptus trees to cut their branches and I earned some money selling the leaves. My mother put me in school again. I was always writing on little papers when I worked at Taniani. I would make notes of things, like what I saw. About then, I had learned to write a bit. And in Mallku Rancho the teacher listened to me recite a lesson as an exam to determine what grade I should be in.

That year we were peaceful until the month of October when my mother became worried because she didn't know where to get money. We were growing and she had to spend more money on clothing.

*Didn't your brothers work?*
They didn't work because I was the oldest boy. By then, my sister was married.

My mother said, "Your stepfather wants us to go to the mine of Cataricagua."

I said, "Let's go. What can we do here?" We went to Oruro, but my stepfather didn't get along with my mother. They didn't fight, they just got angry and wouldn't talk. We children liked our stepfather. They didn't pay attention to us because they were angry. My mother put him out of the house in which we lived, on the street, with the little bed that he had. He took her word for it and went away to live in another house.

My mother couldn't earn money anywhere. I started to work in the city with masons. They paid me every week, enough to feed my little brothers. My mother began to sell vegetables. She sold potatoes, onions, hot peppers, tomatoes, vetch, and beans.

*Where did she find these vegetables?*
She bought them in Oruro from the men who brought in wholesale loads from Cochabamba. She would only buy by the bushel and would

---

[1] A white stone that miners claim holds radium that enables the curer to diagnose the illness.

sell enough to cover her capital outlay. The rest she brought home for us to eat. We had enough, plenty.

I started working for the town in 1935. I worked as a gardener in the *Plaza 10 de Febrero*. My mother was feeling better. Every month I would get paid fifty or sixty pesos if I hadn't withdrawn any earlier. My mother got back together with our stepfather, Luis Rojas, again. He took us to Cataricagua.

I was eleven years old in 1936, and that year I began to work in the mine. When I went to ask for work the manager said to me, "Go bring your mother."

I took my mother to the office, and told him, "This is my mother, and I need to work to support her and my little brothers."

Then they asked for a birth certificate. "I have neither a birth certificate," I said, "nor my mother's marriage certificate here. I need money to get that since I would have to travel far away for it."

When I said that, the manager said, "Go get a work permit from the police."

My mother and I went down to Huanuni and got a work permit, and when we showed it to the manager, he gave me work. My mother went home, and I went to have a physical examination.

I began working at the sample section of Socavón Patiño. We would grind the samples to get them ready to be sent to the laboratory. I gave the little pay I earned – I think it was one hundred and fifty pesos – to my mother. It wasn't much, but it was enough, and my mother was agreeable.

At the sample section I had several companions. One was called Martín Molina. He now lives near my house in Mallku Rancho, in Cochabamba. Two or three of us worked together. One of the boys, who was about to go into the army, was called Zenon. We played a lot with that one.

I was always honorable and respectful, especially with our foreman, Don Urbano Arias, who also took care of the workers' canteen with his wife and his nephew, Arturo. Don Urbano worked in the mine, and left periodically so he couldn't keep track of what the workers consumed. Neither he nor his wife, who had a little boy, could do it. Seeing my behavior, Don Urbano said, "Look, Rojito, will you watch the canteen for me, noting down what people buy? I will give you your ticket [to purchase food supplies] every day. Since there isn't that much work, you just stay at the canteen."

I accepted. "Very well, Don Urbano, I would like that, but in exchange, I want to be sure that if anything gets lost, don't blame me, because I have never in my life been known to take anything from my mother's house or from other people's houses. I am very honorable and I am very concerned about taking or touching something that isn't mine. Please show me everything clearly, so that I know what I can touch or take or eat. You could also tell me, 'This you can eat, but not that, because it costs so much,' right? Just give me instructions on everything. I will act accordingly, and I will give you all the money for what is sold and will also show you what the profits are."

Don Urbano's nephew, Arturo, who had previously tended the store, was a man with an uneven reputation. The canteen made some profit, but very little. Despite all his sales, little money had come in. After everything had been turned over to me, Don Urbano saw an increase of more than 100 percent in his earnings on his capital. I sold everything, and so his earnings were large.

He was astounded. He said, "*Caramba!* Surely that nephew of mine was taking a lot of money from me. He is young and doesn't even drink yet; I don't know what he did with that money."

He began to stock magazines, pastries, the ingredients needed to make *salteñas* [a roll with a variety of fillings], meat pies, roasts, and fried chicken on the stove. He gave me a portion of what I sold each month, as well as a salary.

I was in charge of guarding the store's door. When Don Urbano came in, he had to knock on the door. I would open it for him and he would come in in a good mood. He would look over everything and make a list of what was in short supply, and then he would leave. He brought cakes from Oruro in boxes and I would put them in the display counter. Once his wife, the mistress of the canteen, wanted one, and she came in and asked, "Is it all right if I take a little cake, just one for my little Juanito?"

I answered, "Yes, Doña Juanita, it is yours. Help yourself to whatever you want. I will just note it on the list, so that Don Urbano won't some-day think that it was I eating them."

This must have hurt the mistress's feelings, because she didn't come in again. Don Urbano told me one day, "I will never say anything, son. You can have anything you like in the canteen, you can have candy, meat pies, or cakes to eat. I won't be checking on you."

Doña Juanita must have told him that I was afraid to eat, and Don Urbano reassured me. "Don't be afraid of me. On the contrary, *we* should be afraid of *you* because you keep the accounts and keep them well."

From that day on, Señora Juana came in and helped herself and I didn't say anything to her. Once she said that she came in to make sure I ate something. She passed by again and again with her little boy and always saw me reading magazines, never eating. She would see me passing the time, playing the radio, and she would come in just to urge me to help myself to something in the store. She would take a cake and invite me to have one too. I had to accept and eat, and in this way I got used to it.

When I received my earnings from the canteen I bought shoes and pants. I also had my regular salary from the company. I lacked nothing. Don Urbano's nephew, who was like the son of the household, got angry when he saw how his uncle and aunt cared for me. They had raised the boy since he was very small because his parents had died; but they cared for me more.

Then I got sick again. This was because of a drunk who came to the canteen. Through the canteen window he said, "Write up a pack of Derby cigarettes for me."

"I don't have a whole pack," I told him. "I don't have anything but an opened pack, and I don't know how many are missing." He wanted me to charge him only a half a boliviano although it was worth at least four bolivianos. I got annoyed, because the price was five bolivianos for a full pack.

"Just forget the bill; I still need a whole pack," he told me, but I put him down for five bolivianos. He knew how to read and write and saw what I had done. "Lower the price for me, now!" he said, trying to force me to lower his debt. Then he slapped me with the back of his hand.

I screamed to Arturo, who was in the kitchen, "Arturo, this man is hitting me!" My mouth was full of blood. The drunk wanted to get in and I wanted to hit him with a broomstick. I wouldn't let him get in because he wanted to hit me. He grabbed the broom and I couldn't get it back. I grabbed a sandwich and threw it in his face. Arturo came out, and I also went out, and we got rid of him with blows. I hit him with the broomstick.

At that moment Doña Juanita came back from the commissary. She hadn't gone to get anything, just to pick up her little boy. She appeared at the door of the canteen and threw rocks at the drunk, sending him off toward the camp. He went all the way down. At four in the afternoon Don Urbano came from work, and I told him what had happened. He went to look for this man, found him, and beat him soundly. The company punished him for beating a worker who had come to his store. He beat the drunk because he had come to make trouble at the canteen, but the company didn't care.

From that time on I began to have headaches; it must have been because of my rage. (Ever since I haven't been able to do anything when those spells come over me.) They took me to the hospital where I stayed for two weeks. After that I had to rest for another week. Finally I got better.

My mother went to Oruro because my older brother had called for her. He had started to work for the security police force and earned more than I did, so my mother went to him, leaving me alone. I had some resources, though; I was already eleven, nearly twelve. I was almost grown up, and people already respected me.

I received word from my Uncle Aurelio that my mother was suffering. My sister Francisca was also in Cataricagua, but I had not gotten along well with her when I was young. I was stubborn and didn't respect my sister, so I didn't want to live with her, just by myself.

*How old was your sister?*

My sister was six years older than I. Her husband had an accident while working in the mine at Cataricagua and died in the Guzman section. He fell from the scaffold, all the way down to Socavón Patiño.[2] They took him out in pieces in a dynamite box. It required only half a box to collect his flesh, his bones, a few little things like that, no more. Just a little package was put as a corpse in the coffin. My sister was widowed very young. She married when she was seventeen and they didn't live together very long before he died.

*Did she have children?*

One girl, but she died. Then she had no more children.

With her settlement from the company, my sister went to Oruro to be with my mother. I told her, "Instead of going there to suffer, why don't you stay here with me. Am I not working? Stay and help me. Mother is with Felipe, our older brother. You can stay here in peace."

But she paid no attention to me and went to Oruro. Before a year had passed since the death of her husband, she had gotten together with a man who knew how to respect a woman's rights. This man was very good.

---

[2] Socavón Patiño is the lowest level in the mine.

My Uncle Aurelio came and told me, "Your mother is crying and she has no way to eat because your brother has given himself up to a bad life. He has become very drunk. If it's possible, go see and you can bring her back. She wants to come."

Right away I drew on my account in the company store, although I had never done this. My earnings were counted. I took a thousand bolivianos worth of food from the store as an advance on my wages. They gave it to me quietly, without saying a thing. I went to Oruro immediately. I left my little load in the garage of the bus in which I had come. I went out to look for my mother. I didn't know where she lived, so I went to a lady whom we knew to ask where my mother lived. She gave me directions, but they were wrong. I went to that house, but my mother didn't live there anymore. The tenants told me, "She was behind on her rent and left."

It was already nighttime. I looked all over but I couldn't find her. I asked the porter at the station, "Do you by chance know Francisca Rojas?"

"I don't know Francisca Rojas." Nor did he know María Rodrigues or recognize the name of my sister's husband.

My brother-in-law used to work on the railroad. I went there and said to the gentleman, "I have no place to sleep and I don't want to go to the lodging houses because as you know, there are lots of stories of trouble there."

This gentleman was good. He said, "I have to go to my house. Wait a minute here; come, come in." He let me in his hut. "Soon we will go to my house. You will sleep there," he said. I went to sleep at his house.

I woke up there, and at eight in the morning when I went out the door, I saw my sister coming out of another door. She saw me and screamed, "Juanito! So you came! Where did you sleep? Did you just arrive?" she asked me.

"No, yesterday afternoon I got here. I looked for you everywhere. I couldn't find you. I brought rice, sugar, bread and even meat for our mother."

"Where is it?"

"It is in the garage of the bus company. I left it there," I answered. She took me to my mother right away.

*How was it that you didn't know where your family lived?*

We didn't know because they didn't have their own house. They lived only in rented houses because in those days they didn't let you live as they do now, three, four, five years, with a single tenant. Every month, every two months, they had to move and find another house because there was a law saying that tenants who lived in a rented house for five years had to be compensated by the owner of the house if he asked them to leave. The proprietors were afraid, and so they made the tenants move out to find another place. So my mother and sister didn't have a house and they moved from place to place. I would leave them living in one house and when I came back in two or three months they would be living in another house; it was hard to find them.

I said to my mother, "*Mamita*, come with me. I have a steady job. You will be all right with me with what I earn. Besides that, I am watching the canteen of a man called Don Urbano Arias, and this man likes me a lot and helps me with everything. Let's go, *Mamita*."

She didn't accept. "You have access to the store; just bring me things. I will wait here and you can come." She spoke to me like that. My mother was raising my little brother and sister, Robustiano and Ricarda. I had left and was one less mouth to feed. I already knew how to work, but my mother has always failed me in everything. To this day she has left me to live alone. Many times I told her to live with me, and I had every intention to take her in with me so she could have the benefit of my work, but she paid no attention to me and always left me alone.

In time she died like that, separated from us. Always, from the beginning, I wanted to take care of my mother, but she didn't want it.

I returned to Cataricagua again. It was 1938 and I was twelve years old. Once my mother came to my house. She came in, but didn't find even a single grain of rice. That was her custom, to arrive at Cataricagua unexpectedly and go to my house and look for supplies. On one of those days I saw her at the bus stop. It was in front of the canteen, and I saw everyone who came off the bus. I asked Doña Juanita's permission to go see my mother, and asked her to watch the store for a while. She said, "Go get her immediately, son. We will take care of her."

Well, I brought my mother to Señora Juanita, and she invited her in to have a cup of chocolate and even prepared a plate of meat. She arranged it quickly, because she had everything ready to put on the stove.

After she had been served my mother said to me, "I want to go to the house where you live."

Doña Juanita said, "Take her then, son. I will take care of the store."

"Very well, Doña Juanita," I replied and we left the commissary and went to my house.

My mother came to my house to see if there was anything to feed her family with. If there was nothing, my mother would get very resentful. She always had to complain about everything a lot. She saw nothing there in my house. There was not a single grain of sugar or rice. "How do you live? What do you eat?" she said.

"As you see, *Mamita*, they serve me for nothing at the commissary because I take care of the store. Naturally they don't pay me, but in exchange they buy me shoes, pants, whatever I need. They have my clothes washed by their washerwoman. I don't wash a thing. So that's why I don't cook for myself. I take no advances on my wage, and I save the money." With that, I gave her some money. I don't remember how much it was, but I managed to give her more or less two hundred bolivianos. She was very happy with that and wanted to leave right away, except that she wanted to take supplies. However, it was too late to get them. I went to talk with the manager of the commissary and he said, "It's closing right now. You can't come in. Come back first thing in the morning. I will give you what you want."

The commissary manager knew me, knew what sort of a person I was, everything, because he often came to the canteen to help himself to a plate of beef, either a roast or a stew. I never wrote it down on his account, but made him help himself for free. So he liked me a lot. But Señora Juanita cared for me too, and she said, "Whenever the supply master comes in, you just give it to him without writing it down."

*Caramba!* My heart really fell because I was afraid they had discovered that I had been doing just that. What kind of a reputation will I have when I get out of here? I wondered.

When I came back from the commissary, I told Doña Juanita, "He didn't want to give me supplies because it was late. It is about to close. Even the clerks had changed their clothing to leave."

The Señora said to my mother, "How can you leave without supplies, with nothing? Your son works, after all. You can take whatever supplies you want tomorrow." She persuaded my mother to stay and gave her a bed to sleep in and as much food as she wanted.

My mother stayed that night. The next day at nine in the morning, I took her to the commissary. I went in and asked for authorization to take a three months supply. The commissary manager gave me the authorization, detailing what I wanted, because he had received orders. I took fifty pounds of sugar, fifty pounds of rice, spaghetti, *chuño* [frozen dried potatoes], and meat — I don't know how many pounds, but I got a lot — and also salmon and sardines. There was a mountain of supplies. My mother was amazed. She didn't know what to do. The little bags she had brought weren't enough for what she received from the store. She went back home taking lots of supplies with her.

Doña Juanita and I begged her, "Come live here. You, too, can help here in the store. Bring your other two children. Here we will take care of you. You will need to earn only for your children's clothing, nothing else. We will also be here to watch your children." My mother did not even accept this. She is very contrary. Sometimes, when she was being very contrary, she was afraid people would criticize her. She nearly died of her own rages.

*What is that disease called?*

We call it the disease of rage, *rabiaska wanupun* in Quechua. We have bile in our intestine, and that bile explodes with rage. When it breaks it kills us instantly. One can die quickly while one is going to the doctor. There is unbearable pain. There are many people who get pains in their stomach from rage or cholera. They cannot stand them, and they die quickly. The stomach gets hard. Other people feel a pain in their heads and that gives them a cerebral attack. Anger suffocates them and they die. When the bile is charged up, their livers break with rage. That bile is called *huaqui* in Quechua. It causes sudden death.

When I was fourteen years old, Doña Juanita celebrated my birthday right in the canteen. There were many young men like me, and we danced to a victrola. She bought four boxes of soda. Don Urbano bought cookies, candies; there was everything in abundance. There wasn't a thing missing. It was to praise my good behavior. It was the high point of my career there.

The next day there was a disagreement between their nephew and me. Arturo said to me, "Listen, Rojas, give me five bolivianos. I need them. Why don't you let me in?" I let him in and I watched him carefully. If he asked for something to buy, I would say, "Wait for me a minute. I will be finished in a minute." In this way, I would not let him rush me.

I said to Arturo, "Your uncle told me to watch you carefully and not to let you get cigarettes from me."

He said to me anyway, "Give me a pack of cigarettes and five bolivianos as a present. But don't tell my uncle."

"And if he says to me, 'There's a missing pack of cigarettes, where is it? And so many pesos are also missing.' What do I do?" I asked him.

He got annoyed. "So, is he watching the earnings or are you? Just take it out; it won't be noticed," he said. I refused. He took a pack of cigarettes and put it in his pocket and wanted to take the five bolivianos by force.

He was going to open the cash register when I told him, "Don't open it, Arturo, because I am going to scream for your aunt."

The cook heard us arguing through the window and went to tell Doña Juanita who was in her bedroom with the baby. She came out and heard what we were arguing about. Just then he pushed me against the counter and shouted. Doña Juanita knocked on the door and I opened it for her. She screamed all kinds of words at her nephew that I had never heard before. Arturo went away furious. He shook his head and said to me under his breath, "Well, we will see."

I wanted to leave there. I said to Don Urbano, "Don Urbano, Arturo is beginning to hate me very much because I didn't let him take money and cigarettes. I didn't want to say anything about the cigarettes, but I didn't let him take the money even though he wanted to force me to give it to him. He is getting very angry at me. He has already made the first move. When Doña Juanita scolded him, he said, 'We will see.' I don't want to fight with Arturo. It's best that I just go to my house."

In the afternoon, Arturo came home from his work, and Don Urbano beat him with a whip. On the third or fourth day after that quarrel, he got me when I was alone. Don Urbano had gone to work and Doña Juanita had gone to Harrison to see her *compadre*. That pest took advantage of the opportunity. He came into the store and grabbed me and began to beat me. I was not a fool. I grabbed the bread knife and cut his hand. When he saw me with the knife, he stared at me. He didn't do anything else. Retreating, he opened the door and went out. The store was bathed in blood.

At six in the afternoon Don Urbano arrived a bit drunk. When he knocked at the door, I opened it just a little bit. I had cleaned the wood, but it hadn't come out very well. The counter had been covered with blood, as well as the door where he had grabbed it to open it. I opened the door just a little bit and didn't notice the blood on the ground where he had gone out, so I neglected to clean it.

The next morning Don Urbano asked me, "Where is all this blood from?"

"From my nose," I told him, as the cook had told me to say. "You will tell him, 'It came from my nose,'" she had said to me, and that's what I told him. The cook was Arturo's grand aunt. She had told Arturo to say, "I got cut while I was checking the furnace. I got close to lift the stone and another stone fell on my hand." She told him to say that, and Arturo did. But I didn't like to lie because from the beginning I have always been an enemy of lying.

Don Urbano asked me about Arturo, "When did he come in after the accident?"

"He didn't tell me. I wasn't there," I lied. "The blood came from my nose." But then I took back my words: "Don Urbano, don't believe my words. I will be frank. I will tell you the truth," I said. "That Arturo, since the day that you punished him and your wife scolded him, has been angry and fights with me one way or another. I told you I wanted to leave because of that. Yesterday afternoon, when Arturo got out of work, he saw that you weren't in the house. He punched me and, when I saw the bread knife, I grabbed it and defended myself with it. I didn't want to cut his hand. I just wanted to defend myself. When he punched me again, he hit the knife with his hand. It cut him. He still wanted to grab me, so I defended myself and I wanted to cut him even more. He threatened to beat me with a whip in the face. He went out furious. That's where all the blood is from." I had to tell him the truth.

Don Urbano went out. "Just go on taking care of the canteen. Don't get upset. Let this pass over," he said as he left.

"Thank you very much," I said. He went out of the house to pack up his nephew's things. As soon as his nephew returned from work, Don Urbano threw him out on the street.

"You work for the company," Don Urbano told him. "Go get yourself a room. I don't want any more troublemakers. Juan is like my son. He must live here," he said to Arturo like that. Don Urbano took me as his son. From that time on, Arturo was assigned to another house and lived there.

This was in 1944. I was already eighteen years old. That year Arturo joined the army. Don Urbano always brought him money, which the boy liked. He got out of the army in 1945. I went to Oruro in September. The army was recruiting men, and I joined when I was eighteen, almost nineteen years old.

In Oruro I met a man from Cataricagua whom I knew. He was standing in line chatting with another man and I stopped to speak with them. Some soldiers came by and they said to me, "You, what are you doing? Get back in line now." They thought I was standing in line to enlist, but no, I was just looking. So I arrived with the rest of the men at the examination room, and they found that I was healthy. They recorded my weight. I had become plump. They took me in the army in September of 1945.

Later Arturo met me in the street and I told him, "Now I am going away too."

"When will you go?" he asked me.

"Tomorrow, I have to go."

"We'll see each other tomorrow," he said. "Where are you staying?"

"I am at my brother's house," I told him.

"Well, take me, too," he said, and I took him.

We slept there and when we got up we went to Cataricagua. I told Doña Juanita and Don Urbano, "I enlisted just like that." After this, Arturo and I got along a bit better.

Don Urbano took Arturo back into his house and he lived there again with them. But he got into bigger trouble after that. And he would take cigarettes the way he used to.

"I will let him because he is young," his uncle told me, "but don't let him take them every day. It's all right if he has some every two or three days, but not every day." But Arturo wanted them every day. Our disagreements got worse. We were arguing every day, all the time.

Señora Juanita said to me, "Eh, Juanito, why are you so downcast? I don't see you anymore the way you used to be. You behave strangely, and your way of moping around the house is strange to me."

I told her, "Yes, that's just the way it is. I can't find a day of rest, the way I could before Arturo came back. I can't stand him around me. He always wants to take cigarettes or money from the store. I can't safely leave the store to go outside or to go to the bathroom, or anything, because at that instant he appears and comes in and I get worried. That's why I am quiet and touchy and can't open up more. I'd like to leave, Doña Juanita."

She told this to her husband and Don Urbano caught me in the shop one day. "What did you tell Doña Juanita? She told me that you are always arguing with Arturo."

"That's right, Don Urbano. I am even ashamed of being here. Maybe he thinks that I want to fight with him, but I don't. Any day he might grab me here and hurt me, and no one would see. You know very well that there are times when both of you are out of the house and I have no one to call to for help," I told him.

Don Urbano said, "Arturo will have to leave."

I thought a bit and realized that he couldn't say no to Arturo. Instead of his going, it is better that I go, I said to myself.

October had already come. On the seventh there was the feast of the Rosary at Veinte y Media. Arturo returned drunk from the feast. It was my bad luck that I was in the bathroom when he came into the store. I didn't see that he had come in, but Don Urbano's little boy warned me, "Arturo came in and he is taking everything."

I saw from a corner that there was a five boliviano bill sticking out of the cashbox on the table. Except for that, the cashbox was empty. I was very afraid. I didn't even know how much money was in it, but it was the receipts of two days. Don Urbano and his wife were not home. They had gone to Harrison to see their *compadre*, leaving me with the child. The child was used to being with me in the store. They had said to the boy, "Will you stay with Juanito, or do you want to come?"

The boy said, "I will stay with Juanito and we will watch the store."

They got home drunk from their *compadre's* house. Arturo was sleeping. I had put him to bed myself. I wanted to search his pockets, but his great aunt told me, "I saw what he did. I will tell my niece."

When Don Urbano and Doña Juanita came home, I said, "Your nephew took all the money when I wasn't looking." Doña Juanita was more or less able to understand, but Don Urbano was totally drunk. He didn't hear a thing. Doña Juanita said, "Tomorrow we will advise Don Urbano. He will fix everything."

Well, I stayed awake all that night without blinking a lash, thinking. Now he's going to accuse me, I said to myself, Why didn't I watch carefully? he will ask; Why didn't I keep it in another place, or at least count how much there was?

Preoccupied with these thoughts, at six in the morning before anyone else was awake, I knocked on the door of Don Urbano's bedroom. When he answered I entered and told him, "It happened like this: Arturo opened the cashbox and took out I don't know how much money. I didn't see him, but he made a noise. Your little boy told me what happened." My heart was pounding, because I was afraid.

Don Urbano told his nephew, "From now on, if you behave like this, you will have to go find a house wherever you can. I don't want to see you here in the house or here at the company. I will have you fired from your job," he said.

That month went well. But December came and Arturo committed another, bigger offence. However, it didn't touch me at all. He took one thousand five hundred bolivianos from the box in Don Urbano and Doña Juanita's bedroom. With this he went to Oruro.

"Now I am really going to put him out on the street," Don Urbano shouted when he discovered the loss.

At that moment I came in and said to Don Urbano, "I am leaving also. I have to report to the military headquarters."

Don Urbano said, "No, you have a job. Just take a leave of absence and come back here and work here like Arturo did."

"I already gave you my notice that I was leaving because I couldn't have you put Arturo on the street without feeling responsible for it. Now you can proceed in whatever way you wish," I told him. I found myself very depressed because there was no time when I could speak as a friend to Arturo. I liked Arturo, but I didn't like his way of taking things without permission. I had to go. The company fixed it for me. I don't remember exactly, but I think they gave me seven hundred bolivianos, or seven hundred fifty, something like that. With that money I went to Oruro.

This happened in the middle of December. New Year's Eve came and I got drunk. I got sick with rage when I went out and walked around barefoot on the soil. I went into the hospital that very night. I tried to escape, but there was no way. The doctor came on his ten o'clock visit. After he left, I dressed myself and left because the day to report to army headquarters was coming and I didn't want to go directly from the hospital. I went to my sister's and we had tea with *pisco* [a local wine]. There we welcomed in the New Year.

# 4

## My Military Service

All men in Bolivia are required to serve one year in the
army. In Juan's account of his military service we can
grasp the disorganization of the army, in disrepute because of the Chaco War. Garrisoned in cattle corrals
and outfitted in worn, ill-fitting uniforms, they served
the country in frontier outposts. The regular troops
were stationed in the major headquarters near the
mining centers where most of the action took place in
countering the labor struggles of the miners. For the
miners, military service prepared them to fight the
revolutionary battles that brought the National Revolutionary Movement to power. They learned to appreciate and make barracks jokes about the contrasts
among recruits from different regions of the country,
and from rural and urban backgrounds. Stereotypes
about gender as well as ethnicity were cultivated in the
army. Juan takes note of the flagrant inhumanity of the
officers toward uneducated Indians who barely spoke
Spanish, which went so far as to even cause death or
permanent disability. His release was delayed by the
assassination of President Villarroel in 1946, as the
oligarchy of tin barons sought to stall the reforms
brought about during his presidency and to stabilize
the country by means of a new hegemonic alliance of
mining enterprises.

On the third of January in the year 1945 the recruiting officers were
waiting for us at the army base. I went at two o'clock in the morning.
The line of recruits got very long. At ten in the morning they began to

receive us. Soon a non-commissioned officer came out of the army camp and shouted, "All those who have draft notices form a line here." I was the first to step in front of him. Then they cut my hair and I was ready to receive my uniform.

On the fourth of January they took us to the military base at Velasco Galvarro Avenue. We stayed there all day and slept there that night. On the next day we went to the frontier command post of the Regiment of Engineers, Third Infantry, in Huachacalla, where I did my military service. We left at five in the morning, before dawn. The whole regiment, over five hundred soldiers, went together in thirty-two vehicles, including trucks and jeeps. We got to the post at eleven at night.

There were no barracks ready for us, just some abandoned houses that belonged to a farmer. In one court there were pens for bulls and horses and in the second court, a pen for sheep. Colonel Leoncio Leclerc of the Engineers Regiment, Third Infantry, had ordered the mayor of Huachacalla to move his animals so that the regiment could take possession. We ourselves helped take the animals out to the pasture where there were corrals for the animals. The mayor and the head of the district of Huachacalla had complied like disciplined gentlemen. The army paid them rent. I don't know how much, but they were happy with what the colonel offered.

We each got a single blanket. They were old blankets and some were useless even as covers, with holes here and there, completely worn out. They had given us cloaks in the military region of Oruro. I got one of the new ones, brand-new; others got old but serviceable ones. The coats weren't as old as the blankets. We slept in the corners of the cattle shed using these coats and blankets, because there were neither beds nor cots, nothing. That night a rain fell, such as I had never experienced in my life, not even in the Cochabamba valley. We heard it all night because the roof was made of zinc and you could hear the rain very clearly.

When dawn came at five in the morning a trumpet sounded. I didn't know that they were sounding reveille for us. I thought they were just waking up the other soldiers in the garrison, to call them to a briefing a review. But that trumpet was for us. Paying no attention, we were warming ourselves in bed. With the worn blankets they gave us, we had felt cold all night. At five-fifteen we heard the trumpet sound again. That was for us to get up. One of the old soldiers came in, grabbed his belt, and made us get up with lashes. Fortunately, nobody had undressed. We all had our shoes on and our clothing, just as we were during the day, since we didn't undress because of the cold. He kicked us and lashed us with his belt. We all went outside and left our cloaks and blankets in the cattle shed. After fifteen minutes, the officers took us to the second court to review us and to allow us to wash our heads. They gave us bowls and told us to take them out and get breakfast.

It was half past five and at a quarter of six we had breakfast in the cattle shed. One soldier named Vargas — he wasn't a soldier yet, just a recruit like me — found his little trunk open. His new blanket was gone. Many others also lost their new cloaks or blankets. The older soldiers had come in and rifled our trunks and taken the contents to sell. Many lost the little money they had, their bread, everything. Those scoundrels had opened everything and taken anything of value.

Vargas said to Sergeant Bulucua, "Sergeant, I have lost my blanket and my trunk is open, look!" Sergeant Bulucua investigated and reported it to the commander of the regiment, Lieutenant Colonel López Sánchez. Lieutenant Colonel López Sánchez had all the old soldiers — some twenty-five or thirty men — in formation, and asked them who did it. No one spoke. He sent three soldiers to their dormitory with Sergeant Bulucua. They brought out blankets and coats and showed them to the lieutenant colonel.

Lieutenant Colonel López Sánchez held one up and asked, "Where did this come from?"

The soldiers accused each other, saying, "He brought it," and, "I didn't take any more after that." They threw the blame on one another. Well, everything showed up except for three coats which had completely disappeared. But the older soldiers paid for this. The most guilty got three extra months of service for being light-fingered.

It was already six in the morning when we had breakfast. It was late because of the search. Once we had eaten, they took us, still in civilian clothes, for instructions from 6:30 A.M. to 11:30 A.M. Then we returned to our barracks where we had lunch at noon. After lunch they took us to work at 12:45 P.M. Then they brought us back to the barracks, together with the whole regiment.

The regiment was still not organized. One of the lieutenants sent us out to learn about close formation drill, one of the preliminary maneuvers that we still didn't understand. When we had formed a line, they numbered us. There was a soldier, Mario Choque, who got the number forty. He thought this was to be his number for good.

In the afternoon, when we went out for maneuvers again, none of us knew what they were going to do. They separated us into groups but, at first, without numbering us. One of the noncommissioned officers, Emeterio Pereira — a skinny Cochabambino, a bit foolish, but very good, strict about everything — did the numbering this time. The soldier Choque got another number, but he answered only when "forty" was called. When we answered the roll call, another soldier had gotten "forty" but Choque answered "forty" as well; it was the only number he ever knew in his life, because he had had no schooling.

*Were there miners among the soldiers?*
Yes, there were.

*Were you friendly with the miners?*
Mostly with the friends I had from the city. I still didn't know the mine; I hadn't worked in big mines. In the barracks we were all friends, whether we were miners or from the city or the countryside. There were a few who were a bit selfish, who didn't want to have contact with others, but we paid them little attention. The ones we fought with at the barracks were the Cruceños. The Cruceños called us *Kollas* because the people of the highlands made bowls and plates of clay, wooden spatulas, and so forth. And we called them *Matakos* because in the east, in the jungle, they have a lot of mange on their bodies as well as on their faces.

On January seventh we went on maneuvers in our civilian clothes. We went to the review, to breakfast, to everything at the time we were supposed to. On the eighth of January they gave us our uniforms. Some of us got big uniforms, some of us got small ones. I got the shirt of a large, tall soldier, although the pants were my size [laughter]. I ran around everywhere asking "Who needs big clothes, very big clothes? We'll trade." It was my bad luck that there was one soldier who wanted to trade, but he had gotten tiny pants and the shirt fit him just right, the opposite of my case. I couldn't find a shirt my size.

That day we didn't go on maneuvers, nor did we receive any word about what kind of soldiers we were going to be, how to behave in the barracks, or anything; they just distributed the weapons — rifles, a few light pieces, heavy pieces, mortars, like that. I got a rifle, since I was a rifleman.

The next day we went out at nine in the morning. I was wearing my big shirt with rolled up sleeves, and we formed a line for inspection. Since I always liked to stand up front, I stood in the first row, although I belonged in the second row. Colonel Cleomedes Blechmer noticed me.

"What happened to you?" he asked. "Why didn't you trade with one of the soldiers who had a small shirt?"

We still didn't know how to address him, so I said, "Yes, señor, I tried to trade, but I couldn't find a shirt in my size." The colonel was humane; he didn't say anything. Behind him came Captain Zenon Pérez, who quickly instructed me.

"You are acting as though you were in your own house, or in some office. Here you don't call an officer 'Señor'; you call him, 'my Lieutenant,' 'my Captain,' 'my non-commissioned officer,' or 'my Sergeant,' like that — everything with 'my,' do you understand me?" He was annoyed as he taught me.

When the colonel found a soldier who had a shirt that was too small he made us trade, but even that shirt was too big. Then the colonel ordered the lieutenant colonel of the regiment, López Sánchez, to find a shirt small enough for me. Immediately he sent me with a paper to the quartermaster. The quartermaster took me into the supply room. The sergeant in charge of the keys opened the door and they exchanged my shirt for one that fit me. I chose it myself. I then went out and presented myself in line. The colonel looked at me.

"Now you look like a soldier. A while ago you looked like a freak," he teased me.

Laughing, I got in line again. Soon we found out how he was going to teach us. He taught us how to behave in the army. He told us that the army was a school of discipline for all of the men in the barracks, and that we had to learn to be women, to be men, to do everything.

"A man has to know how to cook," he told us. "A man has to know how to wash his clothes; a man has to know how to sew his torn clothes; a man must never go around dirty; a man has to help himself in everything. And to learn those things you have come to the army. From today on you will be strong men. A Bolivian has to learn to be valiant and in the future, the duties of army life will also be the duties of civilian life," he said. So we kept that in our minds.

We knew nothing about how to address the officers — lieutenants, captains, majors, and generals of all ranks. We didn't even know how to tell whether one was a captain or a lieutenant or a colonel. Lieutenant Colonel López Sánchez taught us the ranks: a corporal wears chevrons on his sleeve, their color, and the weapon he carries, indicating what his station is. He taught us how to distinguish the ranks, all the way from a corporal to a general, what class of stars go with bars, the kind of weapons each carries, what belt a major wears — we learned everything by heart. Every afternoon he taught us.

The next day, the ninth of January, the regiment was divided into companies, sections, and squadrons, and they chose among the soldiers for squadron leaders. I was chosen as commander of the Third Squadron of Riflemen, Second Section, First Company. Then the officers taught us in the courtyard of the barracks how to use weapons, how to carry them on the shoulder, and how to lower them from the shoulder. There was a soldier who fired his rifle accidentally when he put it to his shoulder, passing it from one hand to the other hand. It ripped off a piece of his ear.

The surgeon was a German, nicknamed *"Pajaguito"* because he spoke, with an accent, about birds a lot. Whenever he saw a bird flying around he would point it out, "See how that *'pajaguito'* flies." He said it like that, because he couldn't speak Spanish well. He didn't say *pajarito* but *"pajaguito,"* and because of that we gave him that nickname.

The surgeon went up to the soldier and grabbed the piece of ear and put it in alcohol. "We'll sew it on and see if it sticks," he said, and they took the soldier to the military clinic where they sewed it on, well enough for a piece of grafted flesh. When it healed, they took off the bandages, and it was the same color. You couldn't see a thing, it was so well healed.

Then they took out the sutures and that night, while he was sleeping, the little piece fell off. The next morning the soldier didn't notice. We looked at him and said, "Listen, where is your ear?" [laughter]. We laughed and he started laughing. "Well, here it is." Half his ear was never seen again.

The officers used him as an example: "See how that soldier was disfigured for lack of precaution, for lack of security. He didn't know how to hold his hand to receive the gun from the other when he was hoisting the rifle up to his shoulder."

The next day we went out on maneuvers in a regular formation. They taught us how to describe the terrain, what we were seeing immediately in front of us, at some distance, and even further away. They would indicate a reference point far away. We would say what was there and what we saw. Soon it was my turn.

"Soldier Rojas, come here; describe the terrain." My company commander was Lieutenant Orlando Barba López, a good Tarijeño [a person from the state of Tarija]. He was very good. That man never lifted a hand against us. He got angry with us, but never touched us. He was a gentleman, a very humane man.

I approached him and said, "Present, my Lieutenant . . ." — you always have to say your name and I said it exactly as he had taught me — "Present, my Lieutenant, Soldier Juan Rojas reporting at your orders, my Lieutenant," like that.

"Describe the terrain up to that white point you see there on the top of the hill." There was a cross, the calvary of Saint James. "See that cross there? That target is the enemy," he said. "Now you have to describe the terrain as you see it from here."

I described the terrain in the following way: "In front of me I see a stretch of empty field. Further on there are some ditches which you can't see clearly. It is possible that the enemy may be positioned there. We would have to sneak up there very carefully without making a sound. Further on there are some rocks which seem to have fallen from the mountain. Further on is an area which looks as though it has been ploughed and seeded, and at that point is a cross on the mountain. That is the target where the enemy is."

I had described the terrain perfectly and they applauded me. He made everybody applaud because I was the first soldier to describe that terrain. I was complimented, and because of that, the officers of the regiment began to take notice of me. They saw what kind of character I had and what kind of memory I had. They came to like me.

After that, we got to rest, but during the rest period Lieutenant Orlando Barba López made us play leapfrog. Jump and squat and then a triple jump, that's the way he taught us.

"You have to learn to receive impacts without anger," he instructed us. We played leapfrog, and I was jumping like a rabbit. I could also walk on all fours quickly. Lieutenant Orlando Barba López gave me a nickname, "Rabbit." He didn't call me Soldier Rojas; "Where is Soldier 'Rabbit,'" is what he always said [laughter]. Usually I listened, but when I didn't he called me "Bad Mannered." "Where is 'Bad Mannered' Soldier?" I learned to listen so that I wouldn't be called by that name. But everyone continued to call me "Rabbit." Later, when I came to be considered one of the bright ones, the lieutenant said, "You sure are very lively in everything. *Caramba*, we have to give you another nickname."

Noncommissioned officer Julio Aguirre, who was from Santa Cruz, said, "Excuse me, my Lieutenant, I can give him a nickname. We can call him 'Quevedo.'" So they called me "Rabbit Quevedo" because it is said a long time ago there was a very wily man by that name who was never fooled; because I was so quick, they called me by his name. There were various other men in other companies who also had the nickname "Quevedo." I kept that name in the army.

On the first of February we went out on maneuvers in a tighter formation because we already more or less knew how to behave in the army. They were pressing us more severely. They made me feel, in spite of my being a commander of a squadron, that I had very little rest, compared to the other soldiers. I thought of escaping from the army, because this was serious. When we couldn't do something on maneuvers they used to give us the "chocolate." One might think that this meant they gave us a cup of chocolate to serve ourselves from, but no. The "chocolate" in the army is punishment. They made us walk in a squatting position for some two hundred, three hundred meters. The next day we would walk like children who had recently learned to walk. The legs hurt, the calves, everything all the way up to the shoulders was sore. The only thing that didn't hurt were the hands. I was afraid of that, because every time they did it to us, I would get sick with the rage. My whole body hurt and I found myself almost immobile. I have been that way ever since I was a young man in the army.

Fearing this, I thought of running away. About the fifth of February, five soldiers escaped from the barracks. After these five soldiers escaped, they suspected I might too, because one Saturday when they took us to wash, I was thinking of escaping — the men always escaped on the way to wash clothes — and I had said to my companions, "*Caramba*, I am going, too!"

Someone told Lieutenant Orlando Barba López. He called me, "Listen, Rabbit, what are you thinking of?"

"Nothing, my Lieutenant. Why do you ask?"

"Well, I think you want to escape."

"No, not that."

"You must never do it. A man must bear any martyrdom. That is why we were born men," and saying that, he slapped me on the shoulder.

I thought it over: *Caramba!* Death in the army is honorable. I prefer death to desertion. I will leave with honor and will be a good man for my country. That's what I thought. I didn't think about escaping any more.

Soon after, a peasant came and said, "Chilean soldiers are occupying the hill of Pairumani." There was a very high hill in the countryside where they cultivated green beans, flat beans — everything. The peasant added, "They are stealing many of our sheep. They steal our beans, rip out our potatoes. There are five Chilean soldiers positioned there."

Those five soldiers weren't Chilean, they were the soldiers who had deserted from the army. So we went, with twelve soldiers on the right and twelve soldiers on the left, to surround them. We surrounded them at six in the afternoon in a cave where they had hidden themselves. They had slept there for the four nights they had spent out of the barracks. We approached with Sergeant Bulucua in front. When he was sure it was them, he shouted to us, "Everyone over here for the roundup!"

We collected the five, and took them back to the barracks. We dressed them as women, hung large signs saying "DESERTERS" around their necks, and made them mount horses and go out in a procession with a band in front and the whole regiment bearing arms marching behind. We took them through all the streets of the little village of Huachacalla. These men slept at night tied to their cots. They weren't free to turn over. Near them slept officers who would wake up instantly if they tried to escape again. They were tied like that for a month. They didn't have the liberty to go out even for a minute to the street. During the month they were tied up, three other soldiers deserted. Two were not found; one reappeared. He walked back and surrendered himself.

The tenth of February arrived, the anniversary of Oruro. Since Huachacalla is in the department of Oruro, it is also celebrated there. They cooked cabbage for the soldiers' lunch. We didn't have a kitchen — just an enclosed area in the yard, and when they put the cabbage up to cook, it started to rain and hail heavily — a big storm. This put out the fire and wet the wood. They were using green wood and couldn't cook the food. At eleven in the morning it was still raining. At noon it was still raining. At one in the afternoon, it calmed down, and we helped ourselves to the food, which was still raw. The rice was raw, the potatoes were raw, everything was raw.

When I got out of the army and got married, I told my wife, "On the tenth of February always make me a good meal, because in the army I ate raw food that day. Now in my civilian life, I want to enjoy the day." That day, we didn't eat until seven o'clock at night. They didn't even give us a cup of tea.

I didn't get any news from my family because my mother didn't know where I was. When we reported for duty in Oruro, they didn't let us know any more than that we had been chosen for a regiment, and they took us to the military region without telling us where we were going. They sent us away in the trucks and no one saw us leave. When my mother went to the army post they told her we had gone to Huachacalla. She thought it was only for a few days. I sent a letter in February, but my mother was in Cochabamba, and just my brother was in Oruro to receive news. Almost everyone in the barracks received their letters from home, but a few other soldiers and I never did. The mail would arrive but we didn't expect anything.

In March, just about the middle of the month, the mail arrived. I was sitting on the benches in the barracks, in a corner of the patio, when I heard, "Soldier Juan Rojas." *Caramba!* That instant I leapt up to receive the letter from my sister and my mother. They told me that my mother was in Santa Fe, working with my stepfather. The next week I had another letter from my mother.

*Did she know how to write?*

No, she had the letters written by my brother. It was a very detailed letter, saying that my brother was working in Morococala and my stepfather was working in Santa Fe. They told me in the letter that if they received a letter with my correct address, they would send me a package of food. Knowing that they were in Morococala and in Santa Fe, and that they both were working, I sent a letter to Morococala to tell them where I was, with the correct address. They received the letter and two weeks later a package came, containing toasted corn cakes, dry cheese, and cooked jerked beef.

I had been put in charge of the keys to the supply room, since I behaved well. Once I was in charge, nothing was lost from there, although previously soldiers and officers before had stolen blankets or sold the rice and sugar. During my time of service, there was not as much theft, nor did I take anything for myself, except for a little bread, to eat and pass the day. Every day I went in I would take two or three pieces of bread from the officers' supply, not from the soldiers' supply. The soldiers' bread was badly made, but the officers' bread was beautifully made with pure butter.

Lieutenant Colonel López Sánchez, the subcommander of the regiment, gave me the key to the supply room and said that I was going to be directly responsible until the time I left the army. He told me, "You must never allow anything to be taken from here unless it is authorized.

If you don't behave that way, we will take the key away and you will suffer. You have enough money and you can eat some bread from here if you like, but you can't give it or sell it to the other soldiers."

I understood everything clearly. I didn't need money for anything in the army. Only those soldiers who had vices, who drank themselves into stupidity needed money. Ever since I was a young man I never liked alcohol, and I never set out to get drunk. On exceptional occasions I drank with my companions or at some weddings, but rarely. I am afraid to get drunk because it is bad for me. So, I didn't need anything while I was in the army; everything was there in that room. Anyway, I didn't know where to sell things; in addition, I would have been afraid to do so.

On one occasion Sergeant Bulucua told me, "Listen, Rojita, the review is near and I need some money. Why don't you give me twenty-five pounds of rice? I'll sell it."

*Caramba!* Out of fear, I agreed. The sergeant came with his bag and he took out over thirty-five pounds of rice while I just looked on. I gave it to him because I wasn't going to deny a good friend. I saw everything he took out and where he went to sell it. I could become rich that way, I thought. In the supply room there were also piles of new blankets, military uniforms, belts, and even arms. I thought, *Caramba!* I wish there were some relatives I could give blankets to, to make myself a bed at home. But there was no one to give a few blankets, so that I could have them later when I left the army. So all I did was look and think about it. I was tempted, but I never committed the offense; I never stole.

I had a friend, Vargas, and that poor boy was called "Bones" until he finally left the army. He was a very skinny soldier. He didn't receive a single letter, not a package, no news from his family, nothing. He had a father and a mother who worked in Huanuni and they forgot about that poor boy. He was the only one I would give a piece of bread to — not the officers' bread, but the regiment's, the soldiers' bread. That was the only time I committed the offense of taking bread for a soldier; I gave it to Bones because he was so poor.

The individual review came on the eighth of April. I was promoted to corporal. They didn't call me Soldier Rabbit any more; they called me Corporal Rabbit.

They took us for a day in the countryside. To prepare for the feast, Lieutenant Colonel López Sánchez ordered twelve soldiers to hunt vicuñas. We went in a truck. He sent me not to hunt, just to be in charge, because I was a good soldier.

"You, Corporal, go and make sure those soldiers behave well and watch that they don't steal any wool or leather to sell because they are a bunch of light-fingered soldiers."

One of the soldiers fired his rifle accidentally, and I didn't realize he had hit something. He dug a hole and buried the carcass and covered it with branches. I was counting the shots and went to where I heard them come from. I told them, "For each shot there has to be one vicuña; therefore we should have twenty vicuñas." At one place I saw blood, but no meat. I asked a soldier, "Who was here?"

"Soldier Jiménez was here and put the carcass in a hole in the sand, and covered it with rocks and dirt and branches," the soldier replied. I saw that and forgave the soldier his offense.

We returned to the barracks with nineteen vicuñas, not twenty. I lied at the barracks and said that one of them had missed, but that I hadn't discovered who it was. The subcommandant paid little attention.

The next day they read us the list of those who were to be promoted. On Saturday night we put the vicuña meat in the oven with potatoes. They had asked the owners of the two haciendas, Escara and Huaillas, for a donation to the regiment for our day in the country. They responded and gave potatoes, plus ten sheep for the officers.

Before eating they had us assemble in formation, with all those to be promoted in front. We put on our insignia and wore the colors of the Third Engineers. After they promoted us they distributed roasted meat and cooked potatoes from the stove, serving first the soldiers who had been promoted to corporals, then the rest of the troops.

The afternoon passed, and we returned at five. There was a band. We danced and we ate the roast, the potatoes, everything. All went well and we received congratulations from the officers. Those of us who were promoted were commended, and those who had failed were reminded that there would be other individual, squadron, section, and company reviews, and, finally, a regimental review, and that at each review they could be promoted if they had learned what was required. When dismissed we left at a trot and began to dance with happiness to the music of the army band.

Every Saturday we had a dance at the barracks. After we collected the laundry from the wash, we went into the barracks. The band would place itself in the corner of the courtyard and we would begin to dance.

We all danced, no one was sad. When they played *cuecas* [dance music favored in the Andes] it was fatal for the Cruceños [people from the Santa Cruz lowland area] because they don't know how to dance to *cuecas;* the same went for us, who were from the highlands, when they played *taquiraris* [regional dance music of the lowlands]. When they played the carnival songs — the *taquiraris* — the Cruceños jumped about like monkeys. They liked those songs very much.

There was a Cruceño who bothered me very much. He was only my size, yet he was afraid of no one, except for the officers, and them only because if we fought, they punished us.

On one occasion I was away from the barracks on a Sunday. At seven in the morning I had asked the soldier on guard for permission to go out for a little while. He was my friend and let me go.

I went to Sabaya where a friend, Inocencio, had invited me. It was his birthday and he said, "Let's eat a bit of *picante* [a dish cooked with chiles]. You come, and I will wait for you."

I kept my word and went. When I was at his house I met the Cruceño, my enemy. I was sitting with my friend's father when he came in. We just looked at each other. We didn't know what to do. Of course, we spoke politely to each other, and I behaved myself well. We both had to be passive. At noon they gave us *jayakitu,* a dish with dried beans, cooked potatoes, and roast goat, and we lunched in peace.

At about a quarter to one, we went out on the street with Inocencio, his father, and his sister. (His mother was cooking with other ladies.) Inocencio took us to a bar where he bought beer and we drank three bottles. Then he took us to another bar where he invited us to have some Chilean wine. There was plenty of Chilean wine there, and it was good wine. We drank and we talked.

The Cruceño was a private and I was a corporal, but he didn't address me by my title; he would just cry out to me, "Rojito! Rojito!" I was getting angry because I wanted him to use my correct title. Drunk or sober, he should address me the way he did in the barracks.

I called him — I don't remember his name — and said, "Listen you, come over here. I want to talk to you. Why do you address me by my name alone? You know very well that I am your superior. You have to address me the way you are supposed to. Otherwise, I'll see you back at the post and I will teach you how a private should address a corporal." In spite of all this, he still didn't address me correctly.

At four in the afternoon, we were asked in for the *picante,* and we ate well and drank beer and wine. The return to the post was long, an hour's walk. So at five in the afternoon I said, "We have to go because if we don't, it will get late." We made our farewells and returned to the post. He stayed out on the road while I went into the barracks and took off the cloak I had taken because it was cold on the mountain road to Sabaya. I put my cloak away and went out. He was waiting for me on the street. I walked with him toward the old burial ground.

I said to him, "Let's go find some *camote* roots [a form of potato]. They are very good and juicy. Let's quench our thirst." Once there I grabbed him by the hair and said, "Listen, shit, address me as you were addressing me back there!"

He said to me, "Take off your hat and your shirt." While I took them off he added, "You don't have to be afraid." We fought until we were exhausted and couldn't fight any longer. We did not mark each others' faces, but I gave him a sock in the chin that made his jaw hurt. He couldn't eat for awhile after that.

From that time on, we respected each other. I respected him and he came to respect me for the rest of the time we were in the army. After that, we never saw each other again. We wouldn't know each other now, because he is older, as I am. We wouldn't recognize each other.

One day we went on maneuvers in open formation to Chulpani. In Chulpani our company commander, Lieutenant Orlando Barba López, ordered us to build fortifications with our spades in preparation for an enemy attack. As we were taking our positions, I found myself a barrier some sixty centimeters high behind which to hide myself. Suddenly I saw some bone, then a skull. With my little finger I uncovered a bit more and the neck appeared. I looked further and found a body, seated like this, the bones and even the teeth shining as though recently buried, intact. On the other side I discovered the arm.

I immediately called Lieutenant López. I shouted because he was far away, and I couldn't run to him because we couldn't leave our positions. "My Lieutenant, there is something strange here."

The Lieutenant came running, and we looked at the skeleton. Everybody wanted to run, but the lieutenant ordered that no one should move. No one else came. He said, "Let's dig away this sand. This isn't hard dirt." He used his bayonet and we uncovered the skeleton. It was sitting, hugging the remains of a little child. It had been buried this way in the dirt. We saw the skeleton of the baby was also intact, with its little foot, like this, crossed over its arm. They had died this way. We couldn't be sure whether it was a man or a woman, because it was only bones. There was no flesh, nothing. They must have been there for a long time, too, because the bones were white.

We wanted to take the bodies out whole, not piece by piece. The lieutenant wanted to take photographs, so he went back to the post for his camera and returned in the colonel's jeep, together with the colonel. Later, instead of doing maneuvers we looked for more graves. We dug everywhere. Some soldiers found vessels full of charcoal buried with plates, vases, everything. In many places there were skeletons buried with their heads downward and their feet up. I don't know how they came to be buried. According to what the old people told us, in the earliest times there was no sun, but the people knew that the sun would come out and would burn them. When it was discovered that people buried themselves alive, the old people said that they preferred to be buried in the dirt rather than burned by the sun.

*Maybe there was an eclipse?*

All they said was that in early times there was no sun. There was just the moon.

*Did the people there speak Quechua?*

I think they spoke Aymara.

We found buried skeletons in lots of places. We brought them back to the barracks and we put them together with Captain "Pajaguito." We reconstructed the skeletons of the big one and its little boy or little girl. The big one was 1.40 meters and the little one was 90 centimeters. I saw it all.

In the month of July the anniversary of Huachacalla arrived on the third. We had a military parade. There had been many preparations for this during June. They gave us parade uniforms, and we wore them for the first time on the day of the celebration. At eleven in the morning we were at Mass. Afterwards we marched in the parade from the village behind our barracks up to the school.

After the parade, there was a party for the officers. I was friendly with Lieutenant Orlando Barba López, my company commander. He liked me a lot because I wasn't lazy when he gave me work to do. He took me to the officers' casino and invited me for a glass of wine and some of the roast they had eaten. Surely I was allowed in there only because he, my superior officer, asked me; even so, some of the other officers didn't like that. I spent the fiesta there.

June twentieth was the birthday of Lieutenant López. The day before he had said to me, "*Caramba!* Tomorrow is my birthday. I have nothing to make here to celebrate. I have a chicken, but I don't know how to cook it." I couldn't say anything to him, although I knew how to cook everything. I was afraid to say anything — not afraid, rather too shy — to say anything. He asked me, "Couldn't you cook some roast chicken?"

"Certainly, my Lieutenant, I will prepare you a good dish of *picante*," I told him.

"Fine. Let's go kill the chicken," he said, and took me to his house.

"We are missing some *chuño*, my Lieutenant. Where can we find some *chuño?*"

"You just kill the chicken. I will get it," he replied.

I killed the chicken and put it in salt water. The next day I went to his house first thing in the morning to congratulate him on his birthday. I embraced him.

"Stay here, Corporal. We will cook the chicken together," he said to me.

I stayed to help him prepare the feast. I thought he was going to send me to get the *chuño* but he went in person to a friend to get it. I prepared it well, I prepared the sauce for the potatoes with spices; everything was well made.

Then I said, "There is too much food for the two of us."

The lieutenant replied, "What do you say, shall we invite the colonel and Major Salazar, too?"

"Fine. There is plenty of food here. There is enough for eight servings," I said.

"Very well, we'll serve those two quite a bit. I will go get them," he said. And so he did. Well, I really cooked that food well. He tasted it, and thought so too. "Magnificent, Rojita! This is very well cooked food."

When the colonel came into his house, I was in his little kitchen. He said, "Let's have a dish of *picante*, my Colonel. Today is my birthday. I want to celebrate and have a little party with you."

Major Salazar congratulated him first, then the colonel. Then the lieutenant called me, and the colonel looked at me. He saw me for the second time with officers. He must have thought I was plotting something with them. He looked at me differently. A corporal with officers was not acceptable. It would have been alright if I had been a noncommissioned officer. But even though the lieutenant was friendly toward me, I was to blame for being in an officer's room.

Lieutenant Orlando Barba López ordered me to his side, next to the Colonel and told me to serve some wine. I served them and they drank. Then he told me to go buy six bottles of beer. He gave me the money and I left. I brought the beer back to the kitchen where his aide-de-camp was inside washing the dishes.

Soon the lieutenant came to the kitchen and said to me, "We can eat, Rojita, because no one is missing; we are all here."

"All is ready, my Lieutenant; I will serve," I said.

They went to the table, and I served them. The colonel, the lieutenant and the major ate and I was in the kitchen, preparing to eat with the lieutenant's aide-de-camp. We were listening and heard the colonel ask, "Who made this? Do you have a cook?"

"No, it's a soldier friend of ours who knows how to cook well. He cooks a lot. We spoke one day, and he told me he could do it and so we did it, the two of us."

The colonel said, "Show him to me; I want to see who prepared such good food."

They called me and I came in as I always did.

"For days I have been watching the way you have behaved, and how you comport yourself with us. Bring your plate in here. We will eat together, the four of us," the colonel said to me.

We ate together. From that day on he came to care for me a lot. I had prepared him an excellent meal, although I had never cooked a chicken before. But I had watched how my mother cooked and kept it all in my head, and I was able to make a good meal. We finished eating and we served ourselves beer. I drank together with them. I asked for permission to drink, saying "With your permission, my Colonel, may I have a glass of beer with you?"

He interrupted me, and said, "Don't be uncomfortable. None of us is special; we are all soldiers." They said to me, "We will talk here as though we were friends. If you feel you should serve us, you have to say, 'Help yourselves,' and we will."

The colonel had bought beer, and Major Salazar also had bought beer, and we got a bit drunk. Then, with wine, we did get drunk. It was as though I were drinking with the soldiers, without any fear, in peace.

The next morning the colonel called for me. The soldiers had heard that I had been at a party with the colonel, the major, and the lieutenant and me no one else. I went in and out of the post as though it were my home; I didn't need to ask permission from anyone. The colonel told me not to be afraid of anything, that he was my friend and that I shouldn't be afraid of him.

One day I went to do a census where the Ch'ipayas[1] lived. We were supposed to leave the next day, but our commander stayed another day, telling the regiment commander that our truck had broken down. We stayed at the house of the richest man among the Ch'ipayas. He had many pigs and he made us cracklings with hot sauce. Everything was very good.

*How were their houses made? Are they round?*

Their houses are very small, made of straw. Some are sort of round, some are square. They say that before they lived only in round houses, but now for the most part they are square, with straw roofs. There is plenty of fine straw there, very tall, about two meters high. They feed the roots to the pigs. The ground where the roots grow feels like a pump when you step on it, because it is hollow underneath and the ground rises, sinks, and then rises again. Even people eat these roots. Some roots have plenty of juice and they are good. We tasted this when the Ch'ipayas invited us. There are no fields for planting. I don't know how those people survive.

The feast of Saint James came. There they celebrate for eight days, starting on the twenty-fifth of July. There is a large image in the church of Saint James astride a horse. The horse is larger than real horses. All the soldiers went to hear Mass in uniform but without bearing arms, just like anyone else. After Mass there were all kinds of dances: *diabladas, morenos, cullawas, Tobas, and Incas.* There were also civilian dance groups. When we heard that music, we soldiers felt like dancing.

They gave us time off that day from five in the afternoon until eleven at night. We wanted to dance with the women, with the girls, but the girls there are afraid of dancing with soldiers. They wouldn't dance or even speak to us. They are rude and don't mingle since they are afraid of outsiders.

*Do they speak Spanish?*

Aymara and Spanish. They didn't understand Quechua. They scolded us in Aymara. We didn't understand, so we paid them no attention.

I had a friend from Huachacalla, a bachelor about thirty years old. He said to me, "Do you want to dance?"

"Yes, I want to dance, but I have no partner. They don't want to dance with soldiers."

[1] Ch'ipayas are the indigenous people of the area who speak a language linked to Mayan.

He said, "What do you say, I will lend you my civilian clothes and you can disguise yourself. In addition, I'll give you a cap so they won't recognize you. You will see that they will dance with you."

He took me to his house and lent me his clothes. I disguised myself as a civilian. I thought I was the only one doing this, but there were others who had also disguised themselves, men who were recognized by Sergeant Bulucua. When I saw that I left quickly. I had danced a lot, and the Huachacallans had danced well with me because they didn't realize I was a soldier.

I don't know why the women of this place are afraid of men, especially foreign men. I think they lose friendships because they behave in a different way. In the cities, women are pleasant. When a man speaks to them they answer the way human beings are supposed to answer. But there people are of a different type. I don't know how to describe them, but they seem to have a different character. They don't act like human beings. I think they must be like the Chileans, because they are supposed to be that way, too.

When Sergeant Bulucua recognized two of the soldiers in disguise, he called to them and said, "You, come here. Who gave you permission to disguise yourselves as civilians?" And he immediately took note of who those soldiers were. That was when I went immediately to my friend's house and dressed as a soldier again. The others had said, "Corporal Rojas is also in civilian clothes. He is dancing right now." At that instant I returned from my friend's house, back in uniform, and I went to stand right behind them. They were in front of me and suddenly turned and saw me dressed as a soldier.

Sergeant Bulucua, seeing me, laughed at them, and said "Oh, really? Corporal Rojas is a soldier right now. Why are you putting the blame on him, too?"

And they said, "Genaro is also disguised." By chance Genaro was standing right there, and so he was also seen in civilian clothes. The three who were caught didn't get free Sundays for a month. For those four Sundays, they didn't see the street.

There were eight days of celebration. There were bands and dancers in *tarqueadas, lechehuayas,* and no end of bands. It was very exciting, but we just watched. The people were having a fiesta and we were reprimanded by the officers when we paid more attention to the celebration than to our own duties. Our company commander, Orlando Barba López, scolded us. (He never in his life punished any of the soldiers physically.)

The man who punished us physically was a non-commissioned officer from La Paz named Lucio Gallardo. This man even killed a soldier just before the individual review. Another killer was Sublieutenant Mario Rodriguez. He suddenly killed a soldier by punching him because he hadn't understood an order. All of Rodriguez's comrades beat him, and, when he couldn't take any more, he fell. They took him for an operation in La Paz, but before they arrived he died. They took Sublieutenant Rodriguez to La Paz and he never came back. In his place came Lieutenant Ramallo from Challapata, who was another killer. He drove the soldiers with punches and kicks.

Lucio Gallardo was cruel to everyone. He did not comprehend pain or any kind of suffering. It seemed he wasn't made of flesh. He drove the soldiers with punches, not in the face or the body, but on the ear. There was one case of a soldier, Thomas Chiri, a worker from the mining company of Morococala. He was an Indian. He would look at the other soldiers and if they weren't working, he wouldn't either.

Sergeant Gallardo would give him an order, saying, "You, this is an order just for you." Chiri didn't know what to do. So Sergeant Gallardo said, "I'll give you this to make you understand me," and hit him in the ear with all of his strength. The ear swelled up. Next time he couldn't hit him there so he hit him on the other ear while the first was healing. When he saw that it had healed he made it swell again on the first side. Finally he got him on both sides and both sides swelled.

On one of those days Major Salazar came by. He said, "Soldier, come here." The soldier presented himself and the major asked, "Why do you have swollen ears?"

The soldier didn't speak Spanish very well, but the major understood Quechua, because he was from Cochabamba, so the soldier explained in Quechua, "Sergeant Gallardo has done this to me many times. Why? I don't know. I can't hear because of this, not out of either ear. When this one got well, he hit the other side; when that one got well, he hit this side. It hurt me a lot. Now this side is well, and the other side is, too, but I still can't hear. When he speaks to us, we can't hear, and he doesn't understand that it is because we are deaf from his hitting us." He complained about all of this to the major.

So the major summoned Sergeant Gallardo and said, "You, Sergeant, why have you behaved this way to Soldier Thomas Chiri?"

The Sergeant answered, "He couldn't learn anything, ever. He would watch the other soldiers working and was always last with the operation; that's why I gave him a punch in the ear and it has swollen again."

Major Salazar asked several of us separately, "Why have this soldier's ears swollen like this?"

We told him, "The reason is that every time there was a problem, or whenever he just felt like it, Sergeant Gallardo would punch him in the ears, on both sides, until this soldier has become deaf."

So Major Salazar punished that Sergeant Gallardo. He put him in jail for three days on bread and water. He didn't eat anything else. Mario Choque — the soldier who always answered "number forty" — would give him a bit of extra water because he was humane. We didn't give him anything because we hated that Sergeant Gallardo very much; he was a brute. He didn't understand anything. He was very bad, damned, and that's why we hated him.

He spent the three days like that on bread and water. In the morning for breakfast they would give him soda water and a roll. At noon they would give him a glass of soda water and a roll for lunch, and the same in the afternoon. Three days later he was let out at the same time of day that he had been put in.

He didn't learn even from this. While the celebration was going on in the village with all of its gaiety, this sergeant continued to manage the soldiers with kicks, punches, and abuse. He would order, "Forward, half turn, present arms, backward march, raise up, present arms, raise up. . . ." Like this, he took it out on the poor soldiers, although our company commander, Orlando Barba López, his aide, Captain Julio C. Aguirre, and Captain Emerito Pereira, another company officer were kind and never made us undergo this kind of punishment.

Our company didn't suffer as much as Second Company. The commander of Second Company was Sublieutenant Mario Rodriguez, the assassin who killed the soldier. His aide was Lucio Gallardo, and those officers were bad to that section and to that company.

Third Company had a fairly good company commander, Captain Zenon Pérez. The commander of Fourth Company was good, very good, a Major Salazar. He didn't make the soldiers suffer. Only Second Company had bad luck. We would be playing with our commander, Orlando Barba López, while they were constantly being abused. Even during rest periods the soldiers were abused by Rodriguez and Gallardo. Those poor soldiers had no rest. They always suffered a lot.

After all the suffering we underwent that month, on the twenty-fifth of July — and lasting through the first days of August — and the feast of

Saint James arrived. There were preparations for the military parade. Companies came from posts in Sabaya and Corque. On the sixth of August we marched in review, and on the seventh we had the military parade. It was a spectacle such as had never been seen there, because before there had been no post.

At the end of June an order had arrived saying that we were to be demobilized. Then just before the feast of Saint James there had been a revolution in La Paz. They hanged President Villarroel on the twenty-first of July. Within twenty-four hours the previous orders were revoked; now they said the troops had to remain at their posts until further orders. We lost again.

In the month of September there were new rumors that we would be demobilized in the middle of the month. We were waiting for the announcement, but it didn't come. We stayed there through the month of October. I didn't think we would ever leave; I thought I would spend the rest of my life in the army. By then I was used to it and didn't miss civilian life as much as I had; besides, there weren't so many maneuvers as before.

When we least expected it, at three in the afternoon of the twenty-seventh of October, we were read an order to the effect that the troops were to be dismissed. All the soldiers threw their hats in the air. I did the same from happiness; I would throw my hat in the air and grab it like a ball. Others were jumping with glee.

The morning of the thirtieth arrived and the trucks which had been there since the twenty-sixth were ready. We knew we had to go to Oruro.

We arrived in Oruro at three in the afternoon. Colonel Bustos, the chief of the Third Military Region, ordered us to go to our houses and to report back the next day in our uniforms and well groomed to have our photographs taken for our documents of military service. The next day we reported at nine in the morning as Colonel Bustos had ordered.

Lieutenant Campero called us to the second courtyard and told us that First Company would go first. First Company got in formation. We registered for the photographs, and soon the next company was also called and then the third and the fourth. Meanwhile, the five photographers stood in front of us. We went in, one by one. The photographers must have been in a hurry because they did it quickly and by six in the afternoon we had finished everything.

Still in uniform, we received another order from Colonel Bustos. We were to return to our houses until eight-thirty the next morning.

Those who didn't live there could stay at the barracks. Since my sister lived in Oruro, I went there. My mother was in Morococala with my older brother. I don't remember whether she lived with my stepfather then or was alone.

We arrived at a quarter past eight in the morning. Almost all of us were present. At eight-thirty, on the dot, Colonel Bustos ordered his aide, Lieutenant Campero, to get the Regiment of Engineers in formation and collect the uniforms. Lieutenant Campero ordered us to return our uniforms. There were many soldiers who didn't have their civilian clothes with them, because some were from Santa Cruz, others from Sucre, from Potosí, from Cochabamba, from everywhere. Others had sold their civilian clothes at the post in Huachacalla because we received little food. Everything was in short supply, so, to avoid hunger, these soldiers sold their civilian clothes. These soldiers asked Lieutenant Campero if he could give them old clothes so that they could go home. Lieutenant Campero referred them to Colonel Bustos. He was a thoughtless person with no respect for the dignity of a soldier, and he denied the request. He preferred to let them leave in their underwear rather than give them clothes. The colonel's aide, Lieutenant Campero told the soldiers, "Lieutenant Colonel Bustos will not grant your request. He says you entered the army in civilian clothes, and as you entered, so you must leave. He says he needs clothes for the new recruits and the Major General says they won't supply them. The government says it hasn't the money to buy new clothes for the new recruit."

Some of my friends from the army, asked those of us who lived in Oruro if we could give them our old pants and some old coats. But none of us had any to give away. Lieutenant Campero then went to the colonel and told him that 40 percent of the men didn't have civilian clothes to go home in.

Colonel Bustos finally accepted the request with bad grace and told them "Collect all the oldest uniforms to be found in the post. If possible, give those which are in good condition to the soldiers who are in service, and the oldest to those who are leaving." He gave that order and Lieutenant Campero executed it; the clothing was collected and we got our clothes that day.

Once they gave us our discharge papers, they told us "Come back in six months to pick up your military severance pay." There was a small party for us and the new recruits. We danced and then bade farewell to the new soldiers; we left as civilians.

# 5

# Working in the Mines

Once I asked Juan what he felt when he entered and left the mine.

When you come out after your eight hours of work, you feel light, as though a load had been lifted from your body. You feel about to fly. You feel more happiness, more agility. But when you go into the mine, your body is heavy, as though it were waterlogged. Coming out of the mine is like coming out of water. You feel your own weight, but once you are out, it feels like you are getting lighter, like being filled with air. That's what we feel like. At that moment, we feel calm, free. And that fresh air comes and it feels like a breeze is blowing on us. When we are working hard in the mine, in those very hot places, we are boiling hot and we go wet our heads in water barrels that they put at each level. The first drops to touch our heads, our faces, cool off the whole body. We feel a clear coolness, like taking the air outside.

I asked him how he reacted to the sun when he came out of the mines, since for most of us the terrifying aspect of being underground is the darkness.

When you come from the darkness into the sun, your eyesight is clouded. You can't see for a bit. Your eyes get tired inside the mine and as soon as you come out into the sun your eyes hurt, as though you had been hit, like this, *cam! . . . cam! . . . cam!* This pain goes away quickly; once your eyes get used to the sun, it doesn't hurt any more.

I asked if that was the same happiness as with the fresh air?

It's the same, the same. For example, in level twenty-six there is a place called Hope Vein. It is cold, very cold, especially higher up. You suffer coming from these places out into the sun. When you get out in the sun, you feel as though your hands are defrosting. Your hands begin to move a bit and to have some feeling, after the numbing cold. When you work at these cold levels, you also get a pain in the neck. When you move your head from one side to the other, you feel a sharp pain in the nerve of the neck, as though it were frozen. Afterwards, when you lift your head, it's like the first sip of water or the first taste of something; the salivary glands hurt. You have to taste a bit more until they stop hurting. Both the heat and the cold wear the worker out.

It always struck me when I was working in the mines, that miners lived more intensely than the rest of the population. I realized after Juan told me about his feelings when going in and out of the mine that this was because every entry was like a burial and every exit like a rebirth when they experienced breathing the fresh air as though for the first time.

The other impression I had from Juan's narrative and that of other miners was that the relations of work in the mine are interlaced with those in the community and mediated by them. This comes out clearly in this chapter. Men depend on the work of their mothers, wives, and daughters in preparing the food that nourishes them. When anyone gets sick from the disease of the miners, the women are often blamed for failing to provide the nourishment that protects the workers. Their mental outlook is affected by disruption in the home, and they cannot attend to the details that mean security and survival. At the same time, their motivation to work is inspired by the obligations to family and neighbors. The wages provide all the meaningful accoutrements of living in the culture that mining families create in the community, the festivities, dances, and celebrations that are the reason for

being. This cannot be reduced to "commodity fetish-
ism" or other rational reductionism. Each day that the
workers enter the mine, they must have the desire to
continue to live or they will become victims of the
many dangers that confront them. They prepare
themselves spiritually to confront those dangers when
they enter by chewing coca leaves in solitude at their
work stations. This ritual of meditative coca chewing
is called *akulli* in contrast to *pijchar*, sociable coca
chewing in a group during the process of work. The
sociability is as important as the meditative preparation as workers relate to each other in mutually sup-
portative ways that may mean survival.

---

After I left the army, I went to Santa Fe to get my mother in Morococala. I got there by the Santa Fe company trucks, but I couldn't find
any of my relatives. I didn't know Morococala or Santa Fe, even though
I was born there. I left when I was very young, when I was just six
months old. At that time, they said that there was an evil spirit who
wandered above the houses, and these evil spirits, which we called *larilari*, kill children. My father cared for me a lot because I was the only
male child, and he took good care of me. Because he was worried about
me, he took me to Cochabamba when I was six months old. From that
time, until I left the army, I had never been back to Morococala.

I remember well that I met my little sister when she was coming out
of school. I saw her and we hugged each other. She was going to have
lunch at the house of my older stepbrother, Leonardo, who worked at
the company, and who had his little daughters and his wife with him.
She took me with her, and we met and shook hands. We spoke a bit
about life in the army. He told me a bit about the Chaco War. "You
have followed almost the same path as mine, Juanito," he told me.

In the afternoon my little sister went to school. If she had taken me
to Morococala, to my mother's, she would have been late for school. I
had to wait until she got out of school. My brother was going into the
mine on the second shift at three in the afternoon. He didn't have the
chance to take me either, and my sister-in-law had to cook for my
brother when he came out to eat at seven in the evening. Consequently,
I couldn't see my mother as soon as I arrived. Four o'clock came and
my little sister came out of school. We set off immediately for Moro-

cocala and I went directly to see my mother. My mother, who is no longer at my side [crying], hugged me and kissed me with sadness.

Well, after that, my mother wanted me to come to work at Morococala. I had a godfather at Santa Fe who worked in the accounting office and was the cashier. I met my godfather in his office — he was a godfather at my baptism — together with my stepbrother, Leonardo. My godfather asked me, "Where do you want to work? Do you want to work in the mine, or do you just want work on the outside?"

I answered, "Wherever there is work."

Then my godfather said, "No, not in the mine. It can't be. I don't want you to work in the mine because the mine takes a toll on the worker, Son. You can't go in."

My stepbrother pointed out that I had recently come out of the army and that I needed to earn a bit so as to be able to buy some clothes. I answered my godfather thoughtlessly, saying "I need to earn some money to dress myself, to have some clothes made and to feed myself. If possible, later I'll come out of the mine and work at the store."

My godfather accepted that. He got a job for me in the mine. He took me in person to the administrator, and the administrator authorized the head of the personnel office to give me an entry ticket. With that I set off for registration and from there went to the personnel office.

I started work the next day. I stayed at my mother's house at Morococala and went down to work at the Santa Fe company. When three days had passed, my mother said to me, "It's too far for you to go down and come up every day. You'd better sleep at Leonardo's. You sleep there, and when you come out in the afternoon, come here until seven at night. Then go down there and sleep and the next day you can go in to work. We'll do it like that. I'll bring you your lunch, or you just tell your stepbrother you will eat at his house."

"Fine," I said, and I took my cot to Leonardo's house. I slept there and went to work from there every day.

My mother used to bring me my lunch every day. Finally my stepbrother got annoyed. "Well, if you are staying in this house, why do you tell mother to bring you lunch? You can simply eat whatever we eat in the house. You have to tell our mother not to bring you lunch. In the evening go eat up there, but at noon you can just eat here," he scolded me.

I told my mother "Don't bring me lunch, Mother, because Leonardo is annoyed that you bring it every day. It is tiring and you shouldn't get that tired." My mother agreed and didn't bring it any more. In the afternoons I used to go eat at my mother's house and come down at eight in the evening to sleep. The next day my stepbrother would give me breakfast, and we would go to work from there.

That's the way we were until September of 1947. That year my mother left Morococala, leaving me at Leonardo's house. My stepbrother had been a miner at Colquiri, and they had arranged all his retirement pay. He no longer had any right to work in the mines. The Santa Fe company didn't know this when they hired him as a carter, but when they discovered that he had already received his compensation at Colquiri, they fired him immediately. They said, "You have already received compensation and yet you are still working in mining companies. From this day on you can't work for any mining company."

My stepbrother wanted to say "I can't live in my country then. I can't live without working. I'd better go to another country to make a home." And he left for Mendoza in Argentina.

So it was that my stepbrother left me alone at Santa Fe. Before he left I begged him, "How can you go and leave me, Leonardo. Where will I eat? Who will take care of my clothes?"

He said to me, "You won't lack for anything, Juanito. You see here we have a very close, very good friend right next door to us. You will go stay there with Doña Rosa." This Doña Rosa wasn't a godparent or a relative, but just a neighbor who lived near him. My stepbrother went in to ask her to board me as though I were his son, and the lady agreed to take me on as a boarder. I don't remember for how long, but I boarded with her for more than one year. She took care of me pretty well, especially at breakfast. I was satisfied.

Once I had been at the job for a year, I asked that they give me a room someplace else. The camp boss said to me, "Let's see what you have," and we went. When he saw my house, he said, "But you don't need to change your quarters. You don't have to change anything here. We could only give you a smaller room and you will be fine."

I said to him, "Don Lucho, why are you speaking of giving me a smaller room? I am not asking for a larger or smaller room; I need a room that is nearer the center because, as you can see, it's dangerous here in the outskirts. Someone can come in and take the few things I have at anytime. And as you know, to live in the center of the camp, you need a few years of service. Where will I stay until then, Don Lucho? Do me the favor of giving me temporary quarters in the center of the camp; I have seen empty houses and the keys to them are hanging in the office. The company will eventually give them to the contractual workers, but until then, you could let me have one of those good houses. If there are other bachelors, you can put me in with them. I can certainly live with two or three single men." But he didn't understand my reasoning and didn't want to give me other quarters.

I didn't have a padlock. When Doña Rosa heard about this, she lent me a Yale padlock with two keys. Her husband, Don Telesforo, used to come into my house to sleep when I was on the night shift. I would leave at three in the morning, and Don Telesforo would sleep there to watch over the place.

The celebration of Saint Rafael came. Doña Rosa was an office holder in the celebration. She trained us for a dance group dressed as Redskins. I took part in this, dancing with the Redskins. Before that year they had danced with women, but that year there were only men, because we began to practice too late and the women couldn't join us.

I met my wife-to-be, Petrona, during that celebration. We had known each other earlier, but we didn't have that strong affection that we developed during that fiesta.

*Do you remember when you saw her for the first time?*

My mother wrote me about her in her letter when I was in the army at Huachacalla. My mother told me that she had a friend from our village who had three children, a woman and two men. She told me that whenever she got sick the girl, Petrona, always took care of her at home. I didn't know what she looked like, or what kind of woman she was. But she had a great deal of love for my mother. My mother got sick all the time, she nearly died from the sickness. It wasn't a sickness that lasted for months or weeks, but rather usually for a day or two, and she always had to go to bed. Petrona's mother used to send her to cook and wash clothes for my mother, perhaps because they were from the same village. This girl often came on her own, my mother wrote me. I knew her name was Petrona. When I got out of the army I never went to her house, but my brother pointed her out to me on the street. "That one is Petrona," he said. I looked at her. She was still thin and little. She was barely a young woman.

My stepbrother Leonardo took me to her house for the first time during carnival time in 1947. We went in, I sat down on the seat her father offered me, and we drank almost until we were drunk.

At ten in the evening, her older brother Filiberto said to me, "Let's go out for a walk for a bit. I know how to play the flute and Leonardo can play guitar."

"I can accompany you with a *charango* [a stringed instrument made of fruitwood or the shell of an armadillo]," I told them. My stepbrother played the guitar and Petrona's older brother played the flute.

We went to the house of the fiancée of Filiberto, and there we met Petrona. We didn't even speak to each other or look at each other because we hadn't been introduced. We weren't as friendly as we became after the feast of Saint Rafael.

Later, on the day of the feast of San Rafael, Petrona made a costume for me out of old nickel coins. She made the sash for my chest and covered it with pennies. Then she made me a chinstrap for my hat out of pennies. We were not together yet, just courting. She prepared my costume and I danced well, perfectly, and I was very happy. She was always at my side. I already had her father's permission and her mother's permission to go with her, but they didn't want the girl to have intimate relations with me without first checking our health. I didn't want to disobey them, more because of my fiancee, than her father, because she could be punished for not obeying them. She used to say to me, "If they catch me, they catch me, what do I care?"

And I couldn't say to her, "Well, go ahead," or much less, "I'll carry you off with me."

On the last day of the celebration I got very drunk in the chapel. She and her older brother took me, drunk and dressed up as a redskin, to their house. When I woke up, the floor was painted, as well as the hearth, and in my house it wasn't like that. And the arch in my house was missing! Then I saw Petrona's mother.

"*Caramba!* How did I get here? Who brought me?" I asked and got up in a fright.

My mother-in-law said, "Just rest a while, Juanito, it is early."

I said, "I have to get up early. I have to go to work right now, because our leave is over today." And I left early.

I met various friends on the street. They said to me, "Where did you wake up? For shame! *Caramba!* The boy is just waking up at this hour! Where did you go then? To Morococala?" they teased me. I just laughed and didn't pay attention to them, and I went home. From there I went to work at seven-thirty.

At noon I went to have lunch at Doña Rosa's house. I didn't go back to work. I missed work because I already cared a lot for Petrona and could think only of the affection she had given me. At one o'clock I went to her house.

I told Petrona some of my problems. "My mother is going to leave me now. I don't know who I am going to stay with, but in any event, I have some help; my brother is bound to take care of me."

She replied, "It depends on you. If you want to get together with me before we get married we can, because my mother can't make me stay single, much less keep us apart."

From that moment we planned to get married, whether or not our parents liked it. I said, "If it's your father who doesn't want it, we will have to get married. It won't be here, but any-place else." Our plans were made, and from that time, we never left each other.

The chief of the section, Samuel Quintana, asked me, "Could you work tonight to replace someone else and work half a shift?"

I was delighted and accepted, "Fine," I said. "I'll come in at five in the afternoon."

He said, "You will finish at two in the morning, but will have to come in again at seven-thirty in the morning."

"I don't care. I'll be back at work with you tomorrow at seven-thirty." It was all right with me because I was this chief's assistant. I got there at five o'clock, changed into my work clothes, and at five-twenty I went to work.

I met Chief Francisco Cortez there. He said, "I sent Don Samuel to see if you could work with me tonight, and I am very grateful that you accepted, Rojito. Let's go in and get to work."

We went in, down to level twenty-six, where I worked as his assistant, because his usual assistant was in the hospital. He needed someone who knew this part of the job and since I was Quintana's assistant I knew everything well. That night I worked in peace, with no disturbances.

I came out at three in the morning the next day. I slept at my house and thought Doña Rosa wasn't there, but that she also had slept in the rowhouses above, near where my mother used to live. I thought I would sleep a bit since I had to go in to work at seven-thirty. But it wasn't like that. I was jumpy and woke up all the time. Then it was already five-thirty, and I couldn't sleep. I got up, having hardly slept because I would wake up all the time thinking about work. At six-thirty Doña Rosa's daughter — she was called Teodolinda, and she died very young — came in with breakfast and served me.

My heart relaxed, and I told her, "I thought you weren't here. I was going to the mess hall for breakfast."

"No, we came here after the celebration; we are going to stay just for today," she told me. I had breakfast.

At seven-fifteen I went to work. As soon as I got there, there was a call from the superintendent of mines, Engineer Eloy Sotelo. This engineer had me come to the main office to ask me why I had missed so many days. I don't know if it was a mistake on the part of the time-keeper or what, because our officeholder had asked for a leave of absence for four days, but they gave us only three days. They took one day away from us. The three days were over and I had made up for the day I took off.

He scolded me, "Why have you missed so many days? Your time card here shows three days of absence. How is it possible that you, at your age, are skipping work?"

I answered him, "You know, Engineer Sotelo, you don't understand what's happened. Our officeholder asked for three days, actually four, of leave for the feast of Saint Rafael. The company, probably through you, didn't agree to four days, only three. Since I had a leave, I took it. But anyway, there must be some proof in the time office about our leave."

The engineer asked the clerk in the time office if there had been a lot of leaves for workers. They found the permission for the leave, and there was my name. The engineer said, "I am sorry. I saw that there were several days missing on your card and thought that you shouldn't miss work, at least not at your age. But in any event, forgive me for the misunderstanding. You can go ahead to work."

It was already eight in the morning when I went in to work. Chief Quintana was already bursting with rage, waiting for me because it was my job to divide the dynamite, fuses and the detonators among the hand drillers. He had to assign people to their jobs, and he didn't have time to do both his job and mine. The workers had been waiting for me in a long line. I was jumpy and went in quickly to the chief's booth.

I told him, "The superintendent called me in because of my absences these past few days. They had put me down as absent, not on leave, so he thought I had just decided to watch the celebration or something. That is why I am late."

He told me, "Just go away, and don't bother to explain why you came to work at this hour. I already have a replacement for you."

I told him again, "Sir, the superintendent of mines, Engineer Sotelo, summoned me. I went in and he inquired at the time office about the leave we had taken, because the timekeeper had made a mistake, had missed my name and marked me as absent. You yourself can see the tickets. You were the one who wrote 'He didn't work.' You put that on the time sheet. Anyway, in the office they put it down as absences. That's why he called me in and that's what made me late."

He complained, "Well, I thought you had gotten delayed someplace, or that you were late coming from your house. Now go give out the dynamite. I have to dispatch the workers."

I went immediately to give out the dynamite. When I came to the boss of the work crew, a man named Hilarion Basualdo, with the rush I was in, I dropped some fulminate of mercury on the floor. Hilarion Basualdo stepped on it right where it is attached to the detonator fuse and crushed it. He counted the detonators, and when he missed one, he looked on the floor and there it was, crushed. It was a miracle he didn't step on the detonator itself, because if he had, it would have made a mess of his feet; it would have destroyed them.

He complained to the chief that I was throwing detonators around. The chief rushed in, extremely agitated, and asked "Why are you throwing detonators around? Don't you know that they are dangerous things to handle?"

The boss of the work gang, Calizaya, said, "He is not throwing detonators around. Why would he drop them, knowing they are dangerous? Basualdo probably dropped it himself when he was counting them, and it was he who stepped on it. Now is there something wrong in that?" He defended me like that.

Basualdo shouted at the chief roughly, "Damn it, you shithead! No one is going to yell at me like that. You can go to hell if you think that!"

So the chief dismissed Basualdo from work. "If you go to work at your station, I will have my workers take you out of the section. You better not come to work with me. You will be punished for three days," he told him.

So that bandit Basualdo went to the superintendent to get me in trouble again. I came out at twelve to have lunch without any idea of this and the watchman called me into the main office. The superintendent said, "I hear that you came in drunk this morning and threw detonators around, and that the workers who were waiting for the explosives to be distributed were stepping on them."

"Engineer, how could I have come in drunk? I was in your presence this morning. I came in in good shape. You saw me, Engineer."

"Sure, I saw you, but I didn't know if you were drunk or sober," he said to me. "Quintana saw you come in the door. Let's see, I'll check with him. So he called him in. He had already decided to fire me. I saw the firing slip on his desk, but it wasn't made out. Quintana came in, and he told him what was going on. I don't remember if they punished Basualdo or not; I think they fired him for being a liar. God never left me helpless when I had disastrous moments at work. He has always given me His blessings.

I went in to have lunch at Doña Rosa's house. I was so upset about everything I didn't feel like eating lunch. I ate only a bit of soup. Doña Rosa said, "You're not eating because it's not well cooked, Juanito?"

"No, it's because I don't feel like eating." Since that day, I learned to lie at work. I didn't know how to lie before. I didn't understand it.

After lunch I went in to work at one o'clock, and bad luck followed me again. I was told to give the signal for beginning a shift to the crews. After I gave the order to begin working, I had forty-five minutes before calling out the *akulli*. During those forty-five minutes I went up Hilarion Basualdo's shaft. It was pure mud, but the tunnel was warm and dry. I lay down there on some old sacks. I fell asleep and woke up at three on the dot to call out the *akulli*. I tried to go down but couldn't because a landslide had shut the passage. The chutes were full of ore and I had to shout through the shafts over the sound of the carts as they went by. One of the carters was coming back for his lamp. My luck was always like that. He had fallen off the cart into a shaft and by the time he climbed up, his shift had ended. When he went to the office there was no one there; The second shift had come in. When I yelled, he heard me and said, "Well, what's going on?"

"Tell the chief that a landslide has blocked the way in this shaft and the chutes are full and there is no way to get out. There are no rungs to go up this shaft, and there is no ladder. Tell him to unblock the passage," I said.

Quintana came running up the path which was blocked. "Rojas, what did you go up there for?"

"I came up to see if there were some workers who hadn't heard me when I called out for the coca break. They were working here this morning," I answered him.

However, although they had been working there in the morning, in the afternoon they had fortunately gone to work in another tunnel. In the morning they had set off a charge of dynamite. This caused a break in the side of the tunnel and since the workplace was full of mud, just like clay, the weight moved the supporting rock and it caved in. A lot of rock must have fallen, because air was blowing through the tunnel. The chief and I cleared one side by filling the other.

"I had to come in here," I lied, "because this morning they were working in here and that's why I came up to give the call for the coca break. When no one responded I came up and just as I got here this landslide came down. I haven't been able to get out."

At four-fifteen in the afternoon, we came down the path. Quintana hadn't finished signing the time cards, and I hadn't finished calling the rest period to the workers who didn't have watches. I didn't go to those who had watches because they are under separate control. Workers came to the door of the chief's booth complaining, "They didn't give us our coca break!" Others were saying, "How come they didn't tell us when it was rest period?"

The chief went out to distribute the time cards which are left with him in the morning and picked up in the afternoon for delivery in the card slots.

A man nicknamed *"Chaymante,"* a friend of the crew boss who had corrected the chief in the morning, criticized the chief again. "How can you give us time cards without signing them? Those whose cards aren't signed will be put down as absent. How do you people work? You have to fix this. Your assistant didn't even come to announce the coca break. You spend the day without any cares and you put us to work like donkeys."

Quintana said, "You just don't understand what was happening at the time. My assistant got trapped in the tunnel. I went to open the path up so that he could come out of Basualdo's workplace." Basualdo himself wasn't working there, but he found out soon enough.

We left work at five in the afternoon and I went up to Morococala to see Petrona. We were getting to know each other. I met her and we made a date to go to the movies. I went down to my boarding house, ate, went into my room for a moment to leave my coat, and then went to the movies. We spent that season like that.

I remember that there was an accident in which a person died. There was a narrow passage full of wood and the mine shaft was below. That wood was to support the cross beams over the mine shaft. They put wood flooring over the cross beams, and on top of that other supports so that the men wouldn't fall through. Often, when a heavy weight falls from above, the wood supports cave in below the flooring. To prevent this, they use double beams and on top of that they pile more planks. This is called the scaffolding.

One of those center beams must have broken because of pressure from a hard rock below; this subjected the wooden platform to stress from both sides, and with the weight from above, the cross beam broke. The scaffolding fell some sixty meters. Two men were trapped inside this section which was the Boyadora shaft. It was worked by "Hua-quero's" crew — Huaquero was Viviano Garcia's nickname. There was as much ore as you could dream of. You could fill barrels with it. But once the scaffolding fell down, it was finished. It took us six days to get those two people out. They came out looking like they had fainted from the gas because it was so oppressive inside, what with the heat and the lack of air.

When the collapse occurred, the chief immediately called in a driller named Zapata, who had previously worked at the one hundred-meter level, and had him put in air pipes wherever it was possible. He put in one inch pipe but at exactly sixty meters, they struck against some wood. The pipes also got plugged with dirt and we had to clear them with wires and hooks, whatever way we could. We blew through the pipes to clear them, and when we got short of breath, others took over.

We shouted through the pipe, "Eh, Mariano!" (That was the name of one of them, but I don't remember the name of the other because this happened in 1947 and many years have passed.) "Mariano!" we shouted, "Mariano!" and he heard us. We heard him through the pipe clearly, as though he was shouting on a telephone from far away.

They called in Dr. Liendo, a short man. The doctor said, "We need a little pipe to push a wire through; with this pipe we can send some pills, one by one, so they can take them to alleviate their fatigue and exhaustion."

Some men went to the store to get a cylinder. Tying it to the end of the wire, we lowered it through the pipe. When we shouted through the pipe, they heard us. But the pipe was blocked by a piece of wood and could be pushed no further.

Mariano called through the pipe, "We can hear your voices, but we can't tell where it comes from."

We told him, "We've drilled some pipes through. Just look for it. It must be around there by the overhead arch, or by the wall, or behind some rocks. Look for it."

Mariano looked and found the pipe. He tried to pull the beam over, so that the pipe could go further, but he was unable to. If he had made the beam fall down, it would have been worse, because it would have caved in even further. They opened up a little passage by chipping the wood with some hard rocks. Then they pulled out the wire with the little cylinder tied to it and removed the pills. Then we pulled out the wire with the cylinder so we could put in more pills. In that way, the doctor sent in the pills.

On Monday or Tuesday, Dr. Liendo came back in. "I don't think they are still alive, since there is no one pulling the cylinder out, or anything. They must be dead," he said.

In fact, they had fainted. We were just some ten meters away from the place where they were trapped, when they stopped speaking to us. We got closer on Wednesday but there were some large rocks that we couldn't move. We had to break the stone. Some men went to get very sharp pickaxes and with these we broke the rock piece by piece and opened a little passage. We could see that they were there, even though we didn't have electric lights, just carbon lamps.

Chief Quintana said, "I am going in. Put scaffolding above and below, so the rock doesn't fall in." What would happen? He was fat and tall. Superintendent Eloy Sotelo looked at me as I came to that level, and he said, "You are small; you can get in and see what's there."

We shouted a lot, but no one answered, because they had passed out. In three or four more hours they would die. We had to get them out somehow. We got one of them out; I carried the one who was weakest in my arms. I couldn't carry both of them because it was very narrow and low. I was on my knees, pushing him along when suddenly I bumped into the man who was still conscious and who had followed behind me and passed by me just at the turn. I squeezed to the side, shouting to the men up ahead, "Listen, pull this one out, and send someone in to help me. We'll drag the other one out of here by his hands and feet. One of us will be in front and the other in back."

When Zapata came to help me, he saw that the timbers were beginning to break more, and the other side was starting to cave in. One was still alive, but the second one was now unconscious. Even if this one dies, I thought, we have already saved the other. If I die too, it would be horrible. I moved out quickly. When I had moved some five meters, *corurun!* Thirty meters of rock fell. The whole tunnel broke down completely. Eight days later they took out the body of the other man, who had died when the tunnel collapsed.

I was so frightened I could hardly speak. I remember how much I sweated when I saw the wood breaking on one edge and the side wall collapsing, and in front of me the earth falling down. I was badly scared. I thought I would be trapped there forever. The other man had put me in danger because he was slow. I was small but he was tall, so he couldn't move quickly but wouldn't let me pass, either. He stayed in front of me, barring my way and I was almost lost. I had hardly moved ahead five meters, and then it happened, *corurun!* They would have taken me out like the dead man eight days later. But I escaped. God didn't want this accident to happen to me, and He saved me.

They put me in the hospital once I got out. For three days I had a high temperature, thirty-eight degrees centigrade and more. Then Dr. Liendo came in. I saw him as though I were dreaming. A high temperature makes me feel very drunk. I got better about midnight of the third day, and came to myself. I saw a light, but didn't know what it was; it was a bit yellow, and moving about.

Dr. Liendo was saying, "This man cannot fail, he will live. Give him a hot water bottle." When they gave it to me, I responded suddenly. I was back to myself. A nurse named Alicia, who is a friend of Petrona, gave me some blue pills at twelve o'clock at night. I don't know what kind of pills they were. They made me calm down, but the sweat continued pouring off me. At two or three o'clock the sweating stopped and I was quieter. The fright had been so tremendous that I almost forgot everything at that instant. Later, little by little, I remembered how we opened that rock up, how I went in, how I got him out, and how I saved that young man. Later I remembered everything. But at first I couldn't remember because I was worse than a drunkard.

The celebration of All Saints' Day came. I went to visit the homes of people who had died at work, or in their houses, or at the hospital, to see the tables that their families had prepared. I prayed and the owner of the table would give me a plate with a biscuit, a butterfly cake, dried fruit, and half a glass of wine. I helped myself to this, and went on to another house. I don't remember all the places I went, but I remember that I also went up to Morococala, and when praying there I met a friend, José Rodriguez, who is still working at Santa Fe. He took me to a bar belonging to Rosita Centellas. We went back to the encampment late at night, a bit drunk.

On that first All Saints' Day after that miner's death, I went to his house to pray for him. I was still frightened from that accident, remembering how we got him out, how I wanted to save him, how he stayed there in the middle of the shaft. All this made me bitter. Tears came to my eyes, not because I had so much affection for the man, but because he died in such a fierce accident. That poor man! Who knows with what suffering he died beneath the load, buried alive. I did not speak of this to Petrona, because if I had told her, I am sure she would have made me leave. She never wanted to hear about this kind of suffering. Yesterday afternoon when I remembered the name of the man who had the accident, I told her for the first time what happened to that man.

She began to cry, saying, "You have worked with so much suffering, and you still have come here to Oruro to work in the mine." She told my son, Filemón, "I am going to go in, even on my knees before the manager, to get you outside. I am going tomorrow," she told me. "I don't want Filemón to go to work in the mine. It is better that we do without things, but he must come out. I don't want it, even if they fire you. I am going in, otherwise they will make problems for you. You have to get out." She feels very strongly about these accidents. On one occasion the widow of a man who died in an accident told her of the death of Cabrera, but that wasn't such a horrifying accident. It was sudden, no one saw it, and no one had had to try to save him.

# 6

# Homework

Petrona's account of her life growing up in her parents' home and then forming her own illuminates the
relationship between love and work, money and ties of
kinship. Since her father was an alcoholic and handi-
capped, her brothers became the chief breadwinners.
They assumed responsibility for her needs, and in turn
expected her to care for them. It was they who opposed her marriage to Juan because they would be losing their caretaker. Women provide the motivation for
men's work, and their services to men validate the
worth of men's labor. The mine management is aware
of this tie that holds men to the job, and though they
do not give high rewards, the family subsidies listed as
a separate item on the wage envelope reinforce the
bonds between family and work. Although most mine
women earn money, like Petrona did with her sewing
and buying and selling, this is not recognized as a significant part of a mine family's pooled resources. Yet
her managerial skills and control of family resources
make an enormous difference in the well-being of its
members. Petrona talks about these strategies.

We were very poor. My father had a business traveling back and forth,
taking flour to Tapacari and bringing barley back. But we couldn't get
enough food to maintain the household, so my father went to Cerro
Grande. After two months he sent a letter saying, "I will come back
with money which I have already earned, so I can bring you here. Start

getting ready." So we started getting our things ready, packing them into bags. We sold everything we had, our donkeys, chickens, rabbits, and horses, and we divided up our share of the land and house.

My father came to Cochabamba to take us to Cerro Grande. He said, "We can go now because I already have a room and they have given me a job. I am working and earning well. Let's go!"

The next day we took all our things to Cerro Grande. We lived there for six months.

*How did you live there?*

They gave my father a good house. The company received him because he had lost his hand and his eye there. When he was young, about the time he married my mother, he worked in Cerro Grande. In his youth he had been a tailor. He had a workshop and made suits and skirts, as well as other items, and he earned plenty of money. He couldn't remain single, so he went to my mother and told her, "I want to get married."

My mother and father got married, and they went to Cerro Grande. There he worked inside the mine as a carter. On Saturday afternoon of Carnival he went into the mine to make his offering with the *ch'alla*. It was the custom there to enter the mine throwing dynamite, lighting it in their hands and throwing it up in the air with joy. My father didn't know that custom, and he didn't yet know how to handle dynamite. Before he could throw it away, it exploded in his hand and took away his eye and most one hand. That's how my father became an invalid. That hand had no fingers.

*Which hand was it?*

The left one, fortunately, and it was also his left eye. Even some of his abdomen was blasted by the explosion. They say parts of his stomach burst out and they quickly put them back in and the doctor sewed it up. Then they sent him to the hospital in the city of Cochabamba. There he recuperated quickly and even his stomach mended well.

When he had recovered, he went back to the Cerro Grande mine and they gave him his compensation for the little time he had worked. It wasn't much time, barely six months. Then he and my mother returned to my village, to Mallku Rancho.

In Mallku Rancho my parents looked for a way to earn their living. My father was always very active and worked hard. He knew how to hunt. He had two rifles and knew how to handle them. He hunted guinea pigs in the mountains and hills, far from the village. He raised a little money this way, selling the guinea pigs to restaurants. Over time, it became a lot of capital, and he began his flour business with this. He was the flour dealer of Mallku Rancho. He would take wheat flour to Tapacari, and from Tapacari he brought barley to sell in Cochabamba.

He was doing well in Tapacari until he started drinking. That caused him to lose his remaining capital. Maybe he lent too much to people, or maybe he was robbed — something must have happened. He got discouraged about continuing with the business and fought a lot with my mother. Finally, my father said to my mother, "I already have three children. We can't make enough to feed the children here. I don't know how long this can go on. I haven't killed anyone, nor have I stolen from anyone; I am not a criminal. I am healthy now, so I will go back to the mine to work. Maybe they will recognize me as a former worker. Let's go!"

I was already seven years old, and very alert; I was listening to them. My mother said, "I will stay here with the animals and the children because the girls are in school. You go ahead. If you get work, send us a letter or ask for a leave and come yourself one day."

So my father went back to the mine, and they recognized his seniority immediately. When he returned to get us in Cochabamba we had sold the animals, and he said, "Let's go," and we went. Since he had worked there in Cerro Grande before, they gave him a good house. We were well off.

*When you were a child, whom did you play with?*

With Juan's sisters — they were like my little sisters. We were neighbors of Juan's family in Cochabamba and his sisters and I knew each other since we were little girls. They were named Henriqueta and Silvera and I played most of the time with them. I was never one for playing around with too many friends.

*What did you play with?*

We played with dolls, cooking and keeping house.

*Did you know your grandparents?*

I knew my grandfather, but I never knew my grandmother.

*When did you know him?*

My father's father lived with us.

*And did you know your mother's parents?*

No, just my father's. He was the size of your *compadre* Juan. His name was also Juan, Juan Vidal.

*Was he kind?*
He was a very good, kind man.

*And your uncles, did you know them?*
I never knew any of my uncles. They never worked in the mine. My father was the only one who had that bad luck. Because of his accident, he went back to work in the mine there. "I lost my hand and my eye in the mine, so I have to finish myself there," he said when he went off to Cerro Grande. He didn't want to stay there in Cochabamba.

Soon the bosses at Cerro Grande started bothering my father. I don't know what happened, but they transferred him to Verengela.

"They are transferring me to Verengela," he told us. "Let's go." Because some of the bosses had been there only a short time, they didn't know my father and treated him as a new worker. We went with all our animals and everything. We were there eight years.

*How many workers were there?*
In Cerro Grande there were about 150 workers who came from many places, near and far.

*Did they speak Quechua?*
They spoke *Quechua.*

*What was the house you lived in like?*
There were three rooms, but there were no windows. There was no light, nothing, but it was large. That house had been empty for a long time. My mother got terribly sick there, with a fever. I don't know what spirit she saw in that house. We had to move to another place, one I can't remember.

So in Verengela, we lived like that, bringing in flour from Cochabamba and selling it as before. My mother and I brought candles, ready-made clothes, flour for food, and potatoes. We had to travel all the time. My mother would take in some young single workers as boarders and that earned money as well.

Soon my father was named a dance group leader. He led the dance and he played the flute at the fiestas. For the Feast of the Rosary on the seventh of October — a big important celebration in Verengela — he went to get ready-made clothes, costumes for the llama herders' dance. Every year he would do the fiesta, and he earned money this way, bringing in the costumes.

My father was working in peace while I went to the countryside to collect supplies with my mother. Since she had a business selling petticoats, I had asked her how I could learn to sew.

I had an "aunt," my father's first cousin, whose name was Julia Abasto. She was a seamstress and my mother would sometimes leave me with this aunt when she went to Cochabamba or Arque.

Once my mother had to spend a lot of time in Cerro Grande because of a watch. My father had an Ogival pocketwatch with a case of silver and works of gold. He gave it to a watchmaker to repair. The watchmaker sold it to another, or maybe he lent it or pawned the watch. So when my father went to claim the watch and asked the watchmaker if he had fixed it, the watchmaker answered, "Why didn't you come and get it earlier? I needed the money and that's why I pawned it to another person." He wanted to fight with my father and kept saying, "Why didn't you come earlier to collect it?"

"I didn't have the money. I hadn't earned enough to be able to collect the watch," my father said, getting ready to fight. He went to the police to report the watchmaker, but he had to go to Arque for that because there was no police station in Cerro Grande.

While my mother and father were off on that errand I stayed at home. But I was afraid to be alone, so I went to visit my aunt, whom my mother had left in charge until she returned. I brought potatoes, meat, rice, and vegetables to cook for my brothers at my aunt's house.

When I got there my aunt said to me, "Let's cook," and so we cooked. "Now sit by my side," she said. "You are going to help me sew."

"But, Aunt, I don't know how. How can I sew?" I asked.

"Well, now you will learn. That way, you will always know how to sew. You will know how to use a needle and thread, and you will learn everything."

She would sit at the sewing machine, a little hand-operated machine that she had, and I would sit next to her. I watched everything she did, *Comadre*, with all my concentration. I watched with my whole being. She would give me blouses to baste, and I made little bags for *chola* ladies. She would give me decorative bands for little bead bags. I could already make a nicely finished blouse, with small stitches and everything carefully marked out.

"You have to round off these beads here at the edges," she told me.

"Yes, Aunt," I answered, and I fixed those beads. My eye was always watching the needle and what I was doing, and thinking of what my aunt told me to do. I was very young, only nine. But I wanted to see how she made the machine work, how she cut, what size she was cutting for, and all that. She put a lot of knowledge and skill into making that material, and I watched her hands to see how she did it all. So I learned how to sew, *Comadre*. I even learned how to embroider. She didn't teach me for long — just two or three weeks. I learned quickly and when I grew up I earned money by putting lace edges on handkerchiefs and embroidering the corners, and I made skirts and blouses and petticoats for my mother to sell.

My father had no luck with his work. He had a fight with a worker on the job — what they did to each other was shameful — so my father was fired again. He had no work anyplace, and we had to return to Morococala on foot. It took us almost four days to get there.

*Why did you go to Morococala? Did you have relatives there?*

No, no one, *Comadre*. We were just going like gypsies on that walk to Morococala. We stopped here and there. We stayed in one place called Bolivar for two days. We had run out of food in the middle of the journey, so we had to rest there. The next day, my mother got sick in the middle of the road. She was very ill and couldn't walk. We got as far as a field in Mollepunko where we slept very badly that night in the open air. From Mollepunko we went to Morococala. In Morococala there was a lean-to with no door, like a stable. We took shelter there, and, just as it began to rain, a man named Constantino Gordillo, who is now dead, approached us and said, "What are you doing here? You can come to my house. I have plenty of room where you can rest."

"Certainly, Sir, by all means let us stay at your house," my father said to the man. "But later I shall pay you some rent."

So it was that we went to Constantino's house and lived there for four years because there was no place where we could live by ourselves. We two families were together in their little house. He had his own children, whom my father baptized. When he died, it was my father who wrapped him in his shroud and buried him.

Soon my brothers began to work and when they were old enough they went into the army. After the army they got work in Morococala, and we went there to live.

*What were the houses like in Morococala?*

In Morococala the houses for the workers were pigsties.

*How many rooms did you have?*

They gave one little room to my brother. The whole family had to live in one room, no matter how many there were. In the next room lived another person with another family. So we lived like that, often quarreling. When we arrived in Morococala, the camp was nearly empty. That's why this little house was available. Later, when I married your *compadre*, we had a house with four rooms. He got a better choice of houses because he was a driller; Juan needed a separate room, to get a lot of rest, so I got my choice there at Santa Fe.

*But not your father?*

Not for my father, no, never. What work did he have? He was just a night watchman. As an invalid, he didn't work. They fired him from Morococala for not doing his work, because he was drunk. That's why he couldn't get work afterwards. My brothers supported him.

*Did they always work in the mine?*

My older brother worked in the little mine.

*How old was he when he started?*

He must have been thirteen years old, like Aníbal is now. He earned a lot, even at that age. Aníbal is working now, too.

*What does he do?*

This morning his friends took him to the bus to work as a ticket taker. "Let's go earn enough at least for our shoes," his friends said, so he went this morning. His father was crying, "My son, where will he have his lunch?" Aníbal told him that the boss himself buys him his lunch, his tea, and gives him everything.

*How much does Aníbal earn?*

I don't know how much they will pay him. They will give him his first pay soon, probably this afternoon.

*Did he get the job himself?*

Well, yesterday my sister-in-law came over and when your *compadre* Juan asked, "How is Fructuoso?" she told him that he was working.

"Ah, he is working," your *compadre* said. "Where?"

"At the placer mine," she said.

"At which site?"

"He is working in the Pantipata mine," she told him.

When Aníbal heard this he said, "*Papi*, I want to go to work too. I will go to Santa Fe to work. There in Santa Fe, I'll go to the movies. I'll be earning money and I can stay with my aunt."

Juan said, "No, Son. When I am dead you can go wherever you like to work or study or do anything else, but as long as I am alive I don't want you to leave my side." Juan scolded Aníbal and almost hit him. They were arguing like that when my sister-in-law was leaving. She still wanted to take Aníbal with her, and my brother also wanted him to come.

"Let him come," my brother said.

"I want to see the children," Aníbal said. (He missed my brother's children.)

"You are always mean," my brother said to Juan. "If we take him, he will surely have a good time at the movies. We need money too, to go to the movies. If he comes with us, he'll just go to work with Fructuoso."

"No, no, no, Luciano, I will not let Aníbal leave my side for anything," Juan said. He didn't permit him to go.

Well, that was that, but then yesterday afternoon a boy came over. He had a truck, and knew there were a lot of boys who couldn't find work. So he said, "Aníbal, let's go to work tomorrow. I went to work today to earn money. They need a collector on the bus. Don't you want to go earn some money?"

Aníbal said, "*Ay,* of course I do!" He was almost dancing on his head. "You found me a job, now I am going to work no matter what. I am going to earn some money!" And last night he ironed his clothes and got everything ready. It seems he didn't even sleep last night.

This morning his older brother Filemón also didn't want him to go. "What do you want to go to work for? Are you trying to say my work is worth nothing?" But Aníbal went anyway. He hasn't returned yet, and his father was waiting for him with lunch. But he gets his lunch and tea and everything on the job, he says.

*Do you remember your older brother, when he first went to work?*

He came back happy, very happy. He said to me, "Now I am working, Petrona. Now I can give you clothes, whatever you like. I can give you shawls. I can give you shoes. You go and tell Mother. Don't go play anywhere. Go straight to the store, for now that I am working I will give you whatever you like. First I will buy you some shoes so you can bring me food. Then I will buy you stockings and then I'll buy you a skirt." That's the way my brother, my sweet brother who is in Santa Fe, consoled me. He loved me a lot.

*How much older is he?*

Three years older than my younger brother, and I am three years still younger. We are all about three years apart. I am almost forty-two years old and my older brother just turned forty-nine.

*And the younger one, when did he start working?*
The younger one went to Verengela when he was thirteen years old. The older one was already working at Morococala. He is a good worker. He started working at the mill at Morococala and is still there to this day. The younger was a mechanic at Morococala. He became a mechanic when he was young, after he went into the army. He makes good things and knows how to do everything.

*Did you ever think of working at something — a career?*
My brothers didn't want me to. I wanted to find myself a job or earn money sewing or doing something else, but my brothers didn't want me to.

"That's why we are working," they told me. "You are our little sister, the only one we have. How can you want to go to work like that, at anything?" My brothers didn't want me to work. They cared for me a lot, *Comadre*, those two. As the only sister, I have been well loved. They didn't want me to lack for anything. They preferred to go around in old shoes, old pants, but not me. Every fortnight they would buy something for me. That's why they scolded Juan those times, because he didn't want to buy clothes like that for me when I was still young.

"If you don't want to buy her clothes, we had best take our sister back," they said, "because she is used to being well dressed." And they wanted to take me away, but your *compadre* Juan stood strong.

"I am a man," Juan said. "I will go to work. But I am not going to work just for clothes. I have to work for lots of things," he said. They argued like that a lot.

The daughter of my father's *compadre* — with whom we stayed when we first came to Morococala — and I sold refreshments in the plaza. We made *api* [a corn gruel drink]. I was still young, only thirteen, but very smart. We went together to Oruro to get candies and biscuits. We got along well and we would cook together sometimes. That's the way we were.

I don't like to be always quarreling. Some people like rivalries, but I don't. No matter how much people pick at me or do things to annoy me, I don't answer. That's why I have lived a long time and have been well liked everywhere. No one has anything to reproach me with. I have wedding *comadres* and three goddaughters. I have my confirmation *comadres*, baptism *comadres* and my *compadres* of wakes. I have been first communion godmother to three children, two boys and a girl. I must have about thirty *compadres* in all. I have many godchildren, and over there in Santa Fe, there are many, too.

*When you came to Oruro, how did the city impress you?*

Oruro was tiny, *Comadre.* The houses on Bolivar Street, they were just little straw houses. Now there are two-, three-, and even four-story houses. It wasn't like that then. The Campero market was the only one. The market down below wasn't there yet. We took bread, candies, everything to sell on the street.

*Did you like the city?*

I liked it very much. I thought a lot about going there. My father wanted to buy a house, but my mother didn't want to.

"How will we live there?" she asked. "What will we do? What will we eat? In Cochabamba, we have land and we can eat from that. Don't do that kind of madness," she said to him. If she hadn't opposed it, we would have had our house on Bolivar Street.

He was also thinking of buying a truck, but my mother didn't want him to. My mother understood a lot: "Are you a chauffeur? If you hire drivers, they will make a mess of the truck. And they'll show you up for being as old and rickety as the truck. They will earn money, but we won't get a thing," she said. And so they used up that money just by living. Once he didn't work any more, or do anything, money went fast.

*Did your father receive any pension when he stopped working?*

There was no pension then. They didn't know about such things. They just gave him his severance pay, and there was no social security.

*Did you go to school?*

I was in school for almost a year, but not regularly. Sometimes they sent me, sometimes they didn't. My mother fought a lot to send us to school. My father was a brute who didn't understand — he didn't want us to go.

"Go to school? What's a woman going to do in a school?" he said. "What for? It's impossible for Petrona to go; she has no right to go to school." He'd argue like that with my mother. My father was a crude man who didn't understand what letters were, what languages were. He didn't understand the importance of education.

*Did your father ever go to school?*

No, never.

*Did he speak Spanish? or just Quechua?*

He spoke Spanish and Quechua both. He went to Chile, right next to the Argentinian border, and he learned Spanish there.

*He didn't know it before?*
Before that he didn't know Spanish. He was an Indian and was ignorant of many things. My mother would tell me, "Your father is an Indian, who doesn't understand anything." That's why I didn't go to school.

*And did your mother go to school?*
My mother was well-read and knew a lot. She could write anything. She knew all the answers well. My mother said that she wore dresses during the twenty-two years she lived in Chile's capital, but when she joined my father, she began to wear *polleras* [the full skirts with petticoats distinctive of *chola* dress]. When she got married my father gave her *polleras*.

*Why did he want to do that?*
He said he didn't like the dresses. He was a peasant from the field, and he didn't understand, so my mother took off her dress and wore *polleras*. She cried about it. And the *polleras* didn't suit her. She was very fair, light-skinned, tall, and plump. I look like my father, and my father was an ugly, dark man.

# 7

# Petrona's Account of Their Wedding

*When did you meet Juan's mother?*
It was rather she who found me in Morococala. She sought out my mother and me.

"Where does Petrona live, or María de Vidal?" she asked people. (My mother's name was María.) Juan's mother said she was my mother's childhood friend from Mallku Rancho, where she had taken care of my mother, because, she said, my mother was poor and had no parents, while she had her store and everything. "So," she had said, "you have to live here, María. What are you going to do anyplace else? You have no options, and we have to stay alive. I'll make you a load of *chicha* to sell. We can earn enough for clothes and everything just by selling this. You are young." My mother-in-law had spoken to my mother like that, and they lived there for a long time – my mother married my father in Juan's mother's house.

Later my mother-in-law-to-be came to Morococala when Juan's brother came there to work. (Before that he had worked in the police station.) We had been at Morococala for a long time and didn't know them anymore, and I didn't know her at all.

They had heard rumors that we were in Morococala and sought us out by asking people where we lived, which was near the movie theater.

When she found us she said to my mother, "Little sister, how long have you been here? You haven't forgotten me, have you? You have gotten old already, and I have gotten old too."

"All is fine," we said, and we welcomed her. From that time on, they both cared for me a lot. Juan's mother stole my heart.

"That girl is very good, very able, and very humble," she said of me, and she told that to everyone.

Juan was in the army and his mother wrote him there, describing me to him. Your *compadre* said he had to go to Cataricagua. (Do you know Cataricagua? It's near Huanuni.) Juan felt he had to go there when he got out of the army. His mother wrote, "You must come here, Son. Don't go anyplace else." So he came to Santa Fe — he had worked for some time at Santa Fe, one or two years — and soon I met him. We got to know each other.

My future mother-in-law said to me, "You must marry my son. You are very good." She was very kind.

*Have you had other young men who were in love with you?*

No, *Comadre*, I was young. I was seventeen years old when I got married.

*What did you think when you first met my compadre?*

He just came to my house; I didn't know who he was.

*Did he come with your brothers?*

Yes, with my brothers. They were friends. I thought, Who could he be? But I didn't bother to ask them. Why would I have asked? I was selling some things in front of the movie theater with a friend. I always kept busy. My brothers told me, "There's a young man from Cochabamba here. He always comes with us."

One of my brothers had a separate room, and he took me aside and told me, "This young man is from Cochabamba. He is the son of Doña María Rodrigues."

"Where is he from in Cochabamba?" I asked. He told me Mallku Rancho, but even then I thought nothing of it, *Comadre*, absolutely nothing.

The celebration at Santa Fe came on the twenty-fourth of October. We had some *chicha* at my house and had a housewarming. I was selling alcohol, homemade alcohol, to earn money. So plenty of friends came and drank at my house. Juan also came, to have his hair cut by my father, who earned money as a barber. Your *compadre* always came for his haircut. Juan was good looking, blondish, fair-skinned, young, and plump — very attractive.

Now, it makes you want to cry, every day. Especially now that he is so pitiably ill, *Comadre*. He was in bed yesterday and the day before also. He's been in bed almost all week, yet he continues to want to work.

"You don't want to be like that," I told him. "You have to stay in bed. We can give you whatever you need. Why are you getting up?" But he pays no attention. It goes in one ear and out the other.

"I don't want to," he says. "I'm not one of those soft types that stay in bed. And when I die, how are you going to live like this in an unfinished house? I must fix it up nicely for you to live in," he says. It just makes us cry when he talks like that.

*What happened on the 24th of October [a date Juan had alerted me to]?*

Ah, we met on the twenty-fourth of October. I had a friend named Nicasia, and he went with her to a chapel called San Pedrito. He was dancing as a *chunchu* Indian. I had gone knowing nothing about him, not even if he was dancing or not, when he spoke to me there, saying "I want to dance with you," he said.

"So we will dance," I replied. (When we are young, we are popular and if people want to dance with us, we dance, isn't that right *Comadre?*)

They didn't want to let me leave the celebration. "Go! Go!" said the boys, putting all the girls out, except for Nicasia and me. They didn't put the two of us out. We stayed there dancing, and we ate there too.

Then I was ready to go, but Juan was drunk. I didn't drink, ever; I sold it, but I didn't drink *chicha*, much less any alcohol. Of course he was young, he was a dancer, and the officeholders offered him drinks and he took them. But I took nothing, tasted nothing, but even *chicha*.

He followed us to our house, "Take me," he said, very drunk, "take me to your house. I want to go rest at your house." My friend and I carried him between us. On the way we met my mother.

"Why did you stay so late?" she asked.

"Ah, we were watching the fiesta," we said, and continued on home. I took your *compadre* to my house. He slept at my house. Then he got up at five in the morning, saying that he had to go to work. He was a steady worker ever since he was young.

He left, but he didn't come back to my house until the eighth of December, after All Saints' Day. In that month he came to my house to have a haircut and buy a new hat from my father. My father cut Juan's hair and charged him for the cut and the hat.

"I would give you half of the hat I bought," Juan teased, "but you don't come to Santa Fe any more. Why don't you come to Santa Fe for an outing?"

"I don't have time to go," I said. "And besides, I have no reason to go. When one has a reason, one goes walking. If one has no reason, why would one just go out and walk?"

He said, "There is a reason for you to come. You must come, if only to see the movie. Movies are lovely. Come to see the movie."

"First I will check with my mother to see if I can come," I replied. I was very obedient and never just followed my whims.

So I went to the movies with one of my friends. Since I was the only girl in the family, I said to one of my little friends,

"Let's go to Santa Fe."

"So let's go," she told me. We went there.

I saw Juan there. He spoke to me, saying, "I want to ask for your hand. I want to marry you."

I answered, "It will be the way it will be. I will ask my mother what she would say to that. I'll be able to answer you then." I didn't know anything yet, I was still innocent. "I will see what my mother thinks. Come on up tomorrow afternoon," I said.

He came to Morococala soon after. He had sent a letter to Cochabamba, to his mother, asking that she come with him to ask for my hand.

"I am ready, Petrona. I will always want to marry you. I have been watching you for so much time, and that's why I want to marry you. I don't want you to make a fool of me. I want you to marry me," he told me.

I asked my mother what she thought, telling her what he had said. My mother wasn't annoyed at all.

"You'll have to decide. You'll have to choose your path, and which way to go. I can't tell you what to do." She spoke like that because she was a wise woman. She wasn't just any fool, one of those who would have said, "What were you up to? What did you do?" *Uyy*, she could have hit me. But she never hit me; I never felt a whip, and my mother never shouted at me. She controlled me with her eyes. We never shouted. That's why she said to me, "You'll have to choose your own way on this. I can't say yes or no."

Your *compadre* had told me to give him an answer on a certain day. That day came. "I have to think some more," I told him. "I have to think about it well. I haven't decided yet." Your *compadre* had come to find out what I thought so we could go ahead quickly.

"I sent another letter to Cochabamba. I came to see whether you are going to accept or not," he said. "If you don't accept, I am going to kill myself," he said [laughter].

So I said, "I will think about it."

*Was my compadre* serious?

Well, I believed he would kill himself. I was silly.

"If you are not going to accept, then I'll go throw myself into the shaft," he said to me.

"But why would you do that?" I asked him.

"If you don't accept, what can I do? I want to marry you. I am certain of everything in you. I must marry you," he said.

"But what if I don't want to get married, simply because I am not old enough yet?" I replied, quite angry.

He said, "I want to know," and he was shouting, too, as he added, "By tomorrow afternoon I want to know the answer, whether you will or won't marry. I need to know whether or not to send a letter to my mother, because my mother might come here in vain," he said as he left for his house.

I didn't say anything to my mother. I thought about it. I had a friend and I went to sell candles at the movies with her. I said to this friend, "What should I do now?"

"If his mother comes, your father and your brothers might all get mad at you for going with him," she said. "Where will that leave you? Leave him and you go wherever you like. What do you care? You can live well like this. You could be left waiting and be deceived by him." That friend was a bad advisor. I asked myself all night how it would be.

In the morning I said to my mother, "Mamita, Juanito said 'If you don't accept me, I will kill myself. I will go and throw myself in the mine shaft.' What shall I do?"

My mother told me, "It depends on you. If your brothers catch you, you'll be in trouble."

"But what do my brothers have to reproach me for?" I was completely taken in by your *compadre's* words. Of course he meant what he said, I thought.

But I didn't give him his answer. The next day, I told Juan again, "Come on a certain date if you want to see my mother and father."

"I will come on Saturday night," he told me. Saturday was a payday, and on that day I sold candy at the door of the movie theatre. We sold a lot on all pay days, and I went up there early.

However, his mother didn't come until a week later. Your *compadre* went directly to meet her in Cochabamba.

"I still want to get married, Mother, to Vidal's daughter," he told her. "You have to come right away." Uuuy, my mother-in-law was jumping, leaping as she came.

"If it's with her, I accept everything," she said. So she came. I was well loved. She cared for me a lot. At that point she never had any fault to find with me, nor did she shout at me. She shouted at her other daughter-in-laws in all sorts of ways, but not at us. She seemed to care for me a lot.

She arrived in Santa Fe on Thursday, with everything for a feast. She brought chickens, rabbits, everything well prepared, and vegetables, all from Cochabamba. So we got together.

My father didn't want us to, not for anything. My father didn't eat a plate of food or even take a glass of beer, nothing. He didn't want me to marry.

"My daughter is worth gold," he said. "My daughter must never leave my house." He went to his work. He wouldn't touch his beer, nor his plate of food, nothing, not even *chicha*. He didn't want anything. "I know very well that my daughter will suffer. His relatives will make her suffer. Who will defend her?" It's true that Juan didn't get along with his relatives. They are very bad. Even now, we don't get along with your *compadre's* brother. He is a very bad man.

So it was that we began to live together. We lived well. Soon my father accepted it — what else could he do? And your *compadre* became the most beloved of his sons.

*Where have you lived since you got married?*

We lived in San Pedrito in a little room. My mother-in-law had another husband, after Juan's stepfather. We lived — all of us, including my brother-in-law — in that one room. It was a little room this size, from about here to there [indicating a space of about five meters]. Five of us slept in a single room: my mother-in-law, her husband, my brother-in-law, Juan and me. There wasn't any other room. But there was no other place to live, and it was the rainy season. So we were living well enough.

My mother-in-law turned out to be a stubborn woman, full of rage. She was so irritable it was hard to bear. She would complain over any little thing, and I wasn't used to that. So I went to my house in Morococala for a while, saying, "Mama, my mother-in-law always complains. I want to leave that man. I don't want to live like that. His mother is a bad woman, and I can't get used to it."

"Now you are beginning to realize what you have done. Now you have to suffer for what you've done until you die," she scolded me.

"I am leaving. I am going to tell my father," I told my mother.

"Your father doesn't want to know anything about you," she replied.

I went home crying, wondering what to do. When I got there my mother-in-law was angry again. I thought, what does she want now? but I didn't say anything to her. What she told me to do, I did. If she didn't tell me to do something, I didn't do it. That's the way I was. I told your *compadre*, "Your mother is very quarrelsome. I don't know what it could be; maybe she just doesn't like me. But I am not used to these angry looks, this rancor, and I don't like it. I am going up to stay with my mother. I am going to go there to live. Come if you like, and if you don't, don't," I told him.

"What are you saying? Your father won't want you there. Your father doesn't want to know anything about us," he said. "Leave it be; just bear it. What might he do to you? He might even hit you."

"*Ay*, how can he hit me? I am his daughter. Why would he hit me?"

I was cooking on a brazier, heating our lunch in a pot. There was neither wood nor coal nor paraffin, nothing, and it was the rainy season in December. Just as the pot began to boil, my mother-in-law came into the little kitchen where I was and said, "*Ay*, your pot, why isn't it boiling faster?"

"Because there is no wood; with what wood am I going to stir up the fire?"

"With straw, the way I am stirring it up!" she told me. She kicked the brazier and spilled the pot, with all the meat, everything. I looked at her. I didn't say anything to her. I didn't answer her, not a word. She had become crazy with all her complaints. She is probably accounting for it with God, now that she is dead. It was late, almost twelve. At noon Juan would come for lunch from his work in the mine. What was I to do now? What could I do? Well, I didn't do anything. I didn't go near the kitchen, nothing, nothing. I didn't do anything. I was obstinate, too, and I didn't want to do anything anymore.

I put my shawl on and went to Morococala. I got there before my mother did. *Uuy*, first and foremost my mother was a good cook. When we were at Morococala we had good food, everything. My mother must have started cooking about eleven, because when I got to her house in Morococala at noon, she had already cooked the food. I told her what had happened.

"I can't stand it. I am coming up here," I said.

"Why did you get together with him? Why didn't you ask me carefully? First you have to get used to it, and then you can stand it, all of the anger, all of the quarrelsomeness," she said.

"But you must have known about this. I asked you several times," I argued.

My mother just said, "Now take the food from here." She put it in a pot. "Take this food to your husband. Put some coals in this pot to keep the stew and his second plate of vegetables hot."

I took the food down to Juan. We had a peaceful lunch.

"Now I am going up there to cook for the evening. I'll bring it to you," I told him.

"Your father will protest."

"No, never. He wouldn't mind. I'll just bring some food down quietly, and I will be here before you come back," I told him.

"Fine," he said.

So I went up to Morococala and brought the food down. When he came home from his work, Juan said to me, "I can ask for a room for you. If they give it to me, the two of us could go live together."

"Yes, ask for it. I am depending on you, because I can't get used to it here," I told him. It wasn't more than two or three weeks that we had been living together and my mother-in-law was already impossible.

Payday came. We had been together for a month. I gave my mother-in-law half of your *compadre's* money. I was very generous, *Comadre*. I never took advantage of other people's work. I said to my mother-in-law, "Here is your money, Mami." She didn't want to take the money. "I'll give you half then. With the other half, I'll buy something for your son," I told her.

"No, child, take it and buy something for yourself. You need to buy something. My son has everything."

"No, he doesn't even have a work shirt. I will buy one for him," I said. When I said this, she took half of the money quietly.

"Thank you," she said to me, and she kissed my head, saying, "Thank you, child." That's the way we were from then on.

I had a cousin who was in Quillacolla just then. He had married a girl who sold fruit. He was working alone at Morococala. He came down to visit me and said, "You are living together peacefully now, but my aunt told me that before you were complaining a lot about your mother-in-law. Maybe it will be better if I ask for a room for you in Morococala. That way, the two of you could live quietly there, and I can live with my uncles and their children."

"We'll see. I will ask Juanito what he would think of us living there."

So I asked Juan and he said, "Could we really go up to Morococala?"

"But is that possible for you?" I asked him.

"We have to go because you quarrel too much with my mother. You can't get used to it. So we'll go live there," he said to me. My mother-in-law said that since her husband was working in Morococala, and since she had her trading as well as his income, we should go. So we went to Morococala to live in the company's room which my cousin had obtained for us. We lived apart from my mother-in-law.

*Do you remember when Juan got ill from the gas?*

It was just after we began living together, one or two weeks later. It was about ten-thirty in the morning and he got an attack just as he went in the mine. I was busy cooking. In San Pedrito, we lived in a place that was in sight of the mine. A friend of mine came running from the mine, screaming, "Petrona! Petrona!" and "Doña María! Doña María! There has been an accident!"

I stopped and listened. "What did that woman say? She's not calling for us is she?" I asked my mother-in-law.

My mother-in-law said, "She is running and calling our names."

Then I saw that they were carrying a body on a stretcher, like a corpse, of the side of the mine. The woman approached us and said, "He had an accident and he was calling for his mother or his wife."

I didn't want to go. I feared that something bad had happened and I was afraid. But my mother-in-law said to me in Quechua, "We must see; I'm going." I ran after her instantly, without my shawl, without a hat; I just ran.

When they took Juan to the hospital, the doctor there said to me, "Señora, don't be so frightened. The young man fell down with dizziness from the gas. There is nothing the matter," he said to calm me. "Nothing serious happened. At noon or twelve-thirty he will come to and you should come back then," he told me. He was unconscious when I left. Your *compadre* was lying there as if he was dead. I ran to tell my mother-in-law.

"Nothing happened. He fainted from the gas."

"*Aay*, with the gas," my mother-in-law said, beginning to cry. "That's what work in the mine is. I didn't want him to work in the mine. We should go to Cochabamba."

"Well, I don't understand about that because none of my people work in the mine. My brothers don't work in the mine; one works on the outside, at the mill, and the other works on the pumps," I said, "so I don't understand the mine." Of course I was an innocent. I didn't know about the mine. We should indeed have gone somewhere else, isn't that right, *Comadre?* I should have known that he was going to get sick the way he is now, but I didn't. I was foolish, but I cannot change what I did then.

So around twelve-thirty or one I went back to the hospital. When your *compadre* became conscious, he said to me, "Petrona, you came!"

"Yes. I came earlier also, but you were unconscious," I told him.

"I don't know what could have happened to me. When I was just going into the mine, I felt as though an enormous blow hit me. I never experienced that before. I felt as though I was completely lost."

He left the hospital at two in the afternoon. When he got home I said, "I think it is a serious mistake for you to continue working in the mine. Why don't you work on the outside or do work in the fields?"

"But the money from farming won't support us," he said.

"But do we spend so much that we need so much money?" I asked.

"No, but we need money to live, to do anything else. We have to buy beds, we have to buy furniture, we have to buy other things. I have to earn a bit more money. Then I will come out of the mine," he told me.

"You have to come out now, because that gas could kill you. You'll come out sick or worse," I told him.

"No, we'll do it like I say." And then later he didn't want to come out. He got used to earning money and didn't want to come and work on the outside.

*When did you buy the furniture?*

First we got a bedstead — the one we have, a brass bedstead — then a trunk, then a few tables, and then we bought ourselves some clothes. We dressed well but we also had money. I was never a wastrel and didn't throw things away or spend money foolishly. Whatever we earned, I saved well.

Shortly after that it was Carnival. That time it was lovely. We danced. I was together with your *compadre* in a dance group, and we danced well. Just after Temptations — it was on the Monday evening of Temptations — Juan got drunk. He had seen a ghost. He was coming down the path at three o'clock in the morning, returning from work. He had come to Morococala, since I was at my mother's house.

When he stopped in the path he saw a large man, reaching almost to the sky, very tall, wearing a white shirt, a black tie, a black suit, and a black hat. Juan said he was huge. It must have been an evil spirit. Your *compadre* almost went crazy, but I cured him with the *yatiris* and I saved him. Otherwise your *compadre* would have become crazy. He was cured with medicines, with *k'awas* and with incense. The *yatiris* asked God's forgiveness with the incense and cured him like that.

We lived in Santa Fe for a long time. There I had my first daughter, Sabina, who died. When she was born I was eighteen years old and I didn't know anything.

*Was she born in your house?*

Yes, the one in Morococala. I went for my confinement to my mother's house in Morococala. The pains came and Juan took me to Morococala, saying, "We have to go immediately to your mother's house." Just as we got to Morococala I went into labor and gave birth to a little girl.

*Did a midwife help you?*

Yes, a midwife. Your *compadre* had gone to get the one who always saw me.

*Did you give birth in bed?*

Yes, I got sick [delivered] in bed.

*Did your husband help?*

Yes, I always delivered with him. He knew how to deliver babies. He is half a midwife, himself; he understands. He always delivered my sister-in-law's babies. She never wanted to go to the doctor, or to the hospital.

"If Juanito comes, I will go into labor, and if he doesn't come, it won't come out of here," she would say. She'd put my brother out of the house, telling him "I don't want you to get near me. You have hard hands, and you make me hurt. Go outside. Call Juanito." I would be running around, crying for my sister-in-law.

I cared a lot for that sister-in-law. Just the other day she reproached me bitterly for not coming to see her more often."Why didn't you come sooner? You have left me alone for such a long time. Why didn't you come? Why didn't you even send a letter?" She cried so much. Yet she is quite healthy and plump, no? "You can almost pick me up," I told her, "so you should come get me!" Afterwards she laughed.

Anyway, I got sick with my first daughter, María. I took care of myself for a month in bed. My mother and father looked after me. My father didn't want me to do anything. He got a girl to take care of the baby and paid her salary.

"My daughter is still young," he told Juan, "and she doesn't know how to take care of a baby. She could drop it, or something else could happen. I will pay the girl not only to take care of the baby, but also to breast-feed it and keep it clean as well. You people can do something else. You don't have a crib or enough baby clothes, and some things for the house are missing. You can take care of that, but I will pay for the girl."

So my father gave the girl her monthly salary. I was well loved by my father, *Comadre*. He didn't want me to do any work. That's why I stayed in bed for a month. But soon I got up and I was well and went to Santa Fe.

But after a month and three days the baby got sick and died. She would have been twenty-two years old last October 25th. Filemón will be twenty-one.

*Who helped you with the other children?*

The lady who helped me with the first daughter continued to care for me. She would send her daughter to take care of the baby because I was very weak. What was it? I couldn't manage little Filemón. He was fat, robust, big and heavy. Until he was two or three years old, I raised him with the help of the girl.

*When Filemón was born did you have to burn the placenta? How did you do it?*

Your *compadre* prepared it. He knew how to do that. He got a pencil, some money, a notebook, then some mixtures with carnations, roses, newspapers, like that. Newspapers are burned so that the child will learn to read quickly, and flowers are burned so he will have luck. We did this with each of my children.

I got sick with some of my other children also. They came every three years, and for each child that lived, one died. After the first María, I bore another girl in my house who died, and a boy died, the first Juan Manuel, also born in my house. Three died, and I got terribly ill with a bad pregnancy after Filemón. I felt a big pain as I was getting on the truck to go to Oruro to attend a confirmation. It felt like a heavy blow against my back. When I got to the cathedral for the ceremony I got another ugly and enormous pain, and my stomach twisted. I had been pregnant only three months. I couldn't even sit down in the church. My mother-in-law was with me.

"Come, Mama, let's go have this little girl confirmed," I said. As soon as the confirmation was over and my *comadre* had thanked me, I was ready to go home, but my mother-in-law didn't want me to.

"Just stay here. You're sick now, and I will cure you at home. Let's go to my house," she said, and took me there.

My *comadre* went back to Morococala. She said, "I am going to take care of your little boy and your husband so that you won't worry, and so that he won't worry that you are not well. Soon he'll come to see you," she said to me. I agreed.

That night I gave birth prematurely to a three-month-old fetus. It was a little woman. My mother-in-law washed it and burned it. We burn these fetuses. She took care of me at her home and I stayed there for a week. I couldn't go anywhere; I couldn't even walk.

Soon Juan and Filemón arrived. "What happened?" Juan asked. Little Filemón, three years old, wanted to hold me and hug me.

*Have you ever used anything to avoid conception?*

No. I always gave birth every three years. Anita will be four years old this September, and Juan Manuel is almost a year old.

Anyway, Juan said to me, "We'll have to wait here in Oruro for transportation for two days. I'll put you in the hospital over there. Here you are suffering. Who can come to see you from over there?"

I got up and went to the hospital in Santa Fe. The doctor there said, "This unfortunate event has been very bad for you. We have to get you stronger. You have some blood clots in your abdomen. We will take out these clots with a probe." So they probed me and they cured me. I had no more children until Filemón was six years old. And the one who came then died before she was a year old, sick from scarlatina. The first Juan Manuel and Ana María died of the same disease. This always takes children.

*Was there much scarlatina in the mining camp?*

In the mine it's very ugly, very contagious. It goes in rows, you understand, it moves consecutively, down one row of houses, from one house to the other house. After six years, almost seven years, I had María, and after María I had Aníbal. After that Elena, and after her, the first Juan Manuel who died with scarlatina.

*In Santa Fe?*

In Santa Fe. I have three children buried there.

Then Anita was born and I got very sick. One of my uncles who came to see us said to my father and mother, "Why don't we take her to Cochabamba? There is still time before All Saints' Day. She can get better and wait for all Saints' Day calmly at her father's house."

My father and mother had been saving money for All Saints' Day.

They had thought I wouldn't come, since I hadn't written them a letter. My mother thought she had to look after only my father, since there was no telegram, no letter from me. So she was making money by selling chickens and eggs, collecting money from one thing or another so as to be able to buy "bread babies."

As I was traveling by bus to spend All Saints' Day in Cochabamba, I let go of my baby girl because I had no strength to hold on to her. I had gotten carsick on the bus, but I wasn't aware of it. People saw me fall off the seat on which I had been sitting, the first row; my little girl fell onto the step. The driver stopped the bus and picked us up. The child's face was swollen, and I was half dead when we got to Vinto. At the station I unloaded all the things I was bringing to Cochabamba, since there was no one to help. That night I soon came to my senses. My little girl wasn't crying, even though she hadn't been fed. Poor Anita made no noise.

When the morning came, a woman approached me. She had known my mother whom I resembled.

"Hello, Doña Petrona, you have come. What's happened? You don't look so well," she said as she came closer.

"I got here yesterday," I told her.

"Are you ill?" she asked.

"Yes, I got sick when this little girl was born. What could it be?"

"It's related to childbirth. Why did you get up so soon? You should have rested a while," this woman said to me. "You should have had baths given to you, and that way you would have recovered nicely from the delivery."

I couldn't even answer, so the woman picked up the baby, and just then it started raining. I was catching a bad cold and had a nosebleed. She carried the baby and we went to a doctor in Vinto. He gave me an injection, but I continued hemorrhaging. I lost rivers of blood through my nose, but the injections calmed me. I took a bus. I don't know if I paid or even if they charged me — I don't remember even now what happened, and to this moment I don't remember that woman. I have lost all sense of those days. I got to my mother's house somehow. The driver dropped us far from the house. The woman hadn't given me good directions and I couldn't tell the driver where her house was. Also, Elenita was crying, "Mami, Mami!" like that, crying and shouting, and that bothered the driver, and he dropped us almost half a league from the house.

There I had relatives, nieces, and your *compadre* also had cousins living there. One of his cousins saw me and approached us, saying "Petrona, you have come."

"Yes."

"*Aay*, what's happened to you? You are in pain! You look like paper," he said.

I said, "What's that? Am I yellow? Am I white? What is it?"

He said, "You are very pale. You look like yellow paper."

"Yes, I got very sick, when the baby was born," I told him.

"You are very sick now. What shall we do?"

I wanted to sit down, just throw myself someplace. I couldn't walk or lift things. I had brought dried fruit, cookies, corn cakes, and "bread babies" — little rolls shaped like dolls. I had brought a lot of things in enormous baskets.

My cousin said, "I will take these things to your house and I'll call your mother."

"I wish you would do me that favor," I told him. He went off on his horse and took my things, my sacks and my baskets, everything. Soon my mother appeared; my cousin had brought her.

"She is terribly sick and cannot walk," he said to her.

She shouted from where she was, "Petrona, don't come to see me and then die!"

"Be patient with me, Mami," I told her.

"You came, you came! How are you child?" she asked me. "What makes you sick? How awful that you are sick," wept my mother.

We took the rest of my things on two donkeys that Juan's nephew had brought. They even took me on a donkey because I couldn't walk. I had bled so much that I didn't have the strength to walk. They took me to my house. As soon as I got to Cochabamba, I went straight to bed and stayed there for two days.

When I arrived, my mother said, "Come, I'll take you to the hospital in the center of Cochabamba, because your sickness is serious. Who will take care of your children? Who will care for them if you die?"

One of my uncles took me to the hospital in Cochabamba in an automobile. He rented the car and we paid six dollars for the trip. In Cochabamba they put me in the hospital, and there I recovered, thanks to medicines and serums. I had gotten sick from lack of food. They said that in one or two weeks I would certainly have been dead. My blood level was very low, because with a hemorrhage every day, I was losing a lot. I became as thin as a little stick, *Comadre*. All that money my mother had collected for All Saints' Day, she used to cure me.

"I will get you cured, child," she said. Juan wasn't earning any more; he was just getting seventy pesos as a subsidy. That's why we didn't have money for food. What were we to do? In any case, we had to make do with only the food they had in the commissary.

*Have you noticed any special characteristics among your children, Comadre?*

What does that mean?

*Do they have any special ways of behaving?*

Filemón has always been very lively, ever since he was small. María was a little bit more light-headed. I don't know why. She speaks a lot of Quechua, yes, a lot of Quechua. She didn't understand Spanish. She didn't understand anything, María. The little girl who died after Filemón was born, whose name was also María, she walked nicely. She was beginning to talk. She died of a very common disease, scarlatina, which the earlier Juan Manuel also died of.

Filemón wanted very much to be an engineer, always. When he was four or five years old, he would say, "I'm going to have a permit, Mama. I am going to learn to be an engineer. I am going to have houses built, or else I am going to be an architect." I put him in school when he was six years old. Shall we continue speaking of the children, *Comadre?*

*Yes, and also of their birthday parties.*

Juan didn't like parties very much. That's why in Santa Fe they called him an evangelist. They would say, "Rojas is an evangelist, he doesn't drink." Although he sometimes got drunk he usually didn't like to drink. However, he enjoyed the celebration of Saint Raphael on the twenty-first of December, the New Year's feast. Everyone was dancing and singing at their houses — everyone except us. We didn't go to others' houses; we didn't bother people, drink, or run around.

It is a custom among miners, when someone does us a favor, baptizes or confirms our children, or troubles themselves in any way for us, then they go see them on New Year's. They came with a hot pepper stew at midnight, with an orchestra, some came like that to have a drink or to dance.

One year my *compadre* and my *comadre* came over anyway with their companions. We drank that night and then we were insulted. I think Juan was insulted. Your *compadre* doesn't like to fight with anyone, but the insult was serious. It seemed to me that he was ready to kill. It was a big, ugly insult. That's why Juan was furious. So he continued listening, but finally he couldn't stand it any more.

"Get out! Get out! Get out!" he shouted. But the other fellow wanted to fight and to hit your *compadre*. And so Juan got really angry. He went out and he beat the man who insulted him shamefully. It was Juan's first fight [laughter]. So the poor man who insulted him got beaten badly. He even walked on his knees, begging his pardon, because he didn't like him. That was the only fight he had that time. But the brother of the man he had beaten was the judge in the mining encampment, and his *compadre* was the boss in charge of distributing houses to the workers. So he went to him, complaining and saying, "I want that man out of that place. He beat my brother shamefully. The one who beat him must be the devil. We can put him down there in San Pedrito."

Down below in San Pedrito there are some neglected houses that no one lives in permanently. They are for the people who don't deserve to live in the mining camp. And now they wanted us to go down below to live, like assassins or thieves. They didn't want us to live near that insolent man. So your *compadre* said, "I would rather go someplace else. I am going. I have a house in Cochabamba. I have land. I am not some nobody from no place. I have someplace to go. If they change our house, I would prefer to retire," he said to the mining camp boss. Right away they laid him off and we went to Cochabamba.

*Did he have a promise of work when he returned?*

No, we had no promise. He was a good worker, and well liked in the company, but the bosses had sent him away, saying he had to move out of that house or leave his job. That's what they said. That's why they fired him. We went to live and got married there in Cochabamba. We got to Cochabamba in the train with all our things and went to my uncle's house. After a week my father came to Cochabamba from Morococala.

He said to my uncles, "How long do you think these children will be living together? It's already been three years, almost four. I don't want them to just live together; I want you to marry them."

So my uncle said, "I will marry them immediately and I will save them." My uncle was rich. He had money, lots of cattle, *uuy*, he was a man of possessions was my uncle, my father's brother. He quickly had us married, both in church and at the civil registry.

We bought potatoes, provisions, everything. We started raising chickens with the severance pay they gave him. They gave him forty dollars and that money was worth more then. We wanted to buy a house, or a piece of land, but my father didn't want us to.

"What are you going to buy a house for?" he said. "There is a house here for you with us. You are the only daughter and you have to have this house. Why buy another house? What will you live on? You should marry and save up for a home for the rest of your lives with that money that your husband got as his severance pay."

So we got married, and we thought that with what was left we could start a business or something. We had to do something to support ourselves while we were there.

# 8

# Married Life in the Mining Camp

Most of the workers had nicknames, so I once asked Juan what his was when he worked in the mines. He replied, "I had one in the army but never in the mines, because I behaved more like a grown man. It is because of that that I have been respected since my youth, and nobody gave me any names. One of my old companions wanted to name me *"Awicho,"* which means old man in Quechua, but he didn't get along with the other workers and no one paid attention to him. No one gave me any names because I behaved like a serious man." This was true in his work life as well as in his married life. Marriage in the mining communities involves reciprocal obligations and claims that ensure survival for each of the spouses. When a man gets sick with silicosis, his wife or the other family members responsible for his meals may feel guilty, since poor nutrition is known to be a contributing factor. When a worker dies from an accident on the job, the entire work crew feels guilty, and his family wonders if he went to work in a disturbed frame of mind that caused him to become distracted and lose the self-control necessary for survival in the mines. Suicide — which, when it occurs, frequently takes place in the mines where it is easy to find an instrument of death — is inevitably attributed to the man's domestic relations. The link between home and work is symbolized in the lunches picked up by a company truck and delivered to the interior of the mines. If his lunch does not appear, a man knows he is in trouble at home, and this often leads to trouble at work.

The complementarity of men's and women's work is evident in every aspect of daily life. Juan assisted Petrona in the delivery of their children. It was he who attended to the rituals with the afterbirth meant to ensure a successful life for their children. He dedicated himself to "buying their lives" out of the mine through education, the only avenue he could envision. This dedication extended to his godchild, the son of *campesinos* who spoke only Aymara, whom he was determined to send to the mining school. In the process of acclimating the child to the new environment, Juan learned Aymara so he could communicate with the child until he learned Spanish.

Men are obligated to their family of orientation as well as to their family of procreation. The conflict between Juan's mother and his wife led to Petrona making the break that cut the supplies she received from his commissary account. Her relatives prompted the official religious and civil wedding that went beyond the *makinaku* (exchange of vows) to ensure her prior claims, and, although Juan resisted, his position was weak because of the layoff imposed on him as a result of an altercation in the mining encampment. The close ties among workers in the mines and in the encampment bring both solidarity and divisions. Rivalries involve the extended networks of relatives, *compadres*, and neighbors in numerous and complex bonds of jealousies as well as of communal sharing. Juan's fight with a neighbor on New Year's Eve in 1951 led to a rupture that caused the family to break away to Cochabamba where they lived with Petrona's relatives. Juan finally succumbed to their exhortations to get married and thus established the claims of his wife as prior to those of his mother. Juan insisted that this was his decision.

---

In early December 1947 my mother came from Oruro. I told her, "I want to get married. Now that you have gone, I, too, need some attention."

My mother replied, "Yes, you are right Juanito. You should get married because, as you can see, I can't leave your brother. He can't control himself and is constantly drunk. He could get hurt if I weren't there to watch him, and, even though he doesn't have a job to support your little brothers. I am not going to leave him. He's a good-for-nothing and can't take care of himself the way you can. You will be alright any place because you are as cautious as an old man. Even an old man can stray from the path, but not you. I know you, and you may get married. I'll do whatever you like." She spoke to me like that in Quechua.

It was a Saturday. I got my wages of 1,200 bolivianos and we went out to buy drinks; two kegs of beer, *chicha*, alcohol, and *pisco*. We had a lot to drink when we went in to ask my future mother-in-law for Petrona's hand.

My mother spoke to her mother in Quechua: "Doña Hilaria, I have come with my son. He told me that he met your daughter and he wants to marry her. I want to ask her if the affection she has for my son will last just for a short while, or whether it will last forever."

Doña Hilaria, Petrona's mother, said, "I haven't asked her, Doña Mariá, because I would be embarrassed to ask her how much she cared for him. But now, if you like, I shall ask her. If she wants to marry, she will, because neither I nor anyone else controls her. If anything should happen to her, I don't want to be blamed. It is good that they met — if they hadn't, they might have remained unwed until they grew old."

Her father was a bit annoyed, but after a while he had to accept it. But her younger brother, Filiberto, also got involved. He said to me, "No one is going to take my sister away. She is like a mother in the household. You have to see it. No one has the right to take my sister away."

I said, "Listen, Filiberto, don't raise your voice. Your parents are living. Only if your father were dead could you get angry and raise your voice. These matters are none of your business. If we decide we care for each other, we decide it, and that's it. You have nothing to say about it; you can't tell me that your sister can't love me anymore than I could say it to you if you cared for my sister. It is our business, and our business alone."

He shouted in a rage, "You can do whatever you like, *Mamay*," and left. No one knew where he went; he didn't come back all night.

Later her father refused to give her to me. But we — Petrona and I — had planned everything very well. I said, "What if your father and mother don't accept us, Petrona? What shall we do?"

She said, "It all depends on me. If I want to leave against their wishes, I'll do so, because, as the saying goes, 'No one can stop one who wants to leave or wants to die.'"

Then I said, "But if your father doesn't want you to marry me, as well as your mother and brothers, then you will have to simply leave with me, and come quietly wherever I go. If you don't come with me, you will never see me again. If you were to come to join me one day, later, you would see me, but we would never again have the same love or affection."

She agreed, and everything was decided together. She did not stay with my father-in-law. I said to my wife, "Let's go, Petrona, because it seems to me that he is getting angrier, the longer we stay here. Let them continue discussing it among themselves and we'll just go off to my house. What do you think, Petrona? Let's go." We left and I took my wife to my house. She obeyed me, and since that moment she has wanted me as her husband and she has listened to my every word to this day. May we always continue like this.

We slept at my house. My brother and mother stayed away and slept at Doña Hilaria's house. The next day Filiberto came to take his sister home. His sister paid him no attention.

"Get out of here!" she told him, "Otherwise I'll kick you out." He didn't say a thing. If he had answered they surely would have fought. And then he and I surely would have fought, because I wasn't going to let him lay a hand on Petrona. He left in a rage. We bathed, she combed her hair, and we went up to my mother-in-law's house. By now they were in a good mood. They didn't say anything more than ask why we had left the night before.

We came in and had some beer with [my father-in-law]. He has accepted me since that time and addresses me as his son. He said, "From today on, you have to behave like my children, like real children of the household." And so the *makinaku* [the betrothal] passed. And that was how we became betrothed.

We lived in one of the private houses in the area between Morocacala and Santa Fe called San Pedrito, near a football field. Three days after the betrothal, my wife went down to the camp to get a room for us. The chief of the camp, Don Lucio Hinojosa, knew me well. He was fond of me because I was never a troublemaker. When I was single, I had lived in a house together with a married couple who didn't have any children, and we never argued. The chief of the camp had visited that house to see how we were getting along. He always found my room a bit tidier — those newly married people slept on the floor. They had neither a cot nor a bedstead; I had a wooden bed.

The chief asked me, "Which is your bed?"

I said, "This one." And pointing out to him the one on the floor, I said, "And this one is Coca's."

He looked, shook his head, and went out saying, "Fine."

When I was single, I was happy at San Pedrito. I liked living there because it was more convenient to go dancing. But now we wanted our own house. The Chief gave us a place a bit above the hospital. We lived there for a while and then Petrona asked for a more sheltered house and we came a bit further down the hill.

*What were the houses in the camp like?*

When I got there, in 1946, the houses sat directly on the ground. There was no flooring. The houses were black, blackened by kitchen smoke, with straw roofs. Some had corrugated tin roofs, but they put straw on top of the tin because it was very cold, and also because when it hailed it made too much noise and people couldn't sleep. Then the company's heart began to bleed for the workers and they put tiles over the tin roofs and flooring on the ground. But they also tore down the houses of those who complained. All the houses had electric lights. After 1952, when the National Revolutionary Movement [MNR] triumphed, they changed the houses. Some were enlarged for people who had large families. For example, I lived in a house with four rooms that had been enlarged by the engineer, Aurelio Mendiola.

*Did they heat the houses in those days?*

Oh, no, they did nothing to heat them. We couldn't heat them because, if we did, the company got angry. It was forbidden to use heaters.

*Because of the use of electricity?*

Because of the electricity. They weren't aware that it was the administrators who used the most electricity. They gave electricity to workers only during specified hours. For example, they gave us power from six until seven-thirty in the morning, and at mid-day from eleven-thirty to twelve-thirty; in the evening they turned it on at six and turned it off at eleven-thirty. Imagine! There was no schedule for the administrators. They had electric stoves, heaters here and there in every corner, and no one commented on it. But if one of the workers used a little heater to warm up his house, he was fired. When you least expected it, they would come to inspect the houses. If they found a heater they took it away. Take the light bulbs, for example. They gave us twenty-five watt light bulbs. Of course, it was very dark with these. We would buy forty or fifty watt light bulbs, but if by misfortune we forgot to change them before they came, they would take them away.

After 1952 there wasn't this kind of repression against any class. We used heaters with no problem. Of course there were warnings that it was forbidden to use heaters or light bulbs above a certain wattage, but they didn't send anyone out to search our houses. They said they would, so as to frighten us, but they didn't dare come into the houses. They were afraid, because the worker was free then.

*What other changes have you seen?*

Well, we had always walled our yards with extra rock from the camp to protect ourselves from the wind, and from other people's eyes. The camp chief wanted to take them down, but the people didn't want to lose them. So the housewives made a petition to the administration and they agreed. They let us keep the patio walls around each house.

In February of 1948 I went to work in the morning as I did any other day. Petrona and I had been living together for just a short while, about a week. I was working as a hand driller, and the night before I had set off dynamite just before getting off work. When we went in that morning, we began to work. When he knew that we were all at our stations the foreman, Severino Katari, went to his station without checking anything. I was at my station at the face of the mine. I had a narrow vein, but we couldn't get any metal out of that. We were just moving along, looking for a vein or pockets of ore.

I didn't know then how sick one could get from carbon dioxide. The shaft was filled with ore from previous explosions. I crawled on top of the loader to my station. In those days we didn't have electric lights, but used coal oil lamps. Also, no one had told me that a coal lamp won't burn if there is a lot of carbon dioxide in the air. I went in innocently, never suspecting what would happen. Just as soon as I went in, the lamp went out. As I bent down to raise the wick to relight it I began to feel terrible. I couldn't do anything, not even raise the wick. I heard all kinds of noises in my ears — like the cries of pigs and birds, train whistles, car horns, the sound of iron rubbing against iron, and hissing. I felt dizzy and confused. I couldn't hold up my head because I was getting sick from the gas.

I went out to the passage where there was a little pipe from which water filtered out to a place where the housewives collected it. Lower in the mine was a little tank of water at level twenty-six. I went to wet my head there because I thought it was the heat that was making me feel bad. I didn't know it was the gas.

After I wet my head and neck I went back to my station at the face. I hung my lamp and turned around to pick up my shovel, and I don't remember anything after that. I must have fainted dead away.

When one of my companions from the work gang, Julian Amarillo, came to call me at nine-thirty for the coca break, the foreman still hadn't come by to see me. Julian said my lamp was nothing but a little blue flame, burning in the shaft. He yelled, "Rojas! Rojas!" and when I didn't answer, he came in. When he was halfway in he saw me, on all fours, trying to crawl, half asleep, half dead, on top of the loader. He was frightened and ran out to tell my companions. There were eight or ten people nearby who came running, and they pulled me out to the main tunnel while the others brought up the cart. They pushed me to the office in the cart. Once they got to the office, they called the elevator and took me out. The ambulance was already waiting — they must have ordered it by telephone — and they took me to the hospital immediately.

I woke up at two in the afternoon. I was hungry and thirsty and I had an unbearable headache. They said I had been singing like a drunk, as though I were sick from alcohol. Everyone in the hospital thought that I had had too much to drink.

Dr. Liendo, who took care of me, said, "What, drinking so early? Why?" They hadn't told him anything more than that I must have gotten drunk, but they didn't know from what. Soon they told him that it wasn't from alcohol, but from gas in the mine.

The doctor asked Katari, "Why don't you check out the stations before you send your workers in?" Katari answered that he wasn't used to checking the stations before the workers went in, but rather while they were working.

Someone said, "He only checks the stations during the second hour." Katari got reprimanded because the danger is during the first hours; he was supposed to check things out and he hadn't. Katari explained that he didn't think his workers were so dumb as not to come out when there was gas, and that was why he didn't check out the stations. He worked instead, to set a good example.

I said, "Doctor, my head hurts a lot, and I am very hungry." So the doctor told them to make me a plate of eggs, fried potatoes, and lettuce. They brought it to me within the half-hour and I ate a lot. Before they gave me the food, they gave me a glass of black coffee without sugar.

After I ate they gave me aspirin and that made my headache a bit better, but it continued to bother me.

At five in the afternoon I got so sick in the head that I completely lost consciousness. When I woke up my wife was at my side, crying, and my mother was at the other side, also crying. For a moment I regained my senses and heard the doctor say, "Bring oxygen, oxygen!" So they brought me oxygen. Once, when they put the mask on to help me inhale the oxygen, I again lost consciousness. I don't remember everything, but it was like having something blue over my eyes and being unable to see clearly. Ten minutes passed and again I came to.

I said to the doctor, "Doctor, please give me some medicine to take away this pain from my head; it is making me lose consciousness. I don't remember what happened to me. I don't remember anything except hearing you call for oxygen. Then they put something on my face and I lost consciousness."

The doctor asked the head of the medical department, Dr. Sandi, to have me sent to Oruro, to the hospital in San José. Dr. Sandi said, "The company has no relations with the San José company. We can't send him. We can ask a specialist to come and look at him here, or else we can take him to the general hospital in Oruro. They can look after him there."

My wife insisted that they do this as fast as possible, because my life was in danger, and also cried out, "We have been living together for just a short while. What will my husband's family say to me?"

Just then I became bathed in a sweat as though I had been working and thrown water over myself. Dr. Sandi came in, took my pulse, and listened to my heart with his stethoscope. He told Dr. Liendo, "It's nothing. He's just inhaled too much gas, and it is intoxicating him. It's in his brain. There is no danger."

That's why they didn't take me to San José. There was no cooperation between competing mines as there is now, and, when something serious happened, they took us to the nearest general hospital where they hired a specialist in that particular disease or injury.

I was in the hospital for three days. Once I recovered, I returned to work, and they moved me from Katari's station and put me at Amarillo's vein. When I came in, Julian Amarillo complained. "This is serious," he said. "First we have to empty out the loader with all its debris, because it's hard for us to get in, and the smoke from the explosions can't get out."

In the old days we didn't have anything to protect us from the gas.

The machines weren't automatic the way they are now. The drillers worked blindly. They didn't have any water faucets or hoses to wet the machines; it was all done dry. So we breathed in silicates and got the mine sickness very soon.

The foreman ordered us to empty the loader; I went to Amarillo's station, he to mine. Amarillo didn't want to work there because the gas was dangerous, also, it was a long way in, because that corridor had been drilled many years earlier, following a tiny vein of no importance that they thought would lead to a big pocket or vein. The two of us emptied the loader, and then the foreman sent Amarillo back to his old station, and Hilarion Sabala, a tall man, was sent to work at my station.

Sabala worked there for a month and a half, and in the middle of April the same thing happened to him that had happened to me. There was no explosion; the whole cave was empty. His case was more serious than mine.

In the afternoon he had drilled a lot of holes, because the rock was a bit harder than usual, in which to set the dynamite charges. He began to feel dizzy and fainted. Again, Katari didn't go check the stations. (In the old days it was the custom to have men work without checking on their safety, although it was the foreman's obligation to check the stations before they started to work, and to come by to see if they were working properly.)

On that occasion, Katari was punished with a three-day suspension of his commissary privileges. On the first day he did not feel it too much since he had some food in the house, but by the third day he felt it a lot because he didn't have bread for his children. He had a lot to think about with this punishment that he had brought upon himself by ignoring safety measures — it wasn't his workers who were lazy or foolish.

We got Sabala out barely alive, like me, and we took him to the hospital. He came to at six in the afternoon. He was unconscious from ten in the morning to six in the evening. His wife came at noon. They didn't tell her right away because she was pregnant — they were afraid how she would react. Finally someone told her that her husband had had an accident and was in the hospital.

She began screaming, "My husband is suffering. You have to cure him right now, you shameless ones! He can die like this!"

The doctor said, "Nothing will happen, señora. Be calm. I am here to take care of him." They put the woman in the delivery room and she stayed there talking to some other women. The doctor had told these women to talk with her to calm her down.

But at three in the afternoon, she came out again and began to scream at the doctors. They couldn't do anything. At six o'clock Sabala still could barely talk. After saying a few words he fell back again. His eyeballs turned up into his head as if he were dying. We were frightened, thinking he had died, but the doctor checked him and said he wasn't dead, just unconscious. This happened three or four times. At eight in the evening they took him in the ambulance to Oruro.

In Oruro, he fell unconscious again, although they were giving him pills every half hour. Three of us, myself, Amarillo, and Katari, the foreman, went to a doctor's office on the corner of Bolivar and Potosí Streets. We got there at night and banged on the door and rang the bell, but no one heard us. We pressed on the buzzer and continued ringing until the maid came out. Finally she went off to call the doctor. The doctor came immediately because it was serious, and also because he was going to earn plenty of money from the company. He grabbed his stethoscope and examined the patient. Sabala was unconscious.

"This is something serious," the doctor said, "I cannot be responsible for treating him. I don't want you to tell me that I didn't treat him properly, or that I poisoned him with medicine." We were frightened — especially the foreman who was responsible for the life of this worker.

I went with Katari in the ambulance to the general hospital with the doctor, who had said, "I don't have a clinic here; it's just my office. We had better take him to the general hospital and I will take care of him there."

There one of the hospital doctors said, "It looks like this man needs an operation, because the gas is eating his liver and we can't get the gas out." They tried everything, but they couldn't do a thing.

We were still at his side, sleepless, at three in the morning. At that time, the doctor had a conference with other doctors to decide whether to operate on him; they decided it was too dangerous. They didn't think Sabala was going to live. They went in to see him, and Sabala was quiet. He was much better, but the sweating wouldn't stop. He was sweating a lot.

The doctor asked Sabala, "How do you feel?"

Sabala said, "I'm fine, Doctor. I want to go home."

The doctor said, "You can't go yet. We have to care for you here.

You will get well. Then we'll tell you when you can go home, but for now you are in the general hospital at Oruro."

Sabala looked around the room. In fact, he realized that he was in a different hospital because the rooms at Santa Fe's hospital were tiny, and these were large. He was aware of that immediately.

One of the hospital doctors said to the doctor who had attended Sabala, "Doctor, you can go and rest easy, because your patient has reacted one hundred percent. He is perfectly fine."

*Did he recover because of the medicine they gave him?*

We don't know what injections these doctors gave him. But when he left the hospital, his wife took all the drugs with her. She took them because she was afraid something else would happen to her husband, and so she took all the bottles of drugs and injections. They gave him these injections in the arm and in the buttocks. And before the doctor left, at three-thirty in the morning, they put another injection in his vein. He told us it was vitamin C, calcium glutenate, and other ingredients that I don't remember.

When he woke at six in the morning, we could see the lad was fine. "We had better go back to work because they will mark us down as absent," said Katari.

"But the company sent us here on a job. We have to stay here because they sent us here themselves," I answered. Katari listened to me and stayed. We remained at the hospital until ten in the morning. Sabala was fine; he just felt something hot and very painful in his chest and couldn't breathe properly. He asked for water, but they wouldn't let him have any. They gave him just his medicine in a little cup. It was very cold, and he was to have it in spoonfuls every time he asked for water. He was very restless and wanted a lot of water. We left him at ten in the morning and rode in the ambulance back to Santa Fe.

The next day we heard he had recovered. His wife came to Santa Fe at four in the afternoon to ask the union to have him transferred immediately to Santa Fe Hospital, so that she could be at his side. We ourselves presented the union's petition to the administrator, an Englishman named Gossen Bursman, who accepted it gladly. It was more convenient for him, because he was spending a lot of money on this sick man in Oruro, while Santa Fe had its own doctor. He sent the ambulance immediately, with just the driver and Sabala's wife, and they brought the sick man back.

Near Pairumani Sabala fainted again – perhaps because of the altitude — and his eyes rolled back. The driver didn't know what to do, whether to go ahead or back.

Finally the wife insisted, "Go ahead before he dies!" The driver got him to Santa Fe in a very agitated state. He had started to sweat again and was terribly restless all the time.

His wife then changed her mind. "He was doing well in Oruro," she said. "Let's take him back again." But the administrator paid her no attention.

"You yourself asked me to bring him here. If the doctors here aren't good enough for you, take care of him yourself." That English administrator really got angry.

The union couldn't say anything because it had made the petition for his wife. The union agent told Sabala's wife, "It must be the altitude that is making this happen. But, Doña Severina, don't be so alarmed. Go home, because the more you see of your husband, the more upset you will become."

The next day Sabala was the same. In the morning he reacted in exactly the same way. But finally he got well. He returned to work on the same face he had left. We hadn't worked it while he was away because it was too remote and you couldn't breathe. That station did us no good. We didn't even get a kilo of mineral out of it. We worked in vain. Maybe there was something to be found there, but we abandoned it because it was too dangerous.

In time that whole sector fell down, caved in from the outside. The whole camp almost caved in with it. As a result, they abandoned a corner of the camp in which I lived.

Sabala came to work with me. The tunnel was small, but the two of us worked to make it larger, in spite of the fact that it had no metal. In time the tunnel got better and better as it got bigger. By and by four people could work in it. Finally the ore in other parts of the mine was exhausted, and we all got together in this single tunnel. There was a chimney at the mouth of this corridor which led to the outside. We heard crying sounds coming from inside and the people got frightened. There had been accidents in there because of the gas, and some thought the sounds were being made by the ghost of one of those who died.

But one of the men who heard it said, "It sounds like a pig screaming." They looked outside, and they found that someone had lost his pig.

My wife was already pregnant with my first daughter, Sabina, in

1948. She gave birth to my daughter on the twenty-fifth of October in 1948, at my house.

*Didn't they give birth in the hospital in those days?*
No, at my house.

*Was your wife afraid of going to the hospital?*
No, it was I who didn't trust the hospital, because in those days, many women died in childbirth. I was afraid of putting her there. There was a midwife, a private practitioner named Doña Vicenta, who took care of her. She lived in Morococala. I ran to her house in Santa Fe and back in seven minutes [laughter]. She had told me, "You can come at any time." She was already paid; all she had to do was to come.

When I got there, I shouted, "Come right now. My wife is in labor and she needs you." I woke her up like that. "Come right away. I have got a lot of stops to make, but I'll be back by the time you get there." I stopped by the camp at Morococala to let my mother-in-law know, and she got dressed immediately.

While she was dressing, I rushed on down. "You stop by Doña Vicenta's and bring her. I'm going to go on ahead because no one is at home. My wife is all alone." I ran on down, and I was gone and back in seven minutes.

A woman who was like an aunt to us was there when I got home. She had seen me leave the house because she lived just below us, but she didn't know where I was going in such a hurry. So when my wife called, this woman came immediately, arriving there before I did.

My "aunt" said, "But you just left. How did you get to Morococala and back? It's far away and it takes time to get there." She couldn't believe I was back so soon. She thought I had just gone to the hospital and no farther, but in fact I had gone to my mother-in-law's house at Morococala. Forty-five minutes later my mother-in-law and the midwife arrived. My wife was already getting strong pains. At five in the morning she gave birth to my first daughter. She bore the pain that long.

*Did you see the baby when she came?*
Yes, she was born in front of me.

*How was the child delivered, while the mother was lying down or on her knees?*
Kneeling.

*How did you help?*
I sat in front of her, and she grabbed my knees here. The midwife was behind her to receive the little girl.

*Did she have any medication during the birth?*
Yes, a tea made of orange blossoms.

*And did you have something special to prevent hemorrhaging?*
Nothing. I went to the hospital to get some medicines so that my wife could recuperate faster, but they didn't give me anything. They wanted to make me take her to the hospital at Camilla where they would give me everything. I didn't accept their offer out of fear, because so many women died. Three women had died just before that, having babies.

*When the baby was born, what did you do with the placenta?*
As with all of my children, I didn't trust anyone to do it. As soon as the child was out and the placenta expelled, I picked it up immediately. I took charge of everything. I washed it carefully with soap and water and disinfected it until there was no blood left, and I burned it on a coal fire.

*What did you burn with it?*
I put a small pencil with it, then a piece of white paper, and then those old five cent pieces.

*What is the significance of these things?*
Well, the pencil and paper are to make the child studious, and the money is so that the child shouldn't lack for money when it is grown. After it burned, we buried the placenta's ashes at least a meter deep.

*In the house?*
Outside in the yard, wherever. We can't do it in the house because the floor is made of tiles.

*Who told you it was necessary to follow this custom with the placenta?*
My mother-in-law told me that when you don't wash the placenta well, then the children turn out to be dirty. They won't even wash their clothes. They don't take care of themselves and when they are small they urinate all the time and defecate in bed, or wherever, without shame. If you put liquor on the placenta the children will be drunks all their lives. This is incurable, and that's why we take care of the placenta rapidly before anything can happen. Once it's washed, nothing can happen.

*Do you have to burn it in a clay pot?*
No, in a pan.

*Made of metal?*
Made of tin or iron, made of anything as long as it doesn't melt. When the fire is burning strong, you put in the placenta wrapped in paper. You add a pencil, a piece of white paper, five of the old pennies, and you put all of this with the placenta on the fire. You have to keep it cooking for a long time. It can't just cook quickly. You have to keep on adding water to it, until all the coals are dead. They finish quickly; often the coal will finish before the placenta is burned. Then we have to add more coal and try to make everything burn to ashes.

*What is the meaning of the umbilical cord?*
I don't know whether this is true or not, but there are those who say that if you cut it with a knife, the child will go through his clothes very quickly when he is grown. Nothing will last for him. And if you cut it with something made out of clay, a broken shard of *k'analla*, as we call it, they won't go through so many clothes when they are grown up. These children will be very thrifty.

*Who cuts the cord?*
The midwife cuts it.

*After that do you or the child address the midwife with a kinship term?*
No, nothing. When the mother has just had a child, the midwife has to care more for the mother than for the little creature, because when mothers just out of childbirth are in a draft, they can get sick. Often they will swell for no reason, or else get a toothache. All the teeth hurt and become weak, and it doesn't matter if it is a well-fed woman; they become weak and drawn and they get convulsions.

It's hard to recover from this. There are very few people who recover from convulsions. We have to wrap them around the waist with a very tight band. To this day, I don't know why we do that, but it has always been our custom to tie this band on. But I've never asked anyone why. My wife explained to me that we do this so that the woman's soul won't leap away from her. If it jumps away, the woman will die immediately, and they say that when the waist is tied up tight, it can't move. This is more or less what my wife gave me to understand, but I've never asked anyone else.

*Do they get a steam bath?*

None of that. That's rather dangerous. For their thirst, we give them oregano tea which eases the pain in the stomach. It doesn't affect the woman at all, it just relieves their stomach pains. After a woman has given birth, we have to cover her up well, in bed. Not even her hands should be uncovered. She should wear gloves. Nor should the head be left uncovered, but rather wrapped up in a cloth, because, they say, if a woman's head is in the open, air will get in through her pores. If that happens the woman becomes absentminded. They don't remember anything. But if the head is tightly wrapped, then they don't lose their memories. That's the way I have always taken care of my wife.

When my little boy, Juan Manuel, was born, I was working day and night to earn some money because there was very little ore at my station. I couldn't earn any money. The workers would say to me, "You aren't as lucky as you used to be. Now we can't make any money."

To avoid problems, I would work night and day with those workers so they would cooperate with me. It's because of that that I became careless with my wife, and I didn't arrive in time to attend her properly. She got shamefully sick. She was sick for two years. I sent her to Oruro, and she finally got better. The cold in Santa Fe was very bad for her. While she was in Oruro she was in no pain, nothing. And when she had this last baby, she didn't get sick at all, and recovered very easily.

*Because of your help?*

Of course it was because of my help.

We baptized the first daughter in Oruro with a lady, Simona, and my *compadre* was Salvatierra, the sectional chief at Morocacala. They took the baby and the godmother to Oruro in a jeep. They left at eight in the morning and they got there at nine in the evening. They just took the godmother, and they gave a bottle to the baby. We didn't go, because my wife was in bed recovering from the delivery.

*Why did you baptize her so quickly?*

Because we were afraid she would die quickly. That's why we baptized her within three days.

*Was she very weak when she was born?*

Yes, she was a weak baby and that's why we had her baptized so quickly. I had all of my children baptized very young. Filemón, for example, was also baptized in Oruro before he was three days old. I just went with the little boy and my mother-in-law to baptize him. My older brother, Félix, was the godfather. Afterwards María came and she was baptized within a week, in six days. Aníbal was baptized within two weeks because my wife got very sick, and neither I nor my mother-in-law could go. Elena was baptized in three months.

*When they are newborn, do you have to cover the children to avoid some person's evil eye?*

We hide them from everyone, even relatives. We don't show them to anyone, because we believe that when a woman is pregnant and sees a small creature — a baby less than a month old — it's nose will get stopped up. In Quechua that's called *naskakã*. To avoid this, we don't let them see our babies. Men can see them, but not women. You can't let women see them.

*Women of what age?*

Women more than ten years old. When little babies see a woman who might be menstruating, or be pregnant, this stops up their nose. The baby can't suck. In Juan Manuel's case, he was born by the hands of a woman who was pregnant, the midwife of San José. And he couldn't suck at his mother's breast. He wanted to nurse, but his nose was stopped up and he couldn't breathe. That's why we don't let women see our babies when they are less than a month old.

In April of 1949, Holy Week came. We went out to the fields with my wife to kill lizards and all the animals we hate, especially snakes. We didn't find any vipers, but we killed lots of lizards.

*What does that mean?*

This has a very special meaning. It has to do with Holy Friday. When the Jews were persecuting our Lord Jesus Christ, God said, just as he had to Adam and Eve, "I will make you fight among yourselves." And so that's why our people do this. It means that the Jews persecuted our Lord Jesus Christ to kill him, and we search for an enemy, to kill all reptiles which drag themselves on the earth. We always grab them and kill them, any time, not just on Holy Fridays. That's what it means.

When we got to the top of the mountain, a turbulent and freezing wind came up, and we held on to the rock. When we were on the rock, sheltering ourselves from the wind, a lizard jumped on my wife's skirt. She wasn't aware of it. If she had been, she would have been frightened, and could have gotten sick. Who knows? I saw it and I stepped on it with my foot and utterly destroyed it, then I showed it to her. "Look at that lizard. I killed it," I said to her. She was a bit frightened. We didn't stay out long, and soon went home.

At home, her older brother, Filiberto, was waiting for us. He had gone in another direction with his family, but they wanted to come with us. Filiberto asked me, "How was your outing?"

"Fine, how did yours go?" I said.

"My little boy got frightened of a lizard. Now I don't know what's the matter with him."

The little boy, the most mischievous of my nephews, had been trying to shoot a lizard with an arrow and the lizard ran straight at him. He was sick for two months and then died. Neither *yatiris* nor doctors were able to cure him. When he died that *japeq'a* was still with him. He had almost become a little stick. There was no more meat on his body. He was just skin and bones. From that time on, my wife wouldn't hear of lizards or go out on Holy Fridays to look for lizards.

Once my wife went out to collect llama dung with Filemón and María. She used it for fuel in her cooking stove. Filemón was very naughty. He was always pushing over rocks. Underneath one of these he found a lizard and of course, he got frightened, too. *Caramba!* You couldn't do a thing with that child. But Filemón did not get sick, because he wasn't frightened as badly as my nephew.

When Filemón was born on the twenty-fifth of November, in 1949, he was a very sickly child until a year later. There wasn't a single day in which he was quiet and cheerful. He was always crying. After he was a year old, he began to get better. During this time his body didn't waste away; he was always a plump and robust little boy.

Then when he was a year and a half, Filemón almost died. I was earning well as a hand driller although there were plenty of drilling machines. I was earning between two hundred and four hundred pesos a month. On some months I even got up to six hundred pesos. There was a *k'amili*, one who understands about coca and oracles, whom everyone praised. A neighbor said to me, "This man can cure your son. He understands about babies, especially."

I spoke to him. "Can you cure my son? He is always sick and I want to see him well."

He said to me, "I am going to sell the medicines in my bags throughout the camp. I am even going up to Morococala. I will carry your son in one of these bags with medicine as I go on my rounds. If your son is timid, he will cry a lot, but it doesn't matter what his illness is. I have a medicine for it in my bags. You have to pay me whatever I ask you."

"I will pay you what you like, but I want my son to live. You have to cure him," I said to the *k'amili*.

"I am ready," he said. "I'll deliver your son to you healthy. I want you to pay me five hundred pesos." I had plenty of money available in those days because I was earning well. (The only thing is I wasn't smart enough to build a house in Oruro. But there wasn't anyone there to advise me, to make me think, and to tell me, "That parcel, that lot costs thus and such and no more, you can buy it.") So I gave half of his fee to the *k'amili*. I didn't give it all to him. I kept the rest until I could see that my son was healthy. He took Filemón in his bag to San Pedrito in Morocacala, and he went down to Santa Fe to sell more medicine.

At two in the afternoon he returned. We were waiting to have lunch with the *k'amili* and the little boy. He said, "Your little boy cried a lot, and I even had to spank him to make him quiet. And he defecated in my bag. If he hadn't defecated he would have died, but now, naturally, since he defecated, he is going to live." This pleased us a great deal. I was especially pleased and I sent my wife to Doña Severina to buy three bottles of beer so we could invite this *k'amili* for a drink. He drank two bottles, and we drank one bottle. He got a bit drunk and told me he wanted to drink more beer. So I had three more bottles of beer brought in and gave them to him, because I didn't want to get drunk. He got sick and spent the night at my house. Still, the boy was fine. There had been nights when he had cried so much that I couldn't sleep; that night he didn't cry!

The *k'amili* said, "Keep fifty pesos now and just give me two hundred; in five or six months I will come back and then you can give me the rest." And so the *k'amili* left.

Filemón was much calmer. A month passed and he was well. In a year and eight months he was still well. Four months later the *k'amili* came to my house. We didn't live in the same place, but people told him where we lived. I wanted to become a *compadre* with this *k'amili*, so that he could treat my son every time he came. But God surely didn't want that, and we didn't become *compadres*. I continued to have my brother as *compadre*. So then the *k'amili* told me I had to increase his pay. Filemón was perfectly healthy. He didn't cry much, and he wasn't as stubborn as he had been, always throwing himself on the floor in a tantrum for the slightest thing. So I gave the *k'amili* the last fifty pesos. On top of that, I gave him five pesos for his travel money and twenty-five extra. I had to pay five hundred thirty pesos in all to get Filemón well, but he has been healthy to this day. There must have been some magic in putting him in his medicine bag. Everyone tells me that it must have been magic!

I always wanted to show my relatives who have children how to raise a child properly. Now my wishes are coming true. I just have to wait until Filemón, my example, finishes the university. It's the only thing I am waiting for. But *my* life is in danger, since I am sick with the professional disease of the mine. When I least expect it, I can die and my son will be alone. But if God won't begrudge me five or six more years of life, I will see my son have what I have wanted since before the Revolution.

At that time I had a godson who lived in the countryside. He was the son of an Indian. His parents didn't teach their children Quechua; they only spoke in Aymara. Ever since he was a child, they brought him to my house and I gave them bread, always to the child first. The child was happy and grabbed the bread and bit it without breaking it. His parents didn't even teach him that. I told the father that he should speak Quechua to the children so that they would understand it and speak it well. Their father never paid attention and always spoke to them in Aymara. Every time he came, we had problems because the little boy didn't understand what I said, and I couldn't understand the boy, either.

I said to my *compadre*, "When he is six years old, bring him here. I will raise this godson of mine because out there in the country there is no school. Who knows when there will be a school?"

The years passed, and my godson became six years old. Then I told my *compadre*, "Bring your son and a load of potatoes, a live sheep and some dried sheep meat." He did and he left the boy at my house.

The boy cried a lot. He really suffered. At that time I wasn't in the kind of economic crisis in which I now find myself. So I bought candy for the boy, because with candies he would be quiet. If he had no candies, he would cry. He couldn't understand us, and I couldn't understand what he said to us. By and by I came to understand the Aymara of my little godson. I learned it out of necessity because I felt very sorry for the boy. There were times when his father wouldn't come to visit my house for months. By this time the boy more or less spoke Quechua, which I taught him, but there was no way I could teach him Spanish.

The boy was already in school. The teacher told me, "The boy is suffering a lot. He should return to his village right away." But I answered him, "There is no school in the countryside. That's why we had to bring him here, because he is my godson." They discovered that I had him registered in school and they wanted to take him out because no relative of his was working for the company. However, since he was my godson, I complained in some of the administrative offices, and meanwhile, he continued passing from grade to grade. Finally, since the administration continued to threaten to take him out of school, I went to the manager's office, and the manager agreed to my request. He told me that I was a serious man about the education of children. And so the boy stayed in school. He stayed there for three years and he learned to speak Spanish. He also taught me a bit of Aymara. After those three years he went back to live in the countryside because they built a school nearby his home.

For a while I worked with the carpenters, setting up supports in the shafts. After the Feast of the Assumption, on the fifteenth of August, there was a very heavy snow. It snowed without stopping for two weeks, night and day. After that, the wind didn't stop for a week. Snow was accumulating in the pits and valleys of the encampment and everything looked flat. If you looked at the camp, it looked like a cemetery. There was only one path and one street open to walk on.

There was a worker named Torrico who was a widower. He had two girls and a boy. When he opened the door of his house one morning, he saw another white door. He thought somebody had closed him in with something. He put his hand out over the roof, but there was no air, just snow. It continued snowing. He had three large troughs and with these he carefully moved the snow from on top of the house so he could get out. There was about three meters of snow! His house was completely covered. He forced himself up, opening up a wide chimney to get up on the roof.

A week passed. All the llama dung which Petrona had accumulated was used up, and the Indians didn't bring more because the roads were impassable because of the snow. The miners took leaves during those days without permission. It snowed for two weeks. We weren't sure whether it was really snowing, or whether it was just the wind blowing it around.

After a few days, someone from the camp went out to see if he could find some llama dung to start a fire. Apparently when he went out, he sat on a rock and was so cold that he couldn't look for the dung. There was a drainage canal leading away from the mine that he must have forgotten about, because everything was covered up and you couldn't see anything. He fell in the canal at the deepest place. The snow was soft and he couldn't get a foothold to get out quickly. When he fell, his body stopped up the canal and made it wider.

I went to see what was going on when I heard the commotion. No one knew that he had fallen in there. They say his dog came out of there and went home. His wife screamed for him, "Inocencio!" but couldn't find him. His neighbor went out and saw him in the canal. He was already dead because of the cold. The snow had frozen him. He was stiff when we took that poor man out. I tied a rope around his belt and climbed out; then we pulled the body out.

I never saw so much snow. It snowed from the Feast of Assumption until the fourteenth of September. The snow was very high. There was sun, but it couldn't melt the snow because it had frozen. It had become very hard. People were afraid to walk. There were some women who had to take off their shoes in order to get to the commissary, because they slipped too much with their shoes on. They half walked and half skated. For the most part, it was just the children who went to the commissary. Just a few women who were stronger managed to get there, because the ground was covered with ice.

It was difficult to get to work. For example, I usually left at seven or seven-fifteen and we generally went into the mine at seven-thirty. Usually it took just two to three minutes to get there to punch our time cards. With the snow, I had to go very carefully. I'd leave at a quarter to seven and get there a half an hour later making my own path as I went. Finally we carved a little path out of the ice with our work shovels, but if the wind rose, it covered it up immediately with snow. As we went up the path, we jabbed the ice with our shovels and tried to hold on to the sides of the path if we slipped. It really snowed a lot that winter.

On the thirty-first of December of 1951 I wasn't planning to do anything for New Year's Eve. I had a goddaughter whose father was Rosendo Ticona; his wife was named Rosalia. That night they came to my house to make a stew because it was the custom in Santa Fe to prepare a stew for godparents on New Year's Eve. At twelve midnight, they came with a band.

Our neighbors who lived in front of my house had been drinking and getting drunk ever since the early part of the evening. His nickname was *"K'akchalo"* and his wife's was *"Tiripikina."* He was known as *K'akchalo* because when he was a boy he used to say, "K'akchalo, K'akchalo," which means a student who doesn't study. His wife was called *Tiripikina* because she had very small eyes. When he was good and drunk, about nine o'clock, he came over to insult me. I was still sober because I had had hardly anything to drink.

He said, "Come on out of there, coward, and let's fight it out, you and I." I was small compared to him. His body was tall and strong and robust. I was afraid to fight with him, afraid that he would beat me. That's why I didn't go out. Maybe I would have gone out, but my wife wouldn't let me.

At six in the morning, after he had insulted me all night, I went over to insult him. By then I was drunk too, because we had been eating and drinking with my *compadres* all night. I don't remember how we fought, but we fought a lot. We hit each other shamefully. He gave me a punch in the jaw which hurt me all the next day, and I closed both his eyes. It was a shame the way he was covered with blood, his clothes soaked with it.

The next day an officer came with a soldier to my house. I was sleeping and they found my wife. She told them I had been drunk and I was sleeping. The soldier told my wife that I should present myself to the magistrate in Morococala. The officer told the soldier to follow orders and bring me out immediately, but the soldier refused, saying, "We don't have the right to take anyone out of his house, especially when he is drunk." So he didn't take me, but just left after telling my wife that I should be at Morococala at a given time.

I went to Morococala at five in the afternoon and the officer ordered the soldier to arrest me immediately. I didn't resist the arrest. My *compadres*, whom my wife had brought, arrived, and the magistrate asked them, "Which one was to blame?" They testified against *K'akchalo*, because he had been the one to start it. But since the officer was a relative of his, his younger brother in fact, he didn't pay any attention to the witnesses. They wanted to punish me, to beat me with a whip that night.

*The officer himself?*
The officer himself, or the magistrate.

*Were they hired by the company?*
No, they were put in there by the municipality.

At ten at night, I saw Benancio Arián, the officer, carrying an enormous whip. I grabbed an iron chain from the work table they had in the prison.

"Now you are going to respect a prisoner's rights, or it's going to cost you something. I am serving my term, but I am no criminal for you to come and punish me here," I warned him. They didn't touch me. They went out. Taking all of the chains that were there, I locked the door. They wanted to beat me, even though it was unjust.

The next day they still wouldn't let me go. "Open the door, we are coming in," they said.

"You have a little window through which to talk to me. How long will I be locked up? If you don't let me go, I'll beat the door down and fight my way out," I said to the officer.

So the magistrate said, "How dare you speak to the authorities like that?"

"Because I am outraged. Although he is an officer, he has overstepped his rights in punishing me. What have I done that he should come and threaten me this way?" I answered the magistrate.

"You are going to be rude to me too, huh?" he said, "Open the door!"

"I won't. When you come to let me go, I'll open the door." And I stayed there.

Meanwhile, my wife arrived. I told her what had happened. I told her to get a friend of mine who worked for the mining company of Santa Fe and had influence in Morococala administration. He came immediately and went to call the officer and the magistrate to the door of my cell to hear our stories. The same day he went down to talk to the manager. "This is the kind of abuse which your authorities are committing," he said.

The manager ordered them to let me go because all the evidence had been in my favor. "It wasn't his fault," he said, and he ordered the officer to let me go.

But the officer said to the manager, "We have to punish him because he beat up my brother and I want his face to be just as marked as my brother's." He wouldn't let me go. At ten at night my wife left with my brother-in-law, to get some sleep.

After they left the officer came in. "How about it, are you going to open the door for me or not?" he asked me.

"I won't open it," I said. "If I am to be free, tell me, and I'll open it and leave. Otherwise, I won't open it." By midnight, no one had come. I went home. No one saw me leave.

The next day they sent two soldiers, but I paid no attention. "You'll only get me out of here dead — and the only place I am going is to work." I went in to work. At noon the officer and two soldiers were standing by my house. The officer came in to my house to try and take me out because the soldiers wouldn't do it. I ran to the officer and grabbed him.

"You have nothing to do with me," I said, "I have no quarrel with you!" I wanted to beat him up, too, but he ran outside. They went to the chief of the camp. He, too, was a relative of Benancio Arián, the officer, and of my enemy. The neighbors again went and gave evidence in my favor, but he didn't listen. He was going to send me back to San Pedrito.

I went in to speak to the administrator who was a Dutchman. This foreign administrator said to me, "Rojas, you are a good worker, I know you. Why are you always fighting? They told me you were to blame." We went to the manager's office with the witnesses. I took them to the administrator and made them testify. The foreigner understood then that the declarations were false and that they were wrongly accusing me of being a fighter, a troublemaker.

Despite all that, the chief of the camp wanted to revoke my work card so I couldn't go to work. I said to him, "Well, Señor, you can fire me, and I will leave this house. If you don't fire me, I am going to continue working, and I will go to work from this house. But I have no intention of abandoning this house if I continue working here."

The next day the chief of the camp came to my house at nine in the morning. He continued bothering me in my work and holding back my card. They wouldn't let me work. He came with two watchmen and they wanted to throw my things out.

I made a tight fist and I raised it, "What do you want?" With fisticuffs I threw them out. I hit one of the watchmen when he didn't want to move out of my house. "Out!" I said, and he left after the first blow.

The chief of the camp went to management, saying that I had been disrespectful to him when they came to tell me to change houses. But that wasn't the way it was. They had come to throw my things out on the street, to have them dumped in San Pedrito and send me over there. I wouldn't permit that.

The administrator called me in and asked me, "Now, why were you disrespectful when the chief of the camp came to tell you to move to San Pedrito?"

"But what have I done to be punished this way? You know very well that I am a driller and that I come out of the mine exhausted and sweaty, and that if I were to have to walk home to a house as far as San Pedrito, I would surely get ill. The cold would make me sick, and I could even get pneumonia. Who's responsible for that?"

The administrator said to me, "Oh, Rojas, I am sorry for you, but the order to move is coming from the chiefs of the camp. That's not my responsibility. Why don't you just go, and then come back here after a little while. I'll let you come right back. Take a trip, take a little vacation in your village and I promise to let you back in when you return."

I said to him, "Señor Brusman, are you going to let people who rank below you tell you what to do?"

"I have to follow the orders which the camp chiefs give me as well as those from the mining bosses," he answered me. "As I say, Rojas, you can go with my guarantee that I'll take you back. I'll give you some money, and you go take a trip to your village. Go on a vacation, and come back in two months."

The superintendent of the mine, Engineer Cesar Zuña Morales, was my friend, but he couldn't do anything in my favor because he was also the *compadre* of the chief of the camp. He said to me, "Try to forget any rancor, Rojito, even though these things happen — try not to have any bad feelings," he advised me.

I went to Cochabamba in January. There was no alternative but to resign myself to everything, including my mother's situation. I decided to marry my Petrona.

*You still weren't married?*

No, not yet, not a civil marriage or one in church. Her parents kept urging us to marry, and I said to them, "Not yet. We don't fight and I have no intention of ever leaving her. I have every intention of marrying her and living with her until I die. But I will not marry while my mother is alive. When my mother dies I'll marry her immediately."

My wife had been a bit mean to my mother. She didn't want to send her supplies from the commissary. So I would go to Oruro and take her two or three kilos of sugar, the same of rice, twenty or so loaves of bread, like that. I didn't like to argue with my wife, so I took these supplies secretly to my mother. And my mother accepted it because she didn't have a worker to support her. Other times, my mother would be complaining, having to work in order to get these supplies. Once we had a lot of supplies collected between the two of us, Petrona and I — we didn't eat that much — and I said to my wife, "Prepare some ten kilos of rice and ten kilos of sugar. I am going to take it to my mother. I'm not going to go and give it to just anybody, but to my mother, who raised me so that I could live with you." I scolded her when she complained.

"Take it all, then," she said.

"I don't want to take it all. I just want to take what I want to take."
She packed fifty pounds of sugar and another fifty pounds of rice and I
took it to my mother in Oruro.

This was the reason my father-in-law took me to a judge in order to
force me to get married. I said to my father-in-law, "So you want to
forbid me from taking a few things to my mother. And if I get married,
you will tell me, 'You don't have the right to even go near your mother,'
and it's for that reason precisely that I won't get married, and no one
can force me to."

We spoke to a judge in Santa Fe about our living together when I
had my troubles with the encampment chief, and the judge said to me,
"The laws don't permit it. They can punish you at any time that you
cause trouble at home."

"I am an honest man, a person who wants to build a home and live
permanently with an honest family."

The judge said, "If you have thought it out, fine. I'll accept your
word. But the laws do oblige you to get married."

"They may require it, but as I have just said, I am the master of my
own will, and no one can make me do what I don't want to, and my
position is firm and unshakable. No one can change my mind," I said
angrily.

We didn't worry about getting married after that, since we already
had a son, and my wife didn't want to leave me. She has always been at
my side.

So, after the trouble at the camp, I went to Oruro to see my mother.
She told me that the plot of land we had at Mallku Rancho wasn't sold,
and we went to live in that little house. After a week, my father-in-law's
brother took us to his house and we lived with them for some three
months.

I decided to marry in the month of April. We got married on the
sixteenth of April in 1952, in both religious and civil ceremonies. We
had a big wedding. My godmother paid for the wedding Mass as well
as for the chain of *aras*. *Aras* are ancient silver coins which the priest
places in the man's hands, and the man places them in the woman's
hands. My godmother hired an orchestra in Cochabamba.

*Was your godmother a friend of your mother's?*

She was my father-in-law's sister-in-law, and my godfather was my
father-in-law's brother, his older brother.

Everything was set up to cook: chickens, rabbits, everything, plus a pitcher of *chicha*. We made three extra pitchers of *chicha*. This was enough for the wedding, and there was even a pitcher left over. My wife sold that one.

On the wedding day, we left at nine in the morning. My foot hurt because I had cut it while cutting branches of eucalyptus. I had almost cut the nerve, and I was still limping. We arrived at Sipe Sipe in Mallku Rancho on horseback. The road was muddy because of the rains. When we got there we went to my wife's relatives' house where they dressed us in our wedding clothes. The wedding was at ten in the morning, and the Mass started in the church.

The priest spoke to us about how to live as married people. We understood. I especially understood and am still living according to what he told us. First the priest laid out the coins. Then he put the chain on himself. Finally he gave us the *aras*, lifting them out of a bowl with his two hands and putting them in mine, and I, without dropping them, put them in my wife's hands. The priest said, "This chain and the rings that I am putting on your fingers are signs that you will live in harmony. The rings mean a commitment to this marriage and to the creation of a solid home for all of your lives. The chain should unite you as though it were made of iron and should never break. You must never separate or even think of having a bad home, but rather concentrate on building a good, positive home for all of your lives." He lifted the coins from the tray, saying, "This money is the man's daily wage. I represent God and God is giving his blessing, especially to you, man, so that you will give all your earnings over to your wife's hands, and so that you, woman, will use this money to support your family and to maintain your home." That's the way we got married.

When the Mass was over we went again to my father-in-law's relatives' house where we talked and had several drinks of *chicha* and beer. They brought fifty-eight horses for everyone to ride through the countryside. We came to Mallku Rancho in a procession, and they were playing music on harmonicas and trumpets. In those days, they didn't have accordions, as they do now. The musicians arrived before us and were waiting for us to go into my godfather's house. We entered and sat at a special table with our godparents on either side. One by one our guests came up to embrace us and congratulate us, and for wedding presents they gave us money. That was the custom in those days. In two days we got more than one hundred dollars. Everyone gave the same thing; it wasn't the custom to give presents, but rather money.

The only one who gave us a present was Filiberto, my brother-in-law, who worked at another mine where it was the custom to give presents, and he gave us a dozen glasses. (They were brittle glasses; there is only one left.) At two in the afternoon, they served the wedding stew.

*Was it made of chicken?*

Chicken and rabbit. The chicken stew is yellow; they use *khellu uchu*, yellow peppers, and it's called *wallpa kokho*. Rabbit stew is made with red peppers, *puka uchu*, and it's called *khoi kokho*. These two kinds of stew are served with potatoes and *chuño*, followed by carrot salad.

The groom doesn't have a drink until ten o'clock at night or later. He doesn't even have a glass of *chicha* because he has to attend to his guests. The people from the countryside know very well that he can't drink, and no one says, "Pour yourselves a glass, let's have a toast." No. Only people with a bad reputation get drunk and pay little attention to their guests; some of those people even fight with their guests.

*Is it the same way in the mining camp?*

It doesn't happen this way in the mining camp. When a miner gets married he is not supposed to be serious, and he has to toast all the guests with his bride. If he gets drunk, he just goes to sleep. Another couple represents the bride and the bridegroom. They receive all the money and are supposed to give it to the bride and the groom. When the bride and groom wake up, they are supposed to get up, but if it's late at night, the surrogate couple just let the bride and groom rest. They don't wake them up to give presents.

*Is that ayni?* [*reciprocal exchanges of goods and money*].

It isn't *ayni*. It is nothing more than the guests' goodwill. In order to do *ayni*, they have to announce it before they get married, saying "You who are getting married, do you accept the *ayni* or not?" And if they accept it, they say, "We need drinks. Bring us some drink. We will bring some to you when you get married."

And so we got married. From the beginning, before I even had a family, my greatest desire was to educate my children because, like all men and women, I thought about the future. It wasn't going to be just the two of us forever; people have children. All my hopes focused on the education of my children. I knew the countryside well enough and I knew there weren't as many educational facilities as in the city. And the schools in the cities were better than those in the countryside. In the countryside, the time during which people study is shorter, and the teaching is less effective. That's why I planned on staying at the mine because the education in the mining camp is superior to that in the countryside. The teachers are good. There are no strikes, and if there are, the schools don't close. I thought of this, that I had to leave the countryside and return to the mines. So, when Engineer Cesar Zuña Morales sent me a letter, I returned as soon as possible to Santa Fe. At first, I sent my wife to Santa Fe to take some fruit and vegetables to my mother-in-law. On her way back, she met Engineer Cesar Zuña Morales, and they spoke together.

"Have you come back to live?" he asked her.

"No, Señor Zuña, I just came to bring my mother some fruit," my wife answered.

So the engineer wrote me a letter, and when she came back she gave it to me. I read it, and he had written, "Come here as soon as possible, because there is work for you." I got ready to leave immediately. I said to my wife, "Let's go. There is work for me," and in three days we were back at the mine, hoping to be able to educate my children.

But I didn't know what was going to come later. I didn't understand what the mine sickness was, because that year when I went back to Santa Fe, I still wasn't sick. My lungs were still perfectly healthy. If I had known what was going to happen, as I do now, I would have left the mines. I wouldn't have been so concerned about the education of my children, because they could have gone to school in the cities, although it wouldn't have been the same. I didn't know what was going to happen later, and now I find myself with the mine sickness.

# 9

# The Triumph of the Revolution:
# The Workers Are Lords of the
# National Wealth

Juan judged the revolution in terms of his own ability
to achieve, or even pursue, the goals that he had de-
fined for himself and his family. Ultimately this is the
test of a revolution — not the rhetoric that flows from
the ideological objectives of the new forces, but how
people like Juan actualize the promises in their own
lives. For Juan, the success of the revolution was man-
ifested in improved working and living conditions.

With the change in government came changes in
the organization of work in the nationalized mines.
Workers were paid according to the weight of the load
they took out rather than the mineral content. The
solidarity of each contract work-group gave way to a
solidarity of all mine workers as a class promoted by
the nationally organized Federation of Mine Workers'
Unions. Workers acquired new responsibilities in the
management of the mines through Workers' Control,
a representation of union members in managerial
circles. Although this never attained a significant
decision-making level, Juan saw its potential for re-
ducing the graft and corruption in the administration
of the mines. The miners reinstituted the ritual of k'a-
raku, the sacrifice of an animal to the mines, and the
celebration of independence — which coincidentally
also occurred in August, the month traditionally recognized as the time for k'araku — took on a new meaning.

With the advent of the revolution, Juan was advanced to foreman of the exploration work-group.

The mines were nationalized on October 31, in 1952. The government paid an indemnity of twenty million American dollars to the tin-mining barons, Patiño, Aramayo, and Hochschild, the owners of these large mining concerns.

The government allowed the mining barons some time so that they could withdraw their capital goods. They were introducing a lot of machinery into the country just before the nationalization of the mines. For example, when I started working in May of 1952, they gave me a new drill, but then for a while, from about July to December, there was a great shortage of tools and machinery. All the machinery that had been ordered for the mine was returned to Antofagasta or Arica by the mining barons because they knew the mines were going to be nationalized.

The president signed the decree for the nationalization of the mines on October 31, 1952, in the Siglo XX mine on the field named after María Barzola.[1] A holiday was decreed and all work stopped. The factories were closed and neither the brick-layers, the masons, nor the construction workers in the city of Oruro worked on that day. Miners from all the mines congregated at Siglo XX where there was a big meeting. We set off enormous charges of dynamite, as though we were in a fierce struggle, a state of war.

When the mines belonged to the old barons, there were no power drills or steam shovels for most of us in Santa Fe. There were air compressors only at the very few stations where there were automatic drills. After nationalization they set up air pipes everywhere, including the most oppressive places, where you couldn't bear the heat. Before that the workers had to go around swinging a wet rag to get rid of the dust in the tunnels and shafts where we were drilling out new levels. Afterward, there was good ventilation in all the work sites.

During the year of the revolution, the separate unions in each mining district were reorganized under a single federation, the Federation of Mine Workers Unions of Bolivia (FSTMB), which is the miners' overall organizational unit. The next year the general secretaries of the

[1] María Barzola was a *palliri*, a concentrator of metals, who led the women's organization in Siglo XX Catavi. When the miners protested for higher wages in 1942 she led the demonstrators and was killed by the army.

Federation declared that the managers of each nationalized company — as well as the payroll officers, the personnel officers, the quartermasters, and the camp managers — were getting too much graft. They drew up a list of *maquipuras* — casual workers without a regular contract with the company — who didn't really do any work, but who were on the payroll, got the money, and then paid it over to the mining camp manager. Most of the money the *maquipuras* were supposedly earning found its way into the manager's pockets. When all these irregularities came out, the general secretaries asked that each nationalized company organize a directorate that would act as a supervisory control over the business. They wanted a workers' committee with veto power. Victor Paz Estenssoro's government made every effort to prevent the development of such an organization. The miners organized a directorate, but it didn't have veto power, and without that, it was a powerless committee.

The workers at Siglo XX mine were more adamant than those in other mines. They threatened a strike, the first during Victor Paz Estenssoro's period of office. Paz Estenssoro didn't want any problem during his administration and agreed to the formation of the committee. Finally, in 1953, a worker-controlled supervisory committee with veto power was organized. That stopped the corruption in the nationalized mines. The company saved money because every voucher for materials had to go through the Workers' Control committee. No one could take any commissary supplies, hospital drugs, or work equipment, no matter how urgently it was needed, without the approval of the workers' supervisory committee.

Those of us in Santa Fe didn't know what Workers' Control was, or what it was for, nor did we know why our mine still wasn't nationalized during 1953. All we knew was that Workers' Control would have to stop all the corruption that existed in the management of the companies.

Our mining district of Santa Fe, as well as that in Japo, was finally nationalized in 1954, and we immediately organized a Workers' Control board with veto power. The first secretary general was Don Victor Carrasco, who had been the secretary of the union organization in the Federation. He caught various employees who were drawing off the company's earnings. For example, Señor Manuel Cano built himself a fine house in Oruro with material belonging to the company. He would go in person to Oruro to acquire material for the Santa Fe warehouses, saying that he needed piping, wood, all kinds of building materials; he then used these for his own house. The Workers' Control board discovered this when they looked over all the order slips since 1952. He was dismissed from his job. They also caught a Señor Minaya, who was the head of the office. He was a Paraguayan who had embezzled thirty million bolivianos [about three thousand dollars]. Another head clerk, a Chilean, had sent twenty-five million bolivianos to Chile, but they were not able to recover those funds. Workers' Control set limits on prices at factory stores and, in general, made things work more reasonably.

Before the nationalization of the mines, many workers couldn't get a contract until they had worked for two years as general laborers. After those two years they just worked by the day for the contractors. Under nationalization, after working for three months, they automatically became members of a team and worked under contract. Of course, the money came from the team, not the company, but they were paid by the day. They earned ten pesos instead of the twenty or more earned by the contract workers. But after the revolution, it was easy to get a contract. For example, in my case, having started before May of 1952, I should have had to work as a general laborer for two years before getting a contract. I thought they were going to follow the old system because that mine wasn't yet nationalized. But they followed the new laws laid down by Victor Paz Estenssoro for the nationalized mines.

I went in to work one day as a general laborer and the next day Engineer Cesar Zuña Morales said to me, "Listen, Rojas, you can't be in the *pirkin* [a team of contract workers using hand drills] anymore. You have to work as a machine driller."

I was frightened when he said this to me because I had never in my life worked with such a machine. I didn't know them. My body shook, not because of the mine sickness — I didn't understand then what the mine sickness meant or how you got it — but because I was frightened to hear him say that I had to work with the drilling machine.

I said to him, "But, Señor Zuña, you know very well I know nothing about the machine."

"You'll learn as you work with it," he replied. That Zuña almost forced me to take a drilling contract.

I worked as a contract driller from that day until the twenty-first of April of last year, 1969. I have spent a long time working as a driller and I have had good yields. I have taught many of my friends at work how to drill. I have also had many assistants, and most of them have turned out to be good drillers as well, although a few didn't learn how to manage the machine. They were frightened when I told them of the dangers. They usually gave us young assistants because the older men were afraid of the machine, whereas the younger ones were just starting out and didn't know what was happening. I would tell them, and many of them quit and refused to be drillers. They didn't want to work with the machine because they were afraid of the mine sickness. Some even stopped working in the mines.

I had a young helper named Lora. One day he said to me, "Maestro, I am going to put a handrail on the stairs, but hold on to it with care when you go down, because it is only tied at the end. If we go down by the shaft, we are going to be late."

I said to him, "Good, Lora, put up the handrail. I'll go down slowly. You be careful with the rocks."

"Yes, Maestro, I'll be careful. Let's go," he replied. "We are going to be late because we've spent a lot of time on this handrail."

Taking care, I got up and went down on the side where water was flowing. Below, they were opening up a chimney to ventilate the shaft and to communicate with the tunnel they had blasted out below. They had opened the cavity and from this the water was issuing. I got to that place and, trying not to slip, I got careless about the rope that held up the ladder at the end. I stretched out my hand to advance, and the ladder fell toward me. I held on, fortunately with my feet on rungs of the ladder. I grabbed it by the sides and I fell fifteen or sixteen meters. I rode the ladder like a canoe, as though I were walking on water right down the shaft. I must have fallen just fifteen meters short of level 170. Nothing happened to me except that I got my hands scratched on the sides when the ladder struck the walls. My assistant fell on top of me. When he fell, he cut his ear, but it wasn't serious. After that, my assistant stopped working in the mine.

"It's not very safe to work down here in the mine," he said. "I'd better get out of this." He asked to be transferred to the outside, to the office or to the commissary, wherever. But the company didn't grant his request because he was over the age limit. In those days, they gave the work outside the mine to those who were sixteen or eighteen, and those who were older had to work inside the mine. He said, "I'm not going to lose my life in the mine. I can't support my mother and little brothers if I am dead. I'd better get out of this business."

Another time, when I was working with the Paredo team, there was a young driller named Lucio Zeballos. He just had one son. We worked on a single shaft, eight or nine of us working in a line, on a good vein, the Paniagua vein. As we were working we suddenly heard a sound. It wasn't loud, no more than "Lojon!" I looked behind me but saw nothing. In a while the worker who worked next to Lucio, Eulogio Beltran, called to me.

"Don Juan, come and see this for a minute. Something serious has happened."

"What happened?" I ran and saw the boy under a rock, headless. The head was on the other side of the rock. It was just held on by a tiny little nerve. It had been cut off by the metal ore in the rock. We had to take the metal out, that very rock that had cut his head off.

That was the first serious accident I had ever seen, and I was very upset. I was crying to get out, thinking How long will I last? When will that happen to me? But finally, I saw no reason to leave. We were earning plenty, and I tried not to think of the things that could happen. If someone had told me, "Listen, you shouldn't work in the mine. You are young, you should get out. You are going to get the mine sickness if you don't get out," maybe I would have come out, and I wouldn't be as I am now, sick with the mining disease.

When I returned from Cochabamba and started working at the mine again, there was a different camp chief, since Sejas had been fired. I went to the new chief to get a house and ended up with the same house in which I had lived before. My enemy, Kak'chalo, lived across the street from me. We had to look at each other every day.

I was working as a driller and he was a free-floating helper without an assigned station. One day his boss was absent and my helper was absent. My assistant was my *compadre* — I had baptised his son. So that day I had to work with my enemy, Kak'chalo, and we worked as though nothing had happened, as though we had just met. We worked together for three days. He didn't say anything to me or remind me of anything I had said. He chewed coca at my side, and I by his side. We didn't even start sizing each other up. We were like men with respect for one another.

Ever since the time we fought, that man respected me — to the end of his life. Now he and his wife are dead, because they gave themselves over to evil ways, to a bad life since they were both drunkards. But we remained distant. We would look at each other, greet each other civilly, but we never spoke to each other as friends.

My wife arrived at Santa Fe from Cochabamba where she had been staying. The neighbors told her, "Don Juan is working. He lives in the same house he used to." Since she knew where it was, she went to the house, but I had forgotten to leave the key for her and had taken it to work with me. When she got there she found the door locked. She went to her mother's house to see if I had left the key there. "No, he didn't leave it here. Maybe he gave it to your neighbor," her mother told her.

"No, he didn't leave the key with any of the neighbors," my wife replied. So she sat there waiting for me in the yard, with all of her things, until five o'clock. Actually, I didn't even have to lock the house because there was nothing in it — just my suit and my hat and my shoes. Everything else was in Cochabamba, and she had brought it all with her.

I came out of work at five and found her there in the yard. I was speechless.

She scolded me, saying "Why did you take the key with you? What have you got in there that anyone could take away?" I listened to her without saying a word.

"I forgot," I finally said. And then we began to talk to each other in a better mood.

"Don't you see it was God's will that we got married?" I told her. "Now we are back at the same house where you first wanted to live."

We liked living in that house because it was a well-built house. It was sunny from dawn to dusk.

*Did it have windows?*

Yes, in the doors.

*How did it compare with the house in which your parents lived?*

Our house in Santa Fe had flooring, and there was electricity, whereas my father's house in Cancañiri didn't have electricity and there was no flooring or even a ceiling. His kitchen was outside, and the room was tiny. In our house the room was fairly big — four beds fit in it — and there was also a room for a night table. And the kitchen was bigger than that at Cancañiri.

When I first went back on contract, Gil Sejas was working at Morococala, but he had come down to be a cashier at Santa Fe. That animal was constantly bothering me. Once, it was raining while we were waiting to be paid. When it started raining, I shouted, "Hurry up and pay us, because we are getting wet in the rain!" He saw me from the window and closed it. There were other impatient workers behind me and they threw rocks at the window until it broke. Of course Gil Sejas put all of the blame on me. He wanted to fight with me again.

No sooner had I come in the door than I heard "Rojas did it! Rojas did it!"

I said, "What did you see me do, Don Gil?"

"You Movement people [participants in the National Revolutionary Movement] are always making trouble."

I was no longer afraid of people like him and I said, "Aren't you with the Movement?"

"I wouldn't be part of that for anything."

"So why are you making trouble if you are not with the Movement? Those of us in the Movement can take care of ourselves. Don Gil, you saw who did it. Did you see me break your window? I am young, but I behave like a mature man, and you know that I respect you, Don Gil. You look at those people and then say who broke the window." I was angry, so I left.

On Monday, Engineer Cesar Zuña Morales called me when I was getting my time card. He said, "Rojas, come here. I want to talk to you. What's going on? You want to start fighting again with Gil?"

"Look, Engineer," I said, "it was not my fault and that man is blaming me. He is the one who wants to fight again. But this time I am not going to take it quietly in his office. I am going to call him on it, Engineer, because I don't like these accusations."

The Engineer asked me, "Who was it who did it?"

"I didn't see who did it, but Fernández could tell you. He saw what happened clearly and told me that one of those who did it was from the mill. They started throwing rocks and one of them threw a bigger one. Anyway, it's Don Gil's own fault for closing the window." I said. It was my good luck that Gil Sejas was soon transferred to another mine, so the fight didn't continue.

At the end of 1953 on New Year's Eve we had a grand, big party at my house. Several *compadres* came. I had even more *compadres* than before because I always behaved like a good man and people respected me. Three *compadres* came to see me that night, bringing pepper stew; we ate and drank plenty. When it was morning, I rested with my wife at my side. At two in the afternoon we woke up, both of us, with headaches. We both took a seltzer and went out to visit my in-laws. We congratulated each other for the New Year, and soon we came home again.

On the way back, we met Foreman Calizaya. His nickname was "*El*

*Combo,"* because he was a fighter and whenever he fought with someone, he hit them on the head with his hammer and ripped their faces
open. Calizaya called me over to his house. I went in, but I didn't have
a single drink. He knew me well and he knew that I don't like to drink
the day after I've been drinking at night. So he didn't force it on me
and he let me leave his house gracefully.

I returned to my house and at five in the afternoon I went to the
movies with my wife. Filemón , who was already two or three years old,
was with us, running ahead. That night we saw *Love in Jalisco.* It was a
good film, a Mexican movie, in color. We saw the whole thing, and my
wife said to me, "Let's stay for the next show and see it again, because
the movie is lovely and I don't feel too well."

"Oh, don't ask for too much. Let's go home and rest. I can't stand
this any longer. I came to the movies mostly to escape the neighbors
who are drinking too much." My wife agreed and we went home to
rest. We slept well, and I returned to work again the next day.

In September, Engineer Cesar Zuña gave me a station for the coming year's bonus. "Here you will earn money. I will give you this station,
and you can work it with four more people to set it up."

It was a fairly rich station that had only recently been opened. Martín Cuyku de Sacaca had prepared it. I don't know why they didn't give
it to him to work, but he continued drilling in tunnels. I had also been
a driller, but I didn't prepare stations. I worked on exploration and
found the new veins of ore. That's the most basic job in the mine. The
face worker prepares the places where the explorer has found veins. So
Zuña gave me four men, Severino Katari, Severino Cabrera, who is
now dead — we called him *"Cabrito"* (Little Goat) because he screamed
just like a goat to make himself heard at the station — Miguel Aduana,
also dead, and Constantino García, an old man who is now also dead.
Of the team I worked with at my first station, only Severino Catari is
still living.

*Was it difficult to earn the respect of the group because you were so
young?*
In this kind of work, one's personality is more important than one's
age. For example, there are plenty of young people who know how to
respect people who are older than they, as well as those who are
younger, but what is most important is that they know how to make
themselves respected. In my case, I had assistants who were older than
I, but who respected me regardless of my youth. I have also had various

mining friends who were older than I, but they respected me as much as I respected them, because I knew how to behave respectfully to people. I was respectful to people regardless of whether they were young or old.

*While you are working, do you behave in the same way to older and younger miners?*

Yes, it's all the same. On the one hand, I looked for ways to be liked and respected by the older workers, and on the other hand I also wanted to be liked and respected by the younger men. That is very important in this type of work. Of course, there are times at work when there are no status distinctions, especially during the rest periods. During that time, workers feel free to complain about anything, to tell you things that bother them, because the rest break is supposed to be a happy time, a period of freedom and a chance to catch your breath. Respect is still shown during rest periods, but it isn't as pronounced as during actual work.

Engineer Zuña had told us that if we found a little vein branching off someplace, we should follow it without asking for his authorization, and that he would pay us for the meters advanced, whether or not there was much ore. His only condition was that once we started cutting a shaft, we would have to continue until we exhausted the vein.

Late one afternoon we set off some dynamite, and then we quit for the day. The next day I didn't go to check out the other work stations. We had just dynamited the face and we had to get the ore out quickly because it was in a place where there were many leaks that wet the dirt and made the whole station very muddy. Accordingly, I didn't want to take the time to check out the other stations.

Aduana hadn't told me anything about the place where we set the charges off, but Zuña had gone up and came to inform me.

"You have come upon a vein that isn't quite in the middle of the shaft, but it's a fair vein that looks as though it has good prospects. But one way or another, you must not neglect this vein." So I left my work and I went to Aduana's station.

"Why didn't you tell me?" I scolded my laborer. They had advanced nicely and fortunately had made a good find which lasted me almost four years. It was a gorgeous vein, one that yielded 40 percent ore.

Later Aduana teased me, "Now, remember how you scolded me?"

I replied, "I didn't scold you for starting work on it, but rather because you didn't tell me you were starting. The foreman has to know everything that's going on. If there was a vein, you should have said to me, 'Have you seen it?' and I would have said, 'I haven't, but I'm going to look.' Because I didn't do that, the Engineer got angry at me."

Aduana was alone at his station. I told Severino Katari, the driller, to take a telescope drill to level forty-two and open a passage. He followed my orders and that same afternoon began to drill and set off charges. In less than a week, the passage and the shaft were connected. We got a passage right by the face where we needed it, and we had no trouble taking out the load. I made Katari Aduana's assistant. Katari had been a driller before, and Aduana had been a general assistant.

The old man, Constantino García, was good at sorting the ore, and I put him at the face selecting and preparing the samples. We were supposed to average 57 percent ore from the load removed, but this old man could do better than that. I could never get over 50 percent even when I tried my best to surpass the 57 percent average. I don't know how that old man did it, but he got a lot out, with great care. Not a bit of clay got past him and that's why he got such a high yield. I always hurried that work so as to get it over quickly. Consequently my average was always a bit lower, two or three or even five percentage points lower, than that of Constantino. He had patience.

Severino Cabrera was a hand driller. He was very playful, and a real talker who drank a lot. I got angry with that boy.

"Look," I said to him. "We are earning good money but you, Severino, are spending your life playing around. Moreover, you are always absent from work the day after you get drunk. Why don't you work harder and more regularly? And why do you spend half the day talking? When you are working you should forget about the rest. The bosses are bound to get angry at me, and how can I explain your absences? If you are absent one more time I will have to move you off the team."

Cabrera thought about it and worked hard for the rest of that month, but the next month his absences began again. I reported him to the superintendent.

"You can do what you like with Cabrera, because I don't like his attitude," I said. "He talks too much and he skips work too much. Since I am losing this man, give me another."

Cabrera, however, was a godson of the superintendent who had been godfather at Cabrera's civil wedding. He said, "Listen, Rojas, all this time you have been my friend. Let's not do this to Cabrera. You know he is my godson, and I have to help him one way or another. It would be better if, for a while, you work just with the three, Aduana, Katari, and García."

"Very well, Don Samuel, but please, if you are going to send him back to me, tell him to behave a bit more seriously," I said. So Cabrera worked for a week as a general laborer, and then was sent back to me.

I took him back because he was a pretty good fellow, and because we had known each other for many years. I advised him privately, "It is alright for you to play around when you like, but work while you do it. I don't like it when you miss work because you got drunk." Thereafter when he got drunk he slept it off quietly at home, without any fighting and without missing work. The little old man, Constantine García, also drank a lot, but he didn't miss work. What I didn't like was for my men to come to work drunk, because they could kill themselves or others, since drunks don't know what they are doing.

*Did you work Sundays?*

No, not on Sundays. Every Sunday I made my workers rest. Since I first started working I haven't liked to work on Sunday, because it is the day of rest. We have to rest once a week to regain our strength, so as to be able to start all over again. That's why I didn't make anybody work on Sunday. Occasionally, when we dynamited at the face, we would come in to work through the water passage, but only for a half day. Now, we have to work every day, because otherwise we don't earn enough to live.

*Tell me something about the pace of work during those years.*

According to our own work rules, the head of the team has to leave last, after all the other workers, and he also has to go in before the other workers go to their stations. Also, no worker is allowed to stay in the mine; he has to go to the office and to the elevator when it's time to come out. Sometimes, workers don't want to come out at midday because they have troubles at home. But sometimes the elevator would be broken and it wouldn't come to take us out at noon. We preferred not to leave through the old shafts left from previous works because if we did, we'd be out of breath and more tired than if we had continued working. For that reason, even I have stayed working in the mine throughout the day on several occasions. If the elevator was there at the station to take us out at noon, I would come out; if not, I would go back to my work, and my friends who did leave would go to my house and bring me a bottle of cold tea, some coca, and cigarettes.

My wife was a woman who was ready for everything and took care of me well in every way. If I was five or ten minutes late getting home, she would run to my friend's house to find out quickly where I was and what I was doing. So she knew when the miners had to go back to work in the afternoon, and she would go to the main shaft entrance and wait next to the iron gate with a bottle of cold tea and the coca. I would come out at five and tell her what had happened, but she wouldn't be alarmed, because she already knew where I was.

When there was no elevator, we would come out early, at eleven-fifteen in the morning. We would rest, change, and dress by eleven-twenty-five, and go right back into the shaft. We took scarves because you have to be warmly dressed to come in to the mine, and when we leave we also have to be warmly dressed. If we left through the tunnel with our coats on, we would be bathed in sweat because it is very hot from level 140 to level 42. By level 40 it is a bit cooler, and we can breathe easily because there is some fresh air. By eleven-forty-five we would be outside, resting, sunning ourselves and breathing fresh air. After that we would go quickly to our houses. When we went to the office to leave by the elevator, the bosses would complain, because although most of us were tired from working, some were smart alecks — watching the clock and taking time off to rest as early as eleven-thirty.

I have never liked to exploit my companions. I have always earned my living by my work, earned my daily bread with my own efforts, and I have not taken advantage of my friends. So I always worked until a quarter to twelve. At a quarter to twelve on the dot I would stop and rest. I would change clothes quickly and rush to the office to get the elevator. If I dawdled I would miss the elevator, and I'd have to stay in the mine until five in the afternoon, without any lunch.

*Was there any difference between the days that you stayed in during the lunch hour and the days you came out? Did you feel like working more after breathing fresh air?*

Well, after working inside the mine, I would come out completely exhausted. There were times my hand was too weak to hold a glass of tea. My hands would shake as though I were frightened of something. I would rest a bit, breathe the pure air, and eat my lunch — or my dinner if I was coming back to work overtime — and I would find more strength to go back to work. I would work as though I had really rested at my house. You do have more strength when you come out of the mine for a break than when you stay in all day.

Once I was working on a three-man team. At that time none of us was the leader; all they asked was that we work together. There were

Paredes, a fierce man, Zenteño, and myself, just the three of us as a team on the detonator. We delivered the ore in barrels and also by the detonator, so as to get the work done fast because we were making good money. During that period the scaffolding was collapsing every night. A beam would fall down, and we'd have to replace it the next day. Then another beam would come down and, in order to fix it, we couldn't take the time to come out for lunch. They sent our lunch to the office, and we ate there and went right back to work. We didn't have the same stamina we would have had if we had gone home to have a peaceful lunch and then come back to work. There wasn't as much enthusiasm, and we would tire much faster. Although we could work hard until three in the afternoon, until the *akulli* time and the *pijchar* time, after that we would get up and try to continue working at the same pace, but would find that we couldn't. Our strength had been sapped. There is always that difference. One must come out of the mine, if only for fresh air.

*Why didn't they allow the workers to come out at midday in some mines?*

For example, in San José there was Engineer Melgarejo. Do you remember him, the old section chief who has now gone to Huanuni? A tall, blond man? He was a devil. Many workers wanted to go out for lunch, including him. With what righteousness he suffered and stayed to eat in the mine, with his house just a few steps away! As a chief, he could easily have gone to have a quiet lunch at his own house. But, in order to annoy the workers getting ready to have lunch by the gate — just five meters away from the mine entrance — he would suddenly say, "You, what are you doing here? Get inside right now, and go eat at zero level by the elevator." He always made the workers go inside instead of telling them "Go have lunch in the sun. Go take some air and come right back."

It was just a way of maltreating the workers, since they weren't losing anything when we had lunch above ground. The bosses lost the same amount of our time whether we ate inside the mine or outside. But that Malgarejo didn't understand that. He would send them all back in, and people obeyed him because if they didn't he would fine them hours of work. The section chiefs want to see the work move ahead; they want to see the workers exploited, nothing more, and they don't understand workers' exhaustion or how they regain their strength and their energy to continue working.

That year we had a little *k'araku* [sacrificial offering to the spirits] for the *awichas* (old women who accompany the *Tío*) and the *Tío* (uncle, or *Supay*, the hill spirit) with a little white goat and various sweets. Severino Cabrera went to buy the goat in Inchupalla. On the thirty-first of July, at nine at night, we cut the goat's throat and sprinkled all of its blood on the face in the mine and at the work stations, to remind the *awichas* and the *Tío* that we were inviting them to a feast of goat meat.

We came out with the *yatiri* after sprinkling the blood around. We got to our tool hut and joined our other companions who had stayed behind to prepare the food for us. There were eight of us. The team had gotten bigger.

Cabrera said to me, "They put too much water in the stew and it can't evaporate. With that much water, we won't be able to finish it. There are few of us, and we are supposed to have just a little bowl of soup, but there is enough now for each of us to have four bowls."

I said to him, "If you are dissatisfied with what your companions are doing, the old ladies, the *awichas*, will be even more dissatisfied with what we are offering them. We have to make our offering happily. The fire will burn under the cooking pot and the water will boil off rapidly." And so it happened: the water evaporated and we each barely got half a bowl. When the meat was beginning to burn, we took off the cooking pot and put the tray on a red *awayo* [a handwoven cloth, generally of bright cotton, especially red]. We covered up "Fiero" Miranda's eyes so that he could divide up the meat. If he were not blindfolded, those who received the neck or the tail might say that he was choosing good pieces for his friends. That's the way we divided up the portions, as accurately as possible. The meat was good, delicious. Some of my companions wanted to take it with them, but I made them eat it all up and leave the bones to put in the mine. It brings bad luck if you take meat or bones away from the place where a *k'araku* is held.

While we ate, it got late. We finished at about eleven-fifteen at night. We wrapped up the bones in some red wool, and put them into the mine with the goat's head, its guts, its feet — everything went into a dynamite box and into the mine. We got to the place where we were going to hide the bones, and we blessed the place. We sprinkled *chuara* water, prepared with fresh marigolds, and ground white and yellow corn, together with an offering of white and pink flowers and sweet almond paste, and bricks of bright silver and gold. We put this water in a jar and sprinkled it on the walls of the work stations and on all the scaffoldings where we spent most of our time. Finally we got to the

place where we were going to bury the goat bones. That is the *k'araku*.
The goat's heart is put in the middle of the box where it belongs.

When the infusion of flowers and other offerings was done, we made
a *ch'alla*. We spread out two new burlap bags which hadn't been used
before. With the *yatiri's* help, we made the shape of a goat with the
head, legs, and ribs where they belonged, as though we were making a
goat skeleton. So we left it, ready and well made, and next to it we put
closed bottles of *pisco* and alcohol, red and white wine. We also left
sweets and a bottle of beer and another bottle of papaya juice. We
sprinkled the liquor on the ground and drank it for a while longer, and
then we had to leave, without looking back. Once we got to the office,
we could look wherever we liked, because by then we have gone past
curves and corners, and you couldn't see the place any more.

At the office we drank and offered liquor to the spirits for at least
another two hours. During that time some of my companions stayed
behind, making the offerings in memory of the *k'araku*. We called for
the elevator and the man at the winch sent it down immediately; we
came up and went outside. We went into the winch keeper's station to
*ch'allar* [offering of liquor to the Pachamama, or earth spirit] with him.
The man who ran the winch was pleased and he asked us in. We had a
drink and made offerings to our *awichas* and our Tío. Then we left
there and went to our tool hut. We took out one of my new machines
which we called the "Azulejo." We sprinkled it with liquor because it is
the machine we use most.

That night I was at the mine until at least four in the morning. Finally I left and gave my key to the head man who was replacing me,
Mejía. He wasn't drunk and still had his senses about him. He had to
be sure the toolbox was locked so we wouldn't lose a lot of things. In
my hut there were new carts, shovels, hammers, pickaxes, and burlap
bags — lots of goods which were valuable.

The next day, the first of August, no one went into the mine, neither
the house peons, nor the bosses, nor the foremen — nobody. The elevator was working, but just to let the pump operator in, since if the
pump operator doesn't go in, the pumps don't work and the mine fills
up with water. But at twelve he had lunch and left. On the second of
August, no one went in either. The workers went to their tool huts and
drank with the bosses. Engineer Zuña always stayed by his workers. He
became manager when the previous one was fired. The engineer told
us to go in to work on the third day, but the workers refused.

"This is the first time we have invited the *Tío* for this *k'araku*, and he has to enjoy his food," we said. They had had *k'arakus* before, but not like the one we did that year of 1953. That year all the headmen, not just those of our team, had done a *k'araku*, some with oxen and some with llamas. We stayed out until the fourth day, drinking *chicha*, beer, and alcohol. Oh, it was a *k'araku* that we'll never see again in a lifetime!

On the fourth of August we went back to work, but only for half the day, and only because it was a payday. They had to pay us for the Independence Day holidays of the fifth, sixth, and seventh of August. There was a huge celebration for Independence Day. Management tried to impose on labor a donation of time without pay, and there was a big fight over that. Many of the contract men, including me, complained. "How can they impose donations of time when we earn fifty, forty, or thirty pesos, whereas a house peon earns only ten pesos for the day?"

The secretary-general suggested a compromise: "Then the house peons will have to work for two days on the teams, and those two days will be discounted. It will be fair." We didn't accept it at first, but finally we agreed to the donation of two days' work per contract worker two day's work by each of the house peons. So everything worked out.

The fifth of August arrived. They hired a band, a good band. The president of the committee was a certain Señor Tellez. The students had a parade on the fifth. The supply-master had ordered material for the children's school uniforms, and the company was in charge of making all the clothes necessary for the parade. The parade went peacefully on Saturday, with everyone all dressed up in their uniforms.

On Sunday there was the torch parade and an all-night party. At eight o'clock at night we all met at the San Pedrito soccer field. From there we went in with the torchbearers to the Sixth of August Plaza and there we came to our wits' end, what with all the speeches made for the August celebration of Independence Day. President Tellez spoke first, then the secretary-general of the union, Don Victor Carrazco, and finally the Workers' Control committee chief, Pedro Medina. And so the first meeting ended.

Afterwards there was a gala parade in the plaza. Everyone had floats that they had prepared for a contest. The ball began at two in the morning when everyone was drunk.

On the sixth, the villagers and the workers paraded, and on the seventh there was a bullfight. The bull gored a certain Arispe in the pants, ripping them, but he didn't get his flesh; Arispe escaped without a scratch. The people were horrified when they saw it. The women especially were frightened, and they screamed very loudly.

There was also a contest to see who could eat the most of some enormous breads made of dough. The loaves were badly cooked, not done in the middle, but the people washed them down with beer. Watching it, you had to laugh. There was also a contest to see who could eat most condensed milk while blindfolded. And there was a race in which the people carried eggs on a spoon in their mouths. Whoever got to the end with a whole egg, won.

The last contest was to catch a greased pig. The pig was shaved of all its hair, greased, and let loose in the bull ring. From four to six in the afternoon men tried to catch the pig. They would grab at him, but it would slip out of their hands: they couldn't hold onto it. It was a very strong pig. Finally, a lively man who was drunk grabbed one of the capes they use to pass the bull, wrapped the pig in it, and threw it off its feet. His clothes were covered with grease from being dragged in the dirt, his forehead was scratched from hitting the posts of the bull-pen as the pig tried to get away, but that man finally held him. He was a wild man.

They also had a contest with a greased pole that was twenty meters high in diameter. On the top was a tiny red flag. You had to climb to the top to get the flag. Getting up was easy because the pole was wide at the base and narrow on top, but getting down was something else. A certain Mandani, "Crazy Mandani" they called him, got up as if it was the easiest thing he did in his life. But he wanted to come down without a net because he thought the net wasn't good for anything. He came down, holding the pole as tight as he could, but he slid down at a tremendous speed. When he hit the bottom his legs were driven into his body. His stomach and everything was torn, and the bones in his legs were shattered. That boy lost his legs because he fell with all of his weight from twenty meters. But he got the flag.

And what was the prize? They gave him fifty pesos. They had said it would be five hundred, but in fact he got fifty. He was one of the company's workers. They took him to the hospital in La Paz. He came back to Santa Fe without his legs, riding in a little wheelbarrow.

At night they had dancing contests, contests of *cuecas*, tangos, and many other dances. A Señora Victoria Mamani won. Her brother worked in the supply department as a section chief. Her husband was called "Platillo" [Plate] because he was a short fat man, built like a flying saucer. The tango contest was won by a *compadre* of mine who had lived in Argentina for a long time. And finally there was the float contest. The one which was decorated the best won first prize – a sewing machine. Second prize was an electric iron, and third prize was a set of dishes. When the ball began I went home because it had gotten cold. I couldn't stand it any more, and I was worried that my boy could get sick.

It was a grand celebration, such as I had never seen in previous Augusts when the company ran them. That was the first year that the engineers celebrated with the workers. It was because of the influence of Engineer Cesar Zuña Morales. That was the one hundred and twenty-eighth year of independence, but, for the first time, we were the lords of the national wealth.

1 Juan addresses guests at his retirement party in 1970 as Anita, June Nash, and a nephew watch.

2 The San José slag pile and administrative offices. Oruro, 1970.

3 On the Day of the Cross families go to fields where they dig earth ovens and roast potatoes. *From left to right:* Juan, Elena, Laura Nash, Anita, María, Juan Manuel, and Petrona with their dog Huascar, May 3, 1969.

4 Juan reading Elena's report card as Anita, Juan Manuel, Aníbal, and Elena look on.

5  The entrance to the Santa Fe mines.

6 Water spigots in the street of the mining camp serve many families.

7 The mining camp at Siglo XX—Catavi where Juan's father worked when he was five years old.

8  Children playing next to the slag pile.

9 Children playing in campamento, San José, 1970.

10 Neighbors in the campamento, Santa Fe, 1970.

11 Following the nationalization of the mines, men worked in partnerships rather than in the work groups called *pirkiñeros.*

12 After the revolution the nationalized mines received power drills. In Santa Fe few were used before 1952.

13 Santa Fe camp, 1970.

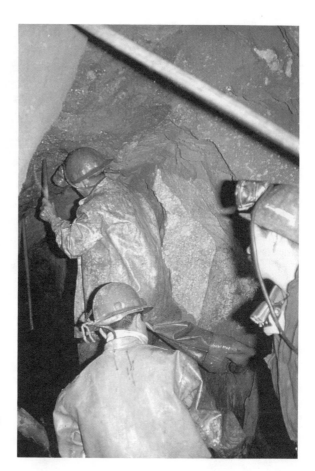

14 The majordomo
is responsible for the
safety of all miners
working on his shift.

15  Supervisors often force the workers to stay inside the mine during their lunch break.

16 Men drinking during a *ch'alla* at their work station.

17 Eating llama sacrificed in a *k'araku.*

18 Burning the bones of a llama after a *k'araku.* The ashes will be offered to the *Tío.*

19 At the festival of San Juan miners and their wives in *chola* dress dance outside Itos mine on the south side of Oruro, June 1969.

20 Mine union meeting, San José FSTMB, 1970.

21  Women listening to mine leaders at meeting of San José FSTMB, 1970.

22  Men listening to mine leaders at meeting of San José FSTMB, 1970.

23 June Nash becomes a *madrina* to Anita at her
confirmation, 1970.

24 The sink-and-float concentration plant that replaced women who
previously hand-sorted metal.

25  Juan's birthday and retirement party, August 1970.

26  Juan with guests perform a *ch'alla* at his retirement and birthday party, 1970.

27  Filming a staged "accident" in Itos for *I Spent My Life in the Mines.*

28  Juan prepares
bread offerings,
*urpus,* on All Saints'
Day, 1970.

29 Women of San José playing rummy to raise money for a mass at the wake of a miner who died of bronchopneumonia, 1970.

30 Filemón goes to work in the mine, 1970.

Petrona and Juan (*seated*) receive a copy of *We Eat the Mines and the Mines Eat* ...*s* when June Nash returns on a brief visit in 1983. With them are a nephew; Elena; ...etrona holding Victor Hugo; María holding her baby; Juan; Aníbal holding Israel; and ...an Manuel.

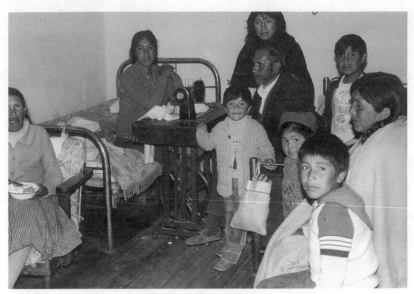

32 Petrona (*left*), a *comadre*, Elena, Juan, Israel, Victor Hugo, and neighbors watch television, 1985.

33 Aníbal dances the *cueca* with his wife during their wedding celebration, June 24, 1985.

34 Filemón with his wife, Ruth, and their children, 1985.

35 Juan Manuel in 1983.

36  Israel blows out candles on his birthday cake while Elena (*left*), Juan, Ruth (holding baby and flanked by her children), and María with her children watch, July 1985.

37  March for Life nears Calamarca, August 27, 1986.

38 The advance group in the March for Life approaches La Paz, August 28, 1986.

39 Women face cannon in Calamarca where the army intercepted the March for Life.

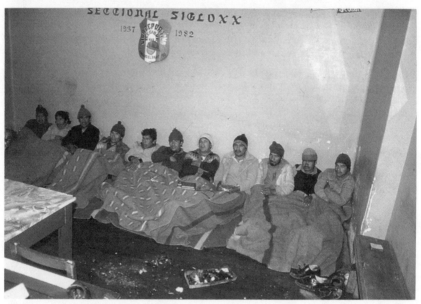

40 Hunger strike in Siglo XX–Catavi following the army's interception of the March for Life, September 5, 1986.

# 10

# We Miners Lived Like Rats in the Mining Camp

Petrona and other women in the mining camps refer to themselves collectively as "we miners." Their lives are as closely linked to the mining administration as are their husbands', since they live in company housing and buy most of their food in the company store. The rows and rows of houses extend outward from the office buildings and storehouses clustered around the mouth of the mine in almost uninterrupted lines. In many houses you can't avoid hearing the sounds of the machines that process the minerals, day and night. The acidic, evil-smelling liquids called *copajira* that ooze out of the mine flow in gutters along the streets of the mining camp. Women deal directly with the camp manager, giving him gifts to improve their lot or badgering him for failing to do so. They take responsibility for bringing complaints to the mining administration about the housing or food. It was around these issues that the women organized in "María Barzola Committees." Named after María Barzola, the martyr of the Siglo XX–Catavi protest movement for higher wages in 1942, the association was co-opted by the right wing of the MNR in the late 1950s as the leaders turned against labor representation within the party and used María Barzola Committees to subvert union meetings and the political action of workers.[1]

[1] Lydia Gueiler talks of this transmogrification of the Barzolinas in her book. *La Mujer en la Revolusíon.* In the early seventies it was replaced by the Association of Housewives that

After the revolution of 1952, Petrona was one of the representatives of the organization bringing complaints to management in La Paz, until her husband objected to her absences and demanded that she remain at home to serve him. It is made clear in her narrative that the private grievances of individuals can become collective issues when the women are organized, but that they can revert to the level of banal complaints — resolved through bribery or backbiting — when the collective base is lost. There is a parallel here to the way miners relate to *Supay*, or the *Tío*, in the mines. When a miner asks the *Tío* for success in his own advancement he becomes enthralled to the underworld lord, or *Huari*, one of the many aspects in which the Spirit of the Mountain appears. But when the work team offers a *ch'alla* to the *Supay* in a collective celebration during which they may ask for richer deposits, the welfare of the entire community is confirmed.

The key role that women play in the mining community, that of forming the basic core of associational life, becomes apparent in Petrona's narrative. Women prepare and invite the guests to the celebrations of family events; the people they choose as *compadres* are the critical members of their support group. Since Petrona's family lived and worked in the same mining camp as she and Juan, her family figures more prominently in such celebrations than his. Men carry the burden of winning respect and honor in the family, but women must intercede so that the men's generosity will not deprive the family of needed resources. In the division of labor in mining camps, women take on the shameful tasks required for survival in order to preserve the honor of the men. Petrona followed her mother's example after she got married.

---

Domitila Barrios de Chungara talks about in her book, *Si Me Permiten Hablar* (1977). Domitila shows how the organization became transformed into a revolutionary movement after the Massacre of San Juan when widows of the men killed in that uprising went to La Paz to seek justice. The Housewives Association was officially recognized as part of the Federation of Mine Workers Unions of Bolivia in June, 1986 and women entered into the meetings more frequently as issues turned from struggles on the job to survival in the mining camp (Nash 1988).

When we were still in Cochabamba, the movement [MNR] triumphed. I couldn't stay there any longer, *Comadre*. I didn't like it very much. I couldn't get accustomed to the climate. Whenever I was in Cochabamba I got sick with pains in my feet or my hands, or my head would ache a great deal. Why would that be?

*The change of altitude?*

It could be that.

We were happily married, but Juan also didn't want to remain in Cochabamba. "Now we have very little money. I have to go and earn some wherever I can," he said.

We were still staying in my father's house near my uncle in Vinto. While we were living there, a mine superintendent, Señor Zuniega — he was like a gringo, tall and blond — approached your *compadre*. He said, "Look, Rojitas, now the movement has triumphed. Before the movement, everyone wanted to beat you up or throw you out of work. But you are a great worker and you deserve your job back. Come on, Rojas, let's go. I am going to pay for the transportation and everything. Let's go."

I wasn't there when they had that talk. Juan came home right away to tell me what the mining chief had said to him. "Shall we go back to Santa Fe?" he asked.

"To Santa Fe? Sure, why not? I'd just as soon go immediately because I can't stay here."

He said, "If you want to go back, we'll go. What can we do here?" We just couldn't get used to Cochabamba at all, *Comadre*. I just couldn't get used to it.

The day we got back to Santa Fe, Juan started working. Your *compadre* was well liked, in spite of having been fired by that manager. The other bosses didn't necessarily agree with that manager, but they hadn't wanted to interfere with his right to fire Juan.

*Did his salary change after the revolution of 1952?*

Hardly; it was just about the same. Actually, he was earning more before we went to Cochabamba, but after we returned he had all kinds of benefits. The management paid for everything. They paid us two or three times a month. They cooperated with President Paz Estenssoro.

*What do you know about Paz Estenssoro?*

He certainly helped the miners, introducing rest periods so they could live better. It is thanks to him that we got this house.

*Did things change for women, too?*
No, hardly at all.

*Have you heard of the "Barzolenas?"*[2]
Ye. I was even a member, and they made me a delegate. I was nominated to investigate everything, to come to Oruro to sign documents
at the town hall. We delegates and members also had to change our
lives. We had been housewives, and some of us had no real understanding of the problems. I was the first to complain about the company
store. When they didn't give us good meat I complained; if the vegetables didn't arrive on time I complained. I was good at bringing all
these things to the attention of the management, and that's why they
named me delegate.

They also elected me to go places, but Juan didn't like that. He said
to me, "You have to resign. I don't like it. What are these things you
are worrying about? Who's going to do the cooking here? Who is
going to do this? Who is going to do that? You will have to hire a
servant."

"No, I had better resign," I said, and so I did.

*How long were you a member?*
In all, I was a member for one or two months.

*Did you take your children to the meetings?*
Yes, of course they came with me

*What kinds of clothes did the Barzolenas wear?*
*Polleras* of wool. Nobody wore a [western style] dress. All of us were
*cholas*. They were all smart, but I was the smartest because I really
understood everything. The women followed me because they couldn't
explain things well in Spanish. They only spoke Quechua, but I could
explain things well to the administration in Spanish. That's why they
nominated me.

The manager liked me. He gave me the money to distribute to my
companions so that we could lodge complaints in Oruro, in Huanuni,
wherever. But your *compadre* didn't want me to do it. "It's too much,"
he said. "It's very inconvenient for you to be going from one place to
the next. Why are you doing it? What can you gain from it? Don't go,"
he said. I resigned because of that.

*In which of your demands were you most successful, Comadre?*
We did best with matters to do with supplies in the company store.

[2] See footnote 1.

We complained about the water; we complained about the lack of proper care given at the hospital. And they gave in to our demands. In time, they got what we wanted them to get for the store.

*How was it after Siles Zuazo became president?*[3]

We were a match for Siles, too. We continued lodging our complaints and making our demands, but we stopped going to other places. He abandoned us, the hypocrite. It was ridiculous. He didn't want to cooperate with us; he short-changed us at the commissary. He was a bad man.

*Did the schools improve after the Revolution of 1952?*

Yes. Before, there wasn't even a secondary school. The miners weren't allowed to have secondary schools. But after the revolution they built secondary schools. They built a secondary school in Santa Fe, and academies for the girls to learn sewing and other things. They opened literacy schools at night for the adults. We even demanded schools for the countryside, and now there are such schools. Now there is a lot of civilization.

*Was there a parents' association in the school?*

The director of the school nominated the parent association members. We went to every meeting. Whenever there were complaints or anything else, we had to be present.

*What work did this association do?*

They asked us for things that would help the children. Occasionally we contributed money to buy things they needed.

*How did Filemón do at school?*

After he was thirteen he continued without failing a year, *Comadre*. You always have to do a *ch'alla*, [a ritual offering to the *Pachamama*] when children are thirteen years old. Soon I will have to do one for Aníbal, to celebrate his thirteen years. With Filemón we had his fortune read by a *k'amili*, an herbalist. He came without Juan knowing and did it all. Your *compadre* doesn't understand these things; he doesn't want to. I paid fifty pesos [about five dollars] to the *k'amili* and he told Filemón's fortune from cards. He said, "He will have good luck. He will never fail at school. He will do well until he graduates." As he fore-

---

[3] When Siles Zuazo entered as president in 1956 his first major act was to approve the Stabilization Plan introduced by U.S. advisor George Jackson Eder (1968). The plan to freeze wages in order to halt inflation was rejected by the miners, who reorganized their party affiliation with the Left Revolutionary Movement under Juan Lechín.

told, Filemón went through school without failing or missing a single year. He was a good student.

*Who came to this party to celebrate his thirteenth birthday?*

My relatives and *compadres:* my friends, my brother and sister-in-law, and their children. We were all together.

*Did Filemón's friends come? Were there presents?*

Lots of Filemón's friends came. They brought him glasses, parchments for diplomas, and little greeting cards; they brought him clothes, underpants, undershirts, that sort of thing. I was very grateful.

*What did you serve?*

I had chocolate and papaya for the children, and also a chicken cooked without hot peppers. For the adults I made chicken with peppers, and we had *chicha* and beer. The children had their birthday party at four-thirty and afterward they left; then we had our party with dancing.

*What is the name of the thirteenth year celebration?*

It is called *Kinsay Chunka Tayoj.*

*Did you have a party like that for María?*

No, I didn't, *Comadre.* We will have one when she finishes secondary school. For Aníbal, however, we have to do it this year, because if we don't, he might have bad luck. We have to have a fine *ch'alla* blessing, and ensure a good future for him.

*How did you arrange the table for Filemón's ch'alla?*

It was at night, and it was just Filemón, the *K'amili,* and me. Your *compadre* was not there.

*Was he working?*

Yes, he was working. We blessed him and the thing was done. I know how to do these things.

*How did Filemón like it?*

He didn't like it, but he had to have his fortune told.

*What else did the K'amili say?*

He asked God to help Filemón be a good student so he could become an architect or an engineer. Then he burned some incense over him, but took him some place else to do the burning. I spent almost one hundred pesos on this [about ten U.S. dollars], for the llama foetuses, and for those sweet charms of glory.

*Do lots of people do this in Santa Fe?*
Everyone does it. There is also a celebration when they get their baccalaureates. But I didn't have such a party for Filemón because we didn't have enough money and there was no one to act as godfather of the ring. My poor son doesn't have a ring, and they say that's why our bad luck continues, *Comadre.*

*I would like you to describe for me in greater detail what you did on a given day: the rhythm of work, what time you got up, whether you turned on the radio, what you made for breakfast — the complete cycle of a typical day in Santa Fe. I would like to know all the details, such as what kind of kitchen utensils and tools you used, what your kitchen was like, and so forth.*
In Santa Fe we got up at five in the morning to make a light meal. We call it *con pica,* because it is made with lots of ground beef and highly spiced vegetables. I would give it to Juan before he went down into the mine, because he couldn't go in the morning without eating. What energy would he have for working? He had to get out of bed at the crack of dawn to breakfast on this meal that I made and served him in a small casserole. In addition, he would eat thick Quaker Oats with milk and bread and then go to the mine. Then I would go to the store to get our supplies, meat and vegetables. I got back at nine and started cooking another meal for when he came out of work at noon. They always went home for lunch at Santa Fe. We never sent lunch down with them as we did at San José.

I would cook him something good for lunch at noon, a meal with porridge or some well-made rice. On workdays I had his lunch and his second course and his tea ready at twelve o'clock. By one o'clock he was back in the mine. In the evening he had another meal, with well-stewed soup and a dessert, ready for him around five o'clock. He always ate three times a day when he worked at the mine.

*How did you cook?*
With dried llama dung or, some days, with wood: sometimes with kerosene, on a metal stove with a chimney. But the smell of kerosene gives me a headache. I didn't like to use that to cook. With llama dung I always cooked on a metal stove. I had a big one but I gave it away when I came here. My cousin from Huanuni came and said to me, "*Comadre,* why are you taking the metal stove? Let me have it. I'll buy it from you, but let me have it because it is old and we can cook on it. Over in Oruro they don't use this kind of stove. There you will cook

on a portable stove or on a brazier, and this won't do you any good."

That's why we left the stove. Now it weighs on my soul that I left it! I might even go back and get it and return the fifty pesos which he gave me. My husband said, "We'll let my brother have it. That stove cost 380 pesos! Your *compadre* is very kind. He is capable of even giving his shoes away and walking off without them.

*And what did you do at the store? Did you have a bit of time to chat with your friends?*
We went to the store early in the morning.

*At what time?*
I had to go stand in line because it was very crowded at Santa Fe, so I would go at three in the morning just to get a place.

*Did you have to wait there until they opened and started selling?*
Yes, we had to stay there in line until eight-thirty, when they opened the store.

*Five hours?*
Yes, and when there was a meat shortage we would go at two in the morning to be in line early for meat. They would let you have four or five kilos of meat for the whole week. I had to go. I would get there early so as to be first in line, so I could be back by nine-thirty or ten.

*And your children stayed at home?*
They stayed at home. I went to stand in line, leaving them at home, and when someone else arrived in line, I would tell them "I am first in line. I arrived at such-and-such an hour." Then I would run home, have my tea, and come back to the line to get the meat. The second in line also went home to have her tea and then came back. I would also leave the line to do my errands, to get my vegetables, or whatever, so that I could get home and start cooking as soon as I got the meat. I looked for ways to get a bit of rest. The women who went down to the store at nine got their supplies at ten-thirty or eleven, and they couldn't have a meal waiting for their husbands. They couldn't get it ready by noon. They would give them a bit of tea, some chocolate, or maybe some roast meat on bread, and the poor worker would have to make do with that. If a man goes back in without his lunch, without his soup, he can't do anything in the mine. And with all the gas in the mine, bread and meat aren't enough for the stomach. Soup is the most nourishing, isn't that so? Food, tea — a good tea with milk — in addition to a solid lunch,

that's what keeps a body going. I always went early in the morning so that I could do my work there quickly so as to find some time to rest, at least thirty minutes or an hour to lie down on my bed.

When my friends got to the store late, I would say to them, "Why do you come so late? Why do you sleep so late? You should come as I do, early in the morning, at five. I am not sleepy then, even though I am already an old lady."

I am not a young girl anymore, able to sleep until eight. I have brains. When I went to the store I wasn't sleepy. One is at one's best in the morning; besides, in the afternoon they would only give us a few kilos of meat, whereas they would give us lots of meat early in the morning. In the afternoon all we could get was *ch'ampa* or head meat, that's all. You have to be lively and smart, *Comadre*, and take advantage of the opportunity to get to the store early.

I also sewed clothes, shirts, everything for the children. I never bought ready-made clothes from the store, never. I didn't like them. I always got material to sew things my own way for María or Elena or Ana.

*What are the most serious and common problems for women in the mining community?*
What do you mean, *Comadre*?

*Well, did you have fights or arguments about certain things? Do you remember specific problems that your friends had with their husbands, or with the company?*

Yes, I do, *Comadre*. There was a man named Aquino, who fought a lot with his wife. Sometimes he beat her, even when she was pregnant; he had no respect for her even then. I had to get between them and defend her like a devil so that he wouldn't hit her. He would come in at three in the morning from where he had been drinking. We lived right next to each other — just a wall separated us — and we could hear everything that went on.

My poor *comadre* would scream out, "*Comadre! Comadre!* See how he is hitting me! He is hitting me now, in my condition. Defend me! Help me, *Comadre!*" she said.

But I would be sleeping with a pillow over my head so I heard her as though she was far away, as in a dream. So the woman would come into our room with her enormous belly, and he was all over her, beating her pitilessly right in front of our eyes. Oh, that was a bad man who worked at Santa Fe! I would smack him as one would a child. I was very

strong; even though I am small and thin, I have lots of power [laughter].
I hit him in the chest and knocked him onto the other bed.

"Why are you beating her like this, when she is with child? Don't
you have a heart? Don't you have any compassion? Isn't she your wife?
What is this?"

"I want to throw this woman out like a piece of shit! This woman is
good for nothing. She doesn't know how to save money; she doesn't
know how to do anything. *Comadre*, you have to forgive me, even
though I am angering you. But she isn't like you — she is not thrifty like
you and she doesn't do anything at all. She doesn't try to earn a bit extra
for the children. You see those children, how dirty and ragged they are?
And their pants aren't even mended. She is always strolling in the
streets, taking the day off, walking without a care with her sisters, while
my poor children are home without food or clean clothing. Do you see
anything good here, *Comadre?* You see everything that happens. And
she calls *me* all kinds of names! That's why I was beating her."

He begged my pardon on his knees, crawling on his knees in front
of me, begging my pardon, because I was godmother to all of his children.

*Was it true that she didn't take care of her children?*
Yes, he said so.

*The woman was not thrifty?*
She didn't save money. She wasn't thrifty. "You see how I work," he
said. "I don't earn as much as your husband, but I work day and night,
and you see how much I earn." He earned around a thousand five hundred, a thousand eight hundred ($150 to $180) a month while Juan
earned one thousand eight hundred to two thousand ($180 to $200) a
month. It wasn't much, but *Comadre*, I'll tell you right now, that man
had no place to sit down.

*Was it his wife's fault?*
It must have been both of their faults, *Comadre*. The man drank a
lot, and no woman is going to save money when she sees her man
drinking. And I would guess she would spend money badly on other
things. It must be because of that. Now she has six little children and
two grown. My goddaughter is growing up, the oldest one called Severina Aquino. She is healthy and tall. But her mother had a total of
eight children.

I lived in the midst of my *compadres*. Over here my *compadre* Segundino Choque, over there my *compadre* Aquino, and behind me my other *compadre*, who is now dead. I always lived in the midst of them, surrounded by my *compadres*.

*Is it better that way?*

It is. They wanted to come and live near me so that I would make their husbands respect them. They have always respected your *compadre*.

*Is it the women who chose the compadres?*

Yes, the women. I have been very good at it and I knew how to make the women behave properly towards their husbands, too. My *compadre* Choque used to fight with his wife the same way; they fought a lot. They would go to parties and it wouldn't do them any good, and on religious celebrations they would come and go, visiting many houses; that wasn't good for them because they drank so much. In the mines there were civil marriage ceremonies. They themselves had a celebration, but it did no good. They went out drinking whenever they celebrated their *aynis* [reciprocal exchanges], but then they always returned fighting with each other. I would have to be dancing around their house to keep them apart nighttime, daytime, or in the afternoon. They always needed me to keep them apart.

They would say to me, "You have been a good person who has taught us how to respect each other and how to behave properly with people. Not even a dog can urinate in our faces." But they would still come and behave badly in my house again.

But what can I do? Everyone has gone. That's the way life is. Some have gone to Japo, others have gone to Morococala or to Catavi, or towards Potosí. I have lots of *compadres* in many of the houses in front of the school, although many have gone to the frontiers. But anyway, in those days my *compadres* would fight each other. And I had to be dancing between them, stopping them from hitting each other. *I* have never fought like that since then [laughter].

*Do you remember how it used to snow in Santa Fe?*

Oh, it was different in the old days, *Comadre*. Now it doesn't snow as much. We used to have snowfalls of five to six meters, that's how hard it used to snow. One night we heard rain. It rained and quietly turned to snow. The next morning, when your compadre wanted to go out to work, he opened the door and snow fell in.

# 11

## Luck in the Mines

Luck in the mines is a combination of appealing to the
right spiritual forces, behaving in accord with rules of
work, and fulfilling responsibilities to kin and co-
workers. Accidents in the mine are a constant re-
minder of the interdependence of mine workers. What
happens in the home influences the worker's frame of
mind at work—so much so that workers regard accidents as the result of upset social relations at home. If
many accidents happen within the same work group,
workers question the luck of the group leader. Juan de-
scribes the tension he lived with as he tried to balance
his responsibilities at home and at work. In his home
life he also conformed strictly to the regulations of the
mining camp and demanded his rights in that context.
As a dutiful son he struggled to get his mother his job-
related benefits in the hospital, confronting engineers
who tried to usurp them. As head of his work group,
he bore the responsibility for any accident or mishap
on the job. The best he could hope for was that nothing bad would happen at home or on the job.

In 1954 I had many difficulties. For one thing, my faithful friend Grajeda, who worked on my team, had an accident. It was his and my bad
luck that he cut his hand and had to go to the hospital.

Then my mother who lived in Oruro wrote that she was suffering
from lung disease. I had a lot of trouble getting transportation to bring
her back to Santa Fe. The manager, Cesar Zuña Morales, was in La

Paz at the time and I couldn't get any help from anyone in Santa Fe. Señor Montaño, the head of the personnel office, knew me fairly well, and I begged him to help me by letting me use a truck to go down to Oruro to bring my mother to the hospital in Santa Fe. He agreed.

It so happened that the superintendent of the mines, Engineer Lucio Rojas who was replacing Engineer Zuña, had to go down in the afternoon with the construction engineer. I went with them at five in the afternoon and was then supposed to return with him and my mother. We got to Oruro at a quarter to seven at night, and I went to my mother's house.

The driver said, "I will come back soon. First I will drop off the engineer and then I will come and pick you up at your mother's house."

When I got to my mother's house, I found that she was almost dying. I waited for the driver to return at eight o'clock, but he did not arrive. He was still missing at eight-thirty. At a quarter to nine he showed up and said to me, "The engineer said he is going back and that we can't take a sick person in the car, because he has to take his family back with him. So you can either stay here or return without your mother."

At that moment I recalled what the manager had said and told the driver, "The order that the manager gave to the garage chief included my mother on the passenger list." I took my mother and made them let her get into the car. When we got to the engineer's house where he was waiting with his family he wanted to force my mother to get out.

There was still room in the back of the truck, so I said, "We'll ride back here, because we can ride any place. We are used to riding in trucks and in any kind of vehicle; we won't mind. However, I should remind you, Engineer, that the return trip was not scheduled for you but for me. I have a written order from the garage chief, Señor Fernandez, and he gave me the vehicle. You were not scheduled to return and came just to be dropped off in Oruro."

The engineer replied that he didn't know that his family, who had been in Cochabamba, had arrived the day before. He hadn't come to pick up his family, but just to wait for them at the train station.

At that moment Engineer Raul Arce arrived. He knew me fairly well and said, "What are you arguing about?"

The construction engineer said, "I want to take my family, who arrived the day before yesterday and were waiting for me, back to Santa Fe. I came down with this vehicle and now I want to take them back. But this worker here is taking his mother back to the hospital in Santa Fe."

Engineer Arce asked the driver if I had authorization to use the vehicle. The driver answered that I had personally received the authorization from the garage chief, Fernández, that the engineer was just supposed to ride down, and that the return trip was specifically for me. Engineer Raul Arce told this engineer to be patient and to wait just a few more hours; then he could go back with Arce who had to return in his own vehicle, a pick-up truck. "We can go back in the pick-up truck," he assured him. "Just wait for me a little while. I'll be back as soon as possible."

The engineer was annoyed when he heard this. "The vehicle came down with me and has to return with me," he said.

Engineer Arce, getting annoyed himself, countered, "This vehicle's return trip belongs to the worker and he has to take his mother."

The other engineer didn't want to ride in Arce's pick-up, so he came up close to the driver and said, "At least take my wife with you in the station wagon." He stayed behind with his children to return later in Arce's pick-up.

Despite all that trouble I managed to get my mother to the hospital in Santa Fe. She got worse on the way and was almost dead when she arrived. At two in the morning I was by her side, not having slept at all. My mother woke up in a delirium and said, "Son, where are we? Now your father isn't here either. Where are we going?"

My father had been dead for years. I don't remember exactly when he died, but it was when I was about eight years old. It was 1954 and I was twenty-eight. I realized my mother was delirious and was afraid she was dying, so I ran to my house to warn my wife.

"My mother is much worse," I said. "We can go see her when she wakes up in the morning since I have a permission slip from the head of the medical department that we can be with her. Her doctor will be there in the morning, too."

My wife and I went down to see her. After we got there, my mother came back to her senses and could speak sensibly. I asked the doctor to give her serum. With this my mother improved 50 percent. By seven in the morning she was no longer delirious, and her temperature had gone down.

The next day I went to work at a quarter to seven. I went to my work site directly, because all I had to do was go to my tool hut and change my clothes. At ten the majordomo's assistant came to where I was drilling to tell me that my wife was calling me. I thought my mother had worsened or was dead. Frightened, I stopped the drilling machine, gave it to my assistant, and went to the office to ask the captain for permission to leave. (We called the bell ringer "captain" because he dispatched the people, the ore cars, and everything else that went in the elevator.)

The captain said to me, "Let me see your order to go out."

"I don't have an exit order, but here is the majordomo's assistant who has come to call me up."

So the majordomo's assistant said, "Yes, he is wanted on the telephone, and that's why I have come to get him. It is urgent that he go out." And so the captain let me out.

Petrona said that my mother had taken another turn for the worse. In a panic I went again to Doctor Sandi. He called me into his office and said, "This is not a serious disease; your mother will soon get well. She is like this now just because she is weak. If I give her the medicines that we have in our pharmacy — and we have plenty of good medicines both in tablet and liquid form — she will get well. But we can't give her too much too quickly because she could get worse."

I went back in to work immediately, because I was drilling and I had to finish by noon so we could set off a charge. There was no ore for the loader as yet and the chutes were empty. As soon as I went in, I went to the compressor to make sure I would have enough air pressure. At five of twelve they turned the air off, which would have made it impossible for me to load. The man at the air compressor agreed to keep it on for a while, so I went in and grabbed my drill again. There was plenty of time for loading, but I still had to drill seven holes for the dynamite. I really hurried and got it done by about twenty to twelve. I set the charges and lit the fuses at five to twelve, letting a little air in so the smoke would clear rapidly.

But it was my bad luck that the charges didn't all go off. I had set twelve charges, but only eight went off. I went out. I didn't want to go back in because it was full of smoke. On one occasion, when I had gone back in immediately, I almost lost my life because I got sick with the smoke and the gas from the explosion.

I brooded about those charges as I walked home for lunch. I didn't even feel like eating because those charges had failed to go off. I wondered if I had made a mistake in setting them, but I reminded myself that maybe some charges went off at the same instant. Still, I was pretty sure that they had all gone off separately.

At a quarter to one I returned to my work site right away. (The elevator took us down only between a quarter past one and two.) I climbed down a ladder left in the shaft from previous works and ran right to my station where I saw that all the detonators had gone off properly. And my assistant had forgotten to take the drill out! Fortunately, I had put it behind a rock where it was somewhat protected. "You take it," I had told him. "I don't have time to check anything because I have to go out." But he had left it, and I hadn't noticed because I was so worried and in such a rush to get out to see about my mother.

I looked for the drill where I had left it, but I saw only the hoses that connected it to the air and water pipes, the piston, and the valves — everything but the machine. I looked, but it wasn't underneath the hoses. It wasn't anywhere to be seen. Then I went back to the face and looked where I might have left it, right where the charges were set. I wanted to move some rocks to look, but I couldn't because there was still some gas; I was afraid of being overcome.

I went to my coca-chewing niche. My assistant had arrived and he asked, "How did it work? Did all the charges go off?"

I just said, "Where did you put the drill? Didn't you take it out?"

"I didn't take it out."

"I told you to take everything out. That was your responsibility! How could you leave it there? Now the explosion has probably destroyed it. Who knows? Are you going to pay for it, or am I? They will probably make us both pay for it. And that drill, how many hundreds of dollars must it have cost?" I was shouting at him.

Without stopping for our coca break, we went back to the work site and turned on the air hoses to clear the air. We shovelled that place out in a flash but still didn't find it. It wasn't there! We searched everywhere but it just wasn't anywhere to be found.

I left in a rage for my coca break and then went back to the work site. We continued to chew coca, bickering about the drill.

Majordomo González came by and said, "Lend me your drill to clear the loose rock from the ceilings and sides of the tunnels."

To avoid that I said, "The machine is in the repair shop. Its braces were loose, and I sent it in to have them tightened."

He said, "All right, I'll borrow somebody else's," and he left.

We went back to the site and, with the luck of a blind man, I found the drill, buried under the load, just as the carts came to be loaded. Luckily nothing was wrong with it except a broken brace. That was quickly replaced at the repair shop, and we brought it right back and set it up to try it. It worked perfectly.

When I was pushing the cart with the load I met González at the turn. "They've brought the machine back to us," I told him. "Take it now if you still need it."

"Fine, Rojita," he replied. "I'll send a laborer to get it and you can give it to him detached from the hoses. He just needs the machine."

So they took it, but, when they used it on the first drill hole, the axle fell apart and the whole machine came to pieces — the whole die-cast body, the barrel, the grommets, everything. I simply told them that I had given them a perfectly fine machine and they were responsible for what happened. I said that they probably hadn't put in enough oil, and when it froze they forced it.

"All you have to do is destroy the machine's cylinder and the rest will fall apart," I said.

We took the drill to the mechanic and he looked it over, saying, "Who is to blame, the driller?"

"Well, it wasn't me," I replied. "Of course it was the driller, but the machine didn't break when I was using it, but rather when a house driller was using it."

They held him responsible for the axle and the grommet used to drill the blast hole. The driller, whose name was Martín Cullco, said, "I think the machine was already broken and they lent it to me because it was broken. At first they didn't want to lend it to me, but then they thought it over and gave it to me. That's how they tried to get out of it."

Since I had already told Gonzalez that we had taken the machine to the mechanic to tighten the braces, and he could see that it had a new one, he asked the mechanic, "Did Rojas bring this machine in just to have the brace tightened, or was there other work done on it?"

The mechanic replied, "Yes, he did, and I just replaced the brace. It wasn't broken, just cracked, so I put on a new one."

What the mechanic said saved me. Only my assistant and I knew what had really happened. It wasn't just the machine itself that was destroyed. The springs of the valves for the fan and everything was smashed, because it was a big explosion bringing down almost four meters of load on top of the drill.

We always ran three to four hundred meters away to wait for the explosion, advising everyone in the passageways to stay put. People admired my blast holes because they took down such a heavy load. Usually it took me many hours to do the drilling, but then our advances were made in less than an hour. The other workers preferred to drill for just one or two hours and then set off the charges. We would spend four, five, or even eight hours drilling and then advance almost four meters in a single hour. And we set off charges every day. In ten days, that would be at least thirty-five meters. Most of the time I had no trouble with the charges. So you see the explosion with my charges was enormous.

After this piece of luck, the engineer, Cesar Zuña Morales, told the supply master to give me a new drill and all the accessories.

"Give this driller a new machine because he is always cutting and finding new veins. He is the kind of worker we need to support and should have a new machine to work with. And fix his old machine for the house teams," he ordered.

*Caramba!* My assistant and I looked at each other. No one else around here has the luck we have! we said to each other with our eyes. So, later the majordomo gave me a voucher to take to the supply master to get a new machine. He gave me an Atlas drill. That's a machine that has more speed and greater strength. The only problem is that it's hard to use when you start drilling a new shaft in a narrow passageway, because it has a very strong recoil. But for drilling in a face with a broad advance it is first-rate, an excellent machine. It's so strong it just pulverizes the rock.

In March I had another problem in the shaft we were working on. My assistant, Zenón Grajeda, went up in the shaft, without telling me. He started down as I was shoring it up with timbers and sweeping out the loose rock in the tunnel. I thought he had already gone out. I covered up the chute with a grill so that loose rocks wouldn't fall through, and shouted down below to where I thought he was. "Be careful! I'm covering the chute up in here," I yelled.

He didn't answer me, of course, because he wasn't down there. He was rolling down in his cart while I was freeing the passage of the loose rock. Some of it fell on him and he lost control of the cart. He fell from the shaft to the main passageway, down the ladder, screaming "Be careful!" as he rolled down. Some rock had fallen right on his face. The poor boy was laid out as if dead in the middle of the passageway, unconscious in the cart.

From the shaft where I was, I couldn't do a thing to help him. He was quite far down, and there was nobody down there to help him. I had to go almost five hundred meters to bring him back to my teammates. He was bleeding a lot, and I couldn't do much to stop the blood.

I took off my shirt and wrapped it around his head. He was snoring like a man asleep. With great care I put his arms over my shoulders and hoisted his body on my naked back, carefully dragging him step by step down the passageway.

Engineer Guerra, who measured the advances, came by. He must have heard the noise I was making, grunting and hauling my assistant along. As soon as I saw his light, I shouted, "Help me! My partner has had an accident! I am coming down!"

He rushed up to help me bring my partner down, and we took him along the tunnel to the main shaft. By the time we got to the end of the tunnel he was bleeding like a fountain. How much blood do we have in our bodies? I wondered. A lot. It wouldn't stop.

Finally, we managed to get him to the office. By holding each others' elbows we made a swing to support him and brought the boy in. He was light and it wasn't hard to carry him that way. When we got to the office we rang the bell hard. Fortunately the elevator came right away; we removed the cart that was inside and came up, ringing the bell all the way. The men on top thought we were just trying to get out without the superintendent's permission, but of course it wasn't that at all.

When we got out he was still bleeding. There hadn't been a telephone at the level below, so we weren't able to call ahead for an ambulance to meet us. As soon as we got out of the mine we called the ambulance, and fortunately, it came quickly. It had been standing right at the hospital door because it's not supposed to move from there.

In the hospital the man stopped making any sounds. He was quiet and looked dead. I was frightened and started to cry.

*Caramba!* What have I done? I thought. But it wasn't my fault; the rock had beaten me.

Dr. Sandi came in and said, after examining him with his stethescope, "Nothing will happen to him. He has just had the breath knocked out of him." He gave him artificial respiration by lifting his arms up and down. Then he gave him injections. The boy was filled with injections, but he still wasn't breathing right. He was just sighing.

I was sure he was going to die. They went to tell his wife that her husband had had a bad accident. Doña María came to the hospital right away, screaming and crying as she entered. My wife also came in.

When the two women met his wife started screaming at my wife, "That is your husband's *luck!*" as though I had forced the boy to work with me!

The two women were fighting because at that time we had had bad luck on my team. There were frequently accidents among my workers, and I had injuries myself, but no serious ones. Previously my team hadn't had any serious accidents, just small incidents. But during the three months after Grajeda had a serious accident so did Fernández — "*Chingalo*" as we called him — then Zenón, and then Gregorio. Those three had accidents during February, March, and April. After that there were no more accidents or even any bad scares. Everything worked out well, eventually.

The doctor gave Grajeda some oxygen and he started breathing normally again. We didn't go back to work that day, but stayed to watch over Grajeda.

This happened near the end of March. We went back to work the next day. That month a cart driver transferred in from the ore concentration plant, and it was the first day he worked in the mine. He was young and recently married. He didn't have children yet. His nickname was "*Terceros.*"

On about the first of April this boy forgot his head lamp and left it outside in the central dispatching area for the carts.

"I didn't bring my lamp," he said. "Send me out, please, Maestro."

"Go get it. Why did you forget it? You are going to make us late," I scolded.

Now, the dispatcher certainly knew the internal work regulations. There must have been some negligence when the cart driver went out, because, somehow, the dispatcher left him alone. He should never have left a man who was in the mines for the first time. They should have gone out together.

So what happened to that boy, *Terceros?* Halfway up the shaft he must have gotten frightened or something and fell from the elevator down the shaft. I was just crossing the shaft when I heard a noise as though a bag was falling, clunk! clunk! clunk! It was him falling down the empty shaft. He was completely destroyed as he fell from level 108 to level 140. I was just about to stretch my leg across the shaft when the worker fell past me, his legless body falling into the water at the bottom of the pit. His legs and fingers were floating there too, but his boots were gone. He was covered with blood, completely red. *Caramba!* I couldn't go backward or forward. I was frozen in my tracks, speechless.

I ran down to Terceros shouting and crying, "Little brother, what has happened to you?" A pump operator named Julio Canedo, who was waiting there at the elevator because they hadn't let him out at the right time and he was late for lunch, helped me pick him up and put him on the elevator. We collected his legs and put them where they belonged. Still weeping, I went back to work. I worked until four in the afternoon. After that I couldn't stand it anymore, I was so upset. I was looking around as though something was going to happen to me, or someone was going to come to grab me and arrest me. I was so horrified!

At four I said to my assistant, "Let's get out, Acuña, Let's leave. I am too nervous to stay down here any longer." So we went out and I went home.

They took the body out for the wake. Wakes were still held at the union hall at that time. I went to the wake that night, and the next day we didn't go in to work. The others went in as usual, but my assistant and I stayed out. We went in for a minute to get our time cards and to meet the mining superintendent, Lucio Rojas. He knew that I was well liked by the administration, especially by Aurelio Mendiola, the manager, and immediately agreed to our staying out.

"Of course, Rojas, take your time card and take the rest of the day off." We went out. He knew what had happened because the pump operator, Julio Caneda, had told him.

*I commented to Juan that a miner's life must depend tremendously on his work companions and that reminded him of another worker who, like the young married man, had died because he had been alone in the mine.*

The veins at Conrado Aquirre's station were running out and his workers weren't earning much money. There was one worker who was very able and especially agile. This man, Mamani, was nicknamed "Little Monkey." He was a young man from Ralinga, near Sorasora. During a rest period this boy, who didn't like to chew coca, went to search for veins. He went off quietly, without telling anyone, and went up an air-shaft that had been abandoned a long time. I had seen that chimney and thought there might be a vein up there. I had put rafters all the way up because I had wanted to check out that shaft. When he saw those new supports "Little Monkey" went up the shaft. He got halfway up and there was overcome by the gas. He died, but no one knew it.

The foreman thought he had left the job, because he often would go out when he didn't feel well. Since he was a good worker, no one paid any attention when he left the station.

It was Hilarón Paiti who saw him go up the chimney and who said to the foreman, "He went up that chimney. I don't know what happened up there, but I saw him go up."

Little Monkey, of course, didn't show up for work from that day on. They went to look for him at his house but he wasn't there. We thought he had gone back to his place in the country. It was when he didn't come back that Paiti remembered he had seen him go up the chimney.

"Let's go see. We'll get up somehow to see that place," said the manager, Arce.

He sent Paiti up the chimney, and when he was half-way up, he shouted, "There's a strange smell up here, Engineer!"

"But what do you see? Go on up and see what's there," said the manager, who was getting annoyed.

"If I expose myself to the gas, who is going to be responsible for me?" asked Paiti, as he came down, refusing to obey the manager. "I am sure Little Monkey is up there," he said, "because it felt as though someone had thrown hot water up my nostrils, it was burning and suffocating. There's gas up there. That's where the Monkey is," he told the engineer.

The men got the air hose and linked it to another so it would be long enough, and we went up, holding our breath. They threw the air hose halfway up in a loop, the way people catch bulls with a lasso. Fortunately, it was long enough to reach the top. We came down immediately, let our breath out, and got away from that place so that we could breathe. They flushed the gas out with the air hose. After that, Ordoñez, the mining carpenter, went up.

"Well, if I die, I shall die with honor," he said. "You are my witnesses that I am going up to save a friend. If something happens to me, you've got to send me some air immediately."

They turned the air on for a minute so that by the time he went up there was no gas. They flushed it out. He saw Little Monkey lying there, dead. He had found a little vein of good-quality mineral. Mamani had gone up to work this.

I don't know why they hadn't worked it earlier. But back then there were veins almost fifteen meters wide, thirty meters wide, huge pockets of ore. So they didn't pay attention to these tiny little veins that we have to work now.

Paiti didn't know that this same bad luck was going to follow him. On one occasion, about five or six months later, a similar thing happened in the same shaft. Some years before, in 1942 or 1943, Bravo's brother had had an accident there. They say he fell down a shaft that was about six meters deep, partially covered. I don't know whether Bravo's brother was careless or what, but he fell and drowned at the bottom of the shaft.

This time Paiti's team had finished drilling, and his two companions went out, leaving Paiti who had just lit the detonators. There was still plenty of air. Paiti then went up to the air-powered elevator and called up to the man who was running the winch, "Bring it up!"

He had gone up just a few meters in the lift when the air powering it ran out. He went up a few meters more with the air that was still in the pipes, but when that ran out the lift started to sink. He screamed at the man who was running the winch to turn on the air and pull it up.

"Turn it on! Turn it back on!"

The man above yelled back, "There's no air pressure. The air is finished."

Hearing this, Paiti managed to climb up some five meters by clinging to cracks in the walls of the shaft. But he couldn't climb up fast enough to save himself. He weakened and slipped and fell into the shaft. The fall hurt him a great deal because it was from a height of about six meters. He broke both legs. Just at that moment the burning fuse was reaching the detonator.

He screamed in desperation, "Save me, comrades! Are you going to let me die here? Save me, my friends!" he shouted. But at that instant the first charge exploded.

The man at the winch got a few cuts on his head from the accident because he wasn't wearing a helmet; he had been working wearing just a *ch'ulito* [woolen cap with ear flaps]. When the rocks dislodged by the explosion fell on him. He was supposed to protect himself by wearing a helmet made of leather.

They didn't find Paiti for three days; his body was all mixed up with the load. The explosion had, literally, made mincemeat of him. There weren't even any big bones left. They were all mashed into pieces. What was left of him didn't even fill up a helmet.

The chief, Rojas, said, "Let's not send this load to the mill before we pick out the flesh." But finally they didn't do this because it was too painful. The whole load went to the mill and was all ground up.

I was about to start work on a new face. It was all loose and crumbly rock, and the job frightened me. Such work is exhausting for a driller because, when you least expect it, the drill can stick and you can't get it out. In order to continue drilling we have to pull out the drill bit by brute force and then pick out the little stones that have fallen in and made the drill bit get stuck. In spite of this, the engineer told me, "Blow it up. Let's see what's in there. If you like, we can give it to someone else to work on later."

I had planned to work there anyway, because I had already spent a lot of time and trouble on it and was experienced at it. I set off the charges, and the first explosion destroyed all the scaffolding in the tunnel. I don't know who had shored up the timbers in that tunnel, but, when they fell, a *Tío* statue sitting on an altar was revealed. His body was larger than a human body. He had a furious expression and was dressed in a blue cape and a red shirt. He had big horns and teeth fifteen centimeters long sticking out of his mouth. Next to the statue was a pile of black coca and white wool. I was so frightened I almost got sick. I was able to leave immediately because it was after work hours. I went home and told my wife what I had seen. It was an old *Tío* statue, left there in 1938, when that section had been abandoned because of flooding.

*As we discussed these accidents and the capricious destiny that workers confront, I began to wonder what kind of spiritual solace workers sought. I asked Juan, "When you were frightened, did you call on the* Tío *or the* Pachamama *to help you?"*

When I was frightened, I didn't call on anyone, because ever since my youth I have been neutral about these things. Before I read the Bible, when something frightened me or loose rock fell all around me, I would say, "*Caramba! Tío*, what's happening?" I would shout that. But after I read the Bible and other books about God I stopped completely.

*When did your interest in the Bible begin?*
In 1961.

*Did a missionary give the Bible to you?*
No. First I bought another book, *Hacia la Cumbre*, a book about how a man is supposed to behave with his family and his wife, and how to make a home — the book tells you about all of that. I bought it on time, and the man who sold it to me was an Evangelist and gave me a Bible as a favor. That's how I came to read the Bible, by myself, without anyone telling me a thing. I had heard people speak of the Bible at Mass and in the churches, but I didn't know what it was about. Many people had told me that only Evangelists read the Bible, and that they have

one Bible and that Catholics have another. I asked the priest who came to San Pedrito in Santa Fe to bring me a little Bible. He did, and I don't remember how much I exchanged the Bible for. [Bolivians use the word "exchange" instead of "buy" when they acquire religious objects since God is in each object and so it is an exchange.] I compared the priest's Bible with the one the Evangelist had given me. They had the same words. Nothing was different. So I got to thinking that our law is one law for all. No one should feel they control it.

The Bible really caught my attention and, to this day, it is still with me. I have a few books about the Bible that I am reading right now. There is another one that Filemón bought while I was working. I have lots of books that discuss the Bible. Before reading the Bible I was very stubborn, very capricious, very degenerate. I didn't even know what my role in my home should have been. I didn't understand anything. I was completely ignorant. When I read the Book, little by little I began to improve myself. I thought a lot, and I stopped being so stubborn. I did it by myself. My success in controlling my bad temper cost me a lot of suffering. When one has a habit it is hard to break. But little by little I changed.

I had friends who took me to the bars and to the whorehouses, and I was getting used to it. I wanted to go out as soon as I was out of work, no matter how tired I was. I would wash and go out on the street, alone, as though I were single and had no family, no one who cared for me. When I thought about it I realized I wasn't behaving properly. That wasn't for me anymore. When I read the Bible it came to me that that just wasn't done, and although now I am still ignorant, I am not as ignorant as I was before.

The Bible leads one to think about two rules that are very difficult to follow. It's easy to say them, but difficult to follow them. The first law of God says, "Love God above all else." That means that we should worship only God, and no other idols. But you can't always follow their advice. For example, there are people who think of the spirits, and even I myself am sometimes confused and say, "Spirits, help me now!" I often think first of the spirits [awichas] instead of calling upon God. Many people also call on the saints before they call on God: "Ah, Saint So-and-so, help me now, please, with a miracle." We shouldn't do this, we should just call on God. God's name should be on the tip of our tongues every second.

And His Son, Jesus Christ's law is, "Love thy neighbor as you love yourself." This is even harder to follow. We can say, "I love my friend;

I love him a lot." But on another day we might hate him. For instance, if a friend disagrees with us over some little thing, *Caramba!* we start looking at the friend as though he were rotten meat, as though to poison him with our look. We are not following God's laws. These laws are very hard to follow. It is almost human nature to have enemies.

*Have you done any witchcraft in the mine or in the community?*

Well, even in the old days, I didn't really believe it worked. At the Santa Fe mining company, under the old boss, Gustavo Amusquivar, they say there was lots of envy even when there was lots of ore. But then, because of lack of development, it became difficult to find that many veins. There was just the Clavo Grande, the big key vein at level twenty-six. So those who worked there were the only ones who made good money; the others were searching for veins which they couldn't find, because the mine was still new and small. The mine needed to be developed much more so that they could find the veins, because it is, in fact, a very rich mine.

So then the workers sprinkled over the Clavo Grande a black donkey's milk that had been boiled with garlic. But they say that it continued yielding the same way. The yield didn't go down at all, and everyone continued earning the same as before. Then, they say, when the vein was ready to run out, the vein moved. Because of that, supposedly, there were many new veins, discovered all over the place. But they were just small veins, no large pockets, like before. I think that happened just because the pocket of ore was finished, and they explored elsewhere. It wasn't the donkey milk.

I saw more of that in 1946, near the Clavo Boyadora where there was another vein, the Clavo Fortuna. That one went from one pocket to another, without a set width. When I drilled straight ahead in the shaft the vein would disappear, reappearing forty or fifty meters, even one hundred meters, away. The vein would jump that much. So it was that the Santa Fe mine did not have regular veins, only pockets — key areas that were easy to lose.

For example, take the case of Calisaya and José Aranibar, whose stations were right near by mine. Where Calisaya was working the rock was pyrite, but where Aranibar was working it was metal. Aranibar had tin, a high-quality metal. But Calisaya's was pyrite and, as with all pyrite, the metal was of very low grade.

Calisaya once said to Aranibar, "Come and work at my station for a few months. I have already suffered enough. My station has lots of dripping water and yours is dry. Let me work at yours for a while, because you earn money I can't earn a thing over here." He got envious, like that. But Aranibar didn't want to trade stations.

"That's our luck," he said. "We each started our veins at the same time, and we have to stick to our stations. We can't trade."

Calisaya had collected lots of hot pepper seeds, and he would burn them, filling the air in the work station with fumes while the men were working. As a result they were constantly leaving their stations because they were sneezing. Aranibar couldn't figure out what kind of gas was making them sneeze. One day he had gone to the bathroom and when he came back smelled charcoal smoke.

He asked himself, Where's that smoke coming from? He followed the smell of the smoke, found Calisaya, and made him confess. They said that in one package there were hot pepper seeds, and in another there were coals burning. Finally, he supposedly threw donkey's milk on the mine face, but nothing came from that either. I myself knew about the hot pepper seeds and charcoal fire. At that time I was working as the majordomo's assistant; I went everyplace and had seen those things. But I didn't see the donkey's milk because that dries rapidly in the dirt.

---

As always, when I asked Juan something, I learned more than I had asked for. I asked about the *Tío* and learned about God. I spoke about witchcraft, and he gave me a lecture on geology as well as the psychology of workers.

# 12

## Union Struggles

All the massacres waged against miners in their struggles are ever present in the consciousness of workers. The most dramatic protest occurred in 1942, in Siglo XX and Cataví,when María Barzola and many other miners and their families were victimized by the repression of the army and government. This history gives the Bolivian miners' union movement its special character. In the following passage, Juan spoke about the massacre on his forty-fourth birthday. He goes on to despair of the internecine violence in which miners became embroiled as competing leaders of the MNR extended their fight into the mines.

I am going to speak a little bit about the massacre in Cataví which occurred in the year 1942, in the park named for María Barzola. That was the year in which the mine workers of Siglo XX asked for an increase in our allowance from general store's supplies. It wasn't a demand for an increase in salaries, only a petition for more supplies from the general store, especially more of the daily ration of bread that we were allowed. In those times the Patiño mine company of Siglo XX-Cataví gave us three rolls of bread a day, and this wasn't enough for an entire family. We asked for more, but the company, Patiño Mines, rejected our petition. Despite that we, the workers who served our nation gathered in a general assembly. This was the largest such assembly in the company's history. The workers decided to march to the offices of the management of Cataví-Siglo XX. The armed forces of the First Regiment were stationed on the hills surrounding the mouth of the mines. As soon as the miners began to appear they fired at them without wounding anyone, and the workers ran back.

One woman named María Barzola, a *palliri*, stood her ground and said, "We are women. Nobody shall ever shut our mouths. As daughters of this nation, as mothers of this nation, as mothers of our children, nobody shall silence us. We shall seize the flag as women and lead the people."

The army stayed put in the hills as the women advanced a few steps bearing the flag. The miners' sons, the sons of these women, were with them. Despite this, the army did not respect the miners' sons or wives and brutally opened fire.

María Barzola, died. The workers had not gone there to kill either the managers or the employers, yet many women died. A woman whose name I can't remember said, "Hurrah for the nation! Hurrah for the mines! The miners are those that give profits to the nation."

There was a second lieutenant, Rodríguez — I remember that officer's name well! He took out his gun and shot her. The woman fell on the ground. She had a small child with her, and they say that the boy also fell to the ground, but out of fright. They say both died. The government's army did not respect either parents or children.

In those times, no workers profited from their work. They didn't know how to take advantage of their daily sacrifice. During those times the families of the miners roamed through the streets crying. They came to my house and I gave them lodging with honesty, courage, and gentlemanliness. The children of the massacred workers did not get an education. They lived by begging. The future of the country is not the parents; it is the children. We have had many governments; some have understood the miners' situation, but others have not. The latter have always kept the worker down. To fight that the miners try to educate their children, but their earnings are insufficient. This is all I can say about the massacre in Cataví on the twenty-first of December.

The elections for our union leadership have always been on the first of May. In 1958 I was elected by the rank and file to be Secretary of Union Conflicts. During September everything was arranged for the installation of the newcomers to the directorate. Meanwhile, the outgoing secretary had to settle all the accounts. He left owing two hundred pesos and said, "We spent some money on extras, however I am responsible for the money missing."

That secretary was against the workers. For example, in 1957 we could leave on vacation and earn the same amount of money as we earned on contract. During our leave, that secretary, Medina, had that taken away from us. We were only given the base pay on vacation. It was useless to reclaim our rights outside the union. We called a meeting to regain that benefit without telling Medina, but it didn't get us anywhere, and we worked in vain.

September arrived, and we dedicated the union building on the fifth. We had a party paid for with union funds. The workers threatened Medina that if he was installed in office, the union would strike at the Santa Fe mine. He wasn't afraid since the people in control of the union liked him. Medina didn't pay any attention to the workers' threats. He joined us at the party and some workers who were more outspoken than most caught him and asked him, "What's wrong with you?" He must have answered that it was done and that they shouldn't speak about that. So the workers beat him up. Well, poor guy, it was pitiful. He couldn't even move. They took him to the hospital because he was beaten badly.

Later in the general assembly meeting, the workers told the council that Medina couldn't come in because we didn't want anyone from the company. But he came in anyway. They said, "If you stay in here, we are going to kill you!" They announced to the general assembly, "This worker must leave immediately! We don't want anyone from the company. We don't want agents!"

*Did he belong to the MNR?*

Yes, he belonged to the MNR, but he was against the workers. Medina was always an intruder. He was cruel with the workers. I wonder why?

During the month of October we had a conflict with Siles Zuazo's government. The president decreed the Monetary Stabilization Act devaluing the boliviano. He had no wish to better our situation. There were many problems around the company store because the price of imported goods went up during those times. But the government didn't give in.

President Siles Zuazo said, "There will be no raise in salaries!"

We only wanted a wage that would make up for the devaluation of currency, not an actual raise in wages. When we had asked for a raise and the government had granted it, we never reaped the benefits. On the contrary, the government took back the little they gave us through the devaluation of currency. The only ones who benefited were those who were paid in dollars, especially the engineers and the office managers. For the workers there was no raise in the wages because the price of products still went up and it wasn't enough for anything. Before, for example, a pair of working pants cost fifteen to twenty-five pesos for a good pair, but after we received the first raise in our salaries following stabilization, the same pants cost forty-five to fifty pesos. The raise was worthless. Those who took advantage were the merchants. We have only seen fraud.

When we chose someone to represent us in La Paz, we did not want any of the general secretaries or leaders to represent us before Siles Zuazo's government. We were mistrustful because they were detaining the union leaders. So we decided to nominate a worker, someone conscientious, but who did not belong to the council. This worker got 100 percent of all the demands we made. Until the end he fought for the workers. After his first term ended in 1959 he was chosen once again to Workers' Control. While he was a leader this youth gained many victories for the workers. He gained a bit of everything.

In the elections of 1957 Victor Carrasco was elected general secretary of the Federation of Miners Unions. He was a short man with a moustache. With the young worker who had become a leader there, Carrasco couldn't hide anything the old guard did behind the backs of the workers. They used to yell at each other during the assembly because they were enemies. On one occasion, during the general assembly they were arguing as usual, and finally the workers turned against them, saying, "We haven't come to see people boxing. We want to have an assembly without any fighting." They reflected on this and didn't fight any more.

On another occasion, all the top leaders had to go to La Paz. They only called for the main leaders such as the general secretary, the secretary of finance, and the secretary of public relations. We lesser leaders did not go. Although the government gave guarantees of safe travel, they were detained in La Paz. We miners went to La Paz to protest because we couldn't tolerate that type of repression.

Siles was guilty of all of those irregularities in the treatment of the workers. Before he entered as president the workers got everything they asked for from Paz Estenssoro. But the cost of living was rising day-by-day to the clouds and we couldn't support ourselves. In the end, we realized that the rise in salaries was leading to monetary inflation. So Siles Zuazo decreed monetary stabilization when he came to power. From then on there were no raises in wages and everything was frozen.

With the stabilization many conflicts with the government began. There was even a revolution in Huanuni. During that revolution, they killed Celestino Gutierrez, who favored Siles Zuazo. The rest of us favored Paz Estenssoro always. In those times, all the mining districts had arms except Santa Fe, because it did not have any regiment. In Siglo XX-Cataví, the workers obtained arms, for example a light piece of equipment, a light gun, and there were also pistols, rifles, and other arms when they disarmed the Colorado Regiment. San José mines also disarmed the Camacho Regiment in the same district of Oruro, and Huanuni disarmed the Ingavi Regiment of Challapata. Then everyone had arms and they weren't afraid to fight.

We left Santa Fe to have a rally calling for the solidarity of Huanuni with Santa Fe, but the miners in Huanuni did not accept us. We wanted to join our friends, the workers of Cataricagua, but Celestino Gutierrez had already called for an assembly in Duncan.

"The mining workers of Santa Fe are coming to assault us, not to fraternize with us!" he told the crowd.

When the miners from Huanuni heard this, they positioned themselves at the curve on the road to Duncan mines. We arrived, shouting hurrays.

"Viva Huanuni! Hurray for the government of Paz Estenssoro," we said as we entered. We were always against Siles Zuazo because he wanted us to fight. When we reached Duncan corner, they stoned us. They gashed many heads with stones, as in the case of a fellow named Victor Lima. They stoned us even in the trucks. When we felt the stones, the driver in the second truck that I was in — his name was Enrique Colque, and he had plenty of experience as a driver for the company — he turned around and we went back. Our truck was small and quick, but other trucks were too big and couldn't turn around immediately. They broke the window of those other trucks, and everything happened to the truck drivers. They split their skulls and bruised their eyes with stones. So we returned because of the way they stoned us.

When they found this out, the workers of Siglo XX, Machacamarca, San José and everywhere were very angry. They took revenge on those from Huanuni. A congress was supposed to take place in Huanuni, and

Siles Zuazo wanted to intervene. The miners came from Siglo XX and everywhere, but those from Huanuni didn't want to receive the unions from Siglo XX or Santa Fe. They treated us like enemies. They only wanted to deal with the mines in the south and Colquiri. Then the workers of Siglo XX came in huge Leyland trucks, up to the bridge on the road to Cataví. From there, they walked. They made a revolution and hanged Celestino Gutierrez in the main square. They were still killing each other with firearms when Siles Zuazo went to Oruro in his plane. In the midst of the revolution, he arrived in Huanuni. He is the one who calmed things down.

He said, "Whatever happens, I don't care if I die, I don't care if they kill me, but I will quiet this revolution."

He came without any guards or police. He was a tough man. When he arrived, the revolt ended. They took Celestino Gutierrez down from his gallows, and his kin took his body to the village where they mourned him.

Once Carrasco entered as our secretary general, he tried to find out ways to regain the benefits taken away from us. We lost the contract payment during vacation time only for one year. Some didn't even lose a year.

For example, in my case, I always had vacation during the month of December, the end of the year. I didn't lose a year because I didn't take leave, since I thought that they wouldn't pay my wage even though I was part of the directing board of the union. Whatever the government said was not reliable. They didn't fulfill their promises. But that time, they kept their promise and paid from the month of December.

Under monetary stabilization we were working well, since the cost of living did not go up any further. During the month of May, 1960, Victor Paz Estenssoro won again with Juan Lechín as vice president. Siles Zuazo wanted to hand over the presidency to Walter Guevara Arce, but Paz Estenssoro had a strong backing, and he won. They had made an agreement after the Revolution of the Ninth of April of 1952 that Victor Paz Estenssoro had to enter first because the revolution was made Siles Zuazo and Walter Guevara Arce while Paz Estenssoro was in Buenos Aires, Argentina. Those two wanted the presidency, but the key man in the MNR was Victor Paz Estenssoro, so they agreed that he assume power. They agreed that he would be followed by Hernan Siles Zuazo, then Juan Lechín, and finally Walter Guevara Arce.

They didn't follow through on the plan, and only Siles Zuazo came to power. Then Paz Estenssoro began his candidacy again with Lechín. Siles Zuazo didn't accept this and they fought among themselves. "Wasn't the compromise this way? Aren't we going to fulfill our commitment? What is going to happen?" they asked.

As a consequence of these internal conflicts in the movement, there have been disturbances. In Santa Fe, there was even a revolt when Siles Zuazo was the president. We were fighting the Morococala mine site. Morococala belonged to Walter Guevara Arce's party and we belonged to Paz Estenssoro's party. Morococala had arms, and Santa Fe didn't. But the workers of Morococala were few and we were many.

*How many were you?*
We were 780 and Morococala had 250 workers.

*Before this conflict, how were the relations between the center of Santa Fe and Morococala?*
We never lived in harmony with Morococala, as brother-workers. In Morococala mostly peasants work and they don't want to associate with people who know more than they do. In Santa Fe, people from Sacaca, Cochabamba, and Oruro, who are more disciplined, more enlightened, worked; those living around the mines of Morococala worked there, those from Chacara, Collura, and Inchupalla. They were indigenous men from the high plateau. They didn't know people like us. When we would go to buy things from their gardens, it was as if we were going to rob them. They were alarmed. This, I think, is why they have always been against the workers of Santa Fe.

Before the revolution, around 1945 or 1946, they said that the men and women from Sacaca were very bad. They say they used to go into the countryside to steal from the peasants. They would go into the countryside to buy something such as a lamb. Let's say it was worth five pesos. Then the Sacaqueños would approach the animal he liked best, choose it, but only pay the peasant fifty cents or one peso, and would throw the money in the patio of the peasant and leave without any fear, taking the animal. The peasant was left behind crying.

During those times, people from Sacaca used to work in Santa Fe. I think that is the reason why Santa Fe is hated by the workers of Morococala. The Sacaqueños are to blame — because they abused the peasants. Sacaqueños had no law-enforcement authorities, and without them, it was worse. They say they used to enter the Indians' houses and demand anything they wanted. Then the Indians had to go to the house of the Sacaqueño with the food loaded on their donkeys. When they would arrive and unload their things, the Sacaqueños would say, "Now you can leave; we don't need any more." And in anger some would even throw the Indian out of the house. This is the reason why the workers of Morococala haven't established any relations with the mines.

*How did the Indians dress when they worked in the mines?*

They would arrive at the mines with their country clothing, their sheep hats, those huge hats, their *ch'ullo*, their poncho, their *huaqui*, their pants and overalls. But once they worked two or three months in the mines and earned enough money, they would wear the same clothing as us. They are no longer Indian. They are refined and a little more enlightened.

*Did their wives use the same clothing from the countryside or did they change?*

The same thing happened with their wives. When they worked in the mines, the women had to be with them. And so, after two or three months working in the mines, the men could buy a *pollera* for their wives. In the countryside, they used *ajsu* — in Quechua we say blue *ajsu*, some say black too — embroidered on the bottom edge of the dress and on the chest.

There was a worker in Morococala called Molina, who was a sportsman. He was always hanging around Santa Fe. He went into Morococala with several workers from Santa Fe to find out the results of the elections. Only a few voted for Victor Paz Estenssoro. Walter Guevara Arce won there. The miners from Morococala were always for Siles Zuazo and always against Paz Estenssoro. Once they found out that Paz Estenssoro won in Santa Fe, they began to jail our workers who were around Morococala. One of the workers from the interior of the mines, Conrado Aguirre, was in Workers' Control. It was only after he took this position that they gave him a little power. When Conrado Aguirre went for a walk to Morococala, Manuel Flores and several other workers beat him up badly. They imprisoned him. Molina from Morococala came down to Santa Fe at seven in the evening and told us, "They are imprisoning workers of Santa Fe because Paz Estenssoro won the elections in Santa Fe."

When we found that out, we hastened toward the gate on the top of Clavo Grande of Morococala. They fired on us, with light artillery, and some died. We escaped to our mine site. At eight o'clock we armed ourselves with dynamite. We had only four or five with rifles and one light artillery piece, but after the first skirmish it got stuck and didn't work any more. They took it to the repair shop, made a new piece, but it still didn't work. That piece of light artillery didn't work because God didn't want us to fight. With it we would have had a bloodier revolution than we did.

We went up there around eight-thirty at night, blasting dynamite. When we approached the gate, there were military police there and they fired at us. We hid behind rocks that were there, huge stones surrounding the hospital of the Morococala mine. By the road was a street trench dug by the men from Morococala. Four boys who had just left the military quarters were walking along the trenches. I don't know why nothing happened to the first three, but the last one was a little bit further behind and we saw him blown to pieces. Maybe they just then turned on the current that exploded the dynamite for him. Further up there was unprotected field. There weren't any big stones – all were small and there was nowhere to hide. We ceased firing.

From below, Cesar Morales, the general secretary, yelled, "Let us pick up our dead. We will take them with us and tomorrow we will reach an understanding with each other." Morales got up shouting, "Even if you kill me, we are going to get our corpses!"

We were about ready to give up. Then a shot was fired, but it didn't reach Morales; it fell short. We decided to surround Morococala completely. We were shooting in all directions when we reached Clavo Grande from behind. It was also mined with dynamite. They threw dynamite but it blew up before it reached us. They had already organized themselves so we left for our encampment. We gathered below, behind the hospital of Santa Fe. There we held a meeting; over half the miners were present.

*Who was the leader?*

We didn't have one. We went on our own. Morococala was led by Julio Negreto. He was in charge in Morococala.

We said, "Dead or alive, we are going back to get our corpses. Besides, there may be some wounded that can be saved."

We went up again. There was a courageous worker, Fernández, a small man, who said, "I will go to make contact so that we will have some representation. It will be clear in the middle of the road and we will get our bodies back, and tomorrow in the daylight we will confront them." He left, walking alone up the highway with his arms up. If we had all gone up, they would have fired on us. Then we went on after him and picked the bodies up.

The next day we arrived at the union hall with four corpses. Parts of the boys' bodies were missing, and we couldn't find them. Searching with a lantern, we had picked up bits of flesh on the rocks and in the hills.

The next morning at seven when the sun was already up, we went out looking for the rest. There were now just bits, only the feet and the finger, that belonged to one of the dead. His whole stomach was missing. We put him in the coffin and lighted the candles.

People were crying, "We must avenge the blood of our workers, of our corpses!" three people swore.

The general secretary said, "They are threatening friends, to send more dead back to our district, because they know very well that you have no arms, whereas Morococala is well armed. Siles Zuazo has given them arms, and so has Walter Guevara Arce." And he told us, "If you want to risk your lives, you can attack them again. But we, I myself, do not authorize it. We cannot have such a dangerous confrontation."

At nighttime, when we reached the union hall, we spoke over the radio with Siglo XX, Huanuni, and Machacamarca. Siglo XX agreed to send us all their armed workers in trucks. Huanuni also promised to come in trucks, and Machacamarca did likewise.

The following day at six in the morning the entire road had been mined by the men from Morococala so that the trucks could not pass. They had to go instead around Pairumani. If not, they would have been blown up. But we already had taken that road and it was now under our command, and they couldn't reach us. When the trucks arrived there were people coming from the other side, but fell back because we were also armed.

First they came from Sorasora, Japo Huanuni, and Machacamarca, to Japo where they arrived by way of Cebada Mayu, along the mountain. There is also a road for vehicles to Japo. They came walking from K'haramayu, from the mountain of Potopoto beyond them, and they appeared on the summit of Santa Fe. We saw a lot of people and thought that Morococala was invading us. We signaled with reflecting mirrors to know who was coming. We thought that they were coming from Huanuni, but instead they were from Machacamarca. They had a light piece in perfect condition, and we had ammunition for it. With that we could battle very well. We were alright, but it was already ten in the morning and neither Huanuni nor Cataví had arrived.

We watched until eleven in the morning. "With this piece of light artillery can't we base ourselves and confront them?" asked the men from Machacamarca.

The general secretary said, "No, comrades, this is too light for Morococala. They have a few machine guns. Ten against one, we can say, but they also have a trench mortar. What could we do?"

We waited a little while more. At eleven-thirty, Huanuni arrived in Santa Fe. They came through the slope of Pairumani on the right road. Four trucks full of people arrived, some with arms, others without. More wanted to go now, and more trucks kept arriving, including some from Siglo XX with more arms.

They drove down to San Pedrito, and from San Pedrito some came marching eagerly, while others stayed there, out of willfulness. The rest wanted to go since they had good arms, pistols, machine guns, and there were plenty of us. Meanwhile Morococala called upon peasants to assault us. They didn't know that people from Huanuni, Siglo XX, and Machacamarca were coming. They thought we were waiting for them all alone, with our arms crossed. They tried to enter Santa Fe at two o'clock in the afternoon.

*Did you know that the peasants were coming with them?*

We had little boys who were spying in Morococala, and these little boys saw everything. They told us, "There are many peasants in Morococala, and they are coming at two in the afternoon."

*Who were the little boys?*

They were the miners' sons. My son, Filemón himself, he was there. He came back also with some information. We were not frightened, especially now that the men from Siglo XX arrived.

At twelve-thirty we left, and surrounded them. They had found out that Siglo XX and Huanuni were in Santa Fe, and that they were being surrounded. They tried to escape by the road around Shokara, by Villacollo. When they arrived at the summit where the people from Santa Fe were posted, they immediately returned to their districts. When Juan de Dios Terrazas, "Negro" Ortega, and then José Lopez and Donaldson got there, they turned back when they saw that the people were already surrounded.

Soon they arrived back at their mine saying, "Comrades, now we are surrounded by the miners of Santa Fe. All of Morococala is surrounded. Let's go inside the mine." All of them, women, children — except for a few who weren't afraid of being massacred and who remained in the mining camp — went into the mine.

The men from Siglo XX entered the camp, shooting their machine guns — "taratata, taratata" — in all directions like that. There were no more people in the Morococala mining camp. Everything was silent, empty.

Those very same Indians whom they had contracted to attack Santa Fe then began to plunder Morococala. Some of the Indians went into the houses looking like savages and left looking like gentlemen, dressed in suits, with everything, even shoes. They entered with hide boots and left with shoes. They were loaded with blankets, with everything. Everything good, radios, machines, everything, was taken by the very same Indians whom they hired.

Some of us surrounded the entrance to the mine. Then the workers from Huanuni entered without fear, without arms, because they knew that people were not armed although there were arms in the mine. They went inside the mine and met with some of the people of Morococala, saying, "Leave before anything happens, because our workers want to place dynamite in the mouth of the mine and demolish it. You will all die in here."

With that, the people went out. The workers who didn't have arms were capable of killing their own companions, just to get their arms. If shooting had started inside there, all would have lost their lives. So they fought over the arms, but most of them were taken by the men from Huanuni and Siglo XX mine, but not many by the Machacamarca because they didn't want to risk their lives.

Then we surrounded the office of the management. "Negro" Ortega was inside the office with several workers in charge of a piece of light artillery. The workers said, "Don't shoot at us. We are workers from the mines! The leaders who started the fight last night imprisoned us."

"Let those people who were imprisoned leave," responded the men from Huanuni. "'Negro' should also come out."

"Negro" fired one shot and killed a worker from Huanuni within our sight. He also killed another worker from Huanuni when he wasn't watching. They listened to his heart and said, "He died."

We all went down to Santa Fe with the bodies. Five dead, all five from Santa Fe, and not one from Morococala. "Negro" was only wounded. They took him too, thinking he was dead, but he revived on the way. When the men from Huanuni found out that he was alive, seven went to get revenge. Of the seven, only one had a rifle. They kicked the door of the hospital and went in. They couldn't find Ortega.

He was sitting in the patio outside, behind a stone, covered with a blanket. I saw none of that, and I know only what I was told by those from Huanuni. They saw him and shot him. He didn't fall. With the second shot, he still didn't fall. Only after seven shots did he die, that "Negro," and they say they killed him in front of the hospital. Then they announced that they killed "Negro," who had killed two men from Huanuni.

Later some men from Huanuni were going down around San Pedrito when a young boy told them, "Donaldson and López are hiding here in Donaldson's father's house." The men from Huanuni tore the door down and captured both. They kicked them all the way down the river San Pedrito towards the entrance of San José where there is a hospital. I saw them bringing them down roughly, with blows from the rifle butt, toward the kiosk in the Plaza Seis de Agosto in the middle of Santa Fe. One worker was ready to blow up José Lopez and Donaldson with dynamite. The hands of both were tied. The men taunted their prisoners, saying "We're going to blow them up."

They tied their prisoners with a handkerchief around their mouths. They lit the fuse of the dynamite. It was about forty centimeters long. At that very moment another worker who felt for those two guys went up and took the ties off the prisoners. He had plenty of time because white fuses burn very slowly. They saved both the prisoners who were condemned to death.

The men of Huanuni wanted to hang them in the plaza, but the women opposed it, saying, "No, we can't do this; we must forgive their guilt and let them pay in jail. We must give them over to the hands of justice."

At least *we* didn't do anything to them. They were in fair condition. But some angry workers stabbed José Lopez in the back right around his lungs. He was bleeding and the other was beaten up. His whole mouth burst open. At nine o'clock at night we handed over both of them to the men from Huanuni.

"Take them away; give them to justice and let justice judge these two men who are responsible for the death of the five boys who died in the revolution."

They disarmed the entire encampment. Morococala no longer had arms. They didn't do anything against the twenty people from Siglo XX. They only yelled, "Get out of here! What do you want? There is nothing here that you can steal. There's nothing more to do. No more shooting."

We down below were ready to run, but someone told us that Mor-ococala was totally disarmed.

So we were calm and patient. They left us there. First those from Machacamarca left, then those from Huanuni, and at eleven o'clock those from Siglo XX left. But some were left with arms, two light pieces and some rifles to carry the next day to the burials. We took four bodies to be buried and those from Huanuni took one to their district. This is how the miners gathered together and saved us. Had they not come, we would have had to fight more, and more would have died. We had four corpses. If Siglo XX, Huanuni, and Machacamarca hadn't come, how many would there have been? They took the arms of the miners from Morococala away. Those from Santa Fe took the rifles without stocks.

When Paz Estenssoro triumphed in 1960, this triumph was also be-trayed. Paz Estenssoro betrayed the working class, but it wasn't the fault of those who entered in the election, Paz Estenssoro and Lechín. The guilty ones are the workers themselves. We didn't know how to make ourselves respected. We sat back calmly and let them betray each other in their own way.

Estenssoro deceived Lechín. Lechín should have taken power after he left office, but Estenssoro told him, "You will take my place in the cabinet as a vice-president. I will be in the presidency, and you will be second-in-command."

Juan Lechín accepted because the following year he was supposed to be the president, for the next term. But all of this was simply deceit, it wasn't serious. Once they arranged this, they began to send the main leaders of the workers to other nations. Paz Estenssoro sent Juan Lechín to Italy as ambassador. Even from there, despite all the prob-lems involved, he opposed them. They didn't let him return to Bolivia because Victor Paz Estenssoro promised to pay him three times the salary he was earning as a vice-president. He didn't let the old man succeed him, even though Lechín had more experience than Victor Paz Estenssoro himself.

In 1964 Paz Estenssoro was elected for a third term, through an election fraud, with René Barrientos Ortuño as vice-president. The workers didn't take this election seriously. They all abstained; none voted for any of the candidates. All the mining centers opted not to vote. There weren't any elections in the mining centers, only in the cities. But Paz Estenssoro gave orders to the soldiers and peasants to vote. Everywhere people voted, five, six, even ten times for the same man. By these infamous means, Paz Estenssoro won the election.

Later that year Victor Paz Estenssoro fought with Barrientos, who left for Cochabamba. I don't know if he went to vacation or on peasant affairs, but Barrientos got together with General Ovando Candia there, and together they took over the government. I don't know which of the captains or colonels it was, but some of them helped Paz Estenssoro get away to Peru. They imprisoned one captain who helped.

Estenssoro said, "I am going to leave on an outing to see how the guards are." Then he went to the airport, and from the airport, he took off to Lima, Peru. And then Ovando Candia took power.

The people of La Paz wanted René Barrientos Ortuño to assume power so badly they cheered when he arrived in the city, "Let General Barrientos Ortuño come to power!" the demonstrators in the Plaza Murillo yelled. So Ovando Candia yielded the presidency to René Barrientos and he took charge.

A few months later Barrientos began to imprison the leaders of the union. He deported Juan Lechín to Paraguay, and then he deported the union leaders, especially those from the federation. Others he arrested and put into the penitentiary. They declared a hunger strike, but the government didn't yield, but rather stood its ground, and the hunger strike failed.

The Archbishop of La Paz made a statement to this effect: "Do not sacrifice yourselves any longer, because this government isn't one of Christians, but animals. It does not understand anything."

The union leaders said, "Let them send us to our death. It doesn't matter. We don't care."

When Paz Estenssoro was overthrown in 1964 we supported Barrientos, because Estenssoro was no longer on our side. He was no longer conscious of our needs, and we regarded him as a traitor. We fought against Paz Estenssoro on the fields of Sorasora. The miners of Santa Fe and Morococala joined with those from Huanuni, Siglo XX, Machacamarca, and Colquiri. We came through Sorasora to Machacamarca where we received word that the troops were positioned in the mountains of San Pedro. All night they shot at us. They didn't let us move anywhere. We were the first to arrive at the crossroad. At the intersection, the miners from Machacamarca told us not to go ahead because the entire road was controlled by government troops.

"They won't let us take a step ahead or they will shoot at us."

So we went along the river instead. We advanced about two hundred meters without shooting, ready with the dynamite. Some had sticks and pick handles, but none of that was useful.

*How did you utilize the dynamite? Did you use arrows or sling shots to deliver it?*

I made myself a sling like those used by natives in Africa, out of a stick with an elastic to throw it like a spear. That's how I had it. I used a thick piece of tire rubber so it would throw far. I made myself three cartridges. If it were heavier, it wouldn't shoot far, but three cartridges would go about fifty meters. A single cartridge would go sixty or even seventy meters. That's what I was carrying. The rest had slingshots, and they shot the dynamite like stones. We prepared this with small pieces of iron from the shop. We used all the tiny bits of iron to make hand grenades in milk cans. We put two hand cartridges in and around it we stuffed the bits of iron, broken pieces of iron with sharp edges. We called those "death bombs."

We took off with those bombs and arrived at a place where they spotted us and didn't let us advance any more. They didn't shoot directly at us, just shot so as to scare us. Ten or fifteen meters in front of us, we could see bullets clearly picking up a lot of dust in front of us. We came a bit closer and shot dynamite with those slings. The soldiers were only five hundred meters away and then they began to leave.

The workers from Huanuni have faith in their ability to fight. They reached the crossroad in a lively mood, but there they were turned back — even those who had light artillery. They returned to the town of Sorasora to quench their thirst. The heat was unbearable at eleven o'clock in the morning. At twelve, in the month of October, it was terrible. So the men from Huanuni left us alone, orphans, without any arms, only our dynamite.

In front of us the army got on their trucks like sheep. If we had had a light piece we could have killed all of them. Without any question, all would have fallen. We could even have taken some as prisoners and then would have had plenty of arms. Maybe we could have even entered the city. But with rifles only, we couldn't do anything against them. They weren't even afraid of us.

Once they were on the road, they went to a sandy hill. They positioned themselves firmly and didn't let us even take a step. We advanced until we were about eight hundred meters in front of them. Then they shot at us and tried to kill us. They even shot at us with a mortar using dead rounds, well aimed so that they fell right in front of us, split in two, without exploding, so as not to kill us yet. We advanced almost one hundred meters more. They were only about six hundred or seven hundred meters away.

They wanted to kill us. They machine-gunned us, a gust of rounds landing about five meters in front of us. I was near the front and Castro was almost five meters ahead of me. The volley of fire fell in front of him and he fell back. I thought he had died, but he had fallen backward out of fright. For a long time they shot at us with mortars.

Several were wounded. They didn't kill any of us, they shot at a distance so that a few fragments of the grenade would only wound us. Several were hurt, and for this reason, we couldn't go ahead.

"They are going to kill all of us. We have no arms! They are going to kill all of us right here!" someone shouted.

Those without arms were in front, and those with arms in back. "What are we going to do without arms?" someone asked. "We must go back." And so we did.

Three trucks arrived from Siglo XX, three big Leylands. The Leyland in front was bringing water because we had asked for it. We were very thirsty and hot on the open field. They wounded the driver of that Leyland, and then they shot the tank of water and it all spilled. We couldn't get near it because they were determined to kill us. They were right on top of us and we were about to be overrun by them. We were only one hundred meters from them. They shot the second truck, but the third truck was able to get through. We returned to the battle, along with those from Siglo XX. They wounded a soldier with a rifle and took him and a second lieutenant as prisoners to Huanuni. The wounded soldier was taken to the hospital.

Those from Siglo XX, who had been in back of us, went forward.

At the foot of the sandy hill one of their soldiers was distributing food rations and water for the canteens of the soldiers. He was carrying a backpack.

"I haven't come here to shoot anyone," he yelled, "I am just rationing water and dried food to the soldiers. I was just sent by the chief of my company."

They hit that soldier and took him prisoner, and someone from Siglo XX shot him. It must have hit his heart since he had a hole in his left side. He was killed instantly.

About sixty soldiers escaped from their hill. If we had had weapons, we would have killed them. Those with arms had stayed behind, useless.

We turned toward Sorasora again. I had gotten cramps in my legs and had to crawl all the way from Chacara on my knees. We went around the plateau, by Aguas Caliente. The trucks came to pick us up, thinking we were wounded. Two men supported me as I held on to their shoulders with my hands. Just as I was leaving, men up on the plateau began shooting. The truck came from Santa Fe and took us to Sorasora, where I got off.

Some soldiers were drinking soft drinks, and miners from Huanuni, Catavi, and Siglo XX stole up on them, seized their weapons, and beat them up badly. Then we went to drop off all the miners, first to Huanuni, and then to Siglo XX. We were congregated on the crossroad of Huanuni and Santa Fe when we heard a plane. We thought they were coming to machine-gun us, but they were only trying to spot the miners. It flew very low along the river. Two men trying to escape the plane jumped down to the river bed where the earth was eaten away by the water flow. They landed hard on the stone bed and, out of fright, tried to scramble away, twisting their ankles. We jumped out of our trucks. There were three trucks and a yellow van still picking up miners, but when they saw the plane, they left only half-filled. Many were still missing, but we left because we thought that on its return the men in the plane would shoot us. But the plane did not return.

We finally reached Santa Fe by truck. Many workers walked back by the hill; others walked along the road. We fought in support of Barrientos, but when he got into power, he betrayed us.

*Did all the miners support Barrientos?*

Yes, because he promised to better the salaries of the workers. He even fought against General Ovando Candia, who tried to oust him from the vice-presidency, since he did not want to betray the miners.

But shortly thereafter, a new decree was announced: the miners' wage was to be lowered! Everyone suffered the impact of that decree, including the retirees. From that time on, workers received social benefits not from their contract earnings, but only from their base pay. Barrientos had promised the workers that he would never abandon them. He was supposed to be on our side, to give us the benefits which were owed us, but he deceived us.

In 1965, when we still had a union, he called the union leaders to La Paz, around the month of May. The leaders of the federation could no longer visit the mining centers since they no longer had any authority. General Barrientos called in all the local leaders of the miners, purportedly to resolve some of the problems that had arisen. Among them was the general secretary of Santa Fe, Victor Carrasco, who was also a member of the federation. There were no secretaries of Workers' Control, since that had already been eliminated. Only general secretaries were left.

In good faith, all the general secretaries of the mining districts went into the room where the meeting was to be held and fell into the hands of the military. No one even said hello to them. They never returned.

We chose someone from among the interior mine workers to become leader, in accordance with the decree of Barrientos' government. It could not be someone from the exterior — neither an employee, nor someone working in the shops or the refinery — and it had to be someone who had never been a leader before. We followed all the dictates of the government, because Barrientos had promised to cooperate with us within the limits of his power. I was elected as a secretary of conflicts, since I had never been a secretary of public relations or held any high-level office.

"We won't have any problems with Rojas," they said, "because Barrientos said that none of the workers could be former leaders, and Rojas seems to be completely clean of the previous leadership."

Some opposed me, but I was elected anyway.

They sent our names to La Paz so that they could check to see whether we had been leaders previously. They probably didn't see my name on the list of former leaders. So we were authorized to be installed.

They called us to deliberate some of the petitions which we had made, especially the one calling for a return to the initial level of our salaries. We went to La Paz and, when we reached the Alto on the way, they stopped our small truck. I was sitting in back with the secretary of the union and the secretary of acts; the general secretary was in front with the secretary of relations.

As soon as the driver slowed down I got off, since we had been instructed that as soon as we arrived in La Paz we should stop the truck and get off. The secretary of acts did likewise, but they caught him by the arm. I went right into the crowd that had gathered around the truck. They looked around everywhere, and I did likewise, as if I were one of them. They did not notice me. Little-by-little I got away. They put the general secretary, the secretary of relations, and the secretary of acts in the back and left with another driver. The authorities and two well-armed military men got in front.

Seeing that, I returned to Santa Fe. I didn't have a cent to leave with, since the general secretary was supposed to pay for our living expenses from the funds of the federation. We had a federation, but it wasn't worth anything. It was only a name and the source of the money we were supposed to get. In Santa Fe we had only a partial list of the members, because the union membership was frozen by the government of Barrientos.

The payroll department had been transferred to La Paz and there were no records of who the workers were, only numbers. That is why they didn't give us anything before we left, and I had only five pesos. I couldn't even catch a bus to go back home.

A truck came by and I said to the driver, "I have come only to miss meeting my family. Now I don't have any money to leave and I can't earn anything either. Can you please take me at least half the way along?"

He took me a couple of kilometers along the way, up to Patacamaya. He left me there. From there, I walked to Caracollo, where I arrived at ten o'clock in the morning. There a small truck picked me up and brought me to Oruro. From Oruro with the five pesos I had, I was able to go back to Santa Fe. I was saved, but the rest were taken to the Alto [the heights, where a prison camp was located] of La Paz. The secretary of acts came back after I did. He was terribly beaten. The rest were even more severely beaten by the government. They even hit them with a whip, because they wanted to know what the union wanted.

*Who beat the leaders?*

Those of the DIC [Dirección Investigacíon Criminal] when the leaders of the union were put in jail. The agents of the DIC came and asked, "Why did you come to La Paz?"

The leaders responded, "We are only coming to know about our economic situation. The workers' wages have been lowered and we have come on their behalf. Maybe we can obtain something for them," they said.

They say the lieutenant, or maybe he was a captain, but he belonged to the army, said, "In the name of the workers, you have come to disturb the governing cabinet, right?" And he placed them in four different cells. They were whipped badly, badly beaten. It was pitiful, they say. They tied their hands on both sides, like Jesus Christ and lashed them with a whip.

Then Alcosa, the secretary of relations, came to Santa Fe. I don't know how he escaped but he came back. The soldiers came after him. He came into the consulting hall of the union. There were many workers but none of them recognized him since he was dressed as a civilian. An agent who was following him caught Alcosa and immediately took him away. The workers tried to grab him but a truckload of armed soldiers surrounded the building. They didn't let us breathe. Perhaps we would have done something, but it was late at night and most of the workers were resting. It happened at ten o'clock at night.

They sent all the union leaders to Puerto Rico, in the department of Pando. There a huge strike was held but it did not achieve anything. They remained jailed until 1968. Management fired them under the excuse that they had missed too many days of work, way too many. They were stripped of all benefits. They didn't even give their wives five cents since "they were fired for missing work days." They didn't mention that they had been jailed in La Paz. They didn't admit that they were in the police station cells.

Then the women complained a lot. Some wanted to begin a huge strike with their children in the plaza of Oruro, in front of the prefecture, but the workers didn't let them because their children were too small. One was one, another three, and the eldest was eight. The women went to La Paz with a petition adopted by the union. It was just an ad hoc group. They gave them something – I don't know what type of benefit they received. They received some money after their husbands were fired from their jobs. Later the men were set free from the jail, but they weren't authorized to go back to the mines; they didn't return until recently. They say they are now working in Santa Fe in the same jobs. Their wives came to Santa Fe with their children and we gave them food from the general store. We gave them sardines, milk, sugar, rice, bread – anything we had in the store. Some of the workers gave them a can of milk or a kilo of sugar. Others gave five or ten rolls, anything they could give out of their own supplies. The women would gather up quite a bit of stuff and give it to them.

The top leaders had to walk around as if they were not in their nation, like foreigners, or spies, hiding, always with a body guard, just as they did with the leaders of San José and many places in Colquiri, Palacayu, and other places. The leaders of the federation of miners didn't come out of hiding until this year [1970], I think, in May or April, when they finally gave them their freedom.

One of the leaders from Santa Fe, Victor Carrasco, was a fairly honest leader, a fine gentleman, who maintained workers' rights in Santa Fe. He never betrayed the workers even though they were controlled by the state. These leaders didn't lower their heads to the floor. They have always kept their pride, demanding what was theirs. From that moment on, up to when they went into hiding, the workers had no rights to demand anything. There were many months in Santa Fe when we suffered from a lack of rice and sugar. They used to send us sugar of very bad quality which stank of lemon and which couldn't be eaten. At least the lemon tasted good even though sour, but the sugar was yellow. There were two or three weeks when we ate no meat. We survived on the fat of lambs. There was lamb or beef when the Indians brought it to the market in the plaza, but we had no money to buy it.

*When did that happen?*

In May of 1965, when Barrientos was already in power.

*How can we compare that period to the period during which Victor Paz Estenssoro was in power?*

When Victor Paz Estenssoro was in power, during the first period when the MNR triumphed on the ninth of April, 1952, for a year or two those living in the city suffered from a bread shortage. In Oruro especially; I don't know how bad it was in La Paz. All the workers suffered the same. We suffered a great deal from a lack of foodstuffs, but they suffered even more in the cities because the government sent it all to the mines. Victor Paz Estenssoro said that the people should suffer a bit so that the workers might benefit. In the cities there was bread made out of the husks of wheat, black bread; in the mines there was white bread, bread made with white flour. So the people from the cities thought we were stealing their bread. But that's not how it was. The government made contracts for too little flour and there was only enough for the mining centers. The government kept doing that for about eight or ten years, and we all suffered very much from shortages of everything.

The cities were up in arms; there were lots of protest demonstrations. While in office, Victor Paz Estenssoro never opposed any of them. He gave them their freedom and the people protested with honesty and discipline, without being abusive to anyone in the streets. The police didn't intervene because they weren't permitted to. However, any demonstration or march close to the stationhouse was stopped by bullets authorized by the superintendent.

There are accidents and even deaths when the government tries to stop a demonstration. During Paz Estenssoro's government, people were never stopped. He let them demonstrate peacefully and there was no noise. Before Paz Estenssoro, there were several casualties. They even used firearms to kill three or four people so as to scare the rest. They didn't use tear gas, but rather bullets, during the Ballivan[1] government before 1952.

During Mamerto Urriolagoitia's government, it was even worse. It was more disastrous. They issued decrees with which they tried to squash people under their feet. The people weren't free at all; the miners weren't free. Mamerto Urriolagoitia wanted to dominate everything. He didn't respect the peasants, or the miners, or the general public. There were many massacres in those times.

There was a leader, Dionisio Villarroel, who was the general secretary during Urriolagoitia's government in 1950. I once heard two agents of the DIC talking at the corner outside my house. They said, "Let's go find Villarroel."

Some people had told them where he lived. I ran to his house immediately and told him what I had heard. "Go," I said. "They are looking for you. They are going to take you and question you. I heard them say your name. They are coming for you. Leave!"

I took Villarroel to Reyero's house nearby. Reyero was a union leader who ran a compressor in the mine. After a while, a soldier stood in front of Villarroel's house. He didn't move from below the window. I kept watch over the soldier. After a while, the DIC agents approached the house and knocked at the door; a small boy with a limp came out. I think his name was Gualberto. When the agents asked for his father he said that his father wasn't there. They pushed the door open and went in. They looked for him, but left when they found only his wife. I walked away and the soldiers followed after me, thinking I was Villarroel. I stopped and one of the soldiers came up to me and looked me over. He didn't say anything.

"Are you looking for someone?" I asked.

"No, I am just watching, that's all I am doing," he answered.

I went back to Villarroel's house at ten o'clock at night to see what

---

[1] General Hugo R. Ballivan was president from May 16, 1951, to April 9, 1952, when Hernan Siles Zuazo took over as interim president until the inauguration of Victor Paz Estenssoro on April 15th.

was happening. The soldier was still on the next corner. I knocked on the main door of Villarroel's house and quickly went in. I suggested that we should dress him as a woman and take him to the mine and hide him inside it. We left dressed as women and we took him to the café and later to the pump powerhouse. We stayed there until the next day, when he left, while I stayed to work. But the agents of the DIC picked him up and took him to Oruro and jailed him.

His wife came to look for him, and I left work and went to her house. I said, "We were inside the mine, but he left, so they must have gotten him."

I went to management later to try to find him, but nobody had seen him. I found out that he had been taken through Calacala to Oruro. They wanted to send him immediately to La Paz, but he resisted them vigorously. He didn't want to leave the work site.

The secretary of Workers' Control, Fructuoso Guzman, was chief of the electric shop, and he told the people in his section to call the rest of us together. We got together just in time to prevent the DIC agents from taking Guzman off with them. We kicked them out. We put them in a small pickup truck and told the driver to drop them off on the other side of the hill. They must have been picked up by some car and gone to Oruro. That's the way the DIC hounded that man and tried to catch him.

Even before the revolution, during June of 1950, Fructuoso Guzman had gone to Oruro to visit his family who lived there. In those times, the police — I don't know what police it was since they didn't have the DIC in those times, but I think it was called "Political Control" — seized him and beat him up. They tried to send him to La Paz. When the miners found this out, we went to Santa Fe to petition for his release. We did not work for a whole day until they released our leader. They did likewise in Siglo XX and in all the other mines. The president, Mamerto Urriolagoitia, gave Guzman his liberty so that we wouldn't do anything.

The company immediately fired him upon his release. It was a happy event for them, because he didn't let them get away with anything. He always got involved and accomplished things for the workers. But since he always did something even after he was fired, they took him to La Paz and jailed him.

We have always failed because we haven't known how to think enough. In those times the lots of land in the cities weren't as expensive as they are now. The politicians thought that the miners would take advantage of the benefits which they received from the government, but only 1 percent of the miners took advantage of Paz Estenssoro's efforts. The rest began to squander their money on drinks, games, on one thing or another. The miners began to lead a bad life. It was the mining leaders' fault. They thought they were kings, and for this reason let the working class become passive. They didn't lead them along the right path. They ignored them and let them become corrupted. Had the leaders advised them to buy some plots and pay for it piecemeal, almost all would have had something. In Papel Pampa, south of Oruro, there were large plots. That's where my mother lived. At that time her house was on the outskirts and now it's in the middle of new homes. The leaders didn't feel anything for their workers.

There were all sorts of abuses in our nation caused by the government, and they haven't let the miners advance in any respect. They only want production and they don't recognize the workers' sacrifice. Now they are looking for ways to improve his life, but it is already too late. They don't earn any more than 280 or 300 pesos and that's only enough to buy potatoes. I don't know where they get the money to dress with, especially those who drink a lot. I wonder what type of sacrifice they must make. Those people who drink a lot have to sell some of their rations from the general store to buy things their children need.

We receive rent benefits from the nationalized mines, especially in Oruro, since the mining camp is too small for all the workers. They also pay us for our fare, but that also corrupts some. They drink less in Santa Fe than in San José, because drinking is prohibited in company houses. There are some days when those people who drink a lot eat only once a day. They intrude upon their neighbors and receive food from them. That is how some live and they jeopardize their children's education. The leaders must guide them, encourage them to reflect. They must tell those people that they are corrupt, and to stop acting in that way. They must guide them in one way or another.

The company itself encourages those vices. The company obstructs the distribution of meat and bread. In San José, the workers don't want to use their coupons in the store. Instead, they buy those products in the tunnel connecting the mines of San José and Itos. The company, instead of allowing those stupidities, should check and see who is selling the meat, or the bread, or any one of the four products that have a standard minimum price. Since the price of these four products is based upon our salary, we may earn little, but at least we are given basic products at a lower price. The secret agents could make a list of the sellers and send it to the union and then the union should take charge of the workers doing that. "Why are you doing that?" we should ask, and we would send them to the management so that they will be punished by not receiving any coupons for a few days or weeks, or they could deduct a fine from his wage. That way the miners would learn. Those who commit such abuses should receive the same discipline as his children. When a man sells his staples, he is selling his children's stomachs. He is not selling something of his, but something that belongs to his children.

By controlling those workers, we can reach an accord more easily. In a meeting I made this point, and the general secretary stopped to think but he didn't accept it, saying, "Once we tell the management about this, they will accept gladly. They will cut down on our staples. Who is this going to favor? Only the company and from that moment onwards the workers' salary will be reduced. Only the company will benefit from it," he answered.

Never in my life have I sold meat, nor any of the products which I received from the store for my work. Rather, I have had to buy coupons because it is never enough. I have six children and all are big and they eat a lot. I need more every month because children's stomachs grow more and more. That's why I buy coupons.

When my term was over, they didn't throw me out with Fernandez and the other leader. A short time afterwards, when Barrientos took office in 1964, they called the former leaders back. We went to the union hall to read some books of the union statutes to remember what type of statutes they were. There was plenty of camaraderie and we spoke like we used to before.

Then other government agents came. They thought we were holding a meeting. A woman, Doña Felina, said, "The agents from the DIC are after you." So I escaped through the window, and went to my house, and from my house to my sister-in-law's house. Despite all of that, they got me. They caught me in my sister-in-law's house and took me to the office of the manager.

The DIC agent asked me, "What do you do every day in the union hall until one o'clock in the morning? What are you plotting?"

I said, "Never in my life have I stayed as late as eleven o'clock; occasionally I've stayed until ten, at the latest. I went because when I go to sleep early, I sometimes wake up early, and I can't stay in bed. I get up sometimes just to walk around and get some exercise on the road down there, but the cold can give me a chill. I once almost got pneumonia. To avoid that, I sometimes go to the union hall and talk to my friend. I wasn't plotting anything."

There was no movement. We had no freedom to act without a union. Yes, there was a union, but it was only a name and had no strength. If a leader went to demand something, he did not get anywhere. The manager didn't pay attention to him.

The manager would say, "Okay, we will do this," and accept, but as soon as the leader left he would throw the paper away and order something completely opposite to the petition. And he had no reason to even meet with non-union comrades. We used to advise those union men how to act, the way we did before, but there was no purpose because they had no strength. If it had no strength, it was worthless, because the manager paid no attention.

In any event the DIC didn't find me guilty. But this is how they came after the union leaders who sided with the workers. Now it's a little better, but we can't trust a military government. Their only mission is to subdue us, the mining workers, by force. Otherwise, why do they have all the army posts in the mining centers?

# 13

## After the Fall

General Barrientos came to power in November 1964 after a coup d'état against Victor Paz Estenssoro. The miners supported him because he promised to ameliorate their situation, but during his first year in the presidency he went against all his promises, cutting wages in half and jailing trade union leaders. As part of the "Triangular Plan," the agreement signed by the United States, West Germany, and the Inter-American Development Bank, Barrientos instituted military control in the mining centers. The miners reacted against this by claiming that the mining centers were free districts. However, the army responded with further repression. Once again blood was spilled when the armed forces entered Catavi, Siglo XX, and San José in May 1965. In the mine of Santa Fe itself there were no clashes with the army, but miners from this district went to Oruro to help their comrades. By the end of May, all the mining districts fell under military control after two weeks of resistance.

When I asked Juan to tell me about the changes in the administration of the mines since Barrientos came to power, he answered my question by describing changes in his own work.

After 1964, when Barrientos took power, ammonium nitrate was used for blasting in all parts of the nationalized mines. In the shafts as well as in the raises connecting the long tunnels. We had to make advances with nitrate. For a few years after 1952 we still worked with dynamite alone. We used very little nitrate, only on the top of the main charge, and only those of us who wanted to used it; those of us who didn't used dynamite.

For each bore (or drill hole), they gave us half a cartridge of dynamite. We used to fight with the management because a half a cartridge wasn't enough. Sometimes we would be drilling late and had to force the cylinder around the cartridge. Then bits of clay sometimes fell in the drill holes, and with bad luck, that would push the dynamite out of the cylinder. In order to load it again, we would have to take everything apart because it didn't come out intact. They never gave us any extra dynamite to replace the lost cartridges. That is why we wanted to use only dynamite, since we had to walk from one place to another. As a result we fought a lot with management.

Almost every day, delegates from the workers of the interior of the mines would demand more dynamite, but it was a waste of time. Management did not pay any attention to us; they said the orders came from above, from the Mining Corporation of Bolivia in La Paz. We began a sit-down strike for three days as a protest, but it didn't get us anywhere. Every time we asked for dynamite, they gave us nitrate. In the end, we were forced to use small sample bags filled with nitrate, and drill a wider bore so as to place it in the cylinder without dynamite. That way it was effective, but we had to keep moving the drill and it was very risky.

On one occasion David Luján — his nickname was Apache — was flushing out the tailings of Clavo Paniagua. The tailings were all bits and pieces, there weren't any big stones. They were drilling a hole to insert the nitrate, and as he drilled he widened the chimney. He thought the tailings had been pushed away, but on the other side there was a chute to go up and it had caved in because of the constant pressure of the load falling on it. He didn't go down to check on it when he went to the pump, so he didn't notice that the load had fallen into the chimney. The chute was jammed from behind the load with the sludge and it covered the chimney. Both David and his helper had gone inside, and, perhaps because he was a coward, he sent the helper up alone to check on it.

After they lit the fuse to blast the load, they couldn't go down because the chimney was lost, covered over. They didn't have any way to escape, but the fuse was nine feet long and it burned slowly toward the explosive. They yelled in every direction, but forgot to go up again and cut the fuse. At the mouth of the mines, Apache could be heard clearly through the cracks, as if he was yelling from closer than five hundred meters. In Quechua he said:

*"Buzoniyku toapay akamun chimeneayayku suruchisques juraykunayku-paj willayku chispeskana,"* or, "From what box has it fallen? What chimney has it leaked from?" They had sworn to tell us when it was lit. There was no space for it to come out. The alley was stuffed. They had to clean it out and as they were cleaning it out, the fuse that was lit was about to go off. He went up again to the box and said,

"Cut it! Cut the fuse! Take it out! Then it will not explode."

Then they realized what had happened and they cut it when about fifteen centimeters were left to burn.

Not even then did the administration give in to our demands, not for the pumpings, nor the small or middle sized tunnels. They didn't give us additional dynamite for anything. They only gave us half a cartridge for every perforation. Only with a lot of fighting did we manage to get a whole cartridge for a drilling. We were forced to economize. We drilled in the easiest places, where there weren't any problems, no salt, nothing. We used half a cartridge tied with a string. It didn't stay exactly in place, but it was safe. The other half we had to save to do the pumping of the load because it was too dangerous to use nitrate. The management didn't understand any of that. They didn't accept our demands and forced us to use nitrate. And now it is used everywhere.

Also, after 1965 they lowered the price on all our contracts. For example, Before they used to pay us twenty-five bolivianos over and above our salary for a cubic meter advanced, but after 1965 they lowered it to seven hundred pesos, and raised the prices we had to pay for produce as well.

In 1965 I was working in Ricardo Bravo's gang. In several sites we failed to find ore. The manager Bustamante said that the team wasn't working well because it lacked organization. But it wasn't due to a lack of organization, because in those sites where there was metal to be found, we worked quickly and that is what Bustamente did not like.

"You are betraying me, leaving this bridge where the best ore can be found, and working on those sites in which no more can be found!"

I told Bustamante to come up and see. He never went up the cracks to the chimney, on the other where we were working. In order to warn him, we fired three shots when we were midway in the tunnel. On the third day, he went up to see whether these were veins and he found that there was nothing. There was no necessity to open up everything to discover that. Ricardo Bravo had gone on vacation and I had taken over the leadership in his absence.

"I am going to call Bravo," Bustamente said.

"But you know that he is on vacation. You should know that, since they gave you the lists of workers who are on vacation," I said.

"They need a driller in the gang of Juan Mareno," he said. Go there and put that site in order because it's in very bad shape. He hasn't had any explosion despite the fact that he has had quite a few good leads. There's a lack of organization here. I want you to go there for a while.

I couldn't leave without putting someone in charge of the gang. My replacement was Raimundo Conde. His nickname was *Banda Cocinera*, the band's cook, because he once acted in a feast of the Coyuma. Two dancing troops came from Koruque, where he had gone to help them take potatoes on a donkey. The cook of the band had said, "Help me cut the meat!" My friends had seen him helping the cook slice the meat for the meal. Since then they called him Banda Cocinera.

I told Conde, "You have to stay here, because the engineer has ordered me to go to the other work gang."

As soon as he could Conde told Bravo, "They have sent Rojas to the other gang."

Bravo immediately went to the manager's office and said, "How is it that you remove people when I am away from my gang? I must be there to decide if someone is to leave or not. I am in charge of the gang. I am in control of all that and I am the one to decide." That is how he spoke to the manager.

The manager said, "I don't want that man in that group. Go in to work yourself; we will give you your vacation on another occasion." Bravo agreed, since he wanted his vacation in December in order to go to Sorasora for the feast of Santa Barbara. I was assigned to the gang of Juan Moreno.

We were working when Juan Moreno fell sick, and had to go to the hospital for a week. When he came out of the hospital he worked for a day and then got sick again. He was sick in his kidneys and had to have an operation. They took him to La Paz to have one of his kidneys removed. When he came back, he couldn't work in the mine any more because he was missing a kidney.

Meanwhile, Engineer Bustamante told me to assume the leadership of the gang. This was the second time I was at the head, the first being in 1952, when there were good veins of ore. This time I was in charge of five people only, Juan Guzman, Luis Mamani, Paredes, Centren, and Mareno. I told Mamani to work on a tapping in order to fill it up; he was the best at that. I knew all the holes because in 1949 there were many veins in that area. After blasting from the side, they filled the sacks. The rock had 40 percent ore content, and the vein was wide, something like twenty meters. They worked the vein with a loading cart. They used two people to load the cart. I had seen all that because in those times I worked as the helper of the steward and followed him as he walked around all the sites. In those times the steward, Eusquio, hadn't found the lode as yet. The tunnel was too long and was crumbling on the sides. Beyond it was another tunnel where they had looked for a vein. They came near it but they didn't reach it. I told him where they had run the tunnel, and eight meters from it Clavo Boyadora cut through.

The next time I was able to reach the site where the lode tilted like a ramp. One of the workers went up fifteen meters to find out where the tunnel led and found the chimney filled with mud. The engineer came to see the floor of the chimney and he found mud. He was dissatisfied.

"This doesn't have much life left."

Truly it didn't have much life. I said to the engineer, "Engineer, we ought to work this tunnel from the sides because it's going to collapse and there is going to be mud pouring out."

The engineer didn't accept my suggestion. "No, just clean it out from the sides and front and get the load out. If the mud falls, let it fall." That was his answer.

Ignoring him, I had the men work narrow alleys on the sides. I got plenty of mineral, sacks of it. There were some big chunks of rock that weighed eight or ten tons. I took out eight sacks, ten sacks, with a good ore content, 35 to 40 percent grade. Bustamante was pleased with the work.

I stayed on that job four months or more. I worked with Mamani, who was somewhat cowardly — not the best man to work with in those dangerous sites. I told him, "Open up three passages on this side, one on the other, and another there in the main passage. When this one is filled with ore, you can go out through the other two."

To hold back the ore there was a slide and further below a puddle of water. The water never dried up because a gutter went by there, and it was the only one. In order to keep the ore from getting wet, he closed the channel off. When he began to tap the rock he was careless and a large stone fell behind and blocked the passage. That very same stone had held back the mud, and mud began to pour down over everything.

He didn't have a ladder to climb up, and it was too high to jump. The mud-slide was coming towards him, from the side of the chimney. When I went to call him for lunch I saw the passage filled with mud.

I yelled, "*Caramba!* What happened?" The other passage was also covered with mud, so I went to the third passage. There wasn't a ladder there either. The ladder was hanging in the middle, and in order to get to the other side, we had to use the slide at level seventy-five. So I yelled to Mamani: "I am here on the side! The load is still coming in! Put up the ladder." The rope was tied on the top of the ladder where it was hanging on the other side from where he stood. I said, "Let it go!"

"I have no space to move to the other side! It is slippery and the platform cannot be trusted. It might fall apart. I could fall all the way down!" he said.

I quickly blocked the passage with wooden beams which were lying on the floor, beams that were no longer in use. I had to make my way with ropes all the way up to the ladder. I wasn't able to untie the ladder because that fool had tied it at the top instead of the bottom where it could have been easily untied. I went down the ladder automatically, but I had to go back up, then down again, taking the "spoon" [a tool] with me so that he could untie the ladder by knocking it. I climbed more than half the way up with a spoon that was three meters long. I had barely untied it when the ladder fell back on top of me. Thank goodness it did not hurt me, but it was close. It fell with the end of the rope still attached above. I landed on the first platform. Later that very same night all three ladders fell with the rest. Everything was destroyed. I immediately asked the steward for more ladders, but he didn't give us any since they were stored outside the mine.

During my break I went down where Mamani was. A lot of the load of rock had fallen in the passage; more was filling the entry. The mud would not stop flowing; it was like water. Out of fright Mamani jumped from a beam, about six meters high. Beams were falling in all directions. They fell on top of him where he was on a slide about four or three meters long. There was nothing he could do. I told him to throw me the rope, but not to move otherwise. With a great deal of effort, I climbed down the ladder to the shaft. His back was hurt by the beams that fell on top of him. It must have happened to him when he jumped.

I carried him to the elevator and called for the ambulance to be sent to the mouth of the mine immediately. When we came out of the mine the ambulance was already there. I took him to the hospital and left him there.

I went back immediately to confront the steward since it was entirely his fault; he hadn't sent us the ladders on time. The steward told me that he would report to the chief of the section, Engineer Campero, that I had come to his office to hit him. He still didn't know what had happened.

While I was in the patio looking for a ladder, Campero called for me and I went. "Why have you disobeyed me? You will be punished for three days," he said.

"Engineer, you don't know what has happened on the job. I just got Mamani out of an accident. His back has been injured because we were missing a ladder. He almost lost his life, and I endangered my own. He is in the hospital," I said. "Last night the tailings slipped and the ladder fell all the way down to level seventy-five. Everything that fell was destroyed. I didn't go down because I knew that all the ladders were destroyed. One ladder with a different end point was left. We were barely able to get it down with the rope. I urged Mamani to come down bit by bit, but out of fear, he jumped six meters from the beams and hurt his back. I went to the steward and asked why he hadn't sent us the ladders we asked for. I don't think I was disrespectful to him. I didn't offend him in any way."

Campero called Gonzáles, and Gonzáles in one way or another tried to apologize. "I didn't send it to him because I was lacking workers," he said. "Someone was missing to tighten the screws on the ladder. We had been waiting until one arrived to get them down."

Well, the chief of the section had already started writing the order for my punishment, but after hearing me, he didn't.

*How do you act when you are startled in the mine? Have you ever reacted differently?*

I felt angry and frightened. At the very moment when it happened I forgot everything, I was so scared. I couldn't remember what to do because the load was close, about to cover us. Yet in the next moment I was capable of risking my own life just to save the other man, because that was my duty as the head of the gang. Had I left Mamani, he would have died there. I thought, if I let this load pour maybe it won't reach him. But then I thought, if the load poured out, it would cover the site even more, because further in there was another site where others were working. It was a good tunnel and that would probably have taken the load away. But to avoid that, I didn't let it drop. Instead I found a site where it could pour out and I yelled to alert everyone. I went around the debris. There was plenty of mud, like glue; it tried to suck my boots off. I can't remember how I got by, but I arrived at the chimney where Mamani was. That mud stank. When we held it, it was as if we were holding red wax, and we had difficulty getting it off our hands. That mud was very strong stuff.

After I got Mamani down, I tried to carry him back, but I could not because the mud was too strong. So I had to go around to the main alley even though it was pretty far away. I preferred to tire myself out rather than go through the mud. If I had let him drop, everything would have been worse. The section ladder was still in the Boyadora vein but I didn't go to look for it, because Mamani was yelling from pain. That jump was tough on him.

I was angry when I went to see the steward, but I can't remember what I told him, except that I scolded him badly. That's when he complained complained to the chief of the section, Engineer Campero. When Mamani was put in the hospital, I said to Bustamante, the engineer, "Look, Engineer, I think I don't have any luck. I want to give up being head of the gang. You should appoint someone else. I will continue working in the same place."

It was already August of 1966. I insisted that I wanted to continue as a member of the gang, but not as the head. He didn't accept my request. "We don't have anyone else," he said. "If you see someone who works better, then he can become the leader." But there was no one else, because that site wasn't like the rest.

When Mamani recovered he came back to work. "Why don't we give an offering to the *awicha?*" he asked. "Since we are already close to August, we can all chip in and buy the things which we need."

I agreed and we did it. He bought a lamb from Chupalla, a ranch where they have good lambs. (They have plenty of herds of fleece-bearing animals around there.) I sent Paredes to get the lamb, and Mamani went to Oruro to buy sweets, corn in kernels and on the cob, alcohol, beer, white wine, red wine, and *pisco* — all of those things. We had a hard time finding a *yatiri;* we had no luck at all. Quite by chance a *yatiri* arrived on the twenty-ninth of July at Juan Mareno's house Mareno was no longer working with us, but he came to tell us about him.

"A *yatiri* has arrived at my house and he knows about the offerings in the mine," he said. I went to Mareno's house, and we made a contract with the *yatiri*.

"Tomorrow night you have to be here with us; from here we will go to our tool shed," we told him.

He agreed to make the offering for sixty pesos. Each of the five of us contributed eighty pesos. We had a lot of money and were able to buy everything we needed. We even had money left with which we bought some extras.

On the night of the thirty-first of July we began our offering. First we killed the lamb. The *yatiri* wanted to kill the lamb by simply sticking a wire through its heart, but we wanted the heart intact. We didn't want it damaged by anything. Since the wire was dirty, when the animal's heart was poked with it, it would have tainted its heart. Besides, we needed the heart blood to spill over the rocks, so we had the lamb beheaded. We caught the blood in a plain white container without blue stripes on the rim. Three people – the *yatiri*, a worker, and I – went inside the mine. While we were sprinkling the blood on the rocks, the others were pulling the hide off the animal and cutting the flesh into cooking portions. We spent only an hour in the mine because it wasn't far – only the second level. When we returned, all was ready, the hearth was prepared, the fire was lit, and they put the meat in. The *yatiri* prepared his things such as the sugar paste, the sugar dressing, pink paste, white paste, *qori llimpi*, *golke llimpi*, *qori banderilla*, *golke banderilla*, *k'oa*, *llama unti* [llama fat], and *cuchi unti* [pig fat], shaping the fat into the form of a llama.

*What do each one of these things signify?*

The six llamas that we made out of the fat mean that we are sacrificing six llamas; they are the equivalent of six llamas. And we cover these with the sugar instead of salt, so that the *awicha* can eat something sweet.

The meat was cooked at ten-thirty. Shortly before eleven o'clock at night we began to eat in our hut outside the mine. First, we covered the eyes of those in charge of the distribution of meat so that they wouldn't favor their friend with the best pieces. I got the leg with a bone. Since there were few of us, we had big pieces to eat. A man came by – I don't remember his name – he wasn't a worker in Santa Fe, but it meant luck to us. We received him with a warm welcome. We called him *Mallku* [condor] and in Quechua we said, "*Mallku, chay wanpis mik-*

*uywanchis mikuysinawanchispa.*" That means "the condor has come to help us eat."

We gave him some meat, but out of bad luck he got the neck where the lamb had been cut. He took the meat, and tried to give us the bones back, but the *yatiri* obliged him to eat it. "You have to eat it; if not, the old woman is going to eat you." That's how he ordered him to eat it.

The man was frightened and finished eating his portion. All of us ate a lot of meat because a lamb was plenty for five people. After we finished we gathered all the bones and wrapped them in red wool. At about eleven-fifteen we put everything away.

When the three of us reentered the mouth of the mine at eleven-thirty, we were quite happy. We said that we were offering the food with all our heart, and hoped that the mine would prosper. We reached the site where we had to place the bones of the sheep and the heart. We put the heart flat down, surrounded by the sweets and carnation flowers, and alongside, a new sack on top of which we assembled the bones in the form of the skeleton of the lamb. First we placed the head, then the spine, then the hooves on both sides, laid in line with the legs on both sides, and then we put the ribs in place. Then we covered it. We placed its hide on top. We placed white wine, alcohol, beer, and papaya in mud cups on each of the four corners. We left it for a while then we made toasts next to it in the memory of the *k'araku*, for the offerings which we made to the Tío.

After that we quickly returned to the office without looking back. We stayed in the office two hours. Then we got in the cage and went outside. We reached the hut and continued with the *ch'alla*. Mamani was still there, drinking with the man who came to visit us. They were pouring offerings from their drinks to the *Pachamama*.

When we arrived Mamani said, "I am leaving because I don't feel well. And I cannot keep on drinking."

I answered, "That's fine. You can leave because we have already finished with everything, and those who want can leave. I too will leave in a little while."

He left while I remained behind with friends and the visitor. We were four altogether. We stayed an hour and one-half more. Then the visitor and my workmate, Paredes, left. I stayed behind alone to lock the shed. It was already four o'clock in the morning and dawning. We slept until nine o'clock in the morning. On the first of August it is not necessary to pick up the time cards. The steward was in charge of them, and he punched them even for those who missed work. He would pass them on to the man in charge of cards. That is the procedure for the first of August.

When I arrived at nine-thirty in the morning I said, "Hey, Mamani, let's cure our heads. Let's finish our *ch'alla*. It's a good time for our *awicha* and our Tío to receive a toast in good form."

We drank until we were dizzy, until six o'clock in the evening. At six o'clock I was the first to leave because I couldn't take it any more. I gave Mamani the lock and said, "The last one to leave should lock the door."

*Why didn't any of the managers attend the ch'alla?*

We asked the managers for authorization to make the *ch'alla* and the *k'araku*.

*Don't they ever come?*

No, none of the managers has ever come. The manager Aurelio Mendiola did a *k'araku* on his own, on behalf of the whole mine, for all the workers, with three bulls. That was the first *k'araku* ever done by a manager in the whole history of the mine. It has never been done for the entire company. In 1957, they did a *k'araku* in Morococala, in Clavo Grande, where they opened up a tunnel. By luck they hit on a good vein. Another manager from Morococala also went and did a *k'araku* with money from the company. He bought a bull that they roasted and ate in the tunnel. They did a good *k'araku*, like the one carried out by Mendiola, perhaps better. We saw it from below. They danced a lot with *tarkas*. There were several bands of *tarkas*. They were happy and drunk too. I have only seen two *k'arakus* done by managers. Since then, I haven't heard of any other one carried out by them. In San José I have heard that they made offerings to the mine, but never in person. They only gave the workers the money to carry it out.

In Santa Fe the manager himself bought the bulls — they sent a commission to several zones to buy white bulls, nine white bulls. He chose the first and bought each for fifty pesos. The whitest were chosen by the manager himself. He was also the one to put the knife to their throats, but of course he didn't kill them. He just put the knife to their heads. Then the butcher began to pierce the flesh. They were great feasts on both occasions in Morococala and Santa Fe.

*Are the awichas the companions of the Tío?*

Yes, they are his companions.

*Do you know any stories about the awicha?*

In Santa Fe there aren't any stories about the *awicha*. It's just that all the workers call them on their work sites even if they didn't do anything. For example, if a tailing falls, small as it is, we have to say: "Keep it, keep it, *awicha*. Don't bother us," we yell.

*In Spanish or in Quechua?*

In Spanish or Quechua, it's all the same. The ones who speak Spanish say it in Spanish, and those who speak in Quechua say it in Quechua, and those who speak Aymara will say it in Aymara. In Aymara he will scold her.

*When you enter the mine, is there anything that you must do? Do you have to pray?*

Well, once we are inside the cage, and the cage is moving we cross ourselves asking God to protect us, asking His archangel to protect us, so that nothing will happen to us on the job.

*When you go inside the mouth of the mine, do you do anything?*

When we go inside the mouth, by the gate, we do the same thing. In the work site we can no longer cross ourselves to begin working. Only when we come in can we cross. Once inside it is contrary to Christ; It belongs to the devil. For example, of all our tools we don't use a pickaxe to fill "bags" when we find plenty of mineral. We only use it to loosen and free the load. That's because the pickaxe has the form of a cross. When you hold it a certain way, it looks like a cross. It often gets lost or the handle breaks off. That's why we must take care of it. We never use it in the tunnels when we work.

*Inside, then, it is the domain of the Tío, and of all the forces which are opposed to the saints?*

Yes, that's correct. Inside the mine, the workers never ask anything of God, nor of the saints or the archangels; we can only ask of things from the *Tío* and the *viejas*. Since I said *viejas*, you must think there are many, but there is only one, in the whole mine. The *Tío*, like God, is everywhere inside the mine. There is only one *Tío* as well.

*And the viejas are in the work site?*

Yes, in all the work sites, but there is only one, but she is in all the work sites.

*Does she have another name?*

No, we only call her *viejita*.

*What does she look like?*

We make a figure with a woman's face when we chew coca.

*Is she a chola?*

No, she has a hat and her hair is uncombed. *Chaska ch'aska uma,* uncombed hair, we say in Quechua.

*Is she the same as Chaskañawi?*

No, she's not. She is the *Tío's* companion, his wife. When there is any movement in the earth, when anything falls, we have to converse with her; according to the older drillers that instruct us, when we sense the darkness, the danger, we must summon her, we must talk to her. That way she gets scared, and stops throwing the stones on the worker.

*And the landslides, are they her fault?*

Well, when they forget to offer the *k'arakus* to the *viejas* they might take revenge. Since 1952, there have been offerings, *k'arakus* constantly. Before, there weren't any major *k'arakus.* There were only smaller offerings that the manager didn't know about. We had to do them without their knowledge; otherwise we would be punished for three days. Everywhere were signs that read "Don't bring any alcoholic beverages into the mines." There were other signs that read "Don't come into the mines the first Friday of the month as if you were walking into a *chichería.*" Nobody complained.

Before 1952 there weren't any *k'arakus.* There were plenty of accidents, but, of course, the mine was new then. The "administrators," as they were called then, didn't concern themselves with *k'arakus,* because there was plenty of tin. Those administrators were only concerned with their own well-being. They took all the good ore out, and left the bad ore behind. They didn't develop the mine. Then, suddenly, after 1952 the "managers" of the nationally owned mines began to believe in the *k'arakus* because production was low. So they reconsidered and, hoping to increase production, allowed the miners to carry out their *k'araku* once a year, and *ch'allas* every first Friday.

After the revolution of 1952, we made the *k'araku,* some during Carnival, some in August. But this did not come about because of an order from management, or from the union. It was the doing of the workers themselves, and thus one of the greatest days in the nation. After Barrientos assumed power they prohibited the *k'arakus* and *ch'allas,* but we have still found a way of offering food to the *Tío* and the *vieja,* so that they will assist us on our job.

On the second of August we still didn't work, by order of the management. After three days we went to work only because on that day they paid us for the celebration of the sixth of August. On the fifth of August we took our time cards and immediately went to the Plaza Seis de Agosto to set up the ring for the bullfight. Everyone working the mine had to go. Some took the wooden planks along, some tied them together, some dug the holes in the ground, and some stuck the planks in. The president of the National Feasts Committee brought half a barrel of *chicha* along and gave it to those who were thirsty. Some worked, but some who were cunning, and who didn't like to obey the bosses, left for their houses. I was in charge of the workers, so I took note of those who left. I had their *mita* taken away because I don't like people who make fun of these occasions and aren't responsible. That's why all of my workers followed through with their jobs except for those who drank too much *chicha*. Before one o'clock everyone left for their houses.

The rings were ready for the bullfight. All we had left to do was to cover the passageways that we had opened so the vendors could settle in. On the night of the fifth of August we gathered in the San Pedro stadium for the entrance of the torches. We left at eight o'clock at night, and I went to my house with my wife. We returned for the vespers, but the open-air band concert was already over. When we arrived at the feast, the people were already drunk. Some were dancing and others were drinking inside the stands. We were awaiting the contest of the vendors' stands. The inspectors in charge of qualifying each stand went past, looking for the one which was best prepared, with the most ornaments. There were three prizes: a radio for first place, a set of dishes for second place, and an electric iron for third. Then there was a contest of dances: *cuecas, taquiraris,* and tangos. In the contest of *cuecas,* Señora Victoria Cana, with her partner, Francisco Basualdo won, and in the tango competition, one of our workmates, the helper of the driller, won. He had worked for a very long time in the mines in Argentina, so he knew how to dance well. In the *taquirari* competition Señora Trifonia Romero, who also won first prize in the contest of the stands, was the winner.

I left at five in the morning to sleep. We awoke at ten o'clock in the morning. On the sixth of August we went to take a walk around the plaza. We returned to lunch. I did not know how to drink and didn't like to get drunk. It was fun to watch the feasts and the drunkards. We walked, all dressed up, further up the Plaza Sixth of August to watch. My friend said, "After eating, I will fetch some beer and we will drink." I agreed.

So he went to buy some. He didn't know how to drink either. Out of friendship he bought the beer since I had invited him to lunch. He brought two bottles of beer and we drank. They were beginning to gather in the San Pedro Stadium to watch the parade. My friend said, "Let's go to the gathering. It's already late, and they will leave us behind at the tail end."

"Okay," I answered. My wife was still getting ready to go out, so I went with my friend, leaving our wives behind with our children.

First, the director of the school, Franz Tamayo, spoke. Then other teachers spoke. Then the union people began to speak commemorating the nation's celebration. They spoke about the amount of land which Simón Bolivar left for Bolivia, and the situation and conditions under which it lost the Chaco War with Paraguay, the amount of square kilometers usurped, and so on. Then we paraded. They gave the children treats. They appointed me to give out packs of candies, cookies, and oranges.

After all of that, there were a couple of popular games in the Plaza Sixth of August. The school children had sack races, partridge races, and wheelbarrow races. A boy would stand on his hands, a second boy would hold his feet, and the first had to run on his hands. Many hurt their faces on the floor. The contest was dangerous. The first one to reach the goal won the prize. The prizes were: five pesos, two pesos fifty, and one peso. Some that fell scratched their faces and even loosened their teeth because they couldn't go fast enough. Years ago, in 1957, there was a Sr. Montano who was the chief of offices. He had a very playful child who was in the race. His father was watching the race from the balcony prepared by the ceremonial committee. His son got on all four feet, and the boy with him picked up his legs. The boy holding his feet was slightly bigger. He pushed him too much. The boy's hands tired and he couldn't race anymore. He fell in the worst area, where there were lots of small stones. All his front teeth were knocked out, and his nose was bleeding. It looked bad. He was left without any front teeth. His father standing above, watching helplessly, tried sliding down the balcony pole, but a splinter went through his hand. Two accidents at once, father and son. They took both of them to the hospital. This is what happens sometime in these games that shouldn't be allowed. But the children liked them, and they wanted to win money. They would say, "If anything happens, it will just have to happen. We want to play those games. Many people come to see them, and we want to show them."

The children were in a good mood, yelling a lot. They continued running. There were always accidents in these popular games. At these feasts a nurse must always be present in case anything happens.

At night there were spaghetti-eating contests. They cook in big pots that hold two kilos of spaghettis each sixty to eighty meters long. They tried to cook without breaking the spaghetti. I don't know how they do it. It must be with a lot of care. The one to finish first gets ten pesos, and the winner — the one who eats the longest spaghetti — gets one hundred pesos; the second place earns fifty pesos, and third gets twenty-five.

We saw plenty of games and everyone was quite happy. I already had several children; all four of them were with me. My wife was expecting our daughter Anna María. My brother-in-law's wife also was with us, in order to look after her husband who was already drunk. He is capable of spending his whole life drinking, even if he didn't work — he likes it that much! He tried to force me to drink with him, but I got angry and he no longer insisted. He went off alone.

"Would you like to go?" he asked.

"Ah, no, no. I don't like it. You can go waste your life. I am going to spend my time up here," I answered. He went alone and drank. A bum insulted him when he was drunk, but since he was weak, he didn't fight. When he is drunk, he only wants to rest. One of the bums caught him by the arm and threw him from his seat, hurting his head. I saw this and tolerated it, but his wife wanted to run and hit the men. Once again the man approached my brother-in-law and this time hit him. He didn't say anything to the bum because he was drunk and could not defend himself.

At this point I went down and caught the man with a solid punch and threw him to one side of the stand, breaking some glasses. I held him by the chest and threw him out of the stand. Once outside I wanted to beat him up, but my friend stopped me. "He's drunk, let him go, Don Juan," he said.

So I let him go. I took my brother-in-law's wife to sleep with my wife at our house. I remained, watching the children rehearse, and then the dance contest began.

After that we went to look at the milk-drinking contest. In this game two partners are blindfolded and given dishes of milk and spoons to feed each other. It was funny to watch them. My wife and sister-in-law laughed until they cried. My children laughed even more when neither of the Indians in the contest could find the mouth of the other. There were times when one wouldn't aim with the spoon, and the other was left trying to find it. In the meantime, his chest would get smeared with condensed milk. In the end when one of the Indians was about finished, the man to his right dropped the bowl over his head. That way the dish was left clean. It was very funny.

They looked for another can of milk for contestants who were drunk. They didn't blindfold them, but they took those who were most drunk. The prize was one hundred pesos, even for the loser, it didn't matter. Four drunkards came to enter. They drew lots, two of them won, Zembrana and another man whose name I cannot remember. He was a fat, paunchy, short man. They began to feed each other. Zambrana was a tall man. They were sitting on empty dynamite boxes. The public was yelling, "Stand up! Stand up!" They got up. The short man's shoulder and chest were smeared. He couldn't reach the tall man's mouth. It was funny too. They were hugging each other, bumping into each other. They couldn't stand straight because they were too drunk. When they finished, they were given the hundred pesos.

The plaza was full of people. Those people who were in front were also smeared with condensed milk and had to go home and change their clothes.

The next game was boxing between drunkards. They began boxing in the field but they couldn't fight there because there were too many people, so they went to the bandstand. The band went to the bottom floor where they played. The drunkards began to box. They couldn't even punch one another; instead with each swing they would fall to the floor.

There was a man named Vargas — "Cantor-of-the-town" was his nickname. Every morning he sang evangelical songs. He didn't sing popular songs, only evangelical ones. Like the priest, he went to sermons in the workplace and that is how he got his name. He was the referee. He was also a little bit drunk but not that much. And it was his bad luck, when he tried separating the boxers, that he got between them. One was trying to punch the other one, just that moment. Instead he punched the referee, right on the nose. Vargas stopped right then to clean his nose, which was bleeding. Instead of the boxers beating each other, Vargas got beaten. The guy who hit the referee was declared the winner, and they stopped fighting. Vargas lifted his hand up and said, "The champion beat me down."

That is how the night went by. The next day, on the seventh of August, at nine o'clock in the morning there was a contest of hand drillers. Despite the fact that on the job I advanced beyond the limits, finishing ten, fifteen meters more than the rest, I was unlucky in the contest. The first prize was a Philips radio. Second prize was six pots, third, an electric iron, and fourth, a shirt.

We began the contest. There was a man who was drunk. He worked in the store with the drills, but before that he had worked in the interior of the Siglo XX mine. They say he was a good driller. After a very long time, he began to drill. He was drunk and didn't measure his blows, and he began hitting the butt of the drill. But once he missed and hit his hand with the hammer. The whole finger fell into the mud with the impact of the hammer. He didn't feel anything because he was drunk. So much blood flowed! They went up to him, but he went on working even more furiously with the hammer completely bathed in blood, his foot as well. The whole ground was covered with blood. A nurse went to him and tied his wrist so that no more blood would spill. Then we held the man and took him out of the contest. He was right next to me; I saw it all clearly.

The first prize was won by an older man, Garcia Alanes. He now lives a little bit below my house. His nickname was *"Cueca de San Pedro"* because he had a *chichería* in San Pedrito. His son used to play the harmonica for the customers. One day when his son wasn't working, the man got drunk with a woman named Olimpia who used to sell pastry. We used to call her *"Rellenera"* [pastry filler] because of her job. Garcia danced with her without music, and then he called for his son in Quechua: *"Localla jamuy!"* (Come lazy one!)

His son approached and Garcia said in Quechua, *"Tokay acordeoman; madrinay-kitatusuy morda cueca San Pedrituyta.* (Play the harmonica; I am going to dance the San Pedrito *cueca* with your godmother.)

His son obeyed him. His workmates heard all this, and from then onwards called him *"Cueca de San Pedro."* This man won first prize, the radio, and took it with him. Second prize was taken by Ramos. He used to be an interior miner, but he left and went to work with the stone-cutting section to make stone reinforcements for the interior of the mine. We called this man *"Largo Rama"* [great branch] because he was tall. Third prize was won by Victor Flores, a small dark man. We went to the plaza with all the diggers dancing a *waynu* in a band that included the president of the National Feasts and his group. When we arrived, they awarded the prizes in the Plaza Seis de Agosto.

At one in the afternoon a driller's contest was planned. I didn't enter the contest because my wrist was damaged. When I was pushing a wagon inside the mine, I slipped and bent my wrist. Maybe I could have won, but the prizes weren't of very high value, because they had made a mistake and given the hand drillers those intended for the mechanical drillers. First prize was six pots. Then there was an electric iron and a shirt — only three prizes. Eugenio Padilla won first prize, Ramon Aguilar was second, and Honorio Vásquez, my workmate, came third. We used to call him *"Papito"* because he had a daughter. That moment he was overjoyed because he really didn't know how to work; he was only an assistant. "I'm not even a driller, but I won a prize!" he said, jumping around. Plenty of men participated, but the machines weren't working well. They took them from the workplace.

The contest of the hand drillers differs from the contest of the mechanical drillers. The hand drillers have to drive the drill in with the hammer. They use only their own strength whereas the mechanical drillers rely on the force of the compressed air that turns the drill. When the machine is running, it is difficult to hold. One has to stand firmly to hold it steady. If one doesn't control it, the machine moves in all directions, and it can even break the bore hole. With the machine, you can work quickly, but only if you hold it well. The driller working with the hammer can shift it around in any direction, and he doesn't employ as much strength. The only inconvenience is the weight of the hammer. The hands and arms get tired and numb quickly. All the nerves seem to become frozen. With the machine that does not happen, but we tremble from the exertion we expend holding the machine.

After the contest of the drillers, the bullfight began. At three o'clock they put the padding up. At four o'clock, the first bull was let loose. When that bull, which was the fiercest, was let loose, a drunkard jumped into the ring. He was my neighbor. He stood in front of the bull holding his hips. He didn't have a cape to make passes with the bull. The bull ran right into him, pierced his stomach with his horns, and tossed him in the air like a doll. He threw him to the ground and stepped over him. They removed him from the arena and took him to the hospital where he died. There were only two bulls, because as soon as they heard the drunkard died, they halted the feast until the next year. The dead man was named Cándido Lero; he died because he was foolish. As a consequence of his death, the following two days of pack-saddling were suspended.

On the eighth of August we were granted permission to go to Candido's funeral. At four o'clock in the afternoon his corpse was buried. When we reached the cemetery one of the members of the committee spoke and afterwards the secretary of the union spoke. The following day we again didn't work. We had to take down all the benches that had been set up in the Plaza Seis de Agosto. We all went, the office workers as well as the interior workers, but we couldn't distinguish which ones they were because they wore their oldest clothing. They helped us carry the poles and planking from the site to the truck. We returned everything, since it was all borrowed from the union. The union used to put on an overseer every night so that nothing was stolen, not even a handbarrow; it was very controlled.

There were plenty of drinks left from the packsaddling reception and some popular games for adults that didn't take place. There were plenty of cocktails left over, and kegs of beer that they brought out of the cellar. They took it all to the plaza and anyone who wanted could drink it. I think there were something like fifteen barrels. There were bottles too, but in a little while they were all gone. It was completely disorganized. If somebody had been there with glasses the bottles wouldn't have disappeared so fast. The committee was in charge of the empty bottles. Before they finished taking down the bleachers, every-body was drunk. Nobody sober was left to finish the job. Even I was drunk with the beer. I didn't drink *chicha* because I don't like it; alcohol even less. It leaves me without any strength to work.

The president of the committee said: "You must finish the work. If you don't finish today, I will have you punished. It all depends upon me, and I am going to tell the administration that none of you finished your jobs, which is obligatory."

We finally finished at four o'clock in the afternoon. The driver was also drunk and in the middle of the road he spilled all of the handbar-rows. He was very close to the mine, right in front of the door of the commissary. But the men with him did not take the kegs all the way inside. The next day the workers in the shop had to pick them up once again, so it was twice as much work. It is always easier if people do their job properly.

On the twenty-fifth of August a friend from the army barracks where we had served arrived. He was my buddy. When he arrived, I took him to my house and I put him up, along with his son, who was three months old. He came from far away to ask me to baptize his son. He was working in Huanuni. I accepted happily. I already had many godchildren. I must have at least nineteen godchildren whom I have baptized. I don't take into account those godchildren I have from health Masses and marriages because they are not as important. He had to go back the next day. He went with my wife to Oruro, had the child baptized, and returned to Huanuni.

During September, the month in which we had plenty of work, another *compadre*, Francisco Aquino, celebrated his daughter's first birthday. She was my godchild. He ruined me all week because he didn't leave me alone, even though I don't drink. He insisted that I drink. I would visit him around midday and leave in the afternoon. The next day I would return to work and he would be still drinking. The following day, however, he made it hard for me to work at all. He slowed me down a lot. In the month of September they begin to count the average production in order to set the bonus.

I got mad and said, "Don't bother me anymore. I don't like to drink, *compadre*. We already drank a lot. If you want to drink, you can go on. But I don't want to, and I won't force myself to drink. I am not going to drink with you anymore." That's how mad I got. He didn't bother me anymore.

He drank alone. On Sunday, he drank the whole day. I went back to work. When he walked by my house, on the way to the privy or to feed the pigs, he would look at me, but he wouldn't say a thing. Nor would I when I walked by him.

In November, my first cousin got married. She sent me a letter with the invitation. I didn't go because it was the last month of work for figuring the bonus. If I had gone to Cochabamba, I would have lost a whole week. I could have taken a vacation during that time, but I didn't want to leave the job because that would have gotten in the way of raising the average production rate on which the bonus is based. She had come to my wedding and helped with everything. She even gave us chickens. So I sent money to my first cousin to buy chickens and thus was able to return the gift to her. With that money she bought chickens, rabbits, and *chicha* in my name and said, "They are not present, but I have this gift from them." After she announced this, she fed the guests with the chickens, rabbits, and *chicha*.

I was on vacation for the entire month of December. On the twenty-fifth of November, I went to the office to ask for my vacation authorization. On the twenty-sixth I had to begin my vacation, because the month ends on the twenty-fifth in Santa Fe. They begin to count from the twenty-sixth onwards for the next month. My paper was ready, except the manager's signature was missing. I had it signed and we left for Cochabamba for an entire month. We left Filemón behind because he was in school. I asked for permission to take María and Aníbal, because they were ahead in their studies. The principal gave them permission. María's professor said, "In Cochabamba she can copy her homework and borrow a notebook from one of her friends. If she does that, she will have no problem since her grades are already high."

The only problem was with Aníbal. He was not so far ahead. He was only granted two weeks, so when I came back to pick up my paycheck, and I brought Aníbal and María. In the meantime, I had left Filemón at my brother-in-law's house. The children ate there every day but they slept at home. My brother-in-law's wife came by to stay with them. When I got my pay I returned to Cochabamba where my wife's parents lived.

I had a good time in Cochabamba. I like to sow and take care of the plants. I arrived at a good time, just when my father-in-law was paying laborers to cover over the maize, potatoes, and other crops that had been sown. My children and I covered over the corn. We finished it all, and spent the rest of the days on vacation.

My father-in-law used to serve lots of chicken, but I didn't want anything. I don't know what it was; maybe I was sick. When I was in Santa Fe my body was plump, but on my vacation I lost quite a bit of weight. I got back to Santa Fe looking as though I had gotten sick in Cochabamba. People were surprised and asked, "What's happened to you? Instead of getting better, you have lost weight. What is wrong with you?"

I told them how it was, what I was given to eat, and I said, "It must have been the climate that didn't suit me. That's why I look bad."

We returned on the twenty-fourth of December, because my children missed playing around the house with their toys. They always had the furniture pushed towards the wall and played in the middle with the entire family. Sometimes they invited all their friends to play. Because of the joy with which they played, I had to bring them back before the twenty-fifth, because on that day the entire family got together, both of my in-laws, my wife, everybody. My own family was missing. Not one of my kin was living in Santa Fe; all were in Oruro. We cooked a hot dish of chicken. We ate it about three o'clock in the afternoon, with beer — the *chicha* isn't good in Santa Fe; it's like water. It doesn't get you drunk. Your belly pops, that is all. Besides, I like beer more than *chicha*. We also had whipped egg cocktails. My brother-in-law Ambrosio wanted to drink. I didn't let him. My older brother-in-law was also enthusiastic. He said, "Come on, let's have a few drinks."

I got very irritated, because with too many drinks, I faint. I don't like it. The drinks don't smell good.

To get away from them, I went for a walk with Filemón, but I couldn't even walk around in peace. Everywhere people were drinking. When they called me, I didn't pay attention.

Some friends caught me by the hand, "Hello, how are you? Come have a drink," they urged.

"I will be there right away," I said, and waved and walked by. They would come out on the street, but I didn't pay attention to them. Everybody in Santa Fe knew that I rarely drank. I went to the street where the movie theatre is. We walked by the hospital, and arrived at San Pedrito.

We returned at five-thirty in the afternoon and went to the movies. We came out at eight o'clock at night and went home where I found everybody. I didn't want to go in, nor stay in the patio. There was nothing to do. I sent Filemón to call my wife and she came out.

"What is going on?" I was annoyed. "Tomorrow I have to hold a couple of meetings with my friends. I can't drink with them," I told her.

I went in and put the drinks away without serving anyone. My older brother-in-law got annoyed and said, "I'm going to leave since he doesn't want to serve any drinks."

His younger brother added, "Let's go to my house. In my house we can continue. Maybe Petrona is bothered by this." After having said that, they said good-bye. I stayed in the kitchen until they left.

We had to go to Cataví for a soccer game between the teams "Racing" of Siglo XX and "21st of December" of Santa Fe. I used to play, too. We held meetings in my house. We held such a meeting on the twenty-sixth and discussed how we were going to get to Cataví. We agreed that the president of the club and the rest of the leaders would ask the company for a car, because in the regulations it is written that the company must promote sports. The management gave us a Leyland, a dump truck. We had asked for a bus, but it was already being used by the housewives to buy things in Oruro.

We left in the truck on the afternoon of the thirtieth so that we could meet the others on the thirty-first. The workers prepared beds for us in the commissary where we slept — all twenty-three of us.

The next morning at seven-thirty they gave us breakfast, and at ten they took us to the social club headquarters. They showed us all the games and sports available there, gave us a cold snack, and took us to the refinery in Cataví. They showed us all the machinery, the way they sew the sacks for tin ore with machines. The workers don't sew a thing, they only feed in the sacks, flattened out, and the machine sews; then the same machine pushes the finished sack into the trough below, where the workers catch it. They showed us everything very thoroughly.

It was noon by then, and at twelve-thirty we went to the workers' ranch where they gave us lunch. We ate in peace without any ill feeling, although we were soon to be opponents. At one-thirty we left the ranch to get ready for the match. First the intermediate teams played, and then at two-fifteen we played. We lost. "Racing" was a tough team. We didn't lose by much, only one goal. They won 2 to 1. In the second round we tied all along until about ten minutes before the end when they goaled us, so we lost.

I had to be back at work on the third of January. We returned to Santa Fe after having been beaten and went home. We were still on vacation. There was plenty of drinking still, but I didn't drink at all. Most of us didn't drink. It is not sensible to ride around in a car drunk; it is very dangerous. When we arrived in Santa Fe, it was a great drinking occasion. They were dancing everywhere on the night of New Year's Eve.

My wife was in bed. She hadn't done anything because I was not there. On New Year's Eve we usually cook a hot meal, but since I had to travel that very day, we didn't. We were kept awake until dawn. I stayed at home, while the rest went from house to house.

On the first of January, I went to Morococala to my friend's house. He, like me, wasn't a big drinker. I told my wife, "My *compadre* is waiting for me. I am going to visit him." I went outside, still avoiding my neighbor. I didn't return home once I went out. I went straight to Morococala, having told my wife, "Come in a little while. We are going to cook in my friend's house. Nobody is going to bother us with any drinks. We will come home late."

When I got as far as the hospital, I saw my wife and children walking behind me. We went together to my friend's house; He wasn't there but his wife was. He had gone to play soccer, so I went with my son to play soccer, even though I had only my regular shoes on since I wasn't expecting to play.

When I found him I said, "We have come to visit because my neighbors are drinking and won't leave me alone. They try to get me to drink too much."

"I am going to play a little while longer," he said, "and then you must come to my house."

My friend told his wife, "Listen, Juan says his neighbors are drinking too much there and they don't want to do that. They want to be home, like us."

They cooked a good meal, and we ate and drank a little beer. We left at six o'clock in the afternoon.

When we arrived home we found that our neighbors had broken three of our windows. My children's toys that had been on the window sills were gone. I don't know if they broke the windows to steal the toys, or if it was just horseplay. My children were left without any new toys, only toys from past years, and María began to cry for her doll. Three days later, María saw our neighbor's daughter with the doll and told me about it.

"Don Marcial's daughter has my doll."

I went to see if it was true. I saw the doll, but missing its hands, eyes, eyelashes. It was completely disfigured.

"It's no longer in good shape, my little one," I consoled her. Then I went to Don Marcial.

"The doll was inside my house on the altar over the bed. My daughter treasured it, and your son took it out of my children's room."

Actually, I don't know whether the daughter or the elder son took it. She was still young and ignorant, about five years old, whereas his eldest son was thirteen. He must have taken them, I thought, and I blamed him for the loss of all the toys. The children began to blame each other: "No, it was such-and-such's child," "No, his son took it," and so on. That way we didn't get anywhere. I could not blame any one person because they all accused one another. I didn't want to have ongoing problems with my neighbors, so I didn't say anything else. But my wife insisted; she wanted to force them to pay up.

I told her, "Leave them alone. I don't want to force them; I don't want to bother with them." But I was bitter.

# 14

## I Bury Myself Alive Every Day

The hazards of working the mines are enormous. Statistics on sickness and accidental death have been a carefully guarded secret. The International Labor Organization team that went to Bolivia in 1946 came up with a figure of 6,000 accidents a year resulting in death or permanent major disability, from a workforce of only 28,000 in the major mines. In addition, disease takes an unestimated annual toll. The most common cause of death by disease is silicosis, called "the sickness of the mines" in Bolivia. The damage to the lungs causes bronchopneumonia that is often the immediate cause of death. Liver and kidney diseases are also frequent because the *copagira* [acidulous waters in the mines] and noxious gases enter the body and affect the major organs of the workers. Women are aware of these dangers and try to fortify the men with good nutrition — the first defence against sickness. They also feel responsible for maintaining the psychological defences: the miner must want to live when he enters the mine, lest he become a victim to the ever-present dangers within. When a death occurs, even if it was clearly an accident, people ask if the victim was fighting with his wife, and they condemn a wife who sends her husband off to work in a state of despair. Coca is considered a friend of the workers as they face the hazards of underground work. Some believe that chewing coca prevents the gases from damaging the internal organs. Coca breaks are designated periods of rest within the mine during which workers congregate to chew collectively. In Quechua there are separate terms for chewing in a group — *akulikar* — and for chewing alone — *pijchar.* The importance of collective strength in the protection of workers is embodied in this most basic ritual in the mines. Juan speaks of these illnesses and how the workers try to defend themselves.

---

The miner is always affected in his internal organs, especially in the liver, because the miner chews coca and coca is hot and can burn the liver. But they must chew it daily anyway. If you don't chew coca, it is worse because the odor of the gas goes to the head and then you get liver trouble. The battery pack for the head lamp also hurts the kidneys because the case is tied to the waist and, as we work, it heats up and this hurts the kidneys.

The gases of the mine affect the worker's entire body. Workers mostly get sick in their lungs, then in their kidneys, and finally in their livers. The liver is a very important organ that enables us to live. Many workers have died from liver ailments.

I almost died from a liver ailment. I was reluctant to go to the doctor since I didn't want to miss work, but finally I couldn't take it any more; I had to go to the hospital. Dr. Madriaga, a Cruceño from Santa Cruz, was there. He was a good doctor and popular among the workers, but he didn't know a thing about the liver. He sent me to Oruro to Dr. Nestor Valdez because my eyes hurt me when I went from the darkness of the mine into the sunlight. I would see a bright star and a black spot that would eclipse the star when I turned. It would then become small and disappear. I told Dr. Valdez about that, too, since he was also an eye doctor.

He put me into the general hospital in Oruro because there were no beds available in the hospital in San Jose. I was completely immobile for two weeks. Every day I had an injection, sometimes two, one in each buttock. I couldn't stand injections in my arms. I got pretty bored living immobilized like a tree. I couldn't move anywhere. In order to get out of bed, I had to have someone help me. But I had to endure it. Finally I begged the doctor, "Doctor, I don't think I can recover with injections only; please give me a rest from the injections, because I cannot move any more. I am like a tree trunk in bed. I feel like a dead man." After that he gave me medicine in liquid form and tablets. I responded better and after two weeks I went back to Santa Fe.

When I returned, Dr. Madriaga had left for his new post in Colquiri.

Dr. Carrasco had come, but there was only one doctor although there had been a request for two. After a while another doctor, Francisco T. Troncoso, arrived. He was a player on the team "Royal Santa Fe." Since I also played on the workers' team, I had met this doctor the twenty-first of December, in the stadium.

When I saw again he looked at me and said, "I used to see you looking fine before, but now you look different. Your eyes are yellow; they look like cat's eyes. You look skinnier every day. Is anything the matter with you?"

At that time, my chest was hurting me, burning me, and I had no desire to eat. I went to work out of breath. When they gave me a glass of soda, or something cold, and I drank it, the pain went away. So even when I wasn't thirsty I had to drink so that the pain would fade away.

Doctor Troncoso said to me, "What do you say about coming by my consulting room tomorrow? Tonight I am going to study about the disease you have. You have a liver problem. I shall give you some medicines. If there aren't any here, I will have them brought from the city. Have you any money?"

"I have eighty pesos in my pocket," I said.

"I think that is enough. With that money we will buy the medicine, Juanito."

That night as I rested, I told my wife what that doctor had told me. The next day, I felt tired. When I left the mine, I went by the doctor's office. I opened the door and was waiting when he saw me. He said to his assistant, "Let that worker come in."

I entered and he greeted me. We spoke forty-five minutes, speaking about how I ached with this sickness, how the pain had begun, everything in detail. He took notes.

Analyzing all this, he said, "You are very sick in your liver. We couldn't find the drugs which you need. Do you have any money with you?"

"Yes, I have eighty pesos."

"That's too little," he said. "We need one hundred pesos more."

"I don't have that much, Doctor," I said.

"Can you go to Social Security? I will give you an order so that they can give you some money in advance." He gave me a medical certificate to buy the medicine.

I went to Social Security and they in turn sent me to the superintendent in charge of accounts. He gave me an order for the hundred pesos and they gave me the money at eleven o'clock. That same afternoon, at about four, the doctor went to Oruro to buy the medicine. He came back at eight and brought the drugs to my house in person. He was a good friend. He always came to my house. We talked, played cards, and ate whatever my wife cooked. He gave me a piece of paper with all the directions as to how to take the drugs, which ones at what time. Everything was noted in detail. I began to take the drugs right away.

Troncoso said, "Tomorrow you must leave your job. I am going to give you an order for external rest, not internal. You must come to the hospital so that I can give you some drugs that will take the pain away. You should rest and take these medicines."

Before I took a leave from my job, I wasn't feeling well. When I was on my way to work, I walked like a drunkard, *chancaqueando* [staggering] from one side to another. I would look for a place to rest. It was always the same. Once I chewed coca I would regain my strength to drill. Coca heals the body. It is as if the body were asleep. In the hospital I had dextrose injections in a serum. With all of that I got well soon. I had been sick for four years, and for the last two years I had trouble breathing. I walked around dizzy.

*When did that happen?*

It occurred between 1958 and 1962. My daughter Elena was already born; she was a year old. I couldn't even hold her in my arms. I had no strength left. But I kept working. In the morning I would walk to work quickly, with energy, but soon I would get tired and I could no longer work. In the end, I followed the doctor's advice and took the drugs which he himself bought. So far I have had no more problems with my liver. But I am not completely well. Whenever I eat something hot, the pain returns. It burns.

*Have you chewed much coca?*

No, not very much. I didn't like it. Before I worked in the mine I didn't like it at all, because it didn't smell good. The workers, my companions, forced me to chew at least a little bit. In the end I grew accustomed to chewing coca. Too much coca is harmful. It can even stop one from thinking.

There was a worker, Juan Callejas, who is now dead. He chewed coca on both sides of his mouth. You couldn't distinguish his mouth from his nose because he stuffed his cheeks with so much coca. He never spoke. Once he started *pijchando* [chewing coca in solitude], he stopped talking and would only make gestures. When he didn't chew, he would get sick. He chewed in his house, and even at bedtime he had to chew.

They took him off of the job because he was very sick. When he retired, there was no money to buy coca because he was so poor. He owed the company six thousand bolivianos. Upon getting his consent, they took that amount from him and gave him the rest. All the money was gone because his wife, Sebasta, was a shrew. She took plenty of money and spent it, even though he didn't have much. He was left with only three thousand, some of which they used to buy on clothing and to pay people whom they owed. I think they were left with something like a thousand bolivianos.

This man got very sick in his liver and kidneys. The doctors told him to stop chewing coca. Once he stopped working he should have stopped, but he could not live without it. He would become bored and fight with his wife and children. He hit his son, Juan, a good boy, now working in Santa Fe.

He got very abusive, and the only thing that calmed him was the coca. And so to retain his senses, he had to chew coca. This is what the doctor was told. The doctor tried to cure him of his vice, but he wasn't able to. In the end he died with the disease of the mines, sick in his liver and kidneys.

After seeing what happened to him, I was always cautious with coca. When I was an overseer, I only chewed coca on the third shift. On the first or second shift, I wouldn't even taste any. There were a few over-seers who chewed a little. I didn't chew it much because it has a bad smell. In my house I chew only when I have to do something difficult which requires plenty of force. Coca gives you strength and desire to work. I can't completely stop chewing it when I work. Whenever I want to do something special, I always chew a little bit of coca. With that I feel good and I work with a will.

During the month of April, 1968, there were three terrible acci-dents. A man fell in the main shaft after having a fight with his daughter and wife. His daughter wanted to go out alone to the movies at eight o'clock one night, without the company of her brother. The man, Do-mingo Sanchez, didn't want her to go out alone because she was nine-teen years old.

"I don't mean a thing in this house," he said to his wife. "You want to let your daughter go out wherever and whatever time. This means that I am not needed here. I am leaving."

The family didn't follow him when he left the house drunk. He slammed the door hard and then he went to the mine. There he got into the elevator cage and as it went down, he fell. His head was knocked off as he reached the 140-meter level, the last level. His body was badly mangled but the only thing missing was his head. His bones were completely smashed. That was how they found him in the bottom of the mine shaft.

The whole neighborhood blamed the woman. From early in the morning, the family had been in good spirits, celebrating the son's birthday with his friends, dancing, giving the company refreshments. But the day went by, and they kept drinking. They had no reason to drink that way. It only led to the accident. Besides blaming the wife, they blamed the girl. The older uncle of the girl, Sánchez's brother, ran up to their house when he heard of the accident, and screamed at the daughter.

"What have you done?" he said, and like a madman he hit her in front of the corpse. Her nose and mouth bled as he yelled, "With what *imilla* [girlfriend] did you go out to spend your money? Do you know that you are responsible for your father's death?"

Some said that he had no manners, and that he shouldn't have said that, especially in front of the corpse which they were watching over.

"You could have lost respect with any one of us, but never in front of the body," some of the people who were watching over the corpse said to him.

They took the dead man to the cemetery to bury him at four o'clock in the afternoon. I didn't go to the burial because I had to work. Every one except myself left work. When I left at five they were already going to the cemetery. From the mine, I saw a big crowd clearly.

"I can't go because I have to work," I told my wife. "You shouldn't go either because you have to prepare my food since I have to return immediately to the mine."

Even though I didn't give her permission, she went. I went into the kitchen and served myself. Before going to work, I told my son to tell her that I had returned to work. I came home at eleven o'clock at night and I found my wife at home and we slept together.

The next week, around the fifteenth, there was another accident. In that accident a man fell in the same way from level twenty-six down to level seventy-five. He tripped over a frame and fell into a tunnel. The man was badly hurt. He was in the hospital a week before he died. His spine and skull must have been broken. He had fractures all over his body they said.

Before the end of the month there was another accident. Some workers were greasing the elevator frame on a Sunday, and a lot of grease spread to the cage. One worker who was greasing moved his foot, slipped on the grease, and lost his balance. He fell with the can of grease on top of him all the way down to the seventy-fifth level. He must have fallen straight down, because his legs were shoved up inside his body. He was a tall, robust man, but when they found him, he was half his former stature.

We tried pulling him back to his normal size, but we couldn't. The flesh of his thighs and legs was stuck inside his abdomen.

*Was he married? Did he have any problems in his house?*

No, he didn't have any problems in his house. He left his home with the intention of going to work. He didn't have any desire to kill himself. He was an older man, about fifty-five or fifty-six, maybe sixty. His name was Ricardo Torres, and his wife's was Victoria. They lived right next to the movie theatre. They called his street the *"Kullukokalle"* because it was narrow.

That morning when he left his house and said to his wife, "I have a dangerous job. We have to grease the frame of the elevator. I have to avoid moving my feet from one side to another, because grease spreads over the floor and it becomes very slippery. Please set out my sneakers. I will wear them."

His wife replied, "But with sneakers it's even more slippery. You can't go with your sneakers. You should wear your shoes with the spikes, because the grease from the cable will make it very slippery when it drips on top of the elevator."

If Torres had listened to his wife and taken his shoes with spikes it would have been better for him. That way he might not have slipped. The sneakers were indeed very slippery. He forgot that the metal roof of the elevator had a crust of grease that got very slippery. If he had taken that into account, he would have worn his shoes with the spikes.

We all went to the burial. We were almost obliged to go because the foremen of the drillers, and all of those in charge of each section made sure that we attended the burial.

So there were three accidents in the month of April and in all three there were deaths. After Torres' burial the people asked Engineer Mendoza to make a *k'araku* [sacrifice to *Supay*, the mine spirit], but he just smiled. He didn't understand what the *k'araku* was all about. Maybe he understood but preferred to spend the money on his own house. So he didn't have a *k'araku*. The workers had the regular one at the usual time in August.

There were plenty of other accidents that same year. There was one in the work site of Castro Bascope. It was a pretty rich vein. That is where the Clavo Porvenir [vein of the future] was located on level 140. It was a very rich vein with a high mineral content, and plenty of men worked in it — at least twenty-seven men. In most work sites only about fourteen men work, and in others there are even fewer. The men are spread thinly all throughout the mine, but there are many men.

The accident happened during September of 1967. They say that at nine-thirty in the morning the foreman said, "Let's chew coca" to all his work mates.

There was an Indian in the work group by the name of Fermín Villca, who was somewhat acculturated and wore *chola* clothing [Juan used the somewhat derisive term, *"indiecito que ya se ha refinado porque tenía ropa de gente chola"*]. He did not go down with the rest; this man was accustomed to going down last and working last, so he didn't get up right at that moment.

Many times accidents happen after the announcement of the rest period. Some lose themselves in the passageways or there is a cave-in, or they fall in the shafts. There are always accidents like that. Without taking into account what was happening, this lad did not obey.

The other men always used to say to him, "Why do you work like that? What do you think you are doing? Do you want to extract metal to sell on your own? Is that why you are always late?" That is how we used to scold him, but this Indian never paid any attention; he was very disobedient. He always opposed those working with him and never realized what he was doing.

On one occasion all the workers of that shaft had gone down to the coca niche where they were already beginning to chew coca. Only Villca was missing.

The foreman said, *"Chay, carrajo, imarayku mana jamunchiri? Rikawaycamuy."* ["Why hasn't that idiot come? Go look for him."] He sent one of the workers to look for him. The worker went yelling out his name in the shafts, "Villca! Villca!" But there was no Villca. He went even further up, shouting, "Villca! Villca!" But Villca was already nearly buried under a load of rock. He hadn't even cried out.

The worker looking for him went back to the coca chewing niche. The men had already given the cigarettes out to everyone, and Villca was still missing. While the others were smoking, Bascope, the chief, went up and found Villca. His leg was caught under a heavy stone. Bascope couldn't lift it alone, so he went back to the coca niche and told the crew, "Villca had an accident! His leg is caught under a stone!"

All the men ran to get their pikes. Villca's leg had been broken by the stone. He was almost dead, but they saved him. When they took him to the hospital, they found that his leg was so smashed it had to be amputated. After that he spent many months in La Paz recuperating. They gave him a cork leg which they brought from Brazil. It didn't work. He tried using it with a brace attached to his right shoulder, but with this he got even sicker. They took him back to La Paz to have a firmer artificial leg made to last him his whole life. They bought him one with a knee that bent and put it on him in 1968.

Pedro Vargas, a man we called "The Town Singer," had an accident. He had had a fight with his wife that morning, and when they told him to go out for lunch at twelve he stayed in the tunnel. He sat there to chew his coca and didn't leave his work site. The foreman of his crew, Hilarion Basualdo, said to the other men, "Why isn't he coming down to eat? I am going to go up one more time to see that he comes."

Basualdo went up and found Vargas sitting on a stone right at the top of the shaft.

"I am not going out because I had a fight with my wife," Vargas said. How can I go out there and face the others? Maybe she didn't even cook my lunch."

"Why don't you go to the restaurant to eat? How are you going to stay here without eating?" the foreman asked. Basualdo tried to pull him out by force, but Vargas — we used to call him "Loco" — didn't pay any attention to him.

Vargas went back to work about one o'clock in the afternoon. The rest of us arrived at our work site at about one-thirty after chewing coca, but by then Vargas was already buried underneath a load.

He had said there was a lot of clay spilling out on one side of the chimney and he had climbed up into it, because when there is clay spilling, there always is metal. He must have wanted to fill his sacks in order to boast about it in front of the others, saying, "I have filled more sacks than you!" While he was doing this, a load that would have filled five carts spilled out, as though it were a chute, and covered him with clay and rocks. You could see only his head. He wasn't hurt badly — only a few cuts on his face and hands — but that shaft was very hot and close.

The men uncovered Vargas with their shovels. He had fallen unconscious, hardly able to breathe, and in a few more minutes perhaps he would have died. They took him down from the shaft. I was working a little distance away and ran quickly, sure that they were taking someone who was hurt. When they brought him into the superintendent's office, they filled his helmet with water and splashed it on his face so that he reacted and took a deep breath. This made all the workers happy. When the lift arrived, they took him up to the surface. He was hospitalized only three days, because the load that fell on him was mostly light gravel and clay. He wasn't hit on his head except for a few sharp stones that scratched his face.

*Was there any security control?*

There were no security measures on that site because it was a new tunnel. If we had put a frame to secure that site, it would have lasted only a couple of days since they would have had to take it down and move it. They were drilling in that tunnel and so they just shot some plaster into the crevices, and that fell out.

The work site turned hotter. The men kept climbing up to the top, and as they went up, the chimney weakened and fell down. This was about forty meters from the principal tunnel that they used to lower wood and stone for the framing. The cave-in was right in the middle, twenty meters from one side and twenty from the other. The men began to clean that tunnel to reach the frame, or to get at least as far as the chimney through which the materials needed to repair the shaft would come. It was unbearably hot. The workers in that site weren't accustomed to such heat, and little-by-little they weakened until they could not work any longer.

The superintendent installed an air tube, but the foreman — I don't know whether he did it out of stupidity or laziness — had the men fill the block in such a way that the pipe got cut off and there was no air coming through. It was useless, and they had to cut it off.

There was a fat man who worked in that shaft. I don't know his last name. We called him "Little Pig" and sometimes *"Mayranito"* ["Fatty"] because he was so fat. He wasn't an old-time interior miner, and had just come to work because he needed to earn money to retire. Before that he worked in the shop. He was assigned to that site when the landslide occurred.

The men were working almost naked, looking like boxers in their short pants, boots, and their hard hats with lamps, nothing else. This fat man began to weaken. His stomach was big, but he began to lose weight. He used to play soccer before, when he wasn't so fat, but when he broke his leg he stopped playing and put on a lot of weight. His stomach was bloated. But working in that shaft, he began to lose weight.

"You must leave that job!" his wife told him. "You're losing too much weight."

But he didn't listen to his wife; he was earning money and wanted to accumulate some more to retire on. When he retired, he wasn't able to regain the body he had before. His wife still sells vegetables in the market, and he is still skinny.

That shaft had plenty of metal, but on the top it was all eaten away. If they had fixed the tunnel on top, they wouldn't have had that landslide. That was the foreman's fault. Everybody lost weight in that shaft because it was too hot. They only worked it two out of eight hours each day. They couldn't work it more because the workers would have to go out and stand together where the air was blowing. It was quite cool in that one spot, but as soon as they moved elsewhere, they had to hose water over each other. That is how they spent the day. But there was good ore. In a short time, they could heap it up and take it out in sacks. If there had been only a little metal, they would have felt discouraged.

I once went up to that site to pick up a load. The temperature was so high that I had to take my shirt off on the way there. Then, when I climbed the shaft, *Caramba!* I almost got cooked.

I looked through the crack and yelled to the men working there, "Look out! Look out below you!" so they wouldn't drop anything while I was climbing. I saw them all wearing only shorts and boots, and I was frightened and thought, What are they doing in here? Some were working, some were resting on the platform. That's how they worked: five minutes drilling, then ten minutes to recuperate.

There was plenty of metal in there. You only had to drill a little. The workers didn't have to select the ore because it was all pure. They gave me three cartloads, but it was like water, all melted. *Caramba!* I couldn't load anything else with that. Once I secured it, I sent it up without nitrate to the top of the tunnel. If I had included the powdered nitrate, it would have dissolved in the liquid.

When they gave me the ore, the drillers said, "We put the nitrate in with it yesterday, but it melted because it's so hot. Instead, we should have used it to blast then."

I said, "You should leave early because I have to explode the dyna-mite." I lit the dynamite fuse and they all left the tunnel. I left last. They went to level 108 where they were cleaning out the tunnel. Here, about fifteen meters from the shaft, there was some air. They had removed some of the load that was blocking it. Behind, the sides were beginning to cave in once again.

At five o'clock all the men went out to fold the sackcloth. While cleaning up they heard a sound typical of a shaft collapsing, the sound of wood splintering. It was about ten o'clock at night, only an hour before quitting time for the men on that shift. One of them said that so little time was left on their shift that they ought to leave.

"Let's leave!" he said, "We shouldn't work more, because it might fall in and cover us for the rest of our lives. How could they save us?" With that, he left.

"It *could* kill us! Let's leave!" another man said, and followed him out.

The next day the first to enter the tunnel saw that about thirty me-ters had caved in. The chimney was completely covered. The men tried to insert tubes so they could breathe, but the stones were big and im-movable. There was nothing they could do. The whole site was weak-ened and there was a ten-meter gap in the upper level. They would have had to shovel the ore out, but they couldn't do it.

They tried to put a chimney up on the other side to communicate with the next level, like a slide, but they had advanced only seven me-ters when the gas started leaking through. They had air blown in, but it was too late and, as the air flowed in, it got mixed with gas. It was like an oven while they were working in there.

On one occasion, the explorer-driller had discharged dynamite at the face, and the work crew had also discharged dynamite in the shaft. When they returned after the charges had exploded, the crew suddenly felt completely exhausted. They thought they had just gotten tired on their way back, so they began work. One by one they lost their senses, as though completely drunk. There was no one there to take them out.

I came down with the cart driver, Bascope, looking for some ore to pick up, but we didn't see anyone. "Maybe they are hiding themselves," he said to me. I helped him empty the block because Bascope was my friend. As I was emptying it, I heard something upstairs, like the moan of someone who has a stomachache.

"Ay, ay!" they said. None of them had the strength to go down the ladder. I looked and thought that perhaps they were all sick with the gas. I went up and let air in so that it would blow on them.

I told my helper, "Let's go upstairs and see what it is. I don't know what has happened." We ran up. As I had guessed, all were seated near the corridor. They were exhausted and dripping wet. They didn't have their pants on. When we arrived in the corridor, my pants were entirely drenched with sweat as if someone had thrown water on me. A little air drifted by in the passage, and they all revived a bit. No one was sick. Even the headman, who was the last to come down and took a little while to respond, was able to walk on his own two feet.

By noon they were all out. They tried to return to that section, but they couldn't get the gas out of the block. So they left the vein, just like that, and went to work on another one. They should never have worked in that area.

---

After rereading this chapter, I felt that a miner had to have a great desire to live in order to work in the mines and confront all the dangers that threatened him. Any problem can take away his will to live and the defences this gives him. I asked Juan if he thought the miners had more accidents when they entered the mine after having an argument. In his response he narrated a personal incident concerning a worker who committed suicide right in front of him at a time when Juan himself felt desperate about his life. This remembrance helped him reflect on the life of the miner.

---

There was an accident similar to many others, but this was the result of the specific kind of personal problems workers encounter. The man had an accident in the Rosario section, a mine near Santa Fe. He was hurt during a dynamite blast and his body was badly cut by the shrapnel, and could barely move. The misfortune this man experienced was caused by his wife.

This man's wife was a bothersome, tricky woman. Although he was a tall fellow, she used to manipulate him like a small child, a street boy. She didn't treat him like her husband; she didn't behave like his wife. She didn't respect him at all. She did as she pleased.

They went to a celebration in Morococala. There they had a fight, and he went home alone, furious at her. He had lost one eye and had problems with the other one. He was going blind because veins in his eyes had popped. He couldn't see very well, and the doctor had said that someday he would be completely blind.

He left the party drunk, and on his way home he thought, "When I am completely blind, she will treat me even worse. It's better that I kill myself now. The weapon is in my hands! He entered his house furious, upset, rebelling against his fate. His children saw him get his dynamite out of a basket. He prepared the dynamite cutting the fuse with a knife and made a circular coil around his body. Then he walked to the cemetery and stood on the tomb of a man who had recently died in an accident inside the mine.

My son, Filemón, was then turning fifteen years old. He was in the tenth grade. That same day, I came home from my job at two in the afternoon and found him home.

"What are you doing here?" I asked him. "Don't you have any classes? What's wrong? Are you behind in your work?"

He answered that he couldn't pass an exam in mathematics and that he had been kicked out of class by the teacher for not studying.

"What have I always said to you?" I said. "Can't you see me? My life consists of going into the mine and coming home to rest. The following day I go to work again, and so on. I have lunch and return home to rest. Why don't you follow some such routine? Can't you pursue your studies the same way? Just as I go to work every day, honestly, disciplined, without missing once, you have to do the same thing. Why don't you study? I have asked you so many times about your studies. But you always neglect them. What's wrong?"

I had left my job feeling disgusted because I broke four drill bits, one after another, and I had none left to work with. I left the job in a fury and when I arrived home I was in an even worse mood.

Filemón answered, "Daddy, I wasn't born to study. I can't. I just can't and I will not. Why don't I begin working in the mine? I will help you."

"Who taught you this, Filemón?" I said, "Who told you this? You can't say that. These are not your own words! Why do you utter them? I don't know who has taught you to say these things! Who have you learned this from?"

He repeated that he couldn't understand any of the lessons that his teachers taught him, and that he wasn't born to study, nor was he going to keep trying.

I am a very demanding father when I get angry. I act like an animal without understanding a thing anyone says. I feel that I am not made of flesh at those moments. I am like a solid mass of wood or stone. Nothing hurts me. I have no heart for anything. When I'm angry I am capable of anything. I looked at the wall and saw a whip hanging on a hook. I still have it. I made it from a rubber band split in two. I used it to punish the children. I looked at it, then I seized it and went into the bedroom with it.

"You must tell me who taught you that nonsense!" I yelled "This is not something that comes from you. Those words belong to someone else, someone who is twenty years old, not fifteen. Someone must have taught you these things. They can not come from you!"

"Nobody has taught me anything. It's just that I don't want to study anymore," he said. "I want to work and I am going to work in the pits and help you."

Then I began to cry. "Why don't you want to study?" I asked. "Can't you see me day and night, digging in the earth for metal? My nails are gone, my fingers are torn. Some days my fingers bleed just where the nails grow out." I showed him my cracked fingers, "Can't you see this? Do you want to work like I do inside the mine? Do you want to bury yourself alive inside the mine every day? First I bury myself alive and now you? Do you want that?" I asked.

"I prefer to be a miner," he answered.

Then I got the whip and beat him furiously with twelve or more lashes. The skin on his legs was split open. He probably still has the scars. I also cut his ear. I left him a scar there so that he would always remember.

"This ear will never hear anything against your studies again!" I yelled at him, trying to cut it off. I stepped on his neck with my boots, in a rage. I should have been tried by the authorities for such acts. I wanted to kill him for saying that he wasn't going to study! His answer infuriated me. It broke my heart. I was in pain.

Then his mother came in. With all her strength she pushed me aside. I yelled at him, "You must study dead or alive while I am alive! When I die, you can stop studying, but God will not take my life away before you become a good man. You must also educate your younger brothers and sisters. Can't you see that I am a miner? Your father's life hasn't been bought nor is it eternal. God gave us life to die and we will all die. So until the hour of my death you must study, whatever happens, and no matter what it costs." That is what I said to him.

So I went with him to his school and I said to the teacher, "If he can't learn what you teach him, then you have the right to beat him. Hit him with a whip if necessary! I will bring it to you." I said this, in front of all the boys, and I beat him again. Blood was running down his legs. I pulled his pants off and exposed his buttocks to all of the boys.

"Because you are stupid and a scoundrel, you have been beaten." And I told the other students, "He didn't want to study. He came home because his teacher sent him home. It was a shame!" This is what I said to them so that they would all think about their studies.

From that moment on, Filemón reconsidered his attitude toward his studies. He never repeated any of his courses, nor did he fall behind again. My words had a positive effect on him. He is now a good man. He is working and is like a father of all of us.

After I left the school, I couldn't remain home because I was so upset. My wife tried to calm me down. She gave me a glass of water to drink, but it didn't calm my suffering heart. What have I done? I thought to myself. I went out and watched the people coming out of the mine. It was five o'clock in the afternoon and I still had my working clothes on. I usually took them off as soon as I got home. If I went to the plaza, the movies, or even just to chat with my friends on the corner, I never wore my working clothes. So I went out in the countryside, walking toward the cemetery. I felt like going back home, but I couldn't control my fury.

Then I thought, I should walk further because I will only suffer more down here. I went up towards the back of the cemetery. When I was about to enter the cemetery I saw my friend, Mauricio Zeballos, and then I heard a loud blast — Boom! I was frightened. What had happened there? The people down below were looking up. From where I was, you could see everything clearly. As soon as I entered the cemetery, I saw a red stream trickling down the path. I looked for Mauricio but he was gone. The dynamite had blown him to pieces. His entire back was gone. There was flesh left only on his right leg.

His wife was responsible for his suicide. She was both flighty and jealous and took advantage of his simplicity. He never thought of having relations with other women. At dances we can dance with anyone — married, unmarried, widows — with whomever we like. His wife didn't like that. She wanted him to dance only with her, but he also wanted to dance with other women. That's why she scolded him in public at the fiesta that day; then he committed suicide. I wouldn't have seen that if Filemón had behaved well and not been sent home from school.

*The teachers can sometimes discourage a student, right?*

Yes. For example, look at the way in which I chastised Filemón. I was like an animal because I was furious. I just couldn't control myself. My only intention is to educate my children. Cursed was the day I entered the mine! If I hadn't I would be healthy, working peacefully, educating my children. If I hadn't entered the mine I could have been a good mechanic working in the shops. My older brother Leonardo, who is now in Argentina, is to be blamed. My godfather, Juan Luca, wanted me to work in the general store, but my brother opposed it. If I had worked in the store perhaps I could have gotten ahead. I have always learned quickly. Maybe I could have become the boss inside the store, or I could have been working at something else, and not be as I am now, half dead.

My only thought is to educate my children. I don't know what else I can do for my children, Aníbal, María and Elena, Juan Manuel, and Anita. I don't know how I'm going to keep alive. My oldest son can't always think about the others. At any moment he could stray away from us and betray his younger siblings. He may forget about them, about their education. God should not let that happen. My wife knows how to sew, and if I die she will educate her children. She also knows how to knit. She has her own machines for sewing and knitting. She will always be able to earn money from that. But I don't want her to work while I am alive. I don't want her to look tired and sick like me.

The women who work on the slag pile get the same disease I have. We have young children whom she must educate if anything happens to me. If I die, and if Filemón abandons them, she will sacrifice herself as she saw me doing. I think about it day and night. In the same way that I have worked, she will have to work, to educate her children and see to it that they live well. I think only about how my children can avoid suffering the way I have.

Everybody looks down upon a miner. They don't know how a sick worker suffers. My children shouldn't have to share the pain of my lungs. They should never have to say, "Let me have your pain; I will help you." They will never say that, I hope. And even if they do say it, they shall never suffer the same pain. It's bad enough that I have to bear it.

Everyone looks at the miners with a bad eye, and they treat us badly. In the stores we receive poor service; we seem to put people in a bad mood. Only the foremen, some of them, understand us and treat us well. The rest don't feel a thing for us.

# 15

# My Lungs Are Exhausted

In 1967 Juan received his transfer to go to Oruro where Filemón had gone to continue his studies. Petrona, along with the younger children, had already gone there to live in the house they had purchased from CONAVI, the national housing cooperative. María had remained with Juan to prepare his meals while he continued working in Santa Fe until he the transfer. The physical checkup required for the transfer revealed that he had silicosis. The next four years he worked, at first in the interior of the mines where he was able to demonstrate his skill as a master driller to his new chiefs. But his failing lungs deprived him of energy, and he was finally transferred to the surface where he worked as a night watchman. He grew comfortable with working in Oruro because, as he states, "While I am working, I can grow accustomed anywhere, even in hell, because I am a man dedicated to work." But he was disillusioned when one of the engineers in charge of measuring production for his bonus tried to deceive him on the progress he had made. Growing ever more desperate to get his children educated before he retired, he finally collapsed and had to be hospitalized.

During the month of July, 1967, some of the workers were transferred to San José. The first time I saw it happen, I didn't pay any attention, but then my son, Filemón, went there to study in Oruro High School and my wife went there to live since the cost of boarding him was too high. I earned too little to pay for it.

*When did you buy your house there?*

We bought this house around 1963. I made several sacrifices to acquire it. When I signed up for the house in the cooperative, my brother-in-law laughed at me because he didn't think that I would get it. "They are only taking money from you to construct the houses," he said when I told him. "You'll be lucky to get that back — without interest; they may just run away with the money."

"Why don't you get a piece of land at least?" I asked him. "Maybe they will come through on it." But he didn't believe me.

We almost lost hope because of the persistent rumor that we were paying money for nothing. "They are making homes for other people with the workers' money," people said, but I was determined and didn't let them influence me. My whole heart went into having that house. In 1966, when we least expected it, they gave us our house. My brother-in-law was amazed. He couldn't believe it.

One day after drinking in my house he said to his sister, "They must have just taken over a house lent them by the company." But when he realized it was ours, he tried to get one from the cooperative, but it was too late. None were left.

The land and the site map cost me 2,500 bolivian pesos [$250]. We paid it in cash. It was our down-payment. From then on we paid fifty pesos [$5] every month for a year. In 1963 we put in one hundred pesos [$10] so that our houses would be built quicker. It was rumored that the government was deceiving the workers and that someday the state would take the houses away and throw them out on the streets, and that's why we had our doubts. I felt, though, that I would have my house there.

The rumors were false, of course. All of us who bought our houses are still living in them, even widows. If the government had wanted to, it could have taken the widows' houses when their husbands died. The widows aren't paying any more, yet they are still living there. I, too, am no longer paying the cooperative because I am not earning a salary. I haven't paid a peso for three years. My next paycheck wouldn't even cover the rent if I had to pay it. If I wanted to, I could borrow fifty thousand pesos from the company with the house as security, but I would need that money later when I'm out of work, so for that reason I haven't asked for anything. According to the statutes of the cooperative, if a worker is sick and can't work anymore, he doesn't have to pay his dues until he finds a new job. After he retires and has no way of earning money, he also needn't pay. His immediate family can live in the house until they all die. That is what the president of the cooperative said. I abide by those statutes and so I won't have to pay anymore.

When my son Filemón was transferred to the high school in Oruro, I didn't feel like staying in Santa Fe any more. No one was urging me to stay and I thought, Damn it, I'm not earning much here; it's best that I go to Oruro. I didn't say anything while I was doing well, but when I didn't earn enough, I went to the foreman to find out about a transfer to Oruro. The foreman said I could go anywhere I wanted.

Vargas, the chief of the employment office in Santa Fe, brought me and six of my friends to Oruro in May of 1968. They checked our lungs. Of the six, only two of us were sick, Juan Iquina and I. Juan Iquina had 80 percent silicosis and I had 100 percent. At the time, though, we weren't told that we were sick.

We waited for the information to come from La Paz where our X-rays were sent. When I asked about them the following month, they said they didn't know yet. In July I was getting restless. I couldn't stand living alone in Santa Fe any more, and I was unhappy. It wasn't good for my children either, especially María who was cooking for me and also studying. She went to school in the afternoon and in the mornings she had to cook. She had no time left for homework, not even an hour. When she came home from school at four o'clock in the afternoon, she had to cook again for me immediately so that I could go to work. Sometimes I would work overtime, until eleven o'clock at night, without eating anything. I drank only a cup of tea. After work, at eleven at night, my daughter had to cook again. If I didn't work overtime we ate at seven-thirty in the evening, or at eight. I saw that she was suffering a lot and decided to take a vacation. I asked for her to be transferred to the school in San José, but they wouldn't do that.

"You must transfer yourself in order for your children to be transferred," they answered.

So there were days when she went to school and others when she didn't. She was my favorite child and I didn't want to make things difficult for her. The other children had gone down to Oruro with their mother. I had gone to the school in Santa Fe and lied to them, saying that they had gotten sick in Oruro. They weren't sick, but I didn't want them to be kicked out of school for not attending. Despite all that, my daughter Elena still lost a year in school. She would now be in the third grade, but she is only in the second grade.

I left on vacation to join my family around the tenth of July. My *compadre* Francisco Juan Iquina, hadn't left with the others in the first transfers to San José. He came to Oruro to talk with me about baptizing his last child — all five of his children are my godchildren. He always baptized his children when they were a year old, and her birthday was on the next Saturday. That very same day we baptized her, and at his house that evening we drank in the little girl's name. The following day we went to my house at five o'clock in the morning. We were upset because Filemón wasn't with the children.

At eight-thirty in the morning my *compadre* arrived and took us to his house in Santa Fe to drink again. He had just received his transfer to San José, and he said it was our last opportunity to join him with our other friends up there. I was very tired, but we went along with him and some other friends who were living in Oruro. They came and drank with us in Santa Fe because we were all from the same mine.

When I picked up my paycheck the next day I informed the supervisor of Santa Fe mines that I wanted to be put on the first list so that I could get transferred to San José. However, I wasn't able to leave until August, since there were no transfers until then. I worked at Santa Fe from the end of my vacation until the fourteenth of August. On the fourteenth I was going to lunch when I saw a notice that those who wanted transfers to San José and had indefinite contracts should come in and sign up. I signed up right away. I ate lunch with pleasure because I was going to be transferred.

I told my daughter, "María, now we are going to Oruro. We will live with your mother and your sisters and brothers once again."

I went up to the supervisor of the mine and had the transfer made on the fifteenth, but on the seventeenth I was still working there.

That day, when I was just about ready to go down in the lift, the supervisor opened the door and yelled, "Rojas, don't go in. You have to go to San José this morning!"

The lift was already descending into the mine, so I had to go down, but I went back up immediately and went to the secretary and said, "What did you say?"

"You have to leave today to transfer to Oruro. Everything is ready," he said. "You can give your clothing and your work tools to security."

I left that moment. I changed immediately and took my clothing to security. About twenty-one of us left that morning. All of us gave our working tools back, but I had left one of the tools at home, so they didn't want to give me the order to be transferred. It wasn't functioning well, and I had taken it home and forgotten it. I went to the personnel office to get permission to leave, so that I would not be bothered when I arrived at the check point in Cala Cala.

I locked the door of my house and returned to the mine at ten o'clock in the morning. I didn't have time to say good bye to any of my friends because it all happened so quickly. The rest of my belongings were sent down to Oruro three days later. There wasn't much left because I had moved most of my things when I went on vacation. There was no one to look after them in Santa Fe when my daughter went to school, and if I worked overtime on Saturdays the house was left completely empty. I had asked management to lend me a large truck so I could move things like the bed, a chair, and my clothing, and they had agreed. But we didn't want to stay that long and left without them.

At a quarter to eleven we were all crowded in the back of the truck, ready to depart.

*Were you sad to leave?*

The day we rode in the truck on the way to San José was one of the saddest of my life. When I moved to Cochabamba in 1952 I didn't feel sad because I had been fired by the company. But in 1968, when I was transferred, I turned around to look at the mining camp. My heart trembled and I didn't know what lay ahead, so I was sad.

My friends looked at me and said, "Don Juan, where are you going? What is going to happen to you?"

I answered, "We don't know what luck is awaiting us there in San José."

When we were about to take the curve on the mountain I looked back and saw the camp in the distance. I began to cry; I had lived there for twenty-three years, since 1946, and I had grown accustomed to that place. My wife also cried when she saw the camp for the last time. After the curve on the mountain Potopoto we could no longer see the camp. When you looked down it was all flat where the encampment lay, and the mountains rose above it. And then I could not even imagine it any more.

When I arrived in Oruro, I felt so far away from Santa Fe that I could not imagine having been there. While I am working I can grow accustomed anywhere, even in hell, because I am a man dedicated to work and I like to work very much. I became accustomed to life in Oruro very easily. I forgot everything about the past and didn't think about Santa Fe, nor any other place I had been. I was happy with what I had. I was happy to have my own house, the house that God gave me as a blessing for obeying his laws.

We went to the San José mine directly from Santa Fe. The man in charge of us went to the office to find out what section we were going to work in. He took us to the superintendent of the mine who told us that we were to be taken to the "Sinkan" refinery [the Sink and Float Concentration Plant]. He took us to Sinkan and showed us around.

"You are going to live here in those white houses," he said. Then he took us inside Sinkan, saying, "Tomorrow you must present yourselves to the supervisor of the mine."

After that, Juan Matos, the chief of the camp, showed us around the camp. The houses didn't have doors or windows.

We asked him, "How are we going to live here? Our families have to come and cook for us. Our families don't know yet where we are going to be working. Today we will have to work without eating." Even though my wife was in Oruro she couldn't bring me, or even send me, my lunch because she didn't know what section we were going to work in.

Then we went to see the chief of employee welfare, Mr. Walter, to protest about our living conditions. He said, "It's all up to you. If you want to live in the camp, come by here in the afternoon on your way out and we will find you a place to live. Those of you who have your houses in the city or in the cooperative can live there. But if you don't want to come such distances, you can sign up to live in the camp here. You should also go up to the chief of the garage so he will pay for your trips." This made us feel better.

The superintendent then told us to go to Sinkan and present ourselves there. We went in our workclothes to Sinkan. We went through the tunnel at eight o'clock in the morning on our way to see the chief of the section, Mr. Adriazola.

"You must be registered according to your occupation. Otherwise, you will have problems," said Adriazola.

I was registered as a driller. There were several who belonged to the electrical shop and others to other shops. A man named Longines Molina belonged to the electrical shop; he is now working in the mill as an electrician. Another man, René Arroyo, is still working as a mechanic in Sinkan. The superintendent wrote each of our skills down and we were given jobs accordingly on the various shifts. Juan Guzman and I were put on the second shift. He told us then, "You can now leave. At three o'clock you must return to the mill."

Isaac Clavijo and Medrano went on the third shift, and Juan Guzman and I went to the mill at three o'clock on the second shift. Finally, after seven they gave us jobs that only lasted a few minutes. We didn't even work half an hour. We cleaned out a load and shoveled it from one side to the other.

"Since you came here without eating," the foreman said, "you can leave early." At nine-thirty we left. At two, when we came back, the foreman said, "Tomorrow you will begin working. We just got everything organized."

The mill wasn't working continuously. It was open only a couple of hours a day. All the workers had to do was help the machinists man the motors. That's all.

The following day we worked the same way. Isaac Clavijo's wife came up to the mill bringing him his things. My wife came with her and brought the rest of my things that had been sent from Santa Fe. The foreman lent my wife a small truck because she didn't have too many things. They also gave one to Clavijo, and his wife brought all their things in the truck — their stove, everything. Since that day I have lived in San José.

We had a second medical check-up. Dr. Carrasco was surprised when he saw my X-ray plates. He was startled because I was very sick. He said, "You must submit your papers quickly so that you can be insured immediately. If not, you could die and leave your family on the streets; they might evict your wife for inability to pay the rent."

I was filled with fear; my life seemed over. Yet I had to transact everything as soon as possible. I was feeling very vulnerable. I sent a telegraph to Santa Fe to find out about my papers, and they gave me permission to go back there for one day only.

I went to see Isoforo Vargas, the chief of personnel in Santa Fe, who received me warmly since we had known each other from the time he was the teacher of manual skills.

"Come in, Don Juan," he said. "I want to talk to you."

Without thinking twice, since I had to return to San José right away, I said, "My job is demanding, Don Isoforo, and I have only come to get my papers cleared up. What is happening? Am I going to be able to go ahead with the transactions for my social security? It is urgent that I know."

He replied, "I want to talk to you about that. Two of the men tested proved to be sick: Juan Iquina and you."

"So be it, but can you take care of my papers?"

"There is an office where they prepare the papers. You do not have to do anything, since virtually nothing remains to be done. Almost everything is done," he told me.

I have waited two years, and the papers are still not completed.

I got an appointment with Mr. Clavijo and he told me, "Your papers are still not in La Paz."

"You have to send a telegram asking for my insurance, when it is going to come and what pension I will get. Ask them to verify everything," I said.

But they didn't send information of any sort. During all this, I was feeling very weak. In Santa Fe I did not feel any pain in my lungs, but when I was transferred to Oruro, although I did not work in the mine as much there, my lungs ached and I felt strange.

They gave me a transfer to the Itos mine instead of San José. I showed my transfer papers first to Engineer Laura and he ordered me, "Go have the papers signed by the superintendent of the mines."

Engineer Arevalo wasn't in the city, so Engineer Araujo took the paper and signed it. "It is too late for you to go back to Santa Fe. You can work in San José," he told me.

I presented myself to the chief of laborers, Don Severino Merida, and he assigned me to be helper in the block. That day we worked and on the following day I reported again at San José. Engineer Laura had not come, and I continued working in San José. On the third day, I again went to San José, and they sent me to level 150 where they were building a turn in the rail lines. It was very curvy. The platform they had made would not last because there was a lot of dripping; also, it ended very abruptly. The *copajira* would have eaten away the iron and raid so since both parts of the corridors had a rail, it was necessary to prepare a siding. They had taken out part of the corner to be able to dump the load to level 280, and from 280 they had to get it to 340 by a chute, and from there it could be taken out.

I was surprised to see that they suffered from the lack of an experienced driller. The men working there knew how to make the machine function, but they did not know how to master the machine when the drill was poised and it was in full function. I was assigned to clean the corridor at first, because no one knew that I was a driller, although my transfer paper stated "Occupation: driller." They did not know what kind of experience I had. No one said to me, "Come help me drill."

On my own initiative I approached them when I saw that the machine was not functioning as it ought to. It had plenty of air, and I thought, *Caramba!* These men are not drillers, they are just assistants.

Without any rain gear I began to drill. Cutting the water, I set the regulator so it would just drip a little and wouldn't drench me. During the entire shift those men had made only three or four holes of thirty centimeters. I made two large holes in forty-five minutes.

When I was making a third hole Engineer Araujo saw me working. Engineer Laura was with Araujo, as was the section leader, Dario Gómez. The gang chiefs wanted me to work with them, especially Engineer Araujo and Engineer Arevalo. (I didn't know Arrevalo well, but apparently Engineer Araujo had discussed my work with him, since he had been there during the shift.)

Laura and Gómez came to realize this.

"Good, but you have to go to Itos right away."

Dario Gómez said, "This worker has to remain here in this section and another of the transferred men has to go there instead of him."

The one who put an end to this was Engineer Araujo. He said, "Someone else should be transferred from San José to Itos; I intend to keep this worker here, by reasoning with him or by force, if necessary."

I stayed there. Gómez and Araujo won. Mr. Pinaya was opposed because he was my foreman in Sinkan and I had been very helpful to him. Gómez assigned me to work wherever I could be free to drill without falling behind — there the machines tend to break down. So it was that they did not assign me to the slag pile, picking out the metal from the slag, hour after hour, tin to be sent on to Machacamarca. I got my transfer, came to San José, and there I was working well.

*Would you have preferred to continue working in Sinkan?*

I could have worked in Sinkan because I liked it a lot. The work was lighter, not like a stint in the mine, very restful. On the other hand, I felt a little ill and every day, especially when I worked on the third shift, I coughed a lot. I didn't sleep well in my house and at work I was not tranquil. I was always coughing. There were times when I didn't have work and I would just go wait in the office of the chief of the shift, Piñaya. There they were working, looking over the tasks of each worker, checking what things were lacking in the machines, what had to be repaired, all that.

Also, I needed to earn a little more because what I earned in Sinkan was not enough. At that time, the plant was not yet completely in operation. During an eight-hour shift, the plant worked only one hour, forty-five minutes. On Sundays we did not work, nor on holidays. We worked only on the weekdays. As a result, I earned only two hundred forty or two hundred fifty bolivianos, and this was not enough for anything. At the end of the first month I came out owing twenty-four pesos. After the second month I owed sixty-five. Well, after the third month, it was about one hundred twenty bolivianos, and I couldn't pay it. I thought, Here I am going to end up a debtor, like the workers at Santa Fe." After pondering this, analyzing it well, I asked for my transfer. They did not want to let me go from Sinkan because all the bosses knew my attitude, the care I took in my work.

Marcelino Choque, chief of mechanics in the Sinkan plant said to me, "*Caramba, che!* With what heart are you leaving us?"

"I want to see what kind of contract wages they pay in the interior of the mine. If they pay me too little or deceive me in the contract, I will come back right away. I believe that I am not causing any harm. I believe that they are going to receive me, just as you are going to let me go now."

Marcelino Choque approved of this, and said, "As a remembrance, leave me your rubber boots to make half-soles for my children and soles for my working boots."

"Why not? I am happy to," I said, and at that very moment I took out my knife and cut four pieces of rubber from the boots I had in the locker. He also urged me to return on Saturday evening.

I left on Saturday at one in the afternoon, and Engineer Adriazola gave me a roll of thin rubber for half-soles for shoes. I still have those cut-up boots, and I still have the rubber, which I am saving as a souvenir. This was the gift I gave to Marcelino Choque, my boss on that job.

The following day I was given waterproof clothing. I already had boots and with that clothing, I went in and Gómez ("The Beast"), ordered me, "Go finish that drilling so we can begin to discharge at three o'clock in the afternoon. At twenty to three you are going to light the fuse. I am going to send dynamite and ammonium right away."

I arrived at eight-thirty in the morning. They gave me the tools to begin drilling immediately. I chewed coca first, until nine, and then got up. I was arming the machine when Beast Gómez came by and tried to scold me.

"You have been in here for a while. What are you doing? Why are you just starting to put the machine together?"

"Yes, Don Dario, I arrived a while ago, but I am not going to work with an empty mouth. I went to the office to get work tools and I didn't chew coca. I just now got a chance to, and now I am arming the machine."

He didn't scold any more, but just said, "You have to finish these drillings by three. We have to make fourteen drillings."

I didn't do all fourteen. I made only nine, but I got us to the corner. The man next to me had widened the corridor more than necessary. It was much more than was needed for the carts to pass by. I discharged the dynamite.

Araujo urged Gómez, "Give this worker a contract immediately. He must work because he knows how to work. He is a real craftsman. We have to give him something else to drill quickly."

Mr. Gómez took me to the vein and said, "Choose whatever place you want."

The vein was enough for three workers. On the right side the driller Calle from Santa Fe worked, and on the other side "*Pulowasa*" worked. (They called him Pulowasa because he was slightly hunchbacked. He died last April or May on level 150. He was buried by a load cave-in while he was working.) He worked on the left and I worked in the center. I chose the best spot. The vein was wide, extending to both sides. One had to walk like a cat. In the center one spot was uncomfortable, the only spot that got in my way. I worked perfectly well in that tunnel. In one month I earned lots of money. I earned about six hundred pesos [about sixty dollars on contract, plus base pay].

*What do you do with your salary?*

All I earn I give to my wife, along with the statement of my wages. Never in my life have I robbed her like other workers do with their wives. In any case, Petrona knows how to read a little, and she can read the statement. She adds it up and if some is missing I account for it. I have to ask her for money, but she must give it to me no matter what. I didn't have any reason to hide the money from her because I respected her, and that's why my salary had to be enough for her.

During that month they paid me a lot. I drilled 145 cubic meters, 80 centimeters in width. They paid me well. By the end of the following month I advanced even more and had a spot in the vein that was between two and three meters wide.

The engineers were told by the managers to deceive us in their measurements. When the vein is narrow, up to about 60 centimeters, they pay us more; if it is 80 centimeters, a little bit less; when it is a meter, even less; and when it is 120 centimeters, less still. It is harder work to make a narrow tunnel, but it pays better. When it is wide, it isn't as hard to work, but they pay us less.

On three meters the engineer based my pay. I didn't know his last name, but I knew him. I had no desire to know his name. Everybody hated him because he cheated us on our contracts. Everybody gave him the evil eye, and so did I. I thought I was going to earn more because I had advanced a lot despite the fact that we worked little during February. But he projected the total on the basis of that one wide spot and paid me less. I earned only slightly more than my normal daily wage.

When we received our monthly compensation on Friday, I almost died of rage. I went to see the chief of the section immediately and protested, "What's going on here? My bonus is less than twelve pesos."

The chief of the section answered, "Don't get excited. We are going to get things fixed. Monday we are going to make a claim. Don't get so furious. Be patient."

I was still very angry. That night I was supposed to go to work but didn't because I was so furious. Why should I go in? Instead of earning money I was losing it.

On Monday I went to the technical office to complain to the engineer who measured the vein. He said, "Get me an order from your chief of the section, and I will fix things up." I gave him the order and went in at ten o'clock in the morning. I was waiting; I didn't do a thing. I didn't even touch a stone.

My helper, "Morito" Paniagua, who died in the last accident from the blast on level 340, said, "He is coming."

I got up and waited for him. The Beast came along and told me, "I think you aren't working, Rojas. You should be drilling already. The work site is waiting for you."

"Why should I drill if I don't earn anything anyway? Why should I risk my life and take nothing home? If you want me to work you'll have to pay me justly. I can't work and earn no money." After reproaching Gomez in this way, I got up.

The engineer had been listening and said, "Everything is the same width as this. According to instructions, a vein has to be the same width everywhere."

I objected. "Is the work site too long? It is only thirty-five meters long and it is still not three meters wide. Despite my efforts, the tunnel was widened by cave-ins. When I began blasting it all slipped down because the surface was very smooth. I tried to keep it from let sliding but it didn't work. Very big chunks fell, and it got wider."

"We are not responsible," he said.

"So who is responsible?" I asked.

"Those who work on the veins," he answered curtly. Then they gave in a little. "We will give you a few more cubic meters and you will earn fourteen or fifteen pesos."

Disagreeing, I said, "Then whoever wants to be abused should work for you. I don't want a contract any more, Don Dario. I will leave on vacation at the beginning of March."

*Did they receive instructions from the manager to cheat the workers?*

I think that the manager gave orders to the engineers. The engineer earns from what he measures, so I don't believe that he would cheat unless the manager told him to, since it would not really benefit him. I think they must receive a benefit for cheating us on top of what they earn. Even the overseers try to cheat the workers.

When the worker is behind in his work he must lie to the overseer saying, "I have put so-and-so many beams along the way." The overseer then goes to see for himself, and, in order to hide his lie, the worker says again, "I put this in," when, in fact, he didn't.

The overseer has to look inside the holes drilled for the charges to see whether or not they are full of dynamite. In one way or another the worker has to cheat everyone from the superintendent to the manager. This is the way we retaliate for their cheating us. And then the superintendent and the man who measures our work areas cheat us further.

Sometimes we drill out of line. Often that is because there are veins in the way and, in order to avoid harming them, one moves to the right or to the left, and that makes the tunnel wider. If the manager has told the engineer to cheat, all the engineer has to do is take the widest place as the measurement for the whole tunnel. The engineer has to comply, and the workers get paid on that basis. This is the way they do it.

I hear they have shut off the shaft that they were exploiting. They say that the engineer supposedly has enough metal from discarded ore, and that's why they have stopped working it. They also aren't exploiting other veins. What they should do is find new veins. I don't know, but I've heard that those working inside the mine are moving beams from one site to another. They are reinforcing only those passageways that have already been worked and are essentially finished. They shouldn't be working on those sites since they don't have any more life. If they worked on other locations, the mine would produce more. The manager's luck, of course, would depend on the explorer-drillers.

*The administrator told me that workers don't know what a cubic meter is, and that they don't know what they are complaining about.*

That's a lie. Even the dumbest worker, one who doesn't even know how to read or write, knows how to calculate distances better than administrators, because we know how to measure with our hands and feet. We also have drills of different sizes, big and small; we have rope that we use to tie the bags and can throw it up into the lifts to estimate the height of a shaft. I always use a rope that is between thirty and forty meters long. Last month I measured my production with it. The levelling of the vein is already determined. We already know which place is high and which is low and we have to level it all. We also calculate the width inside our heads. It's a lie that a worker can't measure by meters. We keep track of the measurements better than anybody else.

Once, when I was working with the drilling machine, Guerra said, "Rojas, you are advancing very little." I had already measured my advance. I measured the passageway with my feet and every month I wrote down in my book the number of meters I had worked. That is how I know how many meters I have advanced. Every morning when I began working, after clearing the debris from the previous day's drilling, I measured with my feet how many meters I had advanced.

"Rojitas," he said, "you are not advancing much. You must hurry up because they are about to begin measuring."

I answered, "I have already advanced more than last month, and it is only the twentieth; by the twenty-fifth I will have advanced five more meters."

"How do you know?" Guerra asked. "Do you have a measuring tape?"

He was a friend of mine, and was quite popular. He didn't have his diploma yet; he still had to write his thesis. He knew that the bosses always like someone who works well, in a disciplined manner, and that is how I worked.

"I bet you haven't advanced that much yet," said the engineer.

" I have so. At least two or three meters more than last month. I have measured my production with my steps."

"How much do you want to bet?" he said.

"Engineer," I answered, "our salaries are too low for me to bet."

Another engineer, one who was just beginning there said, "I will be the witness."

But Guerra left, saying, "Maybe you'll win." He earned far more than I did. Arauje measured the vein and said that I had advanced 320 meters, more than the last month. The engineer was surprised.

"We monitor each other quite well," I said to him. "We know how to check on each other. Everything is measured. Nobody can say that a worker doesn't know how many centimeters there are in a meter. We — the workers — are quite on top of things because we are dealing with these advances every day and experience has taught us how to measure them.

I was finally granted my vacation in March. During February, after Carnival, I didn't pick up a tool. I didn't work at all. The only thing I did was fix the wooden box because it was stuck. I stopped working. The machine was rusting just where it was. I didn't touch it because I was so furious. Dario Gómez gave me my vacation. Then, during March, I got sick and went into the hospital for two days. They took an X-ray. The doctor frightened me when he said, "You should not go back into the mine. You can no longer work in the mine. You are very sick. Your lungs are collapsing."

# 16

## You Can Die Working

Petrona became aware that Juan had contracted 100 percent silicosis when they came to live in Oruro. She felt guilty when she learned about the seriousness of his illness from the doctor, yet defended her care of him. The dependence of men on their wives and daughters is revealed in her narrative when she speaks of how she managed both households. While Juan was waiting in Santa Fe for his transfer, María took care of his meals, and Petrona was setting up the new house in Oruro and preparing meals for Filemón, who was attending school there. Petrona shows her initiative in the move, and Juan picks up the narrative talking about his growing anxiety as to how, with his illness, he can see to the completion of the education of his children.

I [Petrona] came to Oruro because I couldn't pay for Filemón's room and rent. I went to the house where he was living and told him, "We can't send you so much money for your board. I have already borrowed too much money from your aunt and your godmother just to pay for your allowance. What are we going to do?

Filemón said, "Mommy, why don't you think about this: why don't you come live here? I am thinking of emptying the room upstairs so we can live here. You can bring the children here — Elena and Aníbal — and leave Father with María."

I said, "I will talk with your father and see what he says. Tomorrow I shall mail you a letter so you won't have to live at the boarding house any more."

He answered, "Yes, Mommy, that would be best because I have other expenses. I always want to buy ice cream cones, candies. Everybody has a snack except me. I don't know what to do. Why did I choose to come here when I knew very well that my father wasn't earning enough money? I should be punished for coming."

That day I rushed back to Santa Fe and spoke with my husband. "Look," I told him, "this is what Filemón said. He doesn't even have money for his snacks. He has barely enough money for room and board. He told me, 'Maybe you can come live here and cook for me. You can feed me well. They don't give me enough in the boarding house. They give me too little and we pay too much. Sometimes I don't even like what I am eating. My grandmother doesn't even open the door for me. I don't have a portable stove, so I can't even make myself tea at night. I can't live like this, Mommy. You must think about it and come live here with me.' This is what he told me."

My husband answered, "Petrona, maybe you *should* go to Oruro. Elena is getting sick. I think you should leave with her and Aníbal."

I got ready the following day, Saturday. I left with all my things. I brought a portable stove, paraffin, meat, everything. My son had not been eating for two days. He said his grandmother didn't care about him, but the poor woman was sick. I left Aníbal and Elena alone with their father in Santa Fe for one month, until they finished their exams. Elena got terribly sick. Then I went back to get them and left María with her father, to cook and care for him. She was twelve years old. She had to go to the mine store every day to get bread, meat, vegetables, cocoa. She didn't have enough time to go to school. She also had to take care of the pigs.

When I returned to Santa Fe I told Juan, "Juanito, why don't we kill the pigs? They are suffering. Some days María feeds them, others she doesn't. She just doesn't have enough time to take care of them."

One pig was huge and about to give birth. We slaughtered them, and I brought half the meat with me and left the other half with them. Juan continued to stay on in Santa Fe.

"Can't you get transferred?" I asked him. "Why don't you meet with the manager and ask to be transferred?"

He answered, "It's impossible. I will work in Santa Fe until the day of my death. This is where I started so I can't go elsewhere. The papers I sent to La Paz can get messed up if I leave. I have already been sent to La Paz my request to be recognized as disabled. With that, I am sure that I will be able to retire soon. I am 100 percent disabled, so it's certain that I'll get my retirement."

"In the meantime," I told him, "you should live however you can. But my children can't live alone. Elena got terribly sick because she missed me so much. It's all Filemón's fault for having chosen to go to school in Oruro. He could have finished the sixth grade in Santa Fe."

Juan went on to say, "You always let your son interfere in things. He is always bossing you around."

I answered, "He didn't go because he wanted to, or because I wanted him to. But he learns more in the city than here. Besides he can't go into the army unless he finishes this year."

Juan agreed, adding, "He also spends money going back and forth. I don't earn enough money to pay for his trips. Where am I going to get the money if I don't earn it?"

The following Saturday Juan came down to Oruro. He said, "While I'm on vacation, I am going to stay here. Perhaps my papers from the social security will come and I can retire. Then at last we can all live together."

When he went back to Santa Fe he got terribly sick. He stayed in bed because he no longer had strength to work. I went to Santa Fe to help him with his things, to clean his clothes and everything.

A man up there told me, "Señora, they are registering people to be transferred to San José. Don Juan should hurry up and leave in any pickup truck that's going this morning. They are taking names at the entrance to the mine."

I told Juan, "Be careful to pay attention to what others advise. You aren't listening to what they say. You always let the supervisors tell you what to do. You keep your ears closed to what the workers are saying. Submit your name so you can come live with us."

I didn't send him any of his work clothes. I told him, "You should get registered as soon as you arrive at the mine. Maybe we'll leave this very day or tomorrow."

The following day he went to work. The day after that he left for Oruro with María, who arrived looking very tired. The woman across the street yelled, "Doña Petrona, look at your daughter! She can't carry the bags she is holding."

But they just left most of our things two days ago, I thought. What could they be bringing with them? Then I saw that my little girl was trying to carry a sack filled with potatoes, rice, meat, and vegetables.

My daughter cried, "Mommy, at last we have been blessed from the heavens. You prayed so many days, asking God to send my father here, and He finally listened to your words and now Daddy will be working in San José."

Your *compadre* went directly to "Sinkan" [Sink and Float, the concentration plant], where the men were shown around the mill they were going to work in and told the jobs they would be given. He worked there for three months but he didn't grow accustomed to it. He earned less in the mill. They wanted him to be an overseer because they said he worked well. He was liked in Sinkan but he wasn't happy with what he earned. It wasn't enough, it was just enough to buy food.

Then a friend from Santa Fe said to him, "They need drillers. Why don't you ask to be transferred?"

*Did he know he was sick?*

Yes, he already knew that he was sick. They said, "You can't work inside the mine because the air is bad and it stinks." They had told him in Santa Fe that the work would be outside.

"Why don't you come?" his friend said. "In these coming months your retirement may come through; with what you'll be earning you may get a better deal. Why not come? There's a vacancy."

Juan told me, "I want to go back to working in the mine. What I earn is not enough. I'll be able to earn more."

"But Juan," I said, "I don't want you to go inside the mine again. You've been out of the mine for so long."

"It won't hurt. I've already rested a bit. I have worked three months in the mill."

"Well, it depends on you. You should know what's best for you. There's nothing that I can really say. But I wish you wouldn't work inside the mine anymore."

That's how he ended up in San José. He earned over five hundred pesos that month, but with a lot of effort. The following month he earned a little bit more, but his papers still didn't come. For three months nothing happened, and they even cheated him on his pay. I don't know how much, but I know they did.

He was furious, and shouted, "I would be better off if I returned to Santa Fe. I am leaving. You all should be blamed for bringing me here. I came here in such a rush. I can't earn anything. They were about to give me a fixed contract where I knew what I was going to earn in Santa Fe. Then I would have earned a lot. They say that Bravos is earning well, but you had me come here! Why? I am so fed up here! They don't know how to fix the machines, or even when to give us air. They don't understand a thing; they are just a bunch of kids. When will my papers come in? I don't earn enough and I can't get used to this job."

Then he had to go into the hospital. He got something like *rabio*, [a sickness believed to be caused by anger], but he was really sick in his lungs. One morning, after a month, I met the doctor when I was bringing Juan vegetables — cooked with a little bit of oil, with lots of tomatoes — and some lettuce and milk. I fed him all sorts of things to help his lungs.

As Dr. Salinas was coming out of Juan's room he said, "Ma'am, I want to talk to you."

"Good morning, Doctor. How are you? What is it?"

"You are here so early, ma'am. There aren't many women like you who come so early in the morning to feed their husband. It's a very good thing that you bring him food because he is very sick in the lungs."

"Well, why is he so sick?" I asked the doctor.

"He is very sick with 100 percent lung disease, and he should not go back into the mine."

"What can I do, Doctor? I don't want him to work inside the mine any more. He was working in the mill, in Sinkan, but his wage wasn't enough and we have a lot of children. That's why he asked to be transferred back into the mine. He gets too mad inside the mine. He got fed up, and I think this is what made him sicker."

"He doesn't have *rabia* or anything like that," the doctor said. "He has to be transferred out and he can't work in any heavy job because he is sick in his liver and his lungs."

I burst out crying and went in to see your *compadre*. I told him what the doctor told me.

"You have to get those papers and work outside of the mines," I said. "I told you for so long that you shouldn't work inside the mine. He told me that you are very sick in your lungs. Now where are you going to replace the lungs that you have given away to the company for so long? Some earn just by putting their money in their pockets, but you must work like a donkey for so little. I am so bitter. Yet you continue working even if I break my jaw trying to talk you out of it. You were already out but that overseer, whoever he was, tricked you into going back in. You have to be transferred no matter what!"

In the office they said they would send him to the manager and then home.

After Juan was out a month, he was sent to La Paz. There they promised him 170 pesos for food and medicine. But not even that arrived. We thought, Are they making fun of us? After he left the hospital, he shouldn't have had to work any more.

The doctor said, "You have to take care of yourself. You are very sick and you should be happy that your wife has fed you so well. This has helped you recuperate. If you hadn't eaten this well, you would have died already."

Finally Juan realized that he could have died working. They were just fooling him, making him believe that his papers were on their way. They don't care. They expect the men to die inside the mine.

---

Juan's reaction to his illness was one of desperation. He had not yet realized his goal of educating even his oldest son, and he tried to continue working as long as possible in order to earn the higher wages paid interior workers. He speaks of this ordeal.

---

In 1969, toward the middle of April I [Juan] went back to work. I always took my vacation during December, but that year I had gone on vacation in March. Because I was disgusted with my job and I wasn't earning enough, I forced my boss to give me a vacation. On the fifth of April, a Saturday, I went back to work. I worked only until nine in the morning. At that moment my back was hurting me and my lungs were painful. The machine must have affected my lungs.

*What did you feel in your lungs?*

I felt as if there was a very heavy load of metal on my back. I tried to get rid of it by bending forward or stretching backwards. Sometimes it felt like hot pepper had been smeared on my lungs and back. Once the pain went away, my back began itching. Afterward I rested and I didn't feel too sick, but according to the X-rays I was. I didn't have pain anymore, and I wondered why that was. Maybe the food I ate gave me strength.

I didn't want to go to Cochabamba. It's too dangerous because there is greater pressure in the air. The change in climate could give me bronchitis, or something like a heart attack. That is what happens to men who are sick in their lungs and who go live in Cochabamba. It's just too dangerous and can kill you right away. This is exactly what happened to a man from Itos. I don't remember his name. He died last October from a heart attack, according to the doctor; the workers said that he died from the gases. That could be true, since they had let a lot of gas out the day before. I could die like that if I went to Cochabamba.

"You can go rest in Cochabamba if you want to," Petrona said.

"My life is in danger," I answered.

I had a young friend who worked on the same team as Fernando Bravo. His name was Fructuoso Uzeda, and he was my assistant. He didn't work too long as a driller. He left to buy a piece of land in Vinto, in Cochabamba. He was lacking only 18,000 pesos and agreed to put down 16,000 and try to raise the rest. He went to the social security office to get an advance on his indemnity, but I don't think he ever got his pension because he couldn't get his papers processed. While he was trying to get them done he died. He lived in Cochabamba only two months. He was on his way to Santa Cruz to buy bananas when he died. He must have been about thirty-eight years old, fairly young. He worked very hard, but he didn't eat well. His wife was a lazy person who only wanted his money and did not care for her husband's health. Now what was she left with? She was young, with six children, but, even though she had a house, there was nothing she could do without a husband. She rented it to Ricardo López, a worker from Santa Fe who is still working, I think. His wife says that he travels with vegetables to Santa Fe.

The widow left for Argentina. I don't know what luck she had there, nobody knows. Now she's walking in distant lands because she lost her husband. If she had known how to take care of him, she wouldn't have lost him.

I am probably the only one still alive of all the workers my age who worked as drillers. I know that all have died except Rodriguez, and I am not sure whether he is dead or alive.

Anyway, on that Saturday in April I asked Gómez for permission to go to the hospital. He gave me permission until eleven o'clock in the morning. At ten-thirty I was through. Dr. Encinas asked me to return on Monday at ten; he wanted me X-rayed in San José.

On Monday I returned and the doctor gave me a piece of paper authorizing that I be hospitalized. I went down to the hospital and they immediately put me to bed. I met Dr. Vargas, the chief of the medical department. He called for Dr. Sandi, and Dr. Sandi came right away and took me to the bronchopneumonia section. At two I had my X-ray taken.

He gave me the results saying, "Are you already putting your social security papers in order?"

"I already have, but I haven't received anything despite the fact that the social security acknowledges that I am 100 percent sick. Nothing concrete has come through yet," I told him.

The X-ray technician said, "Better get in bed and try not to catch a cold." I went to bed, and at four in the afternoon Dr. Sandi came in with the plates.

"How long have you felt the pains?"

I told him, "I have only felt pain since Saturday morning."

"It didn't hurt before?"

"No, I didn't feel anything."

The doctor looked at me with his eyes wide open. He was startled and said, "You can't work any more inside the mine. You must leave as soon as possible!" He ordered me not to go in the mine.

I made the request for sick leave while I was still in the hospital, on about the fifteenth of April. Dario Gómez didn't want me to transfer because he knew how well I worked and he wanted me to work inside one of the chimneys. They had to open a tunnel of about eighty meters like the one I had done in the month of December from level 100 to level 150. This one was to go directly to level 280.

When I made the request he didn't grant it. "We can't let you have a transfer under any circumstances. If you leave you must bring someone to replace you."

Even after I showed him the medical report he did not accept my request. I went up to see the supervisor of the mine, Engineer Arevelo. "There isn't anything else to do, son," he said. "What are we going to do? Tell the chief of the section to give you your transfer."

"Chief Gómez doesn't want to let me transfer under any circumstances. He has asked me to bring someone else to replace me."

"How does he expect someone else to come in your place, Rojas? Tell him to give me the authorization."

Engineer Arevelo got annoyed at me and sent me back to Dario Gómez. I went to see him again, although I doubted that I could get anywhere with him. When I begged him to let me go, Gómez stared at me fixedly and said, "I didn't want to let you go because you work well. You are diligent and strong despite your illness. What are we going to do? Well, we'll have to let you go." Then he signed the papers.

I told Dr. Sandi afterward what had happened. "You must telephone me once your boss accepts the transfer. You will have to take your papers to the chief of welfare. I am going to tell him that you are on your way."

So they accepted my transfer and agreed to give me a job outside the mine in a location where it wasn't too cold. I talked with them for about forty-five minutes. The chief of welfare, Engineer Saavedra, told me what watchmen did, how they worked, what their responsibilities were, and so on. He spoke about how some of the watchmen behaved, as opposed to how any honest person is expected to behave on the job. He said that he hoped I wouldn't behave that way.

I answered, "You will never be displeased with me because I take my jobs very seriously. Anyplace, whether it's a tough or a relaxed job, I perform well because I don't want the chiefs ever to have to rebuke me."

Saavedra was impressed with what I said. "You can begin immediately, tomorrow if possible," he responded.

"I have to be in the hospital until the eighteenth," I answered. "Then I'll be leaving."

I thought I was going to be in the hospital until the eighteenth, but that's not the way things worked out. Dr. Sandi let me out the following day, saying, "You can leave, but you must go home and take a great deal of care of yourself. You must get up at ten or eleven o'clock and eat well, eat plenty of vegetables."

I stayed at home until the twenty-first. On the twenty-second I was to begin working. Everything was ready. Saavedra told me, "Come and work for me in my office."

I went to his office at seven on the morning of the twenty-second. I waited for him until seven-thirty when he finally got in. He gave me the job in the opening of Itos mine. I left work at three-thirty that afternoon. I wrote everything down: what went out, what materials came from the storeroom, everything. But no one came to get the list from me. I went to the boss and said, "The guards haven't come around. I am now leaving so here are the lists. No one has come to replace me." I gave them to him.

"You should have gone home already," he said. "When there is no one to replace you, you should just leave."

I left, and when I was on the road he called after me, "Tomorrow you won't work on the first shift. You should come in at eleven at night to work the third shift. Go to the gate where the bakery is."

I accepted gladly even though the doctor had told me not to work during the night. But everything went well. Nothing happened, and I worked up to the last day peacefully.

All week I worked the third shift. Toward the end of the month a drunk drove up to the exit gate in a taxi, and I asked to see his identification so I could let him leave. He didn't have it.

"We don't have to show identification to go out anywhere," he scolded me.

I answered, "If you want to go to your house in a car you have to show it, because our orders are to let only those with identification pass. When one does not have it, one cannot pass. Not even the superintendent can pass because that is the order. Up until eleven anyone who wants to can enter and leave for anything, but after eleven they have to carry their identification. You must have been told this by the chief of welfare."

"There is a list with my name on it that you can check to see that I have a pass," he answered.

"The boss told me that I shouldn't let anyone pass, even if his name is on the list, unless he has a pass."

He got out and opened the gate. I got in front and told the driver, "You can't go ahead. I am going to take note of this and inform the transit authorities."

The driver stopped the car. He tried to hit me. I went into the guardhouse and closed the door behind me. I called Saavedra immediately and told him what was happening. The drunkard took the phone away from me and spoke with Saavedra. When he realized that Saavedra took the same position, and that it wasn't my own doing, he apologized. He realized he had done wrong. He left the car behind and walked to his house. Nothing like that occurred on the following nights.

Juan Matos, who worked on the same shift, got to like me a lot. There were plenty of cars without permits that came at two or three in the morning. I didn't let them go through.

Matos watched me from a distance. Then he came up to me and said, "You're doing fine, Rojas. I like the way you work. Have you worked as a guard before?"

"No, I never did. It's the first time."

"It looks as if you had worked as a guard for many years. You know quite well how to proceed with people." This happened the first Sunday night I was working.

In the month of May he gave me a job working in the upper level on the seven to three shift. My workmate was Vasquez. His nickname was "the Fox." Once he came to replace me early, at ten o'clock at night. He worked on the third shift and I was working the second. One day I offered to replace him at nine-thirty since he had done the same thing for me. He came in drunk and I said, "Don't you think you should sleep until about eleven? You don't look too well. You could fall asleep and anything could happen out there. The saltwort is in bags and somebody could walk away with it if you fell asleep. It's best if you go to sleep and I'll take care of things in the meantime."

Vasquez answered, "Do you think you're talking to someone who just began working?" He was quite offended. "I've worked plenty of years here. I'm not going to fall asleep. You can leave." So I left.

Of course he did fall asleep on the job, and about twelve-thirty somebody took eight sacks of saltwort. I knew exactly how many I had left behind. I had counted them with Vargas, and I hadn't gone into the storehouse because I didn't want to be responsible for anything. There were thirty-eight sacks, and they stole eight from Vasquez. Apparently Valverde had counted thirty at about one o'clock at night.

I came back the next day at three in the afternoon and counted the sacks, noticing that there were only thirty.

Somebody must have taken them somewhere, I said to myself. I don't know how anyone got in. I signed the paper in the main office, but it didn't say anything about missing sacks. I went down and got my portion of calcium carbide. It was still early and the sun was shining, so I left my lamp and went into the hut. I wanted to check out the men as they were carrying used beams from the mine to be used on the rail lines. I heard a whistle from the office so I went back.

"Well, what happened?" Vargas yelled. "Some sacks disappeared last night. Did you leave all of them or only thirty?"

I answered that I had left thirty-eight, and that the Fox received thirty-eight from me. They called Valverde who was in Saavedra's office.

Vargas took me to Saavedra's office and asked me, "Rojas, how many sacks did you get from the store?"

"They gave me thirty-eight and I gave Vasquez thirty-eight," I answered.

"He says you only gave him thirty."

"I left him thirty-eight. I don't know what happened to the rest."

"What do you mean? You have to watch over the sacks of saltwort every minute. When there's imported wood, or eucalyptus wood, you have to look after it carefully because thieves are walking around every minute. What do you mean that you don't know what happened?"

"Well, is it my fault that the other guy was robbed?"

Valverde came into Saavedra's office and said, "When I walked by after the first hour, at about one o'clock, I found only thirty sacks. I also found Vasquez sleeping inside the guardhouse."

I knew I was alright then, because Valverde had seen that the Fox was drunk. Saavedra asked me, "Was Vasquez sober?"

"No, he was drunk," I answered. "I told him, 'Rest until eleven and I will look after things until then. Then another day you can come in earlier.' But he didn't want it that way. He answered, 'Do you think I have no experience on the job?' When he answered in that way I left, but I left thirty-eight sacks behind."

Apparently some thieves had come in without the other guard, the one at the opening of the mine, seeing them. He saw a man with a sack going out the gate later, but the foolish guard did not pay any attention to what the man was carrying. He let him go through. The one he let by was called "the old man." He was slightly limp and worked on the fourth gate. The old man's accomplices went down into the city with the rest of the sacks by a back route. Only the "old man" went through the gate, most likely to mislead the guards. He walked right by them without their searching him. He was a worker from San José who was working in Itos.

Later they had his house searched and found the saltwort. They asked him, "Who were the others who took them?" He answered that seven other men came and that each had taken one bag.

When they asked Fox Vasquez what happened he said, "I don't re-member any men going out. All I remember is that Rojas only gave me thirty sacks."

So he lied even though everyone knew that he was guilty. He tried to blame me because I was new on the job. He said, "Rojas is still new here. He doesn't know how to watch things. They must have stolen it from him."

I looked at him and said, "Just wait, because everything is getting cleared up. Let's see who is going to fall." I said this right to his face, and he shut up.

The following day at four, Saavedra had me called into his office and he said, "You are not guilty. This robbery took place at midnight during the third shift. A man was seen walking with a sack and the guard at the fourth gate didn't stop him. He wasn't searched so he walked away with the sack. Well, there is no doubt as to what happened, so go back to work."

From then onward Saavedra trusted me. A couple of days later they installed electricity in the guardhouse. A boy told me, "You can bring along a small heater to get warmed up at night."

I didn't take one to work because my blood is weak. When I use a heater, I get rheumatism, so I usually just endured the cold, keeping warm one way or another. When it wasn't too cold I would go out. During the night it's cold only during intervals, not all the time. The cold is like the wind, it comes and goes, as if someone were blowing at us in gusts. I had to protect myself from that. I thought that with the heater I would get warm, but I also could get sick every time I went outside, so I used it sparingly.

My companion at work said, "I am not accustomed to using a heater. Last night when it was very cold I leaned against the wall and fell asleep. I always fall asleep from the heat of the heater, and they found me sleeping."

One of the men on the round had said that I was a bad man because I was wasting electricity, but I wasn't one to always plug in the heater when I came to work.

The man from the round said, "You will be reprimanded. You will suffer a penalty because you used the electricity. You shouldn't touch it. You are a guard, not an electrician. Why did you play with the electricity?" He accused me like that to Saavedra, but since Saavedra likes me a lot, he told me everything that had happened and asked me if I had done what the man charged me with.

"Yes, Don Walter," I said. "You know I'm sick and that we sometimes need some sort of heating. Yes, on that occasion, I plugged it in." I guess he went to Saavedra because he was envious of me or maybe just to get back at me.

"Don't pay any attention to him, Rojas," Saavedra said. "Just use the heater when you want to, but don't fall asleep like your companion did."

"Maybe he did that because he's irresponsible," I said, "but it won't happen to me. You'll never find me sleeping. You can keep track of me any way you want to. No one will ever catch me sleeping."

"I like you very much, Rojas, and I trust you. I can see you working well in whatever position you are in."

Saavedra liked me a lot. If I fail to work hard it means that I am taking food out of my children's mouths. If I didn't earn enough what would my family eat? I would suffer.

I went with my medical certificate to see Mr. Clavijo. He gave me the written order to travel to La Paz and have my X-ray taken. Saturday morning they came to get me. I was not told of this by anyone because I was on the third work shift. Saavedra had sent someone to look for me, but he could not find my house. I don't know why, but my mother had taken the number off.

Six of us who were supposed to go, but, because they couldn't find me, five went on ahead. I came in at eleven-thirty on Saturday night to replace the man before me and he said, "They looked for you all over the place. Where have you been? Ortuño saw you at the gate, but then you immediately disappeared toward San José on your bike."

"I didn't go up to San José," I said. "Besides that, I have never been on a bike since I don't know how to ride one. You just mistook someone else for me."

On Monday morning I went to see Mr. Clavijo and said, "Saturday I wasn't told anything about leaving because they weren't able to find me. I didn't know I was supposed to travel. The rest have left already. Well, I guess they will look for another chance for me."

Those who had gone spoke about my case in La Paz and they sent for me on Monday. I left Tuesday and returned with the others with a paper that the social security gave me. I gave the paper to Mr. Clavijo and he gave it back to me. He told me that I had to wait until the fifteenth for the results of the tests to come back from La Paz. They didn't arrive. As you recall, *Comadre*, you went with my wife when you were on your way to the United States, and the week after you went to see them the papers came in.

---

Petrona and I found that Juan's papers had been mixed up with those of another Juan Rojas who worked in another mine. We finally got the retirement papers together with the reports on his medical history. Juan thought that with these he would be able to retire and receive his pension from the social security, but it was more than two years before this came about, and, when it did, the pension he received had decreased in value to the point that it was almost worthless.

---

# 17

## How the Poor Get Buried

Workers in the mining communities are ensnared in the bureaucracies of the National Mining Company of Bolivia (COMIBOL) and of the state. They often end up on the losing side because of discriminatory treatment and disadvantages in education. Oftentimes the sheer stupidity of clerks results in months of waiting for pensions, other benefits, or even death certificates. As Juan approached the end of his working career he endured the abuse, corruption, and ineptitude of clerks throughout the government and company bureaucracies as he tried to deal with deaths in his family and with his own impending retirement because of lung disease.

Even when death occurred, workers in the mining community experienced exploitation in the form of local and federal taxes. The high costs of medical and death certificates caused the poor in mining communities to bury newborn infants without certification. The penalties for failure to follow official procedures are high. During the war of the Chaco, the state demanded that children born some twenty years before be drafted, but since many had already died and been buried without official certification, families were forced to send surviving daughters into the mines to work or otherwise compensate for what was presumed to be a draft dodger (cf. "Basilia" in *Dos Mujeres Indigenas*). In 1970, when I lived in Oruro, the corpse of an infant was found in the garbage heaps that surrounded the encampment. The community expressed its horror — in part blaming the worsening economic situation for forcing people to evade expenses for an official burial, and in part the immorality of youth, particularly the *"minifaldas"* or miniskirted young women.

On the day of his mother's death, Juan was forced to run from one office to another to fulfill the demands of state and local governments. It left him little time to mourn her death or to sort out the ambivalent feelings he held toward her. One year later, when I attended the first commemoration of her death on All Soul's Day, Juan spoke to her spirit, which is believed to attend the first anniversary feast. In front of the sumptuous table laid out by Petrona and Juan, with the plucked chicken, the fruit imported from tropical regions, and the steaming platters of potatoes and vegetables, Juan announced to his mother that, though she had been very mean during her life, he hoped she lived in heaven and not in the hell that he suspected was her fate. Even after her death he was competing for her attention, more than fulfilling his obligations as a son.

The death of any family member threatens the lives of all remaining relatives. Juan explained this threat to me during the ceremonies of All Souls' as he reflected on his own mortality and his hopes for his children.

---

During the burial of a close family member — a father, mother, or sibling — we must never look into the grave. If we do, we will die immediately, one by one. They say the grave will be filled with the entire family. That's the reason why, when we take something with us to pray in the cemetery, we never bring it back with us. It's better to throw it away or give it to the poor who are praying. When someone is buried, a few relatives will accompany him or her. When my sister died, for example, my mother went to see her grave and, before my mother's eyes, she was buried.

That very same niche began to summon my older brother, Feliz. So, when my mother died, I didn't let anybody go near the grave. We all remained in a far corner of the room. I held all of them away from the body. We went to the cemetery after a week. Even so, I think a few more of us are going to die now.

When my mother died I buried her. I went into the office on the first of July to return the platform[1] I had borrowed from the company to mourn my mother.

When I went in to return it, the clerk asked for the death certificate. I had to walk all over the place to get it. I didn't have any money, so I had to walk. First I went to the hospital in San José to get the death certificate. They used to just give it to us, but now we have to pay for it. On the morning of her burial, when I went in to get the certificate from the hospital, they told me to go to the Health Center. I ran over there to get it, but when I got there I was told that they couldn't process one without a medical report indicating the cause of death. So I went back to the hospital and returned to the Health Center with it, but this time I took a bus.

The clerk at the Health Center processed it immediately. Then I went to the Plaza 10th of February to a building where they keep the workers' savings, so that I could borrow some money. From there they sent me to the Section for Public Assistance. I left on the run again, but when I arrived at that section, nobody could help me. They just said, "You have to go back to the Health Center and they will do everything for you right there. From there you have to go to Town Hall where they will give you the certificate to have the burial."

I went back to the Health Center and found someone who did everything just as I was told they would. The paper cost me five bolivianos. I had paid sixty bolivianos for the medical report, thirty bolivianos for the death certificate, and fifteen bolivianos for the municipal death certificate. I spent over one-hundred bolivianos [the equivalent of about ten days' pay].

They get so much out of you! It's very expensive to bury someone. I don't know how someone poor gets buried. In the countryside you don't have to do any of that; they only have to go to the judge for the certificate and then they bury the body. That's all. Meanwhile, in the cities we pay so much in taxes! When you die, it costs plenty to get buried. How do the poor get buried? It's a pity.

We also had a lot of problems with my brother's certificate. My sister lost it. I went to see the man in charge of the cemetery and told him that I knew when he had died, but I didn't know his registry of death number. The day before he was buried, I received the letter I needed to bury him, but it came without the number. I knew the year, everything, but I didn't know the registration number.

---

[1] The funeral bier is an elaborate platform with built-in lights and flower urns.

The man in charge of the cemetery told the secretary, "I will look for it and then tell you what it is. The registration letter you are now holding is worthless unless we give you a numbered certificate."

I thought he was probably right and that the certificate I had been given in the cemetery was worthless, and that I needed one from the municipality.

"Can you give me the number of the registration so I can look for it?" I asked. "We'll pay you ten bolivianos. You won't be looking for it in vain. And when you find it, we'll use it to get a certificate."

He didn't want to give me the number even though I offered to pay him ten bolivianos. He said, "I don't need ten bolivianos to look for it. If you have a written permit, I will look it up for you, and you can pay me thirty pesos."

I didn't like what he said. I have a friend who is a judge. I went to see him in his office on Santa Bárbara Street and I said to him, "Don Apolinar, I have lost a death certificate and the man at the cemetery doesn't want to tell me the registration number I need to get another certificate at the municipal office. He also says that only that old number is valid and I cannot get another."

Don Apolinar got annoyed, "That is none of his business. Who does he think he is to demand that? What is his claim to authority?"

I went with Don Apolinar to see the man in charge of the cemetery, but he still would not give us the number we needed. The judge asked me, "What was the year that he was buried?"

"In 1963, on the day of San Juan, the twenty-fourth of June."

The judge said to the clerk, "Let me see the book."

The man in charge of the book hid it, whereupon the judge went behind the counter to look for it. Lola, the woman in charge of everything, came in. She was also opposed to Don Apolinar looking for the book.

"Miss, I'm a judge. I have the right to go through this book. I can come any time I please and go through it. Please let me continue my search."

So she let him go through the book, and he found the number. Then we went to the registrar. There we found the registration and the certificate. The judge took it to the social security office because my niece needed it. Without it the law did not recognize that her father was dead, and we needed it to get some money for my niece who was sick. She is now under the care of my sister, who has taken her in like a daughter. I think everything will be resolved in about a month.

After we buried my mother, Roberto Mendoza called me to his office. He said, "My boss is looking for you; he needs you. Come in."

I went in and met his boss. I didn't know that it was for my retirement pension; my papers were all done by the first of July. I went up to him and Clavijo said, "Are you Rojas?"

"Yes, Mr. Clavijo. I am Rojas."

"We have received an order from La Paz for your retirement. Your pension checks will be coming through soon."

I replied, "First of all, I would like to know how much I have coming."

"You will be getting 290 bolivianos, so you can retire now."

I signed my retirement papers. I was scheduled to go to Itos to work in Sinkan where I was supposed to work the whole month. Instead I went to the doctor's office. He wanted to hospitalize me.

"I have retired Doctor," I said. "I am not going to work anymore. I will come in every once in a while to see you in your office, but it would be worse for me to stay in the hospital."

Dr. Encinas told me, "Very good. If you don't work, that's fine." He gave me medicines and told me I could leave.

I had gotten to the city in the car of "Old Hat." That is the nickname of the contractor, Eugenio Mamani, who had replaced Saavedra. He said to me, "Go along with the driver. He'll pick you up later."

So I went down to the hospital, and the driver went to pick up cement from the ball field. I got my medicine and waited for him at the door. He went to leave the load of cement at Sinkan. After that we came back.

Eugenio told me that my son had called me from the second gate and was looking for me. My wife didn't know yet that I had retired. It was after two o'clock in the afternoon and she had sent Filemón over to find out what had happened to me. I was still wearing my regular clothes since I had not even gone in to work. I spoke with my son, and he said, "It's past two o'clock, Daddy. What time are you going to get your work clothes? Shall I bring them or are you going home to change?"

"Bring the clothing here, Filemón. I'm not going to work, but I need you here."

I had my retirement card made, and a job card for my son. Mr. Walter wrote the letter for me. He was a small, bearded fellow. I needed my son to sign it and then gave the letter and card to the manager to sign, I got my card back and the letter stayed in the office. I then asked for work for my son.

I spent the whole month having my papers processed and signed. They didn't get things moving. I still didn't know how much money I was going to receive from the social security pension. One day when I was waiting outside the office to find out, Walter Saavedra saw me and asked, "Are you retiring?"

"I am not retiring voluntarily. The company is retiring me. They say my pension is on its way and that I must retire. Now I am going to rest until my death. I am not going to work anymore. If I do, it will only be part-time, not every single day. I will have plenty of days of pension."

"That's fine, Rojas. You deserve a rest because you have worked a lot."

He congratulated me for the work I had done for him while I worked in his section.

I was going up in the elevator when I met Mr. Clavijo. He asked me, "How is everything going? Have you gotten everything straightened out?"

"Mr. Clavijo, I don't know what I'm going to do. A paper goes into an office and sleeps there three or four days. I come back and they always tell me, 'Come back at such-and-such a time and we will have it ready.' When I come back, they simply reply, when I ask them where it is, 'It's not ready yet. It will take a couple of hours.' I am just wasting my time. Nothing works, and I don't know who to complain to."

"Go see the supervisor and complain."

I went to see Mr. Gallegos. He received me well. I complained to him, saying, "My papers have been sitting in the office for a whole month. They never leave. They should have had everything ready this month. Besides, I need some money to make purchases for the up-coming feasts."

Mr. Gallegos said, "We have already paid you three months' pension." He didn't let me reply, so I left quietly.

The month was ending. I didn't want the second month to pass because medical attention lasted only through the second month. My wife went to the hospital with my youngest daughter who had hurt her leg. She told them, "He no longer has any medical attention. He has already retired."

A friend of mine was working there, and he said to her, "We are going to give you a card in Filemón's name. You'll have to go with your husband to the hospital to pick it up, but there won't be any problem. They'll take care of it."

If he hadn't been my friend, my daughter wouldn't have been attended to. I no longer have any medical assistance. If anything happens to me, I have to wait until the social security clears my papers. If they don't I'll just have to die for lack of medical care. That's why I wanted things to get done quickly. I'm still behind on any payments. My leave pay came in from La Paz at the end of the July and I went to the bank immediately.

*How much was it?*

It was eight thousand seven hundred pesos and something. It was too little. I left my youth in the mines, and that's all they gave me in return. I invested it in the patio here in my house. I also had to pay back my son-in-law. He lent me money a couple of years ago to pay for Petrona's parents' burial. I bought a pair of shoes for myself and my wife. I couldn't buy her any underwear. All the money was gone. I thought of working a couple more months to increase my retirement payment.

I told Mr. Clavijo, "I would like to work three more months to increase my retirement payments."

He replied, "This retirement order is from La Paz. There is nothing we can do." They didn't let me work in the mine even for a few more months. I just had to accept the sum of money I was given. They cheated me. I should have received at least one thousand pesos more.

*Does your leave pay reflect incentive increases you received?*

You know very well that they give miners an incentive payment above their salary in order not to raise our salaries. Minister of Work Gallardo offered us a higher and higher incentive every month. I think he gave us four pesos for a work day. Those who work outside the mine earn 50 percent or, at most, 60 percent of the wage of interior workers. The guards earn two pesos a day. Those working in the mill 180 pesos a month, and the clerks earn sixty pesos. They say we'll have paid vacations. After twenty-five workdays we were supposed to be given four pesos incentive a day. Then they gave us one hundred pesos a month as an incentive. They said they were going to add that to our vacation and retirement funds. But, at least in my case, they haven't given me anything based on the incentive payments. I still haven't seen Mr. Clavijo about this, but I already made my claim in La Paz.

The supervisor of labor relations just nodded his head and said,

"This problem belongs in San José. There is nothing we can do about it here."

I haven't had time yet to see Mr. Clavijo. I won't say anything until they fix my cancellation papers. They are probably going to round it off. But they should pay me on everything because it was really part of my salary. I have to make a claim. According to the previous government's promise, I should get paid. But we didn't want to accept Colonel Gallardo's word. During President Paz Estenssoro's and President Barrientos' governments they gave us two pesos every day above our salary. Each month they gave fifty pesos to those working in offices and eighty to those working in the mill. We always protested this. Plus, they didn't pay us two pesos! Plenty of workers were fired because of union problems and they didn't get paid at all. For that reason we had them add those two pesos onto our salaries.

We asked Gallardo to add it on to our wages and he answered, "It can't be. If it goes through, the cost of living will rise. Things will just get worse."

We realized that the first to take advantage of a raise in our wages would be the merchants; the workers would not have benefited at all. So we accepted the incentive. Our wage had to go up every six months. At the end of the first period, we would get paid four pesos more, at the end of the second period six, and so on. But they haven't paid us more than five pesos in all the years since 1964. They have paid only one peso more in six years and the rest has been in bonuses. They have cheated us. I am going to see Mr. Clavijo as soon as I have time. I don't have any money to buy things for my children.

They are paying Filemón only fifty pesos a month. That is only enough to buy two bushels of potatoes and some vegetables. After that I have no money left to spend on my children. While I was working I earned 124 pesos. I could buy shoes for my children at least.

*Does your son give you his salary?*

I don't see his salary; he gives it all to my wife, the same way I did. He gives her the whole thing. He doesn't even ask her for any. If we give him some money, he takes it. If we don't, he doesn't say a thing. He knows how much we scrimp even to buy something small. I may not receive my paycheck until November. I don't know how we're going to live. We do not have enough money right now. We don't have rice. And, as children grow, their appetites grow. Every day the cost of rice, of sugar, of everything is going up. All I have left is what I harvested last year. We are managing with just that. Today we went to the general store. We didn't have time before because we were busy with my nephew's marriage and my mother's burial.

This is all that has happened to me and my family up until now. If you want to ask me something you can. It will bring back memories to me.

---

Juan uttered these words in December, 1970. I asked him, "Did you want a big family?"

---

When I only had one son, things were alright. I had everything. The times were better too. I wasn't the way I am now, like a tyrant. When I had my second child, María, things were still okay. I wasn't worried about anything yet. After María, Aníbal was born in 1958. The two older ones were already in school when I had another child, Elena. She was born in 1961. After her, Ana María was born in 1966. And last of all, Juan Manuel was born. I don't know if I'll have more children. It all depends on God.

*Have you used anything to prevent your wife from becoming pregnant?*

No, no of course not. I only expect God's will to work. It is all up to God.

*Do you prefer boys to girls?*

I like all children. Some men don't want their daughters to study. They only want their sons to study. They think a woman can't study or that her studies won't get her anywhere. But they forget what is ahead of them. When a father is of a lower category than I, a poor man who doesn't know how to speak well, he won't have any standing with the neighbors. He will be looked down upon by those who know how to speak and express themselves well. And if the children follow the same course as their parents they won't have any prestige either. My wife is the child of a very poor family, just like me. She is following, just as I am, the steps of her mother and father. In my case, I lived like an orphan from early on. My mother could not educate us. She could only feed and clothe us. She raised us on what she earned in the market. I can't blame my father because he died early. That's why I fell behind in my studies. But despite all that, I have learned how to use my ability.

When I worked in the mines, I bought the "ABC books," a notebook, and pencils. I wanted to learn how to write. That's how I learned. I bought a great many notebooks and wrote as much as I could when I had breaks, and after work instead of going out to play. The books were my sole teachers.

Once I had many illusions. I thought that the day I had a wife and children I would educate my children. That's what I always thought of doing. My wife is the offspring of a poor woman just as I am, although her father lived until she was older than I was when my father died. He died when she was thirty-five. She could have had some education because both her parents were alive and her older siblings were boys. If they had thought of it, they would at least have made sure she learned to read and write. They would have taken her traditional dress off and given her a modern one. But her brothers are a bunch of dogs who don't even remember her. They even go against her now that she has a husband and children. They are envious because we have a house here and in Cochabamba and they don't have a place to live. Once they retire where will they end up? Her brother has a lot of sons and only one daughter. Where will this poor man live? He works inside the mine. He wasn't a driller, nothing of that sort. He worked as a pipefitter. He didn't work on hard jobs; he had light and clean jobs, and that's why he doesn't have the miners' disease. Now he has begun working as a driller. In time, he'll get sick. Where is he going to live? Where is he going to rest once he's sick? Where are his children going to live? He doesn't have any brains.

My wife has to do everything. She has to wash clothing, cook, patch the rags our children wear, clean the house, and take care of the children. She has to do everything. Why? Because she lacks education. Also, to be sure, because she has a poor husband who doesn't give her enough money to hire help for her work in the house. That's why one must stop and think about what's going on. That's why I think that both girls and boys must be educated.

If a girl is well educated, she will have a better chance at getting a husband who is prosperous. Her husband may even have gone to the university. He will be someone who will know how to respect his wife and know how to make a home. My daughters will not suffer like their mother does. Their husbands will earn more and get a maid to do things for them. Some people don't think about that.

My brother-in-law said, "Ah, I have a daughter. I am only going to educate her up to a point." If she could become a nurse, she could probably get married to a doctor, and since the doctor earns good money he could hire a servant for her. Once their daughter marries, they think, She's not going to be a nurse anymore; it would just be a waste of time.

Males are never stopped from studying, but it's best that a woman also be educated, since if anything happens to the man, an educated woman can always take over. Some men just don't think ahead. They can't imagine things that might be ahead. That's why they don't educate their daughters. I want to educate both my daughters and my sons.

Nobody ever told me of the problems that rearing a family brings, nor of what one should do. I had to figure it out myself. But despite my efforts, I didn't realize what was coming.

When Filemón started school, I didn't spend nearly as much on school materials. A pencil lasted two months, and he never lost one. I taught him how to use a pencil sharpener. Then, when María began school, Filemón had me buy a larger sharpener that fastened to the table. He said it was much more economical. He said, "At first you'll feel the cost, but it will only be once, and you won't have to buy things over and over. The other boys always have to buy things over and over, or borrow pocket pencil sharpeners."

I wanted my eldest son to get ahead in his studies. I always thought about that and tried to guide him. I also wanted him to help me educate his younger siblings. He's the one in charge, now that I've retired. I can't pay for anything because I don't have any more money. They haven't been sending me my pension; since the twenty-eighth I haven't received a thing.

Last year, when Filemón came to study in Cochabamba it was hard on us. He came in February to register, but it was too late, so he lost some time. They told him, "There is no more registration. Everything is closed. It's too late. You must come back next year. You have already lost this year."

He came back very sad. But I have old friends from my military service days who got an education at the university — two are now professors there. I went with my wife to their house in Cochabamba and we lived there a month. Petrona asked them for their help. They advised her to write a letter saying that our boy hadn't been notified of the exact date of the registration at the university. She did, and they reconsidered; at the university they asked my son what he wanted to study and accepted him.

I wanted my son to be an agronomist, at any cost, even if my other children couldn't be educated. I liked that profession. They don't have enough agronomists in Cochabamba. In Cochabamba there is only one and he is very old and doesn't work any more. If they need help they have to go beyond Cochabamba to get an agronomist to find out what is causing the animals' diseases.

I intended to start a farm on the land that my wife's father left her. I also wanted to build a cattle clinic. But we didn't have luck. That's partly why we wanted my son to study agronomy. I have been unable to contribute the money necessary for his studies. It was too much. His trips cost an awful lot of money. He asked for a hundred pesos or so, over and above his living costs. I couldn't give it to him so I told him to stay with us.

"Don't leave until I can afford it," I said. "But next year you have to be at the top of your class and continue working hard at your studies."

When he came home on his vacation, I talked to him about his working.

He said, "Well, if you want to sacrifice yourself so much, Daddy, so that I can be a good person, I accept it. But my position is the following: when I finish with my studies, I will help educate my younger brothers and sisters, but as for María, there is nothing I can do. You will have to help her. She's already in high school and I can't work yet. You will have to make the sacrifices for her. If I have a wife someday, she will not get in the way. I will consider my wife an older sister. I will only give her 25 percent of my earnings. The rest will go to my siblings."

I told Filemón, "If you take the same course we did, in a short time you will have a wife and forget about us. Then where will we be?" I sent him back to Cochabamba, but then I had bad luck and became ill; I had to bring him back to Oruro before retiring.

That year was a total loss because we lacked resources. When the students went on a trip to Santa Cruz, they needed extra money. They also went to Chapare, to Tamboriri, and many other university towns. But the school didn't have a car, so the students had to chip in to rent a taxi. Filemón needed money, more and more money.

I felt awful. I cried because it seemed there was nothing I could do.

Then I decided not to finish the patio. I put the money in his name and told him to use it for his education. This is what I told Mr. Pelaes when he came to my house while I was still working.

He came on a very windy day so we closed the door and began to talk about education.

"How many children do you have?" he asked.

"Six," I said.

"Do you have an older son?"

"Yes, I do. He is studying in the University in Cochabamba," and I told him all that was happening. He was surprised when I told him that I was going to have to interrupt his studies soon if I didn't get my pension; that I was going to retire and would be waiting for my papers to come through; and that it could take up to four months.

He agreed with me. "You can't afford it even though you want to. I'll make a suggestion: if you have an eldest son, bring him. He can still study while working if you bring him home and he studies at the university in Oruro. We will help you process your papers. Once you retire, your son can go in the mines in your place. Do you think that only an agronomist earns money? The electrical or mechanical engineers earn even more, and there is greater demand for them. He can study here while he works."

I brought Filemón home to Oruro. They assured me that my papers would come soon. But, despite all their efforts, there was nothing they could do at the social security. With your help, *Comadre*, we got things going. My papers finally came in soon after you went to La Paz the last time.

When I retired Mr. Pelaes gave me guidelines on what to do, and I followed his advice. You also told me that it would be better if I brought Filemón back to Oruro because he could continue studying here at lower cost. And now he's working. I am glad I have a male child. Who would help me otherwise? I might have died.

I have suffered enough; my brain is spinning. But my situation is such that I can't realize my wishes, and I have little time left. I hope that my son doesn't forget what I have taught him. He is the one who has to take care of the children. God must have known that I was going to get sick, for He gave me a son so that this son could support the household. God probably doesn't want us to suffer all the time.

María must study one more year in Oruro. Then she is going to go to Cataví. There she can study to become a nurse. She can't study anything else because it is too expensive. I want her to be a good student. I grieve because I won't see the rest of my children grow up. I am exhausted and no longer have full use of my lungs. I can't work any more, and my life is drawing to a close.

# PART TWO
# Fifteen Years Later

# 18

## The Rich Are Richer and the Poor Are Poorer

In July 1985 I returned to Bolivia. The country was involved in one of the sharpest crises it had faced in the tumultuous decades since 1952. The teetering democracy of President Siles Zuazo had not found solutions to the problems of rampant inflation and a stagnating economy. The election scheduled for later in the month failed to rouse the public; in fact, many of the candidates themselves appeared to have little concern for the impending decision. While the biggest crowds went to hear General Banzer and Paz Estenssoro, many said it was only to get the plastic bags and other gifts that they handed out. The next major runner-up, Jaime Paz Zamorra, had only a few dozen listening to his talk winding up his campaign in Oruro.

The apathy regarding the election seemed related to the sense of frustration in the face of the enormous debt and inflation. From the time I arrived in the country, the exchange rate for the U.S. dollar had risen from $b350,000 to $b1,000,000 and prices for many commodities kept pace. Even products grown or manufactured in the country had become "dollarized," i.e., prices were pegged at the exchange rate. Market women carried pocket calculators to figure these astronomically high figures in the transactions that occurred daily. They were doing better than professionals: doctors working in public institutions were making about $US50 a month while vendors raised

prices almost in direct relation to the "parallel market," a euphemism for the black market in currency
exchange.

When I arrived in Barrio Minero Santa Fe I could
hardly find the Rojas house. It was no longer on the
outskirts of the mining encampment surrounded by
fields of *paja brava*. New houses had been built right
up to the foothills. Tenants living in the old house directed me to the back courtyard where I found the
family on the balcony of the new extension. Petrona
was the first to recognize me. She had become the
main supporter of the family, selling housing lots,
meat and vegetables, woolen caps and sweaters that
she knitted, and a line of watches and jewelry. Juan was
working as a night watchman in the stadium. He raised
guinea pigs, using the grass he cut on the stadium field
and selling it to others who raised animals in their
yards. Anita and Elena were still in high school and
Juan Manuel had just run away from the army. Victor
Hugo seemed to be the best student in the family, but
he was outshone by Elena's son Israel. Petrona called
Aníbal, who arrived with his new wife, and María, who
lived in the same barrio, soon arrived with her three
children and Guido. Filemón, who lived across the
railroad track, did not appear until the following day.
Juan caught me up on the events of the past fifteen
years.

---

Well, the devaluations of currency have not favored the poor people.
Everything is for the owning class, for the rich, because the government is not one for the poor but for the rich. They have made the rich
richer and the poor poorer. In each devaluation, we lose 50 or 40 percent. For those in troubled industries, such as miners and factory workers, and for pensioners it is even worse, because while the active work
force will get a 60 or 70 percent reduction, we will get 85 percent reduction. It's for that reason that the retired people are completely
ruined with the rise of the dollar. We suffer as the market prices rise to
the clouds. There is not nearly enough money. So the poor people
don't eat meat. They don't even know what it is. If we should eat any
meat, then we would pay for it the whole month. You know that every-

thing is very expensive in the market. For example, with my pay of $b3,500,000, $b2,000,000 is for electricity, water, and telephone, and then I just have $b1,000,000 left to buy vegetables. I don't have anything left. My daughter Anita who studies in high school needs carfare, and my daughter Elena has to go to piano classes in the center of town. I have to scratch up money where I can to pay for these costs, for shoes, to buy rice. The only one who helps me is Aníbal, or at least he did help me up until next Monday. We have to give him back his commissary book then, and I don't know how we are going to live. We are completely strangled. I don't know what we can do. This is the way the poor people suffer.

*How much was your pension in 1982?*
In 1982 it was $1,200 U.S., a year.

*And it has gone up, but it isn't worth anything?*
Yes, the state increases it according to the official dollar, but we have to feed and clothe ourselves with the prices of the parallel market, or you could call it the black market. So there is a great inequality in levels of living. It's something very grave in our country.

*How are the others affected?*
The bankers, the factory owners, and the politicians can make out because they close their doors, and the market is suffering from the lack of financing. The people scream, and the government accepts the higher wages for their employees while we do not get anything. If we try blockading the roads, they send out a police detachment and disperse us by firing on us. It is unreal; I don't know how we are going to overcome it. There could be some outburst, some subversion of the state.

*What would happen if there were a military coup?*
There are some who say that maybe tomorrow there will be one. In La Paz, the one who is trying to move this is Banzer of the Democratic National Action party. It really concerns me that he will try a coup.

*They are taking advantage of the situation. It is a shame. I think it is worse now than when I was here before the entrance of Juan José Torres in 1970.*
In those times we were living on the body of the king. We had everything. Wages were good, but from 1980 on we are totally strung up. The prices of merchandise are in the clouds. Nothing is enough. The people who work in the small masonry companies do not eat. The con-

struction material is very expensive and there isn't any work, because the people are making their own small houses here in the fields. They can't earn enough to pay for a mason so they do their own work.

Our problems here in Bolivia are very serious. The workers are pleading for jobs but there are many unemployed. A lot of people are complaining. The construction companies pay the workers what they want to and the farmers give the field hands what they want to. For example, here in the Ayala Construction Company there were more than forty workers and they laid them all off and hired new people. The ones they laid off were under social insurance and had benefits, but the new people are not insured and they keep them on just two months and twenty-five days because after that they gain job security. They fire them so they won't get their social benefits.

*Is this what is happening in the whole country?*
Yes.

*In the new enterprises here do they have any benefits?*
Here it is worse than in some other places. There ought to be some law or some work for the unemployed to go to immediately when they are laid off. But instead we don't have anything because there isn't any organization either for the state or in the farms. If a man tries to go plant something in the new lands that are opened up in the colonization areas, they throw him off and clean out his crops. So the lands are going to waste for lack of sowing seed. Here in the highlands near the city, the poor people used to go to the fields around Caracollo, about thirty-seven kilometers from the city, and there they could use lands that were not sown for a year. They could bring their food from there. But now they don't let them. If they could do that, there would be more production for the rural people. For example, in Chapare the hills are going to waste for lack of sowing, but the State has failed to distribute these lands to the people who go asking for it. They just want to give them land in the jungle so they will clear that out.

*And after the poor campesinos go down there and open up roads and clear the land, do they give them any materials to work with?*
The state doesn't even take part in opening the road. They don't do anything for them. They are just throwing them out as soon the forest is cleared and the stumps have rotted out.

*So they lose all their work?*
Yes, that's what I have been thinking about. There is a great deal of disorder in this country.

*Who is saying that there is going to be a military coup?*

This afternoon I heard it in the street, at the door of the courthouse a friend of mine told me. I think that someone knew about this and talked to him. It is very possible that there will be a coup because Banzer is not going to get many votes. Some of his collaborators said that he is going to take power either by good means or bad.

*But at least Banzer ought to await the elections to see if he wins?*

But that is what they say. There is a threat here.

When we were in Santa Fe, we used to have those colors, black, red and white, on our banner and when we came out on a march, the orators always said that the black is mourning for the Bolivian family, the white is the innocence of the people and the red signifies the flow of blood. When Banzer himself was in power this occurred.

---

Petrona, with all her resiliency in the face of disaster, was finding ways of coping with the crisis. Added to her sales, she went to Cochabamba to harvest corn, receiving part of the crop rather than money. She talked to me about how she was coping.

---

*How much is bread in the commissary?*

It is only four hundred pesos. Every one hundred pieces costs us $b15,080. In the external market, ten breads cost $b35,000, so it is more expensive.

*And rice?*

I haven't checked recently. I bought some at a very low price in Cochabamba. My *compadre* sold me some in the form of a gift because he has lands in Chapare. I came with a great deal of produce from there.

"*Compadre*, don't you want some rice?" he asked me.

"For how much are you selling it, *Compadre?*"

"Ah, you can take it with $b3,000,000 for a hundred pounds." And so he gave me a hundred weight.

*How much is it in the free market?*

Now it is $b240,000 for a kilo. I brought another variety from Cochabamba, what we just ate. Beautiful. My *compadre* wanted to have me take more.

"You can send me the money for it when you get your paycheck," my *compadre* told me. But Juan is very sensitive and I was afraid of getting indebted. He doesn't like that at all.

*What else did you bring back from Cochabamba?*
Nothing more than the produce from my land, just corn. About a half a *quintal.* It only produced a little.

*And how much did you earn picking crops?*
A few *arrobas.* [25 pounds]

*How long were you there?*
I was there for a week. But I didn't work every day. I just worked three days and in those three days I earned three *arrobas.*

*Did you have any other sales to make in Cochabamba?*
No, I didn't have any money to invest. I earned a little knitting caps, sweaters, and so forth. Last year I went to Cochabamba with clothing and I earned some from that, but I spent all the money. I bought rice. I spent my last peso on the rice I bought, so I had to make these sweaters and hats to earn my passage. It cost $b9,000 for the passage. We can hardly get by, comadre. There isn't enough to buy meat, comadre. Aníbal is not going to take back his book for the commissary just yet because of that. Since your compadre has come out of the mine, we have not had enough. I haven't bought a skirt for some time. Elena has to have uniforms, and each year she asks for a new one for the procession. Since it is a school for teachers she has to wear a new one.

Ana has to have pens and paper, and so does Victor Hugo. Five hundred sheets of paper, pencils in color, ball point pens, covers for notebooks — they need all these things.

*Do you get any other help? Aren't there any Mothers' Clubs?*
None of that. They didn't want to register me because my husband is a pensioner and has income. They say it is for people who do not have any income. Elena is included, however, because she is a student and has no help with her child from anyone. The help is from the United States. They give money to mothers to buy food. Before they used to give her milk, and now they give money.

*Petrona then told me about the trip she had made to Copacabana to improve her luck with Virgin of Copacabana.*
We bought miniature houses with floors, very beautiful. I also got a miniature truck with a complete cargo of coca, sugar, rice, noodles, sardines, and alcohol, and everything was blessed well by the priest. Since then, until now, nothing has been lacking in my house. Since then

I was able to construct and finish my house here, and we put on the second floor. My greatest desire was to do this. The Virgin collaborated very well with me. One has to have a great deal of faith in the Virgin of Copacabana. She helped me do everything, almost with nothing.

Juan and Petrona put their cares aside on the fortnight before the saint's fiesta that María and her husband Guido planned. The entire family, with grandchildren, neighbors, and tenants who rented parts of their house gathered to drink chicha and chew coca, light candles, and pray to the saint. Whatever surpluses they had were used up and they even went into debt. But these ceremonies give them the faith to go on in an uncertain world.

# 19

## Petrona

Petrona's resourcefulness was tested to the utmost as inflation cut in to Juan's meager pension and his wage as a night watchman. She intensified her selling activities, adding jewelry and even house lots, as she used her connections in the Santa Fe mining community and in Cochabamba to buy wholesale and gain entry into new markets. She deferred to Juan's judgment as she undertook each new venture, but he assigned full blame to her if things went wrong. Although he had approved her renting the new wing she was constructing from the profits of her sales, when Elena became pregnant as a result of her relations with the son of the tenant, Juan blamed Petrona. And when the sale of the lots backfired, Juan again went into a rage. But even while Petrona takes the blame without complaining and allows him to feel that he is making all the decisions, she becomes central in most of the actions that ensure their survival in difficult times. She attributes her successes to the collaboration of the Virgin of Copacabana and takes responsibility for her failures.

From the moment that your *compadre* left his work, Filemón entered in place of him. After working for two years he thought about getting married. "Ah, great!" we said. We accepted it. But at the time he said he was going to get married, we had no money, not a cent.

What can we do? we wondered. All night we thought about it, your *compadre* and I, discussing what were we going to do. Then I had an idea and I proposed it to Juan.

"Why don't we lease for a loan the house in the southern part of town that we got from your mother?"

"That's a good idea you thought of, Petrona," Juan said to me.

So since he said that, we went to the house in the southern part of town. A woman named Juana who fixed shoes was renting it. We spoke to her.

"Look, Doña Juana, we want to make you an offer."

"What could it be? Tell me no less, Doña Petrona," she said to me.

"Do you want to lease the house? I would like you to take it in return for a loan because I need the money for the marriage of my son."

"Well, I might want to do that, Doña Petrona, but what would my husband say? It all depends on him," she told me. "I can come to your house," she said.

"Well then, come and tell me as soon as possible so that I can speed it up, because I know very well that I could offer it to someone else. In that case you would have to leave it right away because the person who is going to want the house is going to say, 'Hand it over to me!' There are many people that would want the house on a loan. Who wouldn't want it for a year without paying rent? You could be earning even less than you are from your sales, and still you would have something left to buy food. That's in your favor."

"Yes," she said. "I will come and advise you. I will ask my husband right away and see what he says."

So we gave her a little time to think it over. She came later on in the afternoon of the same day. She said, "Yes, Doña Petrona. I am going to take the house. We are in agreement. I spoke with my son-in-law and with my husband. So we are going to give you the sum of money."

"Well, very good then. On what day, more or less? I need it by the sixteenth of February, for that is the date we are proposing to have the marriage. Her father told us that they were going to just have a civil marriage."

"Ah, no, Doña Petrona," said Juan. "Do both at once. There is enough money."

I leased the house for four thousand bolivianos (about four hundred dollars). It was real money then, in those times.

*At that time, what was a peso worth in dollars?*

To this day, *Comadre*, I don't understand anything about that. And your *compadre* can't explain it to me.

Anyway, we wrote up the papers and arranged it in good form. Filemón got married on the sixteenth of February in 1972. Then they didn't want to live here. But this four thousand was real money in those days. You could exchange it with any money then. It was like a million today. I covered all the expenses of the marriage with that money. I bought clothing for both of them. I got two suits for Filemón and two dresses for Ruthy [his wife] — a wedding dress and a print dress. I bought her two pairs of shoes, one white and one black, I think. For Filemón I also bought shoes, trousers, underwear, shirts, ties — I bought everything with that four thousand. And I bought vegetables and *chicha*, I bought beer, a liter of alcohol, and meat.

*Were they already living here?*

They were living here in the room that is now rented as a shop. It turned out that Ruthy didn't want to live here. Her family would visit here and wouldn't leave her alone. They gave her no peace. Apparently, they didn't want her to live here in my house. As a result, they moved to her parents' house, but there they couldn't live well. They returned here, but they couldn't live here in peace. Better they should get a house on loan, they said, one near her family in Barrio Machacamarca. They took it on a loan of two thousand bolivianos. But even there they couldn't live.

Your *compadre* called their attention to our needs. "Why don't you help me out a little on supplies? I need help. You have abandoned us, Son. What has happened to you?" he asked Filemón. Filemón replied that his wife had to have an operation after their daughter was born, and they didn't have enough left over to share with us.

So they had their troubles. They moved again, I don't know to what place. They gave back the money I had put up as a loan for the house. The owner of the house said to me, "Your daughter-in-law doesn't want to live well. Why doesn't she want to live with you, Doña Petrona? You are so good."

"I don't know, Doña Filomena. I can't say anything. I can't force them," I told her.

*How many were there in Ruthy's family?*

She has a sister Rita who is younger than she. Her elder sibling was Freddy, who died. She also has a sister younger than Rita, René, who is married and has a little girl.

The poor woman cried to me when she talked about her childhood. She came here alone when they were not yet married, when she had just fallen in love with Filemón. Filemón had told her, "Go get to know my mother. My *mamita* is a little bad tempered."

"I came here because I love your son," she told me. "If I didn't love your son, I would never have come here to know what you thought about it."

So we stayed there like that, short of supplies. It turned out that I had to go looking for some other business. A jeweler lent me some money. I knew him because I used to wash his laundry. I would go get it and bring it here, or his servant would bring it. With what he paid me I was able to buy food, one thing or another.

Then the jeweler said to me, "Look, Doña Petrona, why don't you go travelling to sell things? You are very lively." He is a very good person, this gentleman.

With the thousand pesos he lent me, I went out buying and selling things. I decided to go to Challapata for meat, because that was what was scarce here in the mining community, for the children, for everyone. I brought the meat here and sold it. I brought toasted pork fat. I bought it cheap. I would get twenty-five pounds of meat for six pesos, but after awhile, this price rose. I would then get the same amount for ten pesos, then fifteen, and so on. It was good that I went out on this selling. I would take the meat to Santa Fe and exchange it for coupons to buy supplies in the company store, which I then brought back here. I brought loaves of bread, sugar, rice, soap, milk, and other supplies from Santa Fe, where I had taken the meat to sell. So we no longer had to buy from outside in order to live, to eat. We couldn't buy with the little pay your *compadre* earned. It was only $b190. So I sold things very well. Certain afternoons I would go to Santa Fe, especially on payday, not just any day, because you can't always sell things.

*In Santa Fe you could sell things for more?*
Everything sells for more. Here there are plenty of sellers. Everything is here. There they want lamb because they can only get jerked beef.

I punctually repaid the jeweler the money he had lent me to start the business. I earned a lot. I sold the meat, but always kept some for the children to eat. When I gave the money to the jeweler, I thanked him a thousand times for what he had done for me.

"Oh, you have a lot of luck, Doña Petrona. You haven't been at it even a month, and you have brought me back the money. I thought you would be at it at least a year," he told me.

"No, I am very considerate. I don't like to spend money in vain, because you need it also for your business," I said.

"Doña Petrona, I want to tell you something," he told me. "Why don't you sell jewelry?" he asked me.

"Jewelry?"

"Yes, jewelry is what you ought to handle also. You could earn more. You ought to have some stock. I can let you take a few things."

"Let's see. I have to ask my husband what he thinks about what you said. Depending on what he says, I can take it on. Since I am always going up there I can carry some more," I said.

"Yes, Doña Petrona, you ought to carry jewelry along. I advise you that washing clothes is bad for you. Since you are so clever, I would give you ten watches, five for men and five for women. And you could take gold earrings like these and sell them to earn real money."

At that time Juan got an offer of a job here in the stadium, working with the engineers. He had been laid off a long time; it was four years that he had been laid off. So I said, "If you can work, it depends on you. I don't urge you to work. You could damage your lungs. Then what could you do?" I asked him.

"I can work as a mason," he said. "I was a mason at one time. I know how to do that."

"But if you mistreat your lungs, then you cannot cure yourself. Now you are very healthy," I said.

"I want to work with this engineer, Jucuchima. He wants to take me into his crew. I will give it a try to see how it goes," he said.

"Look, I want to tell you about this offer. Don David said that he would give me some merchandise to take to Santa Fe to sell," I told him.

Juan said, "Think it over carefully."

"Let's see. I can try it, anyway."

He said, "It seems like a good deal, but I can't tell you whether to take it or not."

So I went to the jeweler's house. As I mentioned, I had been traveling with merchandise like meat, pork fat, and all those things. He gave me the five watches for women, five for men, and three sizes of earrings. He then gave me ten pair of *chupetitos* of gold. I bought a little notebook to write down how much I charged, how much I gave him, in order to keep a record.

So I arrived in Santa Fe. I displayed the watches. Mmm . . . everyone

wanted to grab them and buy them. I came back here without any earrings or any watches. This merchandise you couldn't exchange for
things in the company store then; they had to pay me cash. So I had to
bring back a lot of cash with me for the jewels and the watches. I asked
the jeweler if I was doing well.

"Oh, very well indeed. If you agree, you can take ten more," he
told me.

So for a second time he gave me watches, earrings, adding to my
debt because a part of the money I had earned I spent on clothing for
the children. And I also had to support your *compadre* because he didn't
earn much with the engineer. (Although they didn't pay him well, at
least it passed the time because he couldn't be idle. He had turned almost crazy resting so long a time. Anyway, they liked him a lot; eventually they increased his wages.)

So both of us worked. We put our earnings into construction on this
house. We raised the walls and made a second story. Aníbal, when he
was still young, was working on it. He won two prizes in school. He
followed in his father's work while he was still studying in the Arce
College to get his degree. Then he went into the army.

*Did he have to go in or was it his choice?*

It was his own choice to go. He said, "I want to go once and for all
into the army in order to be able to work for a company. I am going to
earn my workbook," and saying that, he went. I did nothing more than
bid him goodbye, crying. And he went very far away, to the Paraguay
border. Far away. Your *compadre* went there on a trip, and it took four
days. Aníbal was there a year in the army. He was very much loved.

Then he came back. He worked at everything that he could get employed to do. He made ices, but he didn't like that. He went into construction for the company. It was assured work, and he had access to
the company store. He had everything, that young man; he was well
set up. Then during Carnival, I believe, his friends said that he could
get work in the San José mine. That very moment he went there, and
they hired him because he had his work book. He started work but as
a temporary. He worked as a temporary for three years, very conscientiously. But, because he wasn't a regular employee, they charged him
the outsiders' prices in the company store. And we received very few
supplies from the store — bread, a little meat — it wasn't enough. Sugar,
those things, I had to bring back from my trips to Santa Fe. I bought
those things with my merchandise.

*With jewelry?*

No, with meat and pork cracklings that I carried there; they gave supplies to me.

*Does Aníbal have his high school degree?*

No. After the army, he studied radio technology. Now he is a technician of radios and television, but he still doesn't have a degree. He wants to get a degree in Argentina or Brazil. He did not graduate; he just received a diploma. He has to graduate still, *Comadre.*

What is lacking is money. We haven't been able to send him to those places. Working for the company, he couldn't go. He studied through correspondence school at first, but now he doesn't have time to go to La Paz. It takes a lot of time and money for him to go to La Paz to take an exam. One day to go, and one night to return. So we have had to get his transfer from Machacamarca to Oruro. Here he can go to the university and become a technician. But still what's missing is his graduation from high school.

*You haven't told me about how Victor Hugo was born.*

Ah, we haven't spoken about Victor Hugo? He is eleven years old. Victor Hugo was born on March 31st, 1974. I carried him on my selling trips. What else could I do? I couldn't stop doing those sales and I like to earn money. That's the way I was able to have that little house added on the corner of our building, and the store as well. I improved the rest of the building. We also bought out the tenants in the little house in the southern part of town that we got from my mother-in-law. My mother-in-law did not give it as a gift. We bought it with money.

*Ah, I thought that it was an inheritance.*

No. No, it was not an inheritance. We paid money for it. We couldn't charge much rent, because the tenant who lived there so long paid practically nothing. Finally we had to put it up for sale and we sold it.

When Filemón got married, we told him, "Why don't you buy back the lease and go live there in the south because you can not live here beside us? We bought this house for you." We consulted with his wife.

Ruthy then spoke to her aunt, who said to her, "That house is too far for you to go and live. There all the thieves and the killers live. How can you live so far away? That house is at the very outer edge of town."

Based on that advice, Filemón came and said, "It is very far for us to live. Do you agree?"

So I said that in that case we would sell it.

Later we sold the house, and the man who bought it paid in installments. We sold it for sixty thousand bolivianos dollars, no more.

*When was that?*

In 1976, I think. I am not sure. We have done so much since with this house. The people have a great deal of envy of us. Maybe it was 1978 that we sold the house.

*And what about Elena and her child?*

Israel is now five years old. He was born in 1980. I had many problems talking this over with your *compadre*. It was a disgrace the arguments we had. The mother of Israel's father lived in the lower floor of our new apartment, and her son and Elena were acquaintances at high school. We had no idea of what was going on. For me it caused a great deal of suffering.

Anyway, this woman cried a lot. She rented a little house in the San José barrio. The owner came and took the house and turned it over for another loan. She knew I had the apartment here that I was fixing up, and she said, "Let me borrow your house for three months, no more, so I will have a place for my children. It is vacant." She pleaded a lot, and this woman was my friend. I did not know that her son was going to have relations with my daughter or anything else. I used to use it to store potatoes, clothing, and things that I sold. I rented it to them innocently.

The way it happened was that a neighbor here in front was in her doorway, and I went up to her and said, "Don't you want some potatoes?"

"I do want them, Doña Petrona; potatoes are just what I need."

"Come over and I will select some potatoes for you," I told her.

Then one time she came over with her friend, and the potatoes were in the empty room. She said, "Your room is empty, Doña Petrona. My friend here, Doña Plácida, is looking for a place. Give it to her. She is crying a lot."

"Doña Placida?" I asked.

"Your friend, here, don't you remember? She sells meat coupons for the commissary." She was a very good woman, this one now the grandmother of Israel. Very pleasant.

Then I said, "She wants a house? But I don't know what my husband will say. I store things that I sell there. This has not been fixed up to live in."

"Ah, Doña Petrona, give it to her. You can charge some rent to fix it up. It's going to fall in if you don't put a roof on it. The poor woman can't go anywhere. She'll be there just a short while."

I said, "Let me see what my husband says. It doesn't even have a door yet. It's just half built. We've been doing it bit by bit as we got money. If she gives us a little bit, perhaps we could buy the materials. We haven't been able to put on a roof yet to protect it from the rain. Anyway, I will suggest it to my husband, but I think that he is not going to want it. He doesn't like to live with people." I spoke to her with complete frankness. "It doesn't even have a floor, just dirt. There's no plaster on the walls."

When I carried lunch to Juan in the stadium I told him, "Look, Juan, this woman is a friend that I have. She sold me coupons for meat and for bread. She is very friendly. I gave her some potatoes. She is very good."

"Everyone knows you. Everyone is friendly with you. Walking here and there, you always make friends," he replied. "But how could she live on the ground like that? The floor is nothing but dirt, and it's cold."

"But the woman said that we could buy these things little by little and it didn't matter to her," I said. "We can buy the door with what she pays us. We could rent it to her for fifty pesos."

"Fifty? That's not much."

"She would give us a three-hundred peso advance," I added.

"Give it to her then. And get the advance to buy the door."

So I gave the room to the woman and she came with all her children, and not just for three months. Elena knew her son in high school – he had gone to San José and she went to Carmen Guzmán de Meir – and both of them were continuing their studies.

And then, months later, this thing happened. I didn't know anything, but your *compadre* noticed it. At his work he asked me when I came with his supper.

"Petrona," he said, very seriously. "I want to talk about something," he told me.

"Yes, what is it?" I asked. Brrrr! my body shivered. What could it be? I was frightened. What could he be thinking?

"Haven't you noticed that your daughter is with child?" he said.

"What?" I was incredulous.

"Your daughter appears to be expecting a family. I know very well when people are expecting a family," he said.

"*Ay*, what are you saying?"

"You know, but you are trying to hide it from me," he said.

"Truly I don't know anything. I swear to God that I do not know absolutely anything. Why are you blaming me?" I replied emphatically. I really didn't know, *comadre*. Both of us began to cry; right there at his job, your *compadre* was crying. I noticed a day later what he had seen.

She was looking at me when I was realizing what had happened, and said to me, "Oh, I don't know how this has happened. I didn't realize anything."

"No, you have been hiding everything from me," I said.

"I don't know anything." And she didn't know, *comadre*. As Señor Jesus Christ is listening, she did not know anything. Why should I lie to you? How can we lie?

When I came home that night, Juan was drunk. "For this you have brought in people!" he said. "It's a very good way to hide things. You brought these people to the house." Clearly he blamed me.

"What foolishness you are speaking. The señora is a friend of mine. I brought her with no intent of this happening."

"If you hadn't been so reckless, this wouldn't have happened," he insisted.

I approached Elena carefully, asking her about her condition. "I see how you look, and I notice you do not go out of the house." She polished the floors, arranged everything, cleaned the house, but she didn't look well. I couldn't see her face as she continued studying her book.

Finally she said, "Yes, it is true, mama. This has happened."

"So, what does he say?"

"He wants to marry me," she answered.

"And what do you want? Do you want to marry him? Are you going to continue studying?"

"I am going to continue studying," Elena said. "But he said that he wanted to marry me. The other day his mother came when you were gone and told me that." So she confessed everything and I advised her of everything. She was five months pregnant. Now what should we do?

"That boy has made a fool of me," I said.

"That is why I don't want to marry him or even study with him," she said.

The real truth is that we have to have an understanding with our children. We have to show solicitude to our children and humor them because our children are our children. She didn't want to lose credit for her studies. Now that she was pregnant, she could ask for indefinite leave from school.

Juan continued berating her, but what could we do? Chastise her, beat her? Certainly not, especially given her heart condition. We couldn't mistreat her body. She had thought it over. And so we were resigned to it.

Then he came to ask for her hand, crying. "Yes, I love Elena," he said. He did not abandon the girl; he came here directly, with his mother.

Well, Elena did not want to marry him. "I don't want to get married yet," she said. I have to fulfill all that my father wanted for me. He wanted me to study. I do not want to fail my father."

That year she did not graduate. But after she had her child, a short time later when the child was a year old, she got her degree and continued studying. She wanted to be a nurse, so we sent her to Cochabamba, spending a lot of money since she wanted to enter school there to be a nurse. But she couldn't. Everything there was done with bribes. All the employees, including the nuns, wanted a bribe, wanted you give them money before they would help your child. She performed well in the exam, but they gave her a poor grade. She had to come home. Twice she went there to ask for her degree, but they never gave it to her. There were *campesinas, indiacitas* as they appeared to me, who did not study well, but they had enough money and their parents gave enough money to all the employees; they received their degrees.

Elena came home crying and asked, "*Mami*, what can you do?"

"You have to choose another profession. Here there is a normal school that is opening and Carlos [a neighbor] has just graduated as a professor. You ought to enter there. It is near and you won't have to pay carfare. You can study there in peace near our side."

*And Israel was here while she went to Cochabamba?*

Yes, she went alone.

So she said, "Yes, *Mamita*, I want to be a professor of music."

"That ought not to be too difficult," I said. "But we do not have any instruments."

"Even so, Mama, I would like this profession. I want to be a teacher."

She enrolled in the school. What was lacking was an accordion. They cost a lot of money. And now that I am not selling anything, we hardly can meet expenses. I had begun to sell house lots.

*When did you begin that?*

In 1975 or 1976, I think. Everyone was envious that I had a house. I traveled to Santa Fe where they said me, "Doña Petrona, there is a man who has acquired some land. Why don't you get some of it for us? We can pay you a good fee if you get it for us."

Especially eager was the father of my godchild who comes every night to sew, Julieta. Now he is still working in Santa Fe. I got this house near us for them, and that is the way I began. People continued to ask me to arrange these purchases. At that time they gave me a fee of one hundred pesos. The money was enough for me to buy vegetables. But because of this business, I fell into this fight. I was able to sell many lots, more than forty it must have been — Almost all this zone.

*And this man with whom you worked took advantage of the sales?*
Yes, and he didn't give me anything.

*Now how much do you have to give back?*
I have to return the money to three people. One person gave me 45,000 pesos.

*We talked a bit about the elections. Petrona said she was going to vote for "El Mono" [Paz Estenssoro].*
I like "El Monito" because I have my house because of him. At first I didn't like this house, *Comadre*, because it was at the far end of town. I had a house in the center, at the entrance of the station that the mine company assigned to us, but there was more noise and a bad odor. I had not often come to this area. But one time Juan and I had a fight. I went to my mother-in-law's house.

"I am going to my mother-in-law's. What am I going to do here suffering your insults," I told him. So I went there, with my baby, Juan Manuel. (The old lady was still living then.) I went by the cemetery and nearby there was a sewage disposal that was very smelly. Surely many flies came from there into my house. Ugly, smelly place. I didn't like that. But I liked the house on the south side that the company supplied us. When I entered this house, I complained about it,

"How am I going there in the north at the foot of the hill? I am not a thief nor have I killed anyone. I cannot live there." That's the way I complained to your *compadre*. "So I am going to live alone," I said. It was far away, where the hospital for workers is. The buses came as far as the hospital. There are plenty of houses there now but at that time there were none. We were all alone. It was enough to frighten you. Only the wind ran here.

"I am not moving to that place. I haven't killed anyone to go there. Also I am afraid," I said to your *compadre*. "I just have to go back."

"If you don't come, I will have to go alone," he said.

"So I will go with two children to the corner house that the company gave us, and you with two children, to the place you have bought," I answered.

Days passed. Up there in the north there was no electricity, nor was there any down in the company house. We had to combine living in the two houses. We came and went, back and forth. My mother-in-law also did not have electric light. My sister-in-law finally put it in. The thing I wanted most was to have electric lights, and finally I had electricity installed. I didn't have any money, so I had to hock my sewing machine. I had this little sewing machine, a "Tumex," and when I got the loan on that, I finally succeeded in getting electricity. I did what I could, for a person who had no profession and had never worked in any place. But I always had my work selling. I sold merchandise, skirts, anything. I was always good at it. If a wife doesn't earn something selling or otherwise, she suffers, *Comadre:* the wage of a husband is not enough. In Santa Fe I always helped sewing clothing, shawls, overalls, petticoats, and even hats. I made all the clothing for the children. I dressed María like a rose. When she was in her teens, she bought suits, but before that I made everything. María also is able to take advantage of being able to sew. She just buys the cloth. Other women don't do this to save their husband's wages. All they do is take it and eat. Mining people just waste their money.

So that is how I see things. God has given me a good head. I think about the future. I have thought a lot about matrimonial life. I have perservered.

*For the rest of the children, what hopes do you have for them?*

For whom? For Anita and Juan Manuel? *Comadre*, I cannot think much about that. I haven't any thoughts. Juan Manuel doesn't want to take advantage of his studies. Sincerely, I cannot answer.

Aníbal told Juan Manuel, "I am going to go over there [Sweden]. You have to work in my place." But Juan Manuel can't do that without his discharge papers, and he has to buy clothing to replace what he had in the army. I don't know what to think of that. What is going to happen?

Anita has a great capacity to study. "I am going to graduate," she told me. She would have finished, but she lost a year. It was Filemón's fault. He told her that she ought to study in the Valencia college, so she went to the school, but it didn't go well. The two years she was there turned out badly. I didn't know what was going on. Apparently, there were just young people teaching. But then Anita realized what had happened.

"I failed," she said. She cried, the poor child. But she is very determined. "I am going to get out when I am twenty years old," she said. But now it looks as though she will be twenty-one. She is in the second year of high school. The third and fourth year remain, but she has a good outlook, Anita. "I might have to work like a burro here in the house, but I have to graduate," she says. "I have to study. I cannot fail. I have to become somebody."

As for María, she just had her little boy four months ago. He was in an incubator in the hospital until recently. They told us that he was going to die.

His father was preparing us for a funeral. "The baby is going to die," he said. "Now I have the money for the Mass." He was very upset. But when the baby was three months old, they let him out. Now he is very lively. He's quite a rogue, very macho, very well developed. He was nursed on a bottle in the hospital, but María kept her milk by nursing her sister-in-law's baby while her own baby was in the incubator.

# 20
# Juan

---

The central importance of work in Juan's life continued even after he left the mines. With Petrona's income from her sales the family was able to stay on in
the expanded house, renting out rooms to augment
Juan's earnings as a guard at the stadium. He was able
to use the grass clippings from mowing the lawn at the
stadium to feed his guinea pigs. Aníbal now provided
the family with coupons at the commissary. Juan was
still recovering from a stroke when I arrived in Barrio
Santa Fe, but he moved vigorously. He occasionally
attended rallies with me for the presidential campaign
scheduled in July. Bolivian politics seemed to have
come full circle: Victor Paz Estenssoro was again running for office after two decades of exile and living on
the margins of political life; Hugo Banzer had outlived
the coup and the intense reaction against his six years
in power; some people longed for the prosperity of the
1970s when U.S. loans were still available and the
mines were active; Jaime Paz Zamorra had little
chance of winning an election after the debacle of his
party's occupation of the burned palace; and the Left
was fragmented into seventeen parties. Juan had
reached the point in his life when the great dramas
were his illnesses and the familial rituals that marked
the life crises of his children and grandchildren.

---

After I left work in 1971 I had economic problems despite the fact that
my son was working in my stead. He was still a bachelor. In the month

of August we had spent all that we had, and I was not working any-where.

*You didn't have social security?*

I spent the entire year walking around trying to get my social secu-rity. But my retirement benefit failed to arrive in San José. Instead, it was granted to a Juan Rojas Rodríguez of Catavi. So all my attempts to gain retirement benefited him. The employees in the offices don't know what they are doing and did not take responsibility for filling out the papers for Juan Rojas Rodrígues of San José, who was me. They just retired me. I waited two months without receiving any pay. Finally I went to La Paz and discovered that all my papers were in order and recorded in the National Social Security office in La Paz, but under the name of Juan Rojas Rodríguez of Catavi; my retirement records re-mained in the basket or in the files.

The result was that in October 1971 they told me that my social security was going to start that month. This did not happen. It was delayed still further. I had spent the whole year waiting. There was nothing to be done.

In January 1972 I went with the same goal of completing the pro-cessing of my documents, but they were still working on the documents of Juan Rojas Rodriguez of Catavi. In April I went to La Paz to Dr. Saavedra. He told me, "Your papers are not assigned to you but to an-other person."

I left the office and immediately went to see the lawyer Quevado. He was not a real attorney with a degree, just someone assigned to the desk. He carried out the task of looking for my files to send on to San José. When he found them, I looked at the picture and it was of some-one else, thinner seemingly taller. I removed the photograph, and he wanted it back.

"This isn't me," I said. "Every time you take this out, but it isn't me. My papers are in the files of the social security."

Then he said, "Go to Dr. So-and-so (I don't remember the name). He is in the Avaroa Plaza."

I went there and he confirmed the fact that the documents were those of Juan Rojas Rodriguez of Catavi and that mine were in the files. He said, "I am going to carry out the procedures for you. I am going to have to take out your papers. I myself will arrange your registration as a worker with 100 percent disability. The other Juan Rojas Rodrí-guez is registered as 80 percent disabled, so I will have to revise everything. You can go back to Oruro in peace and come back next month. I am going to arrange everything for you correctly."

The next month I went to La Paz, but the doctor had left on vacation. I couldn't go to another person because they did not know of my affairs. So then I had to wait the whole month of May.

The following month I returned and found the doctor. He said, "Now your case is in order. You can come back on the fifth of August. Your pension is going to arrive." He gave me twenty pesos to return. I came back in August and my social security had finally arrived.

*Did you get an indemnity bonus?*

I received only eight thousand pesos. I used it to make the patio for this house and for clothing for the children and me. The money was gone right away. It wasn't enough because they hadn't let me work until I had accumulated free benefits. I was totally incapable of entering the mine because my sickness was very advanced. Doctor Sandi had told me that I ought not enter the mine any more. He gave me, through Dr. Encinas, a medical certificate to take to the laboratory where there was a man called Gómez. Gómez didn't want me to leave, but when he saw the certificate he gave me a transfer to the exterior where I had to look for another job with the watchmen. That's when they contracted me as a watchman.

My son Filemón was working, but we were a large family. I was working but not making enough to support them. I looked for work everywhere. The work I had been doing was that of a mason. Finally I had found a job in the stadium setting posts in cement and attaching the wire. Working there improved my economic situation a little.

*How much did you earn there?*

I don't remember. I think it was twelve pesos a day. I asked the engineer, Kochima, who was in charge of the work for more money. "I am earning very little and it isn't enough for me. And the work is very high pressured. I do everything rapidly."

So the engineer raised my salary. He said, "Yes, Rojas, I understand your situation; you need a raise. This very month you are going to earn more." Throughout that year, I received various increases without demanding them. I was content in my work.

But I had problems in my family. Filemón told me that he was going to marry. I couldn't say no just because he was supporting the household. On the first of February in 1974 he got married. Again I fell into the same condition as in the past, because he took back his workbook and gave it to his wife. For us there was nothing. Since the girl had very little experience in running a household, she abandoned us for a time. Although we still had six children to care for, she completely forgot us. It was because of our great need that I requested some help from my daughter-in-law. She did not quarrel with me. Since she is very intelligent, she did not say anything more than "Yes, *Papi*, thank you." That was her reply. She never said anything more that would undermine my dignity.

So at least I was working in the stadium. I used to feed my guinea pigs with the grass I cut mowing the playing field. Senōr Calderon had fired one of his employees who was lazy and put me on instead. And when I was working there, I was supposed to work half a day and sleep in the stadium at night. But I earned the complete month's wage.

One night while I was there, I don't remember the date, something happened that I had never seen before. At midnight a sound came from far off in the direction of Cochabamba. A moment later, it came nearer, getting louder and louder. It was like a toad crying, like this, "Ugh, ugh, ugh," like that. It seemed clearer and clearer as it approached, like a pig, "Ugh, ugh." Then it seemed as though something blew up. Twenty yellow flares burst into green, rose, and white lights, like powerful light bulbs. Then whatever it was went on to the south. A month or two later I heard news that the same thing had been seen and heard over Argentina. I do not know what it was, but it gave me a very disagreeable moment when it passed. I felt as though someone was throwing hot water over me.

*Was it one of these flying saucers?*

It was flying, but it was not round; just some lights that approached like this [demonstrating a zooming motion], all together, without separating. I felt strange at that moment. I could not stay in the room where I was sleeping; I felt restless. I took a walk on the other side of the stadium before going to bed. It was then one in the morning. Just as I was falling asleep at two there was a riot of sound in the stadium. I did not yet have a dog to accompany me in my work, so I went out alone to look and found nothing. All this disturbance had passed. That's what I heard and saw in the stadium — on a night that was very clear.

Once a woman asked me "Do you have hay to sell?" So, for her, I used to cut hay in the night. During the day I could not do it because the administrator was a very stingy man. I had to carry hay to his house, but outsiders were not allowed to take advantage of the rest of the hay.

It would turn yellow, but he would rather have it rot than give it to people. After it was cut, the grass grew again. He didn't notice anything since I was cutting some of it during the day for him. I had a mower that was almost useless, so I cut it by hand with a scythe. And I took this to his house for his rabbits; I took a load just big enough for him each trip, but he had a lot of rabbits.

So the year passed and the sale of the hay helped me. Finally, in December of 1974, I had even more success with this pasture. The heat had made it grow rapidly and there had been rains, and the administrator said, "Don't you also have rabbits? Take some of this. Or some of your relatives can come to take some. But they can't cut it; only you can do it, using the machine at the same height that you do to mow the grass."

Thereafter I had greater access to the pasture. Every day I got ten or fifteen pesos — never less than eight — for the hay. This helped me a lot, since it was enough to buy vegetables for the entire week. Also, we did have rabbits, as well as guinea pigs. I had all that my mama left me, and we didn't lose one of them. In fact, the animals had increased.

*Did you have enough to sell some?*

No, just enough so that we ate meat.

In December 1975, when we were cutting hay, the renovation of the stadium itself began. In February it was inaugurated. Then I went to work in the construction company. Engineer Sandoval received me readily because I knew the whole organization of the stadium. I received a wage of eight hundred pesos a month.

There was a mason there by the name of Emilio Mamaniel whose nickname was "Natacha." That is the name of a woman in a popular television serial. She attracted the attention of all the viewers by talking constantly about her suffering. That's why we called him Natacha, because he was a great complainer. And he complained to the engineer that I was earning more than he did and that I was not even a first-class mason. So the engineer said, "Rojas, you are not a mason. But you have to work in masonry as well as you can because there won't be much work for you otherwise. I think all you will need are your tools and you can start work."

So I bought a level, plumb line, and tape. I laid the bricks perfectly well. We built it very high. I have a memento of sorts. Whenever I go to the stadium I look at my hands that suffered so much. I recall very well how, when I mixed the mortar, my skin was always sore. My skin was sensitive because of my being sick with the illness of the mines, silicosis. My hands still feel somewhat sore and the ends of my fingers bleed. In the cold months I could not lift the bricks. No one was supposed to know. I had to work with a stick because I could not handle the "duck" — that's what we call the rods. Finally I managed with gloves my children gave me; otherwise I could not have done it. Up to then, the bricks I laid were always bathed in blood.

While I was working, Engineer Sandoval asked me if I could work as a watchman, and I said, "Why not? I worked awhile as a watchman in the San José mine and I know their movements and duties." So I became a watchman and I worked at that for a long time.

In 1975 there was a South American championship soccer match in August. Various teams from Peru, Chile, and Bolivia participated. Those nights passed very badly because the people didn't leave us any peace, what with all the noise they made, the youths, and the drunks cheering the teams. They had housed the athletes who had come from the interior of the republic at the stadium. They complained repeatedly, demanding that we send away those making noise, so that they could get some rest before the competition. So I went out and told the people to go away because the athletes were resting here. They laughed at me and didn't pay any attention.

On Saturday they had the matches. There was a new administrator who knew nothing of the organization of the stadium. Everything was in my charge. If anyone had a question about using the field for some activity or with certain equipment, they had to come to me. I had to analyze the situation and decide whether or not to allow it. Sometimes, even if they pleaded with us, we had to deny them; sometimes we could accept them with a word. Or I would tell them to come tomorrow at the same time. Some of them would have destroyed the field with the shoes that they wore. The grass was mixed with mud or was stripped bare. So to avoid making this worse we made sure that the field suffered no damage that would affect the professional teams that were paying much more for its use.

During August the eliminations for the championship took place. They put me in charge of all the movements. I remember that on Sunday — I don't remember the date — they had the match between Peru and Bolivia. I don't even remember the score. I had many problems with the police. Some of the officers wanted to enter without paying admission, but the gates were crowded with people. If I opened it for them, many people would push in, and the commander of the Bolivian Police Department would have to force them out. When I refused to open the gate they would ask me "Are you the administrator?" I told them that I was filling in for the administrator. A police captain objected and tried to force me to open it.

I said, "You do not give the orders here. I have greater responsibility than you. I carry the keys here and I represent the owner of the stadium." That's the way I spoke to him. "You can't force me to open the gate. If you want to go out, you can find your own way and leave, but there are many people outside here, and I can't open the gate." I was very angry.

So I went into the office. There were some telephone calls from people encouraging the team to win. And, while I was answering the telephone, the same police captain appeared in the doorway and urged me to let him in.

"Please let me in," he said. "I won't let anyone else come in. It is urgent; you have to open it! I *must* get in."

So someone had to open it for the police, but if anyone opened the door the crowd would rush in, and they would blame me. There were ten soldiers there and I called them over to help me. Even with all the crowd there we managed to open it, but the stupid captain couldn't squeeze through. Only the policeman accompanying him entered. I had to open it again with a great deal of care to let just him in. No one else entered.

In this championship match I earned a lot of money. I bought shoes, pants, and underwear for all my younger children.

*Was it extra money that they gave you?*

No, it was a gift that the people gave me in the name of the team. The admission fee was high, and I let some enter for less. Some gave me five pesos, others gave me two pesos, and this added up. The understanding was that they were employees of the stadium. Although it was a lie, I had been told to let them in, but they did give me something to take home to the children.

After this, I began work at the construction company. They took me on a kind of loan from the stadium. This suited me, because the stadium administrator was a crude man who was very bad to his family. He didn't give his pay to his wife; he just kept it. His wife earned money making sandwiches of grilled meat. With this she supported herself and her children. This character made a fool of his wife and abandoned his children. I don't know why, but I had a strong reaction. Any man who is so evil, so angry, I have to challenge. When he got drunk he was very bad to his wife. On one occasion there was a match between the engineers of the University here in Oruro and the San José team. There was a huge crowd and this administrator was among them. He told the guards that people were crawling in under the gate, yet the guards came to the field to watch the match take place. Meanwhile the public was entering. I was attending to the interior gate and had no authority at the entrance gate. Actually, I had authority, but a civilian has less control than a military man who commands more respect.

I told the administrator, "A lot of people are entering over there. The guards are not paying any attention. I already told them to go, but they ignored me." I was trying to help four soldiers carry out a ferocious character who was forcing his way in. Meanwhile, the administrator was having an argument with his children and his wife. This was while his wife was going on her route selling sandwiches. He beat her badly and the children were trying to stop him.

I went to him and said, "Don Celestino, please, let's go and take care of the public. Don't bother your wife. She is trying to sell her sandwiches and this is upsetting her."

He stared at me, enraged, but he did take heed. His wife thought that we were going to fight. She sent her younger son Rudolph to see that we settled it in peace. I didn't say anything else.

That afternoon when the match was over, he said that his wife had not come home and that he was going to take off. I recommended that he not do this.

"Don't do that," I said. "Go lock the doors and leave the keys with the porter and I will come to the house. Don't do anything, Celestino, please." I got authorization to leave and I went to the house. His wife had not returned. She also had a *chichería* [saloon selling fermented corn liquor] with which she supported herself. She left him once and for all. Now she has died, poor woman. I don't know where he is. His children left home. One went to Tarija.

Anyway, we passed the year 1975 fairly well from the point of view of finances.

*Was Aníbal working in the mine?*

Aníbal was still young. He could not yet work anywhere. In 1978 Aníbal entered the army and left in 1979. Since then it is he who has supported the household with his commissary book. He does not give money, just food from the store.

One of the men was having problems with the director of the stadium who was not behaving properly. He said, "Let's ask for our salaries because he hasn't paid us for two months." I hadn't complained even though I had a little to live on. Although I suffered, I endured it because keeping the job was more important to me than any other thing.

I said to my wife, "If they are not going to pay us, we are going to claim what we have lost."

Finally I went to the director in December and he said, "We are going to pay your wage and your bonus also. However that will be the end of your service here, Juan. We don't need you any longer. We are going to hire someone else."

So I said, "Well, that is alright, but I need my pay right away because my family is crying for bread."

They paid me all they owed me on the twentieth of December. Everything was paid up. In January I went back to the construction company. They welcomed me with open arms because I had worked there before, on loan from the stadium. Shortly thereafter, the lawyer who had taken over the administration of the stadium came looking for me and asked me to go back to work there. He said that he would pay me more than I was earning. The wife of the former administrator of the stadium, Don Celestino, came to me. She said, "With that kind of man [her husband] you don't have any desire to work because he does not keep his word. He doesn't realize that people have to eat." She really rejected him.

At the time, during the months of March and April — and that is the time for rainfall — the sports field was completely bare. There was no grass at all, because they had not attended to it as I had. I used to leave my house at four in the morning and arrive there at four-thirty, sometimes in a downpour. I got the field good and green again.

In 1977 I went back to work at the construction company as an assistant mason. The walls of the stadium were complete, but they were installing prefabricated benches. I did the finishing work. I have always been liked by the bosses. They always offered me increases in accord with the work that I did.

Aníbal entered the service in 1978 and came out after a year. I continued working in the stadium as a mason in construction work, so both of us were working. We lived in a more relaxed way since we had enough income. He took out supplies from the company store and I was able to buy supplies in the market. Filemón already had his chil-

dren. He could not continue supporting my family because he had his
own to support. Then Aníbal started work in February in the San José
mine as a temporary worker, or as we say, a *"makipura."* They don't
receive benefits. If an accident or something happens, they are not
compensated. Of course they care for them in the company hospital
when an accident happens, but they do not earn anything during the
time they are incapacitated. Also, they can get supplies in the commissary, but only at the same price as in the market; they aren't entitled to
the controlled prices allowed the regular workers. Aníbal was there four
years as a temporary employee, working on the maintenance of machinery in the mine and also keeping up the grounds.

In 1982 María got married, and that year in February Aníbal became
a regular worker at the Sink-and-Float plant in Itos. He worked there
until he was transferred to Machacamarca, where he still works. He was
married on the thirteenth of April. My daughter-in-law is someone we
know, someone who is aware of the needs of our household. They continue giving us supplies from the company store. We keep his book
with us since she cannot go to take out supplies so early in the morning.
She is not accustomed to our schedule since she lived abroad for a
while.

But there are some people who have given ideas to my daughter-in-
law, saying "You ought to take back your book. You ought not to have
confidence in them because you are married now." They haven't yet
married in church. I do not know who spoke to María. She didn't want
to tell me. What are we going to do?

*It wasn't her father or mother?*

No. Her father and her mother would complain directly to us, not
through the girl. It is another person who has said this. But I do not
know what the motive was. There is a great deal of envy.

*How have the changes in government affected you?*

There were changes of government. In each change, the workers
always suffered. But when Siles won the last elections in 1978 and was
supposed to be seated they did not let him take power. Natusch Busch
seized power and began the devaluation of the currency. After a short
while another one – it might have been Torrelo – was inaugurated.
That was the one who turned over the presidency to Siles in a peaceful
fashion, without a coup. Siles reentered in October 1982 and from that
moment on we have suffered a great deal economically. My son is working but he is supporting the entire household, and his earnings do not

nearly cover our costs. My income is so little, so miserable, that it is not enough for a pair of shoes. It is only $b3,500 [about fifteen dollars in July 1985] per month. With this new devaluation, we have not yet been paid. My wage ought to rise to about $b4,500. There is not enough to live on. That is why I say it can't buy even a pair of shoes. The widows, retirees, and others who deserve increases remain at the same level. Today I sent in my card to be transferred to the mixed pension fund. I think there will be a difference.

*But you have 100 percent disability, don't you?*

Yes, and that is what I am trying to have adjusted. I think they will give me a little more, because my income isn't enough for anything. Look at my children who are still going to school. They cannot get enough. Elena is the one who needs the most since she is in the normal school. I don't know what to do. In addition, her studies are in jeopardy because she lacks an accordion with eighty keys. And she also has to study ballet. I don't know how I am going to solve this problem. And with this problem that my wife has [the legal suit against her for having fraudulently sold lots for houses]. I am totally fed up with living. I am very pressed with expenses. Today I need one or two hundred thousand pesos. I have to go somewhere to borrow the money. If I do not pay these amounts it will jeopardize her studies. To avoid this I have to find more resources. I haven't been able to buy anything for the children. I have only old clothing and everything is getting more expensive. I don't even have enough for a pair of pants. Elena asks for eight or nine hundred pesos for extra expenses. When my pension comes I have to repay the amounts that I have borrowed. Then I will have even less. And there are still children in school. Ana María is in the third year of intermediate school and she needs school supplies. With the reduced income that I have, I can't do it. I have to borrow money until my pay comes. And when it is distributed, everything is gone.

*We haven't talked about the changes of government since the*
*Banzer coup.*

True. The government of Banzer treated workers miserably. That man exiled all the union leaders to various nations of the world. For example, my neighbor, my *compadre* José, who is now executive secretary of the Departmental Workers' Center, was deported to Switzerland. He took his whole family into exile. His three children are still there. Banzer had a government that was very bad for workers. He tortured various workers who were leaders. José was tortured here in the police station. At midnight they threw cold water on him to make him reveal where the rest of the leaders of the revolution were. Since he didn't know he denied knowledge of them. He couldn't say anything. That Banzer was a very bad man.

*Did he lower salaries and wages?*

He didn't cut wages, but he devalued the currency and that raised prices. Bread, for example, used to be six for one peso. He converted it to three for one peso. And then there was another devaluation with Natusch. In each devaluation the government made, the people lost buying power. The workers in the mines have lost a tremendous amount; we have lost 50 or 60 percent. Our wages were paid according to the official dollar exchange, but our clothing and food prices were changed in relation to the dollar in the parallel market. If the official exchange is 100,000 pesos to the dollar, the dollar on the parallel market brought 500,000 pesos.

*And the prices of things made in the country rose at the same rate as imported articles?*

Yes, they rose. So it is that we are poorly fed, mistreated, and there are no machines for work. They have let everything slide.

*What else has happened since I left in 1970?*

When Banzer was still in power, life was more or less in line. But the consequence was that now we are paying for the deeds of Banzer. And he is now considered blameless.

I don't know if the people take into account the propaganda that is pasted on the walls. It shows a Bolivian flag embracing a black condor. And this means that our nation is in mourning, or is going to be in mourning. Alongside of this is a black, white, and red symbol that also has significance. It is an insult to the Bolivian people, that much is very clear. I don't know if people know what the colors signify. For example, the black signifies the public in mourning, the white signifies the innocence of the pueblo — no one can know what the government is doing — and the red represents the flow of blood. This is very serious. It is an insult to see it.

I remember well when Victor Paz Estenssoro himself was inaugurated in 1952 on the ninth of April, they gave us colors for our union banner and they were white, black, and red. They explained to us that the black was the mourning that we had when the tin barons were in power, that the white was the innocence of the public, and the red was the flow of blood. And now again they want to impose these same designs on us for better or worse with Banzer. If Banzer regains power, democracy in Bolivia will not exist. Again we are going to see depression, the conquest of the unions, and the destruction of democracy. Salaries will be lowered and we will lose bread. Banzer made several union organizers disappear without a trace. And now people are demanding that they give information about this. There have been various programs on the television where they assert that Banzer has made people disappear. To this very day there has been no response.

*And with García Meza was it worse?*

With García Meza in power it was even worse than with Banzer, if that is possible. It remained more or less the same with Natusch Busch, and the repression was just as bad, but Natusch Busch was more savage than García Meza. The most cruel repression of all the governments took place under him. It was worse than with García Meza, who just had a mouth, and under whom the poor people had no voice. But Busch wanted people to work like in the times of the oligarchy when Mamerto Urriolagoitia was in power; Busch was going to kill opposition. Even so, new leaders appeared to fight him. There is never a lack of people to fight.

*It really is phenomenal!*

It is something very moving. It is something that one must analyze with care. But never again will the government fall in the hands of that kind of leader, because now people know how to fight. If one falls, another fighter will stand up in favor of the workers.

*And you have given advice to your children about the nature of these regimes?*

Yes, I explained to them all that had passed. For example, in this recent period when Juan Manuel was in the army, he said that the military leaders of his regiment gave instructions saying that they were going to shut up the miners.

Juan Manuel told me, "The military are going to seize the miners and machine-gun them down. They are going to work with guns at their throats."

"You are turning mad," I said. "You do not know what you are saying, Son. This father of yours is a miner, a worker. Are you going to raise your hand against your own father and your own brothers? That is what your officials are saying, but you ought never to take it seriously. That is a bad thing for you." That's what I said, and I went on. "If anything serious happens, like a revolutionary battle, and if the workers take a stand, then you have to liquidate the officials that command you to fire. So it ought to be."

I have always explained this to my children. Many sons of miners are in the regiments, along with children of *campesinos*. These youths ought to consider what their fathers say. And when there is a revolution, they ought to liquidate the officers who command them to fire. And if they threaten to imprison them, the officers themselves should be imprisoned. Nothing is as important as the lives of their parents. That is the explanation that I give to my children about repressive systems. It is very important that they learn this.

*What was happening to your family during these years of repression?*

Victor Hugo was born in 1974 when I was working in the stadium. He was one more burden in the family, another mouth to feed. But he is the blessing of God. I always earned something extra from someone in order to meet the economic expenses of the family. Juan Manuel is a troubled child. I don't know what happened to him. I could not understand it in another's child, let alone my own. He behaves badly. He has made a lot of trouble in my house, including economic trouble. He began to sell food that we needed to eat. And he has done many other things. For example, I had two antique watches of the best quality. They were in good repair and I was saving them to give to my sons. It turned out that he sold these watches when he was in school. When he did this, we decided that he had to go into the army. They took him and sent him to Kolque. But it was difficult for him to become accustomed to the army. I went there to see him one time, and the kid seemed unusual.

"I want to go home," he said. "Let's go. I don't want to stay here. Let's go to the colonel and tell him 'This youth can't stand it here.'"

But I read his thoughts and I said, "Juan Manuel, you went into the army believing that you were capable of enduring it. I told you what suffering there is in the army and that's the way it is with a soldier. A soldier has to bear this suffering until he gets used to it. I warned you about everything. You remember what I told you? You have to bear it, cost what it may, bear what you must. If you run away from the army I will bring you back like a child, so that eventually you will have your army records in order."

So he listened to this and put up with it until April, when he went AWOL on the day of his birth. And for what? For nothing. After so much suffering, he escaped. On the twenty-sixth of April this kid was sent to Cocala to accompany a sergeant that was going there. In Cocala he stayed; he did not return to his barracks. Then he caught a bus and came here to Oruro without the authorization of his commander. He arrived here, and we gave him a party for his birthday. We did what we could to feed him, and on Sunday he left. My wife took him to the bus station and put him on the bus. It's clear that she didn't know what was going to happen with Juan Manuel.

He left on the bus, and my wife came to take care of me. But it turned out that after Juan Manuel left on the bus he got off at the nail factory. He escaped into the fields, where the Huanuni guard seized him and put him under guard. And he was there one month working in Playa Verde in a factory where his wages went to the batallion that is there. After three weeks they brought him here to Oruro and an officer of the regiment quartered here brought him to my house. They asked that I or my wife return him to his regiment where he had given his service in Kolque.

My wife took him and left him there. He escaped again. Three weeks he was in flight without coming to the house. We did not know anything. From the twenty-sixth of April until the fifteenth of May he had not come to the house. After that we took him back to Kolque. All his sins had been pardoned, they said. All his things were in the barracks; all was in order.

But after we left a sergeant punished him with ten lashes. He said, "You have to get lost by tomorrow morning or I will give you ten more lashes." And it was only three days until his release. We received word that he was in Cochabamba. On Saturday his regiment had certified his release, but he had not showed up. One of his officers who is my cousin told us that.

I was in bed, having just come out of the hospital. My wife went to Salitra and they told her that Juan Manuel was not in the barracks. The past week he had disappeared.

Eventually he had to go to get his book back. So I went with the boy. Aníbal was in Cochabamba and from Cochabamba had come here, having to take a leave from his work. When he got here we three, Aníbal, Juan Manuel, and I, went to Kolque. There Lieutenant Vargas said, "I think that his book is in Oruro in the Second Division."

"But I can't believe that. We just came from there," I said.

"The best thing is that you speak to the colonel, but the colonel isn't here," he said.

We had to return on Tuesday. We slept in the barracks with good enough accomodations arranged by a sergeant. He made me a mattress with blankets to sleep on.

On Wednesday the colonel returned. The sergeant said, "Last night the colonel and the commander of the guards arrived. When I spoke to him about your case, he said, "It's a pity that we were not here.' Now that the colonel is here, you can talk with him."

I could hardly say anything because this child had committed these errors. Two times he had escaped, and he had to face up to this. I waited for Juan Manuel who was in the dungeon. They brought him out, along with some others at eight-thirty in the morning and forced them to trot while carrying truck wheels. With all that weight, they were still going at a trot. The colonel was watching this at 11:10, and at that moment he let them put down the wheels and gave them liberty. He didn't want to continue this punishment, because it is very cruel. So we went in with the colonel and talked.

The colonel said, "Wait until the fifteenth of June. Come back on the fourteenth and I will give you your son's book, and he can leave."

So I left him in the month of May. Again Juan Manuel escaped on Sunday. So I didn't go back. What would have been the good of it? Your *comadre* was in Cochabamba working in the harvest and had not yet returned. I was waiting to send her to reclaim him because I couldn't go another time. I was sick: the pain in my shoulder hurt a great deal, my feet were immobile, and I was totally worn out. I waited for him and waited but he didn't come.

Tuesday came, and then Wednesday. Juan Manuel still had not come back to our house. As it turned out, he was still in Cochabamba; he had gone directly there, I don't know with what money, with one shirt no more. In the afternoon I met my *compadre* José, who said that on Saturday they had found Juan Manuel walking in the street, totally without clean clothing. They gave him some old clothes and took him to Quillacolla to eat a chicken stew. They kept him there until Aníbal went there and brought him back. I took him back once more to the barracks, and again he escaped. Since then he has been with us. He has no service record and no book.

*How can he get his records back?*

I think that if he returns the military clothing he was issued, the three shirts, two jackets, a campaign belt, and two uniforms, as well as used boots, he will get his book. He will have to return them first and then they might give him the book. But I do not know in what state his book is. They might have it in the Second Division, but when my wife asked them for it, pointing out that the book was not of any use to them, they replied, "We are going to burn it because he has not finished his military service honorably."

*And what about Victor Hugo?*

Victor Hugo is eleven years old. He is still in school. This year he finished the fifth course of the primary school. We raised him with all the hopes that we raised the others, in a very serious form, especially in regard to his education. From the time that he was small, he was very passive, very quiet. He doesn't react to anything. He always had to struggle with the older ones. He is like a grandchild, and he fights a lot with my grandchildren. He still plays with toys, and little Israel always wants to take them away. And I always tell him he has to give them to the little one.

"It was like that when you were little and Juan Manuel had to give toys to you," I said. But he still wants to play with toys. But it seems to me that this child might have a future with his studies, because the grades that he gets are good. Every time that I go to his school to find out about his progress, about his behavior and his achievements, they always praise him and congratulate me. He sometimes gets behind in his notebooks, but on the whole he is good.

Ana is also very good. She would have graduated if she hadn't lost a year. But this year she has been doing very well. I went to find out about her conduct, and they approved of her and told me that she did well. There were no complaints. She has received her records. They congratulated me that I had taken responsibility so that she would take advantage of her studies. I am just a little concerned about her.

*What troubles you about her?*

When she lost that year, she used to play a lot with her friends and was often absent from school. That was in the intermediate school. She would come home very late. Her friends finished the year and they got out of school. Afterward I went there and discovered all this. They told me that she had had many absences and was failing many courses. That is a headache for a father. It is the most serious problem because the studies of any person are a part of their life, just as for adults, work is a part of their life. Because without work, there is no food. In the same way, without study, there is no work. When you have to work without having finished your studies, life is difficult; one has to work hard every day. But when you finish your studies, the work is light, like in offices or in the administration of businesses. But those that do not study have to labor.

*And were you angry when María married without finishing her studies?*

María had to leave her studies. She was studying hard, trying to finish, but none of them really paid attention to me, with the exception of Elena. Elena is studying and is completing her courses with good grades. The only difficulty is that she needs an accordion. I cannot buy one for her because I don't have enough money. They cost a lot of money. I have to try to get one somewhere because she can't practice without it.

As for María, she was studying in the seminary and she met Guido and they got married. But her choice of a husband was a little bad. I wanted to discourage him because he is not a boy of our level. He is of a lower level, not educated. His parents didn't have any concern with his studies. I, on the other hand, have fought day and night for the education of my children, while his father hasn't. His father was lazy, selling hats from door to door and forgetting about the needs of his children. He didn't make any of his children study; none of them earned a degree. So this kid does not deserve María because she is a little more civilized. He wants to enslave my daughter. He beat her. When he finished work, he would go out on the streets as though he were a bachelor. He didn't have any respect for me. Finally I told him "I am going to take my daughter back with me, even though she has two children. I shall raise them as my children. I am not going to bother you with anything, but I want you to leave my daughter alone."

So I brought her here with me. She was here a week, and then he came promising that he would never behave like that again; he got her back with promises. He has been a little badly behaved with me. Clearly he never exchanged words with me, but he had behaved badly with my daughter. But from that day on, he has reformed, and now they live very well.

*And did he marry María against your will?*

No, he entered to ask for her hand. I laid down the law that my daughter had to get married formally. He had not thought of that, but agreed. So he prepared the marriage. I had paid 100 percent of the costs of the marriage of Filemón because he is a man. Here the custom is that a male child's family has to pay for the marriage, and for a female, nothing. The father of the girl did not pay a single cent for Filemón's marriage. As for María's marriage, the father of the groom should have paid all the expenses, but he did not like to work. He lived on the small income that he had selling hats. He would go into the field with the hats and other items. His father didn't have money, so we paid half the expenses. We had to make an exception because she is my daughter. If we hadn't given anything, I am sure that María would have been upset. As parents we had the responsibility, and we had insisted upon the marriage. There were many guests, at least two hundred. I took care of all the drinks. But because of this, the youth is now behaving well. Today he took us to Vinto for a plate of sausages. However, he got drunk there and we came back with María and his brother-in-law; he slept there.

And Elena became involved with the father of her son. As strict as I was as a father of the household, things came out differently. It is all the fault of Petrona. I would have said that no one could come into our house when Elena was studying, but at the time he was renting part of the bottom floor of the house. (It still didn't have a roof. It was covered with cartons, no more, while we were constructing the top floor.) The youth entered to do his homework, to study with Elena since they were in the same courses. And they had a love affair and Elena became pregnant.

I almost committed a grave error when I first said that she had to get married. His father and his mother had accepted my demand; they had even chosen their godmother of the marriage. Then it occurred to me that I was doing the wrong thing. They were students, and they could not do anything without both leaving their studies and the man dedicating himself to work to support his family. And Elena would have had to maintain him and she would have lost her studies. Then I saw what should be done.

"Both of you will have to end your studies to marry," I said. "This should not happen to my daughter." Doña Placida, the mother of the father of Israel, was in agreement.

I called the young man and I said that he should study with all his heart until he finishes. I did not press anyone. If he had the luck of marrying my daughter, then he could marry her. But only when she finished her studies. Both continued with their studies, for the future of their child. Meanwhile I am going to raise the child.

He will devote himself to his studies until he becomes a professional, and I will take care of his child. He has continued studying, thinking of the future of his child, just as Elena has, thinking of her son, who should also study. When they finish, if it is their luck to get married, they will become professionals. I am not going to think about Elena or her child. I am only going to think of the future.

And now they continue studying, and the father of the child will become a professional in December of this year. He is in the polytechnical military school. But I am not going to permit them to marry until the youth is sure to be a professional and has his salary and everything under control. His specialty is in airplanes. If the youth wants to marry Elena after he finishes his studies, I also am not going to permit it until Elena has become a professional. Then they can get married.

One year more, I believe, that is a lot. Even two years more, if there is love, then they can marry. But before finishing her studies, Elena cannot think of getting married, because she could have another child. Elena lost a year when she was sick with Israel, and the same thing could happen again. So to avoid problems and to become a professional, Elena did not get married. Whether they have luck or not, each one can live from their profession.

It is my one proposal for her that she does not need a husband to maintain her child. When she becomes a professional, she can support herself. Moreover, she can cooperate by helping the young children that I have. But I do not know what proposition her lover will have when he becomes a professional. He has not said anything.

When you become a professional and are earning money, then if you want to get married, I think that you will be less likely to commit an error. It would be bad for my daughter to get married before she gets her degree.

*But she could get married and avoid having children.*
I don't know. Love does not say that.
*What are your hopes for the future?*
My hopes for the future are so great I don't know if I am going to get them. I want to continue making possible the studies of my children, to give them some degree so that they can live well. Because if this cannot be I will not be happy. A lot depends on my health. If I live, I am going to make every effort to enable them to study, even if I end up without eating, but I will not leave off trying to save them with their education. They have to study, until the end of my life. If not, I would not be able to accept them. With study, they will become something, perhaps not great, but at least they will improve their position. I have

fought so hard for all of them, from Filemón to Victor Hugo I have sacrificed myself. At least with your cooperation things have gone along. I always have problems in surviving. For that I say thanks to you that my life is more or less improving.

*Well, we ought to talk of your sickness some day.*

Very well. As for my sickness, it was very serious. I never thought that I would get sick like that. Before I had the same illness, but it was not as bad. I was eight days in the hospital, but I came out healthy. But then at the marriage of Aníbal I drank for four days. And the day of the fiesta, on Friday, I was in bed but I felt pretty good. I did not have a headache but I couldn't walk. My legs trembled. And on Saturday, I was losing consciousness, but I remember that I had diarrhea. And on Sunday I don't remember anything. I lost consciousness. I was completely disoriented by the illness. I also don't remember anything about Monday but they told me that Doctor Esteban Torbo attended to me. My wife was holding me all the time. I was very ill.

Finally, on Tuesday the doctor said, "Let us take him to the hospital. There is nothing I can do to cure him here." And they took me to the hospital. In the hospital, they put me on oxygen with intravenous feeding. From the moment that I entered and for three days they had me on that. Every day I woke up with that. I fell from the bed trying to move. They said that I was talking with someone and no one answered me, but I continued talking as though someone had answered me. Elena told me everything that happened.

Then on Wednesday I woke up between dreams and with a headache. I saw myself in a battalion, but it was nothing more than the oxygen tank. Only my arm had the injection of fluids. And Aníbal and Filemón were holding my hand. I was in a crib such as they have for children. They had put up a rail so that I would not fall out. When I saw this, I fell unconscious, sleeping again for about fifteen or twenty minutes. And again I opened my eyes then with a greater level of consciousness. Then I asked what time it was. It was about eight in the morning.

I asked Filemón, "Where am I? Why did they bring me here?"

"You are sick, *Papi*, since Saturday. You were unconscious. They did these things, but you didn't feel anything." When I tried to move, my body had no strength. My nerves were gone. I felt that I was falling. I couldn't hold on to anything. When I tried to eat with a spoon, I could not do it without trembling. That's the way I was sick that month, on the point of death surely. Thanks to God that he did not want me to die. The injections cost 100,000 pesos each one. The social security did not pay for the injections. They do not cover these medicines. Finally the doctor gave the idea to Aníbal and Filemón, to tell the administrator of the hospital our problem, and he helped me a lot. He charged the bill to Aníbal, who was covered by the company. But I spent a lot for the injections: 100,000 pesos for each injection, and there were four injections every twenty-four hours. But it was the blessing of God that made it possible for me to recuperate from this sickness.

*Yes, but you shouldn't drink any more.*

At my son-in-law's fiesta I will have to drink at least one drink to *ch'allar.*

# 21

## Juan Manuel

---

Juan Manuel had just escaped from the army for the second time when I came to stay with his parents in the summer of 1985. Although only fifteen, he was tall for his age, so Juan was able to lie about his age at the recruiting center and get him into the service. His experiences in the army were even worse than those Juan had undergone during his military service, yet Juan was not sympathetic to his son's repeated attempts to escape. Because I was a godmother at a health Mass for him when he was two years old, Juan urged me to discuss with Juan Manuel his plans for the future. One day while we were discussing what he might do to train himself for employment, I asked Juan Manuel what his aspirations had been from his earliest memories. With the encouragement of Elena, who had joined us, he spoke of his life with greater humility and insight than I had ever before perceived in him. But after I enrolled him in a clerical course that he abandoned after the second lesson, I could also understand Juan's frustration and the cause of his desperation.

---

I remember back to the time when I wanted to write and read but couldn't. When I reached the age to study, they took me to the school in San José to enroll me. I didn't want to stay and returned with Mama. She took me back again, but still I didn't want to stay. I cried about going to school.

"You are a sissy, a sissy!" they said.

Little by little I got accustomed to it, because my parents and my brothers and sisters both scolded and encouraged me. I got accustomed to it to the point that I went to school and returned accompanied only by Anita.

In first grade I was bored and did not have any interest in studying. Again, my parents and my sisters and brothers scolded me. For a time I would listen to them, but then I would forget what they said. The only thing in my head was to play rather than study. I would go to school and study there, but when I came home I would not do my homework. I would just become lazy.

Little by little I began to pay attention for longer periods, but then I would forget or not hear, and they would reprimand me and sometimes spank me. But even then I would not understand. That's the way the years passed.

In fourth grade I began to have even more problems with my studies, because I wasn't interested in anything. I had to repeat that year. And the next grade, I would have had to take over, too, but they issued a decree that all children had to be advanced regardless of their grades. This decree made us all very happy. The teacher wanted me to repeat the grade nonetheless, but Mama went to school and told the teacher that she did not want me to be held back because she was afraid of what my father would say.

[*Elena, who was sitting and listening to all this, interjected a comment.*]

Juan Manuel was always distracted in his studies. He was more interested in playing. Even up to the time he went into the army he was playing with toy cars and with a ball. He was a child, practically.

*But now you are changing, Juan Manuel?*

Yes, a bit. When I was in the first grade of intermediate school there was a serious discussion in my house with my parents. The next day I went to high school but I did not go back home. Instead, I went to Cochabamba and stayed there a week. My mother came to take me back. My parents' attitude had changed because of my decision to run away. I, myself, thought that I ought not to have done that. I stayed with my uncle in Cochabamba, but I was disturbed. I couldn't eat and didn't want to do anything.

*Why was that?*

I felt estranged from my parents because of what they had said. I stayed two days more with my mother in Cochabamba and then we returned here. Then they told me, "Everything depends on you. Are you going to go on studying?" my father asked, and I said I was. But then I went to high school and I didn't want to enter. I was afraid of what the teachers would say. So I went home and told Papa that I just didn't want to study.

He said, "That is your decision. Everything depends on what you want. I cannot make you study."

From that time on, I have been going wrong. I had to repeat the second year of intermediate school. My teacher tried to help me but it was useless. I didn't want to understand or even listen. I was as stubborn as a mule.

This went on until things finally began to enter my head, but still not always. I did not always pay attention, and Papa punished me and beat me. Mama also, and my brothers and sisters, especially Aníbal. But everything was in vain.

*Did they beat you or only scold you?*

[Elena] They beat him with a *chicote*, because he had pushed them to the limit and they couldn't stand it.

[J.M.] I couldn't stand it the way they beat me.

*And what did you think your future would be?*

More or less the same.

[Elena] If one could see the future, what kind of a person would he be?

[J.M.] Maybe a good person.

[Elena] Perhaps with a profession, not like Mama and Papa who suffer so much trying to get a little money. A professional earns more but Juan Manuel could never understand that.

[J.M.] So in June 1984 I entered into the army when I was fifteen. I thought things were going to be better there than in my house, but it was not so. It was worse. I could not get accustomed to the food, to the tea, to the bread.

*What type of meals did they have?*

They had crusts of yellow bread and the tea was Sultana. At lunch we had gruel and the same for supper. I was getting thin; I was down to fifty kilos. Moreover I couldn't fire the rifles or the machine guns. But little by little I got used to things, except to the fact that our superiors beat us. One officer in particular wanted to reprimand me. He said, "You have to be a good soldier. You have to earn your grades." He tried to make me do this, but I was neglectful. I didn't like my instructors.

*You were very young?*
Yes.
[Elena] Yes, he was almost a baby.

*How old were you when you entered?*
Fifteen; now I am sixteen. Before the first review, I came here. In preparation for the first review they abused us a great deal. They seized us and put us in the guardhouse; they beat us. They wanted us to do well, but there were some who failed. Some were only interested in eating, especially those that lived in the rural areas, and some from Uncía. The rest of us couldn't get along with them.

It went alright for me at the review. The colonel and the lieutenant congratulated me. We had polished ourselves up for the review to gain qualification. Three days later they called us, Juan Manuel Rojas, Roberto Mamani Condori, and Edgar Fuentes, and they gave us four days' leave. We left on Thursday and were supposed to return on Sunday.

Papa was happy to see me, as were all my brothers and sisters. I arrived in my uniform, and seeing me wearing it pleased them all. On Sunday morning we went to await the truck, but there was none, so we had to leave the following day at noon. When we arrived, they were waiting for us, they were choosing people for the second review, but because we were late they beat us.

*Was it very high up?*
It is on the border with Chile. It is on high ground and very cold.

Upon our arrival, they gave ten lashes to each of us. Then they reassembled us and gave us instructions. I was in the third section, the most difficult one — you have to climb mountains. We learned to blow up bridges, destroy land mines, and make antitank and antipersonnel attacks. They also gave us instruction in mathematics, and I couldn't learn this.

We were supposed to come here to Oruro on the twelfth of December, but we didn't come because they postponed it until the sixth of August. For that reason, I didn't want to be there any longer. Some other recruits also did not want to stay. The veteran troops bothered us. They stole our belongings, they took our sugar, our toast, whatever we had. My folks sent me milk and they stole that. The corporals were the worst about bothering us. The instructors were always reviewing us. There was one sergeant who was particularly bad. He took every-thing from us. He lived on the sweat of our parents one could say. Some of the other recruits had sugar, preserves, or sardines, and he would take it all for himself. He was an evil one, a bloodsucker. In the third section they punished you with weapons. They held you on your feet and struck you with them for one or two hours. Sometimes they shot off the rifles from midnight until five in the morning.

*And for what acts did they punish you soldiers?*

For failing, for complaining that they did not leave the soldiers in peace.

*Even if you didn't do anything bad?*

[Elena] For the fault of one, everyone paid.

[J.M.] Yes, for what one did, everyone paid. Those who were in ser-vice longer than us got off free. They could order us around like an instructor, and one had to respect them as if they had rank. If we didn't, they would beat us with a stick. There was one poor fat boy that they made eat six plates of food; then they punched him in the stomach and made him vomit.

One time when I left the encampment with permission, the second time in February for Carnival, I encountered this evil sergeant. I had forgotten about the reviews and he caught me with a whip. He almost broke my shoulder hitting me there and on my buttocks. I couldn't walk or bend over. My shoulder was very bad.

[Elena] That was very bad, very unjust.

[J.M.] Another thing this sergeant did was to kill a soldier.

*Did his parents complain?*

They gave the father of the soldier a wage equivalent to the rank of a sublieutenant in the reserves, and his father agreed.

[Elena] They say that his parents were *campesinos* and did not know how to speak Spanish well. They took advantage of them because they were illiterate.

[J.M.] Yes, they took advantage because they were illiterate. And they didn't say anything to the instructor. Now the parents live in La Paz. They have a good house thanks to the death of their son. The sergeant shot him. We saw it all. He was ridiculing the soldier while we were standing at attention. The sergeant fired a volley and a bullet struck him. He died immediately, just that moment. The bullet struck him in the throat. After two months . . .

*But this person is very dangerous!*

Yes, they ought to have taken away his rank, at the very least, but they didn't. He's crazy. In the nighttime he would sing when he was on guard, and singing loudly he would pass the night. After two months, there was another death in my squadron. We were 108 and then we were 106.

*How did the other one die?*

He fell from a large rock. We were climbing it and he jumped with a rope and it strangled him. I also nearly died there, hanging from my foot. Several recruits had already climbed up and they caused rocks to fall down on those that were still climbing. This frightened those of us who were climbing and so he jumped and fell. And I was so frightened that I also jumped, but it did not hurt me because my foot was caught in the rope and I hung there. It was better that that happened or otherwise there would have been two dead. But God did not want me to die.

After that I left again with permission, but I didn't want to go back. I came to my house without anyone but Elena knowing, at first. Then I told them that I had asked for a longer leave. Then, since I didn't want to return, I went off to Cochabamba again. When I returned and my parents sent me back to the army. Again I escaped, but Papa wouldn't let me stay. Then, because my father came, the army received me and told him that I should stay, and that they would treat me well.

When Papa left, they put me in the guardhouse, and days passed. Every day I used to have to trot over a course strewn with huge tires and many rocks, half nude with shorts on. They kicked us and beat us with a rubber fan belt. So that is why I left to come here.

*Did you have to go into the army? Was it absolutely necessary?*

Yes, it is necessary in order to get the workbook.

*What workbook?*

[Elena] Here the discharge from the military service is very important. After you are in the military service a whole year they give these books. But Juan Manuel couldn't get it because they were so abusive he couldn't stand it. His workbook is ready to pick up, but they want him to come for it so they can beat him; then maybe they will give him his book.

[J.M.] My father doesn't want me to go.

*Your father had some problems but came out finally.*

They used to call him "Skinny" because he was very small. I was the youngest and the smallest in my army group, but he was even smaller than I. When he was in the army he weighed forty-three kilos; I weighed fifty.

*And were the other soldiers about the same age?*

[Elena] They were all older than he.

[J.M.] Yes, they were eighteen or nineteen years old. I was the youngest.

*And why did you have to sacrifice yourself so?*

[Elena] Because he didn't want to study.

*And now have you changed your mind?*

[J.M.] Yes, now my mind is changed, or you could say that I am aware of what I do and I repent for the problems I have made for my parents.

[Elena] He has matured.

[J.M.] I said to Papa, "I am going to succeed in becoming something. And with what you have taught me, I am going to try to be a help to you. I am going to think about my studies."

[Elena] Juan Manuel was born on the very day that Barrientos died, General Barrientos Ortuño, exactly on that day, April 27th, 1969. And it was at that moment, at three or four in the afternoon, that he was about to be born and we were very anxious. We went to the hospital with Papa and my brother. He was born in San José hospital. He was very fat and continued to be so. His nickname was "Fatty" despite the fact that now he is thin. We still call him Fatty.

*Were you happy when he was born?*

[Elena] Sure we were. I never left my mother's side when she was in bed with him. I love babies because they are beautiful. I like to hold them when they're little. But when they get older, they are badly behaved and too heavy to carry. I do not remember a lot about him because I was small, too. The one I remember is Victor, the youngest. I bathed him and everything.

When Juan Manuel began to walk he was two or three years old, and he was always wetting his diapers. So I used to get angry because we girls had to wash his clothes. So sometimes we didn't put anything on him because he was always wetting. We just put a long shirt on him.

When we were little, we didn't have television in the house. We liked to see television since we never went to the movies, so we used to visit our neighbors. We always went at suppertime and it was a bother because they invited us to have a plate. "Try this," they would say, and so we would try the dinner, but it always needed salt. They ate without salt. The rest of us didn't want to eat, but Juan Manuel ate all that they gave him and wanted more. But we were ashamed to ask for more, so the woman of the house would make his plate with a little extra. He kept eating and eating, and therefore he got fat. He ate along with Anita, and they even ate what they gave the dog.

# 22

## Elena

---

Elena is the child who remains closest to Juan both emotionally and, as an unwed mother, in her continued dependency on the family. She tried to fulfill Juan's ambitions for her career at great personal cost. She is sensitive to his needs; she stayed with him night and day when he was hospitalized after a stroke. Yet she is able to discern his compulsiveness with some objectivity. Her description of her childhood illness (possibly rheumatic fever bringing about the heart condition she has suffered from) is lyrical in its metaphoric allusions to broken toys and dreams of setting things right. Just as she has played the role of a little mother with Juan Manuel, so she has nurtured all the members of the family when they were in trouble.

---

When we arrived in Santa Fe, I had recently turned six. This is the first thing I remember. We came just at the beginning of the school year. They put me right into first grade because I liked to study. I was always more preoccupied with that than any other thing. I had a good teacher who taught me things that to this moment I have not forgotten. My father liked the way I behaved. Even now he says how good I was, how well I applied myself to my studies.

We used to go to school in a bus that picked us up and brought us back. As soon as I got home I did my homework. Afterwards I would go out to play, to jump rope or play *tuncuna* [hopscotch]. I played with friends from my class.

I also had a friend who taught me how to sew clothes for my doll and how to knit. When I had nothing else to do, I would go outside alone. I remember one August when the wind was blowing so strong that it filled a hole in the back yard with sand, very fine sand, and I would play there. One time when I went out there alone in the wind I found some dolls completely destroyed. I wanted to put them back together and take them home with me because I had hardly any dolls. But none of the dolls had a complete body, not even the heads or arms or legs were intact, and their eyes were all turned back. I returned home late, leaving the dolls there, and in the night I had a temperature, a very high fever. Papa was traveling to La Paz to arrange his retirement and he returned at eleven at night. I was waiting to see my father return but when he did I thought he was coming out of the closet. With the temperature, I was hallucinating; he seemed to be coming to embrace me, but I couldn't even rise from my bed.

On the following day I didn't have strength to do anything. I still had the fever but Mama did not think of taking me to the hospital. She went to call my grandmother, the mother of my father, who was a kind of curer. She said that I had been seized by a fright, a *japeq'a* and that evil winds had blown on me. Since my grandmother told me to tell everything, I told them that I had been playing with the dolls. They went to see the hole, but said there were no dolls. There was nothing.

This is the thing that I remember most clearly to this day because it made such a big impression on me. They told me they found nothing, not even sand. Afterwards my knees swelled up like balls and my chest was swollen, all because of the fright. They said that it was some evil, perhaps evil air that affected me. My grandmother cured me with quinine and with home remedies. But after she cured me I had terrible diarrhea.

When I went to intermediate school I loved to play basketball. I always brought home good grades and this made Papa happy. When I went on to secondary school, I became very engrossed in my notebooks, and also with doing a little housework and sewing, embroidering and knitting. I completely forgot about playing. Now I am in normal school, and it is still the same with me.

*Did you get any prizes?*

For my qualifying exams, no; they weren't that good. But, as I said, it pleased Papa that I had these reports. He liked them even if they were not "superior," but rather "good." One year I was elected queen of my class, not because of beauty but because of good grades. There were three of us girls nominated, and I was elected. They had a coronation in class and Papa made a fiesta for me.

When I was in the third year of intermediate school, and earlier, in the third year of basic school, I became sick, and the doctor said that I had heart trouble.

*I remember when you were sick with heart trouble.*

Yes. That time they put me in the hospital and I was there three months. They had to operate on me and decided to take me to Catavi for the operation. I don't remember much about it because I was very sick. I was always in the arms of my mother. I was large, but she carried me with a great deal of strength because I had had a lot of hemorrhaging from my nose. They said that it was because of my heart, and because I had long hair, so they cut it very short, because they said that long hair was causing me trouble, by sapping my strength.

*What kind of an operation was it?*

I didn't have an operation after all. There was a woman in Catavi who said that they shouldn't operate because heart operations were very dangerous. She said that it could leave one crippled and mentally unbalanced. Mama got very frightened hearing this. She wrote to Papa and told him that she was going to bring me home to prevent them from operating on me. *Papi* said, "You do what you see is right. I cannot say anything," and *Mami* took me and all our things from the hospital and we came back here.

*Were you still sick?*

Yes, I was sick.

*How did you come back?*

We came in the bus. I don't think the trip helped me, but once we arrived here I got better. And I have never had to return to the hospital.

*You haven't had any problem since then?*

No, not so far. But sometimes when I am very angry or upset, I get an attack of nerves, but not a bad one. It isn't like the time when I hemorrhaged from my nose. That time two veins broke. They took care of it in the hospital in Oruro where the pensioners go. They sewed them up, but one burst again and I had another hemorrhage. I think that that is the only sickness I have had, when blood flowed from my nose.

*When did you have your son, Israel?*

Ah, Israel was born when I was in the third year of secondary school, in 1980. I stopped working to have him. He was so little. Papa did not want me to go to school because there was no one to take care of Israel, and also because of my own health. Papa takes good care of me. Afterwards, the following year, I graduated.

*You didn't want to marry?*

That's true, I didn't. We were too young and we couldn't have continued our studies. We entered into an agreement with his parents and mine that first we should become professionals and then we could get married when it was convenient.

*When do you think you will get married?*

If he gets out this year, he will become a professional.

*And do you still see him?*

Yes. Just yesterday he came here to visit during his vacation.

*Where did he come from?*

From La Paz. He is studying at the Aviation Polytechnical College.

*And do his parents still live here?*

Yes, they live here in San José, and he always comes to see his son. He comes to talk with my father and mother. I think it's better this way, because if we had married, he wouldn't have graduated and neither would I. We couldn't have studied anywhere.

I was so afraid of telling my parents that I was pregnant. I was particularly afraid of advising Papa because sometimes he reacts very strongly to things. I didn't even want to tell Mama because she is weak and would have told Papa, and then he would have said that she was at fault, because he always blames Mama for everything.

So at five months I told them. I went to my father's place of work to tell him. True, he complained and everything, but he did not beat me. He scolded me strongly and told me that he was going to call upon the boy's parents, because he wanted to talk with them.

Afterward I spoke to them and we agreed to get married the following Saturday. But during those intervening days, I thought about it, and I said to myself, I don't want to marry.

I said to my parents, "I don't want to marry; we are too young and are going to have many problems because we lack experience."

Of course Mama is good, and she understood me. But as for Papa, I was afraid of telling him. Finally one day my papa was in a good mood, feeding his rabbits with me helping him. So I said to him, "I lied to you about wanting to get married."

And since he was in a good humor he said, "That is all right, Daughter, that you are not going to marry. This sort of thing happens in the best of families, to everyone." So later he [the father of Israel] came home from college and I told him that we weren't going to get married. I explained all my reasons, the first of which was that we had to continue studying. Well, he agreed with me and so he graduated from high school and, in the following year, went into the army. He didn't even see his son born because he was in the army in Tarija, which is far away, and he could not come.

I didn't go back to school for a year, but the next year I returned and received my degree in 1981. Afterward he came here and worked a year. With his wages he was able to buy a few things for his son — milk, a few clothes, but not much because he didn't earn very much.

*Does he help you now buying food?*

No, because now he is still a student. His parents have six other children, and they are all young so there isn't enough to give me anything. My father also understands this because he knows that he is studying. He realizes that even next year Israel's father will still be studying and he will not be able to give anything. I have two more years to go, but perhaps when he gets out the year after this and begins to work I shall get what I haven't received.

*What is that?*

A little economic security for my child. Israel will be starting school he will need more food and clothing.

*How did you choose the name Israel for your son?*

I was still in the hospital. The day that he was born I did not recover well. My oldest brother Filemón came with his wife. Aníbal also came, but Papa was in the hospital. They asked me, "What are you going to call him?" And without thinking, without saying, "Juan, Roberto, or perhaps Carlos," without even thinking, I said "Israel." That's the way it was, completely spontaneous. So in my house and in the house of Filémon they all knew that he was called Israel. The next day when they came to visit me, everyone knew that he was named Israel except me, because I had fallen asleep and forgotten.

*Do you know someone with that name?*

Well at that moment I did not recall anyone with that name.

*[Juan Manuel interjected a comment.]*

From that movie "Daniel Boone" that you saw. I believe you got that name because he named his son Israel. Remember?

Well, at that time I did not think of the movie or of his name. I don't know why I picked the name, but at that moment I was not thinking of that.

*Did your friend come to visit you in the hospital?*

No, he never came because he was still in the army. He didn't even come within the year because he stayed on in the army.

*And did you remain in contact with his parents?*

Yes, they never abandoned me. And I am very grateful to my papa, and more than anything to my mama because she helped me most of all. Also my brother Aníbal helped me. He baptized Israel — he is my *compadre* — at his first year birthday. It was beautiful. We had three days of fiesta, like a marriage. We had pork; we killed two pigs for that day. My papa loves Israel so much. He adores him. Israel sometimes hits him or kicks him and he doesn't do anything. When we were little, we did not play like that with him. When he called us he said, "Come!" I remember coming with my hands behind me, trembling with fear. It was like a fever you could say, but Israel is not like that with Papa.

*It must be like that because your father knew you had so many problems related to the birth.*

More than anything else, he probably saw the fatigue that I had carrying him. I am fine now, but when I was pregnant I was all worn out. My papa always wanted us to succeed, but unfortunately it wasn't possible when I was pregnant.

*Your father always thought about your education as a means of succeeding?*

He always was preoccupied with that, especially for Filemón; that was his greatest anxiety.

*When Filemón went to college in Cochabamba and then came for vacation with his school friends in that singing group, Juan got so angry with him for taking time away from his studies!*

Ah! My papa didn't like those things. Nor does he like to have my girlfriends and boyfriends come to the house. I never invite them to study because it would bother him. He says, "I did not know my childhood. I have been an old man since I was eight years old because I lived alone." That was because his own papa left him at a very early age, and he lived without his father and his brothers and sisters. He wants us to be like that, but you know that youths nowadays are not so closed in. We need to be with our school companions. But Papa does not understand. Well, he does understand, but it does not come easily to his mind because he never enjoyed his youth. He was always working.

*But he ought not to blame his children for that.*
That's what I say.

*But he always thinks about your education.*
Yes, its as if he were saying "I didn't have any fun and you shouldn't. You have to be the same as I."

*And your mother?*
No, Mama doesn't say anything to me; she keeps quiet. Only she doesn't want us to say anything to Papa because he blows up even discussing things. That's why we are afraid of him. And blowing up is bad for his health. Just last month he went to the hospital twice. The last time we carried him almost dead to the hospital. He couldn't even climb the stairs. He had lost his sense of balance, and the attendant had to help him climb.

[Juan Manuel]: Someone told us that in twenty-four hours he would be dead, that he was not responding to anything. I didn't see him, because I was in the army.

[Elena] He couldn't feel anything. We took him to the hospital after he was lying here two days. The doctor who lives here in front attended to him, but he is only an anaesthesiologist. He put Papa on intravenous feeding and all, but he didn't improve. So the doctor said we had to take him to the hospital, and we called the ambulance.

*What illness did he have?*
It was a stroke the doctor told me. He doubted that Papa would recover. He had a hemorrhage in his brain, and that's why he couldn't respond. He was in the bed and they poked him with these great needles — this size — all over, but he did not respond, not even his hands. He couldn't move either his feet or his hands. They scraped the bottom of his feet with a knife, and he still didn't react. He had oxygen and, after they took him up to his room, the doctor who is a specialist in this illness examined him. He cut him here and there and he didn't react. Blood came out, but he did not respond.

After that he began to feel things, and this gave us hope. They put in intravenous feeding and continued the oxygen, and so it was for a while. They also took blood because they said he had high blood pressure. It was pure intravenous feeding and injections that finally made him well.

For two days he was unconscious and didn't remember anything. Before, when he had the same illness, it was our bad luck that the doctors were on strike. Of course he was given medicine, but not as it should have been. I was there with him from seven in the morning until seven at night, tired out and with a pain in my shoulders from knitting. I had to be at his side because after they put the intravenous injections in he was always moving. If the needle became dislodged it would not have been effective, and his arm would have swollen. Someone had to hold him by force if he tried to move. Drop by drop, I had to wait until the injection finished and they put in a new one. Each day for three days they put in three bottles, nine in all.

I suffered a great deal with my papa. I had to go to the hospital, leaving my son who did not have anyone to take care of him well. Since I was the oldest in my house, and since my brothers and sister had their families and couldn't spend much time with Papa, I had to be there. My sister Anita was cooking; my mama was going back and forth, bringing meals for us. It was hard, but this doctor had told me that I couldn't leave. It was almost like sticking a dagger in my body when he told me that — I didn't know whether to laugh or cry or scream. I didn't know what to do. But now everything is good, not *very* good but just so.

*How did he recover? It was a miracle really.*

Yes, it was a miracle. And helped by good nutrition, by the vegetables, meat, all that we brought. We hardly had anything left to eat — often just a little tea and leftover meat.

*But now he is walking well and remembers everything.*

Almost everything. Sometimes when we are talking he will say, "What did you say?" He wouldn't have been listening. It's as though his mind had gone away, as though he were preoccupied with something.

*He is preoccupied. He says that he fell ill because he was preoccupied with the financial problem of your mama.*

Yes, and in addition his preoccupation was even greater with Aníbal's marriage. We were stripped clean and we didn't have any money in the house. She had arrived suddenly for carnival, Aníbal's intended, and within two weeks they announced that they were going to have a wedding. We didn't know where we would get the money. So we had the idea of putting this house up for a loan. The lenders gave us $b40,000 and we have to give this money back in a year. Papa is very disturbed by this too. It was partly because of this that my papa ended up in the hospital. They postponed the marriage celebration when he went into the hospital. Since he was upset we were trying to do everything to calm him down, but he was still raving. Then he got a little better, and we had the ceremony. He had recuperated enough so that he was even dancing at the wedding. But then a week later he had to go back to the hospital with the same illness. The doctor had told us before that he ought not have even a drop of liquor.

*And he did drink some?*
Yes, of course, during the wedding.

*We have to be careful that he doesn't drink at the fiesta on the twenty-seventh of July.*
Yes, for the fiesta of María we were thinking of going to the house of my sister-in-law near here, Aníbal's house, so we could take care of him there. Because if he stays here, he is going to get upset with all the drinking, and it is going to happen again. For example, in order to enter into the bathroom people have to knock at his door, and as he gets upset by this he is going to be very angry. He told me, "I am going to be here. I don't have to drink, but I am going to be here. Upstairs here we can be quiet because they are not going to drink up here."

I said, "But you are going to get angry because the drunks are going to be coming and going to use the bathroom, and the music is going to be very loud, and you will get bored upstairs. Why don't we go some-place else, in the *obrajes* or wherever we ought to go, and the day after we can come back here to sleep. If we stay here the family of my brother-in-law will come here, and they will invite you to drink, not understanding that you are so sick."

Papa always says that I am the one who gets most upset. We have discussions in which I do not agree with him and he wants me to agree. So finally I shut up, and he does too. Then we begin to talk again and discuss things, and invariably we get in an argument.

# 23
## Epilogue

Each in their own way, Juan and Petrona's children act out the contradictions that their parents faced or suppressed in their lives. Elena tried to fulfill Juan's goal of at least one of his children acquiring enough of an education to become a professional. Her desperate attempts to acquire advanced degrees, first in nurses' training and then in music ended in failure even though she had sacrificed the offer of marriage to the father of her child to pursue that end. Juan Manuel acted out Juan's own suppressed desire to escape the army, only to incur his father's wrath and the nearly lethal reaction of his sergeant. Filemón escaped the claims of his parents when his wife initiated their move to the house of her parents. María, who had greater success in school than did Elena, was fully occupied with her three small children. She was resentful that, in the eyes of her parents, she had married beneath her station; they had little regard for her hardworking husband since he had never gone beyond two years of schooling. His commitment to the labor movement in the oil refineries in which he worked did little to redeem him in the eyes of his in-laws. Aníbal, urged on by his wife, was just beginning to escape parental claims on his commissary coupons when I still lived in their house. Anita disappointed her father by dropping out from school in her last year of secondary school, but she was attempting to get her degree at the same time she was doing most of the domestic chores while her mother was in jail. Victor Hugo's strategy of remaining totally quiet meant that he could escape any demands put upon him. (Juan would only refer to him, when reminded of his existence, as "muy pasivo es.") Juan centered his hopes for the future on his grandson, Israel, whose lively antics and precocity gave Juan another outlet for his own aspirations. For each member of the family, undertaking their own independence entailed a rupture with the claims of the father, over their own needs.

Petrona emerges in the later chapters as the center of the household, calming Juan when his sudden rages threaten his health, discretely removing Juan Manuel before his father can strike him, supervising Anita and Elena in the household tasks, and sewing outfits for Israel as she tuned in to her soap operas. She mobilized the family to watch Juan round the clock when he was receiving intravenous nourishment after his first stroke so that he would not rip the needle out of his veins as he constantly threatened to do. Even when confined to prison, she was able to turn her time to profit by knitting *gorras* — the distinctive Andes highland cap with earflaps — for her fellow prisoners. Her energy, resourcefulness, and good humor sustained the family, creating a field of energy that gave direction and purpose to the whole enterprise.

Juan and Petrona voted for Paz Estenssoro at the polls in July 1985. Referring to him as "El Mono" (the monkey), Petrona said that he did, after all, get her their house. Shortly after the election, President Paz Estenssoro signed the decrees formulating the New Economic Policy, declaring the closing of all mines operating in the red. Nothing could forestall the sense of doom that fell over the mining community.

When I returned in 1986 I went to their house in Barrio Minera Santa Fe. The bottom floor of their residence was occupied by a new tenant. All of the furniture was piled in one bedroom upstairs where I found Anita. She told me that her parents were living in Cochabamba where they had gone when the doctor warned Juan that he could not survive living in the highlands. He was working as a night watchman in a ceramics factory. Elena had accompanied them and was working as a waitress in a Chinese restaurant. She was in love with a young man and was intending to get married. Aníbal had gone to Sweden with his wife, who had spent several years there when her father sought exile during the Banzer regime. Filemón had left with his family to go to Santa Cruz where there were rumored to be more opportunities after the mines were closed down. She was not sure what Juan Manuel was doing, and, as he might have preferred, I forgot to ask about Victor Hugo.

Anita was waiting for two Mormon missionaries who had promised to return to prosletyze on their evening round. As she told me about the fate of each family member, I helped her clear the sofa of the piled up furniture so that she could seat her expected guests. When I heard

Epilogue 375

the dogs barking in the courtyard promptly at eight o'clock when they were expected, I ran down to open the door for the two young American missionaries. Without explaining my presence to the astounded young men, neatly attired in their navy blazers and black ties with their blond hair slicked down, I waved goodbye to Anita for the last time.

The unity of the family exploded when the mines closed. It was a precarious unity, held together by the ferocious will of Petrona that had provided a refuge for each family member—when the economy of mining allowed some margins for what used to be called the "family of mining community members." But the security that was once provided by the pooled resources of family and community was now threatened, as the sum of the demands of each member exceeded the total pooled resources of the group. Survival meant that each of the nuclear units that once shared their fate with the extended group had to seek their own escape.

Since 1986 the plight of the mining communities has worsened. Men left for Santa Cruz, for Beni, but mostly for Chapare—the only viable economic area where coca production utilized the workers released from the mines. Women and children were left in the mining centers, often without resources to survive the diaspora. They will become the new statistics as the census of the 1990s begins to reveal the aftermath of policies designed for Bolivia in the financial orbits of the global system.

# REFERENCES CITED

Barrios de Chungara, Domitila (with Moema Viezzar). 1977. *Si me permiten hablar: testimonio de Domitila, una mujer de las minas de Bolivia.* México: Siglo XX.

Buechler, Judith-Maria and Hans Buechler. 1981. *Carmen.* New York: Schenkman.

———. 1992. *Manufacturing against Odds: Small Scale Enterprises in an Andean City.* Boulder, Colorado: Westview.

———. Film "The World of Sofía Velasquez" with Hans Schanfülrich Schlumpf, based on biography of same name.

Canelas O., Amado. 1966. *Mito y realidad de la corporación minero de Bolivia.* La Paz: Editorial los Amigos del Libro.

CEDOIN (Centro de Documentación Información). 1987. *Informe R. No. 125* April 25. La Paz.

———. 1988a. *Informe R.* No. 145 March 3. La Paz.

———. 1988b. *Informe R.* No. 147 April 1. La Paz.

———. l988c. *Informe R.* No. 150 June 1. La Paz.

Crapanzano, Vincent. 1980. *Tuhami: Portrait of a Moroccan.* Chicago: University of Chicago Press.

Crapanzano, Vincent, Yasmine Ergas, and Judith Modell. 1986. "Personal Testimony: Narratives of the Self in the Social Sciences and the Humanities," *Items.* New York: Social Science Research Council.

Dunkerly, J. and R. Morales. 1986. "The Crisis in Bolivia," *New Left Review,* 155:86–106.

Eckstein, Susan. 1983. "Transformation of a 'Revolution from Below' — Bolivia and International Capital." *Comparative Studies in Society and History,* 25, no. 1:105–135.

———. 1988. *Power and Popular Protest: Latin American Experience.* Berkeley: University of California Press.

Eder, George Jackson. 1968. *Inflation and Development in Latin America: A Case History of Inflation and Stabilization in Bolivia.* Ann Arbor: University of Michigan Graduate School of Business Administration, Bureau of Business.

Escobar, Filemón. 1984. *Testimonio de un militante obrero.* La Paz: HISBOL Instituto de Historia Social Boliviano. Imprenta Papiro.

Goslin, Thomas. 1985 "Bolivia: A Nation in Crisis," *Christian Century* (Feb.): 6–13.

Gueiler Tejada, Lydia. 1959. *La mujer y la revolución*. La Paz.

Laserna, Roberto. 1985. "La protesta territorial." In R. Laserna, ed., *Democracia y conflicto social*. La Paz: CERES.

Lewis, Oscar. 1961. *Children of Sanchez: Autobiography of a Mexican Family*. New York: Random House.

———. 1964. *Pedro Martinez: A Mexican Peasant and His Family*. New York: Random House.

Malloy, James. 1970. *Bolivia: The Unfinished Revolution*. Pittsburgh: University of Pittsburgh Press.

Menchu, Rigoberta. 1984. *I Rigoberto: An Indian Woman in Guatemala*. London: London Verse.

Mintz, Sidney. 1960. *Worker in the Cane: A Puerto Rican Life History*. New Haven: Yale University Press.

Nash, June. 1974. "Ethics and Politics in Social Science Research." *Transactions of the New York Academy of Sciences*, 36, no. 6:498–501. Reprinted in M. Rankiewich and J. P. Spradley, eds., *Ethics and Anthropology: Dilemmas in Fieldwork*, and in Gerrit Huizer and Bruce Manheim, eds., *The Politics of Anthropology*. The Hague: Mouton, 1977.

———. 1979. *We Eat the Mines and the Mines Eat Us: Dependency and Exploitation in Bolivian Tin Mines*. New York: Columbia University Press. Reprinted 1992.

———. 1980. "Bolivia: Consolidation (and Breakdown?) of a Militaristic Regime," in J. L. Nelson and V. M. Green, eds., *International Human Rights: Contemporary Issues*. Standfordville, NY: Earl M. Coleman Enterprise, pp. 135–46.

———. 1988. "The Mobilization of Women in the Bolivian Debt Crisis." In B. A. Gutek, A. H. Stromberg, and L. Larwood, eds., *Women and Work: An Annual Review*, vol. 3. Beverly Hills: Sage Publication.

——— 1992. "Interpreting Social Movements: The Response of Bolivian Tin Miners to Conditions Imposed by the International Monetary Fund." *American Ethnologist*, 94, no. 2.

——— with Manuel Roca. 1976. *Dos mujeres indigenas: Basili*. Mexico: Instituto Indigenista Interamericano.

——— with Juan Rojas. 1976. *He agotado mi vida en la mina*. Buenos Aires: Nueva Edición.

Ramos Sanchez, Pablo. 1986. *Consequencias de la política económica sobre el movimiento popular*. La Paz: photocopy.

Strengers, Jeroen. 1985. *La pesada carga de la deuda*. La Paz: CEDOIN.

Wolf, Eric R. 1969. *Peasant Wars of the Twentieth Century*. New York: Harper and Row.

# GLOSSARY

*ajsu (aysu)*, loom-woven black or blue skirt worn by women in the countryside

*akulli*, meditative coca chewing accompanied with alcohol

*akullini*, reunion of miners to chew coca outside the pits

*api*, corn gruel drink

*apu*, piece of women's clothing

*aras*, ancient silver coins placed in the hands of the groom by the priest in wedding ceremonies

*arroba*, a weight equivalent to twenty-five pounds

*awayo*, cloth used in ceremonial occasions

*awicha; awicho*, old woman; old man; related to supernatural beings in mine who look over miners; feminine form refers to *Tio's* companion in the mine, of whom there is no graphic representation

*Aymara*, Andean language of northern highland area of Bolivia

*ayni (aini)*, exchange or loan of services or goods, usually with interest added

*Barzolina*, female member of Maria Barzola Organization in the mining camps

*boliviano*, unit of Bolivian currency

*burro* (Sp.), small donkey

*callawayas*, dances

*camote*, (Sp.), root vegetable variety of sweet potato

*campesinos* (Sp.), farmers living in rural areas

*carajo, caray*, (Sp.), damn it; shit; expletive

*caramba*, expletive

*Catavi*, tin mine located near Siglo XX mine in the department of Potosi

*chakaykachay*, stagger

*ch'alla*, n.; *ch'allar*, v., pre-colonial ceremony in which coca, cigarettes, and alcohol are offered to the earth or hill spirits

*ch'ampa*, scrap meat from head or parts of animal

*chanchaqueando*, staggering

*charango*, a musical instrument, often made of shell of armadillo

*ch'askañawi*, bright eyes; nickname for a sorceress

*ch'aska uma*, hairy person; one giving the impression of being disheveled

*chasqay*, search for; clean up

*chasquear*, to clean up after a load is taken out

*chasquiri*, workers who clean up the interior of mines

*chaymanta*, "and so on;" also used as nickname

*chicha*, fermented corn drink widely consumed in Bolivia

*chichería*, bar at which *chicha* is sold

*chicote*, (Sp.) whip

*ch'illami*, clay container for domestic use

*Ch'ipayas*, indigenous people, speaking a language linked to that of the Maya, living in eastern part of Bolivia

*chiri*, cold; the cold

*chispear*, ignite an explosive

*chola, cholo*, ethnic identification of distinct cultural group in transition from indigenous patterns

*chuaro*, infusion used in *ch'alla* ceremony prepared with flowers, yellow corn, sugar, and white corn

*ch'ulo*, woolen cap with earflaps

*chunchu*, indigenous dance

*chuño*, frozen dried potato

*chupetitos*, jewelry

*chuseka*, owl

*chuwis*, dried beans children play with as marbles

*Clavo Porvenir*, (Sp.) "Key Vein of the Future"; name favored for discoveries in the mine

*Cochabambino*, (Sp.) individual from Cochabamba

*comadre* (Sp.), ritual godmother of one's child

*COMIBOL*, (Sp.) *Companía de Minas Bolivianas*, Bolivian Mining Company

*compadre* (Sp.), ritual godfather of one's child; close male friend

*con pica* (Sp.), dish with spices

*copajira*, acidulous liquids from mines

*Cruceño*, (Sp.) individual from Santa Cruz

*cuadrilla*, (Sp.) work unit with its own organization and hierarchy

*cuchi unti*, pig's fat; llama unti, llama fat; used in rituals in mine

*cueca*, (Sp.) dance introduced by Spaniards

*cullawa*, dance with inverted wheel

*diabladas*, (Sp.) devil dance performed by miners representing the struggle between good and evil; the dance takes place during the carnival in honor of the Virgin of the Mineshaft, the patroness of miners

*golke banderilla*, white darts used in offering to spirits of mine

*golke llimpe*, white paste used in offering to spirits of the mine

*golpe de estado* (Sp.), overthrow of state

*gorra* (Sp.), knitted cap

*Huachacalla*, town in the department of Oruro near the Chilean border

*Huanuni*, town in the department of Oruro formerly belonging to Patiño Mines, Ltd.

*huaqui*, piece of clothing

*Huari*, hill spirit, underworld lord often equated with *Supay*

*imilla*, girl

*Inca*, preconquest Peruvian empire; also identified with a type of dance group

*Inchupalla*, indigenous town near Santa Fe mine

*indiecitas*, diminutive for indian, with derisive connotation

*japeq'a*, fear illness, its symptoms correspond to the *susto* found in other parts of Latin America

*jarka*, strong wooden beam

*jayakitu*, dish prepared with dried beans, cooked potatoes, and roasted goat

*jukus*, those who steal minerals to sell clandestinely

*k'akchalo*, dirty; lazy; nickname

*k'amili*, herbalist diviners who come from northeast region of the department of La Paz

*k'analla*, pottery shard

*k'araku*, ritual sacrifice of an animal inside the mine in honor of *Supay*, or the *Tio*

*khallari*, the beginning of a task

*khellu uchu*, yellow pepper

*khoi kokho*, rabbit stew with red peppers

*kinsay chunka tayo*, thirteenth birthday party

*k'oa*, grain offered on a ritual table during a ceremony

*kollas*, individuals living in highland near Lake Titicaca

*larilari*, evil spirit causing contagious diseases

*lechehuayas*, dancers representing milkmaids

*llama unti*, llama fat

*localla*, lazy one

*loco* (Sp.), crazy

*macho* (Sp.), male, masculine

*makinaku*, request of hand in marriage; exchange of vows

*makipura*, temporary workers in mines without regular contracts, paid according to delivery of metal and lacking benefits

*malayar*, to long for

*mallku*, condor

*Mallku Rancho*, town in the Cochabamba valley, in the province of Quillacollo

*mamay*, mother, endearing form

*maskaynaypikas*, captive soldiers

*Matakos*, jungle dwelling indigenous group

*mayordomo*, (Sp.) low level administrator who controls the flow of people, materials, and instruments in and out of the mine

*mayranito*, nickname

*millu*, stone used in curing believed to contain radium

*minifaldas*, (Sp.) miniskirt

*mita*, work shift that may encompass days, weeks, or months

*morenos*, *morenadas* (Sp.), dance (or dancers) with masks representing blacks from Yungas valleys where they worked in vineyards

*Morococola*, mine in the department of Oruro belonging to Hochschild before nationalization

*muk'ju,* jerked beef sometimes used in the making of *chicha*

*nask'aska,* stuffy nose, applied to children's illness

*obrajes* (Sp.), work site

*oca,* vegetable

*Pachamama,* time-space representation often referred to as "earth mother"

*Pairumani,* place near Santa Fe mine

*pajarito* (Sp.), little bird

*palliri,* concentrator of metals

*papalisa,* (Sp.) kind of potato

*pasanaku,* type of lottery organized by groups of workers

*peón* (Sp.), common laborer

*phiri,* cornstarch meal

*picante* (Sp.), dish cooked with chile; spicy

*pijchar,* sociable coca chewing in the mine

*picaro* (Sp.), playful, often applied to man fond of seducing women

*pirkin,* self-managed group of contract workers typical of older work system prior
    to nationalization

*pirkiñero,* worker in self-managed group

*pisco,* wine of the Andes

*pollera,* wide gathered skirt worn by cholas

*polgue llimphi,* coins, gold and silver

*p'olqo,* cowhide shoe used by miners and peasants

*puka uchu,* red pepper

*puluwasa,* hunchback; also a nickname

*Quechua,* language of highland Andean people

*qori llimpa,* pink paste used in offering to spirits in mine

*qori banderilla,* pink darts

*quinoa,* highly nutritious grain grown in high altitudes

*rabia* (Sp.), rage

*rabiaska,* illness caused by rage resulting in death

*salteñas* (Sp.), turnovers with meat and vegetable filling

*San José,* mine in the outskirts of Oruro that used to belong to Hochschild before
    1952

*Sapuy,* the spirit/owner of the mountain, often identified with *Huari* and venerated
    in the mines

*Siglo XX,* tin mine in Potosi that used to belong to the Patiño mines near Catavi

*Socavón Patiño,* lowest level of mine shaft, named after the former owner of the
    largest mines

*tango* (Sp.), dance originating in Argentina

*Taniani,* mine located in the department of Cochabamba

*tarqa,* flute

*taquiraris,* folkloric dance of lowlands

*tarqueadas,* folkloric dance

*Tío,* the familiar name for *Sapuy,* or the spirit of the mountain *tipanaku*, gift of money offered by guests to the host of the party. In a marriage ceremony the money is pinned to the couple's apparel.

*tiripikina*, nickname meaning "scarface"

*Tobas*, dance group representing indians of the jungle

*tucuna*, game similar to hopscotch played by children in mining camps

*tundiques*, dancers now called *Negritos*

*urpus*, butterfly shaped bread prepared for All Souls' Day on the first and second of November, and given to those who offer prayers to the dead.

*viejas* (Sp.), old women, literally; companions of the *Tío* invoked when miners are scared

*wallpa kokho*, stew with peppers

*waynu*, popular melody of pre-Hispanic origins

*yatiri*, native healer who presides at all important ceremonies

# INDEX